EXPLORING IBM AS/400 COMPUTERS

Ninth Edition

Other titles of interest from Maximum Press

Exploring IBM Technology & Products, Second Edition: edited by Hoskins, 1-885068-31-X

Building Intranets With Lotus Notes & Domino 5.0, Second Edition: Steve Krantz, 1-885068-24-7

Exploring IBM Personal Computers, 10th Edition: Hoskins, Wilson, 1-885068-25-5

Exploring IBM AS/400 Computers, Ninth Edition: Hoskins, Dimmick, 1-885068-34-4

Exploring IBM S/390, Sixth Edition: Hoskins, Coleman, 1-885068-30-1

101 Ways to Promote Your Website: Susan Sweeney, 1-885068-37-9

Business-to-Business Internet Marketing: Silverstein, 1-885068-35-2

Marketing on the Internet, Third Edition: Zimmerman, Mathiesen, 1-885068-26-3

Exploring IBM's Bold Internet Strategy: Hoskins, Lupiano, 1-885068-16-6

For more information, visit our World Wide Web site at:
http://www.maxpress.com
or e-mail us at *moreinfo@maxpress.com*

EXPLORING IBM AS/400 COMPUTERS

Ninth Edition

Jim Hoskins
Roger Dimmick

MAXIMUM PRESS
605 Silverthorn Road
Gulf Breeze, FL 32561
(850) 934-0819
www.maxpress.com

Publisher: Jim Hoskins

Manager of Finance/Administration: Donna Tryon

Production Manager: ReNae Grant

Cover Design: Lauren Smith Designs

Compositor: PageCrafters Inc.

Copyeditor: Janis Paris

Proofreader: Julie Cameron

Indexer: Susan Olason

Printer: P.A. Hutchison

This publication is designed to provide accurate and authoritative information in regard to the subject matter covered. It is sold with the understanding that the publisher is not engaged in rendering professional services. If legal, accounting, medical, psychological, or any other expert assistance is required, the services of a competent professional person should be sought. ADAPTED FROM A DECLARATION OF PRINCIPLES OF A JOINT COMMITTEE OF THE AMERICAN BAR ASSOCIATION AND PUBLISHERS.

Copyright 1999 by Maximum Press.

All rights reserved. Published simultaneously in Canada.

Reproduction or translation of any part of this work beyond that permitted by Section 107 or 108 of the 1976 United States Copyright Act without the permission of the copyright owner is unlawful. Requests for permission or further information should be addressed to the Permissions Department, Maximum Press.

Recognizing the importance of preserving what has been written, it is a policy of Maximum Press to have books of enduring value published in the United States printed on acid-free paper, and we exert our best efforts to that end.

Library of Congress Cataloging-in-Publication Data

Hoskins, Jim.

Exploring IBM AS/400 computers / Jim Hoskins and Roger Dimmick.

— 9th ed.

p. cm.

ISBN 1-885068-34-4 (alk. paper)

1. IBM AS/400 (Computer) I. Dimmick, Roger, 1932- II. Title. III. Title: Exploring IBM AS/four hundred computers

QA76.8.I25919 H665 1999

004.1'45—dc21

99-6044

CIP

Acknowledgments

Many "IBMers" assisted us in preparing the ninth edition of the book despite their demanding schedules. Some provided information about their products. Others read the manuscript and provided helpful comments. To all those who assisted, we thank you. We would especially like to thank John Plansky for helping coordinate this edition.

We would also like to thank Dick Odell, Kathy Slowinski, Rod Ehni, Mark Anderson, George Weaver, Deb Landon, Ron Peterson, Carol Woodbury, William Pence, Dave Marshik, Randy Grimm, Elaine Case, Carol Miner, Dave Boutcher, Bill Rapp, Craig Johnson, John Rush, Rui Fan, and Rick Stevens.

Disclaimer

The purchase of computer software or hardware is an important and costly business decision. While the author and publisher of this book have made reasonable efforts to ensure the accuracy and timeliness of the information contained herein, the author and publisher assume no liability with respect to loss or damage caused or alleged to be caused by reliance on any information contained herein and disclaim any and all warranties, expressed or implied, as to the accuracy or reliability of said information.

This book is not intended to replace the manufacturer's product documentation or personnel in determining the specifications and capabilities of the products mentioned in this book. The manufacturer's product documentation should always be consulted, as the specifications and capabilities of computer hardware and software products are subject to frequent modification.

The reader is solely responsible for the choice of computer hardware and software. All configurations and applications of computer hardware and software should be reviewed with the manufacturer's representatives prior to choosing or using any computer hardware and software.

Trademarks

The words contained in this text which are believed to be trademarked, service marked, or otherwise to hold proprietary rights have been designated as such by use of initial capitalization. No attempt has been made to designate as trademarked or service marked any personal computer words or terms in which proprietary rights might exist. Inclusion, exclusion, or definition of a word or term is not intended to affect, or to express judgement upon, the validity of legal status of any proprietary right which may be claimed for a specific word or term.

Table of Contents

Introduction xix
    What This Book Is xix
    What This Book Is Not xix
    How To Use This Book xx
    A Glance Backward at the System/3X Family xxv
    How AS/400 Computers Differ from System/3X Computers xxviii

Chapter 1:
What Is An AS/400 System?   1

    Application-Centric Computing 3
        Open Systems Computing 5
        Client/Server Computing Systems 6
        Distributed Computing Systems 7
    AS/400 Advanced Application Architecture 8
        Why RISC? 11
        RISC PowerPC AS Microprocessors 12
            The A10 Microprocessor 14
            The A35 Microprocessor 15
            The A50 Microprocessor 16
    Meet the AS/400 Family 19
        A Closer Look at the AS/400 Family 20
        System Unit Members 20
            AS/400 Advanced Entry Model 150 Specifics 20
            AS/400e server 170 Specifics 25
            AS/400e server 720 Specifics 27
            AS/400e server 730 Specifics 31
            AS/400e server 740 Specifics 34
        Custom Mixed-Mode Servers 40
            SSA—BPCS Client/Server or Mixed Mode 40
            MAPICS—MAPICS XA 41
            JBA International—JBA System 21 41

International Business Systems—IBS - ASW 41
Intentia—the Movex System 41
Baan—BaanERP 42
Infinium—Infinium Suite for IBM AS/400 42
Acacia Technologies—Acacia Suite for AS/400 42
Lilly Software Associates—Visual Manufacturing 43
SAP-Base R/3 Package 43
SAP—Ready to Run R/3 43
Custom Applications Servers 43
System Availability 46
OS/400 Subsystems and Logical Partitioning 48
Multi-System Coupling 49
Data Resiliency and Application Resiliency 50
AS/400 Continuous Availability Clustering 50
Disaster Tolerance 52
Continuously Powered Main Storage (CPM) 53
AS/400 Upgrades 54
Upgrading Within a Model 54
Upgrading Through a System Unit Swap 54
Upgrades Between Models 55
Performance Overview 56
Benchmark Testing Overview 57
System Default Priorities 61
Interactive Jobs Favored 61
Server Jobs Favored 61
CPW Benchmark Test Results 61
Symmetrical Multi-Processing (SMP) 62
Server Performance 62
RPMark95 66
Interactive Performance 66
Opticonnect Performance 66
A Closer Look 67
Hardware Architecture Overview 68
AS/400 Clustering Technology 71
What Is OptiConnect/400? 71
OptiConnect/400-Enabled Functions 74
OptiConnect/400 Environment 76
Main Storage 76
Storage Management 77
Virtual Storage 80

Auxiliary Storage *81*
    Diskette Storage 81
    Disk Storage 82
    Optical Libraries 84
    Tape Storage 85
Packaging Technology *85*
Fiber Optic Bus *87*

Chapter 2:
Options and Peripherals   88

Workstations 89
    InfoWindow II 3486/3487 Display Stations *90*
    InfoWindow II 3488/3489 Modular Display Station *93*
    Operations Console *94*
    Personal Computer (PC) Terminal Emulation *95*
    Retail Workstations *96*
    IBM Network Station #8361 .... *97*
Printing Technology and Printers 100
    Printers *103*
        Impact Printers 104
            Wire-Matrix Technology *105*
            Band Printers *105*
        Non-impact Printers 109
    Workstation Controllers *112*
        Twinaxial Workstation Controllers 113
        ASCII Workstation Controllers 114
        LAN-Connected Terminals 115
    Protocol Converters *116*
Main Storage Expansion Options 117
    Model 150 Main Storage Capacities *117*
    AS/400e server 170 Main Storage Expansion Options *117*
    AS/400e server 720 Main Storage Expansion Options *119*
    AS/400e server 730 Main Storage Expansion Options *120*
    AS/400e server 740 Main Storage Expansion *121*
Auxiliary Storage Options 121
    Diskette Storage *122*
        9331 Model 11 and 9331 Model 12 Diskette Units 123
    Disk Storage Overview *123*
        Integrated Hardware Disk Compression 125

Entry Model 150 Disk Options 128
Model 170 Disk Options 128
AS/400e server 720 Disk Options 128
AS/400e server 730 Disk Options 129
AS/400e server 740 Disk Options 130
Model SB1 Disk Options 131
Model 2100 Versatile Storage DataServer 131
AS/400 Disk Adapters 132
Tape Storage *136*
Internal Tape Units 137
2.5-GB ¼-Inch Cartridge Tape Unit 137
4-GB ¼-Inch Cartridge Tape Unit (#6382) 138
13-GB ¼-Inch Cartridge Tape Unit 138
7-GB 8-mm Cartridge Tape Unit 138
External Tape Units 139
Tape Libraries 139
AS/400 Optical Storage Overview *141*
CD-ROM 141
The #3995 Optical Library 142
Auxiliary Storage Controllers *143*
Communications Options *143*
The AS/400 and Local Area Networks *145*
Ethernet 146
Token-Ring Local Area Networks 148
FDDI LANs 150
Integrated PC Server 150
Integrated PC Server (#6616) *154*
The Integrated PC Server (#6617) *154*
#6618 Integrated NetFinity Server for AS/400 .... *155*
PCI Integrated PC Servers (#2865) *155*
PCI Integrated PC Servers (#2854, #2851,
  and #2857) *156*
Product Preview *157*
Statement of Direction *157*
Asynchronous Transfer Mode (ATM) 157
Wireless Local Area Networks 159
Wide Area Networks (WANs) *161*
Six-Line Communications Controller (2629) 164
ISDN Basic Rate Interface Adapter 164
The Async Protocol 166

The Bisync Protocol 166
The SDLC Protocol 167
The X.25 Protocol 167
The IDLC Protocol 167
Frame Relay 168
Integrated FAX Adapters 168
Modems 169
   Integrated Analog Modem #2761 169
Remote Workstation Controllers and Lines 171
   5394 Remote Workstation Controller 172
   5494 Remote Workstation Controller 172
Power and Packaging Options 174
   UPS for Models 150 and 170 174
   AS/400e series Packaging Expansion Features 174
      System Unit Expansion (5064/9364) 174
      1063 Mbps PCI Expansion Tower #5065 176
      SPD Bus Card Cage (#9331) 176
      PCI Card Cage (#9329) 176
      3½-Inch Disk Unit Cage (#7128) 177
      5¼-Inch Tape Unit Cage (#7130) 178
      Storage Expansion Unit (#5058) 178
      System Expansion Tower (#5073) 178
      Storage Expansion Tower (#5083) 178
      Advanced Series Base Optical Bus Adapter
      (#2696) 178
         *Advanced Series #2686 Optical Link Processor
         (266 Mbps)* 179
         Advanced Series Optical Link Processor (#2688) 180
Other Adapter Options 180
   Cryptographic Processors 180
      Cryptographic Processors (#2620/2628) 180
      Product Preview PCI Cryptographic IOA (#4800) 181
   0059 Transition Data Link 181
   *Terminal Multiconnector and Telephone Twisted—
   Pair Adapter* 182

Chapter 3:
AS/400 Software   184

AS/400 Software Architecture Overview 184

System Licensed Internal Code (SLIC)	188
How the AS/400's Software Layers Are Different	189
How the Layers Work Together	191
Software Compatibility	**193**
AS/400 Software Compatibility—Will S/3X Programs Work?	193
Inside AS/400 Compatibility	194
Applications Architecture	195
Program Portability	196
Welcome Center	197
Program Interaction	197
Standard User Interface	198
Application Programs	**198**
Can Prewritten Programs Fit the Bill?	199
Cross-Industry Application Programs	200
OfficeVision for AS/400	201
OfficeVision JustMail for AS/400 (5798-TBT)	209
AFP PrintSuite for AS/400 AFP	209
Advanced Print Utility (APU)	210
Page Printer Formatting Aid (PPFA)	210
AFP Toolbox	211
SAP R/3 AFP Print	211
AnyMail/400 and POP3	211
Query/400	212
Encoded Vector Indexing	214
AS/400 Business Graphics Utility	216
ImagePlus/400	217
Facsimile Support/400	220
CallPath/400	222
Multimedia	223
Client Access Ultimedia Tools for AS/400	224
Ultimedia Business Conferencing/400	225
IBM Job Scheduler/400	227
Data Warehousing	230
Data Mining	233
Performance	234
Capacity	235
Scalability	235
Open Interfaces	235
Multiple Data Structures	236

Data Mining Example 236
Collaborative Computing 236
    Lotus Notes 238
    Lotus Enterprise Integrator (NotesPump) 239
    Client Series and Application Development Programs 241
    Industry-Specific Application Programs 242
    Custom Application Programs 244

Chapter 4:
Operating Systems   246

Operating System Products 247
   Introduction to Operating System Concepts 247
   Batch vs. Interactive Processing 248
   What Are Multiuser and Multi-application
      Computer Systems? 249
   OS/400 in the Client/Server Environment? 250
SSP—An Executive Overview 252
OS/400—An Executive Overview 254
A Closer Look at OS/400 256
   Integrated File System 257
      Stream Files 259
      Integrated File System Support 260
      DB2 Query Manager and SQL Development Kit 262
         SQL Development Kit 263
      Network File System (NFS) 263
      Remote File System 264
         Client for Windows NT File System 265
   Advanced Function Presentation 265
   DB2 for AS/400 266
   Product Preview—DB2-Universal DataBase Support ... 270
      Complex Object Support 270
      Datalink Data Types 271
      User Defined Types 272
      User Defined Functions 272
   Built-In Database 272
      Telephone Book 274
      Physical and Logical Files 275
      Concurrency and Lock Management 277
   Distributed Data Management 279

DB2 for OS/400—An Overview 280
DB2 for OS/400 281
    DataPropagator Relational Capture and Apply 282
    Open DataBase Connection (ODBC) 282
    Java DataBase Connection (JDBC) 283
    Data Striping 283
    Partitioned Database 283
    Database Monitor 284
    Database Management 285
    DCE Base Services/400 286
    CICS Translation Server for AS/400 (5769-DFH) 289
Communications Support 290
    TCP/IP 292
        Virtual Private Networks 294
    Systems Network Management 295
        Systems Network Management Example 296
    Systems Network Architecture (SNA) 297
    Wireless Local Area Network 297
    Display Station/Printer Pass-Thru 298
    S/390 Communications Support 299
Client Access 300
    AS/400 Client Access Family for Windows 301
    AS/400 Client Access Family 309
    AS/400 Client Access Express for Windows
    (5769-XE1) 310
        Lotus Notes 5.0 Client Support 312
SystemView 313
    Commitment Control and Journaling 316
    Backup/Recovery 317
        Operations Navigator 318
        EDMSuite OnDemand for AS/400 (5769-RD1) 320
        Backup Recovery and Media Services (BRMS/400) . 321
        Adstar Distributed Storage Manager (ADSM) 324
        System Managed Access Path Protection (SMAPP) .. 325
        Hierarchical Storage Management 326
        Utility Failure Recovery 327
        Disk Failure Recovery 327
    Systems Manager/400 328
    Management Central 329
        Management Central Methodology 331

AS/400 Performance Tools (5716-PT1) 332
Managed System Services for AS/400 332
NetFinity for AS/400 333
Application Development Facilities *334*
Application Development Tools Set/400 336
Application Development Tools—Printing 338
Application Development Tools—Program
   Group 1 340
Other Application Development Tools—
   Program Group 2 341
Application Development Tools—Debugging
   and Maintenance 342
Application Development Tools Programming 343
Application Development Tools—Other
   Methodologies 343
AS/400 Kernel Threads 345
Integrated Language Environment (ILE) 347
Emerging Application Development Environments 349
   Client/Server Computing Model *350*
   Object Technology *353*
Emerging Applications Environments 358
   Frameworks *359*
   OpenDoc *361*
   ORB Support *362*
   Java *362*
Product Preview—Enterprise Java Beans 369
   Using Java at the Client *369*
Open Standards (UNIX) 369
   Open Standards-Based Interoperability *369*
   UNIX C Portability *370*
System/3X Compatibility *371*
Software Solution Packages *372*
   AS/400e server 150 BasePak (5649-EP5) 373
   AS/400 Operations Productivity Pak (5716-OPK) 377

Chapter 5:
AS/400 and Communications—An Introduction   378

Computer Communications in the
Office—An Introduction 378

What Is SNA?	379
IBM Electronic Customer Support Communications	380
Remote Workstations	383
Distributed Computer Communications	386
AS/400 Distributed Networks	*387*
Distributed AS/400 Network Example	388
APPC/APPN	*390*
Filter Lists	391
AS/400 System Clustering	*392*
ObjectConnect/400	*393*
IBM's Overall Networking Blueprint	393
Applications Layer	*395*
Application Support Layer	*396*
Multivendor Application Program Interfaces	397
The CPI-C Interface	*397*
The Remote Procedure Call	*398*
The Messaging and Queuing Interface	*398*
Transport Network Layer: SNA-TCP/IP-MPTN-APPN	*399*
Multiprotocol Transport Networking (MPTN)	399
Advanced Peer-to-Peer Networking (APPN)	401
Subnetworking Layer	*401*
Intranet	*403*
AS/400 and Retail Terminals	*403*
Intranet/Internet Security	404
Internet Connection Secure Server	*405*
Cryptographic Access Provider	*410*
Hardware Cryptography	410
HTTP Server for AS/400	411
SET Internet Security Manager	411
Digital Certificate Manager	*412*
IBM Payment Server V1.2 for AS/400	*413*
Security Wizard	*414*
Firewalls	414
WebSphere Application Server (5769-AS1)	418
AS/400 and the Internet	*418*
Electronic Business (e-business)	420
Net.Data	420
NetQuestion	421
Net.Commerce	422
Domino 5.0 for AS/400	423

Domino.Merchant 427
Net.Commerce vs. Domino.Merchant 428
OS/400 Directory Services (LDAP) 428
Internet Terminology 429

Chapter 6:
Application Systems and Your Business 432

What Are My Business Computing Needs? 433
What About Personal Computers? 435
What About RISC System/6000 Computers? 436
What About System/390 Computers? 438
When Should I Consider Application Systems? 439
Choosing the Software 440
Choosing the Hardware 442
   *Small Business Environment, Retail—Anatole's
     Sub Factory* 442
   *Small Business Environment, Manufacturing—Bob's
     Gearbox Co.* 444
   Medium Business Environment—Johnson & Thornbush 446
     Hardware Configuration 449
     Johnson & Thornbush Software Scenario 449
   Large Business Environment—Atole Enterprises 451
     Atole Solution Scenario 452
   Server Selection 454
   The Competitive View of 64-Bit Processing 456
The Business Decisions 458
   Cost Justification 458
   Costs 458
     Hardware Maintenance 458
     Software Maintenance 458
     Technical Support 459
     Facilities 459
     Education/Training 460
     Communications Line Costs 460
     Environmental Costs 460
     Enhancing Applications 460
   Benefits 461
     Improved Business Cycle 461
     Inventory Reduction 461

Improved Productivity	461
Improved Quality	462
Improved Customer Service	462
Competitive Advantage	462
Lease or Buy?	464
Education	465
Ergonomics	467
Comfort for the Eyes	468
Workstation Comfort	469
What About Noise?	470
Security	471
Loss Prevention	472
Theft Prevention	473
Service	474
Year 2000 Challenge	475
Migrating from System/3X to AS/400	475
Sizing a Replacement AS/400	476
Migrating System/3X I/O Devices to the AS/400	478
Migrating Programs and Data from the System/36	479
Migrating Programs and Data from the System/38	480
Migrating Programs and Data from the System/34	482
Migrating C, D, E, and F 9402, 9404, and 9406 Models to the Advanced Series	482
Migrating Advanced Series 20X/30X System Units to AS/400e server System Units: CISC to RISC	483
System Performance Tables for AS/400 Systems	483
Appendix A	489
Appendix B	494
Appendix C	496
Appendix D	500
Appendix E	505
Appendix F	510

Introduction

What This Book Is

This book is dedicated to IBM's midsize business computers, namely, the **Application System/400 (AS/400)** family. These computers make up IBM's strategic direction in midsized business computing. For convenience, the AS/400 family is referred to as IBM's **Application Systems**.

First, the Application Systems are introduced. The features of these new computers are compared with those of the earlier System/36 and System/38 family in a way understandable to the business user. The AS/400 family was introduced in 1988, and the first edition of this book, which described the AS/400 family, was published in 1989. IBM has refreshed the AS/400 family in performance, capacity, and application support each year since 1988, and on an average of every three years has evolved the systems areas of applicability. Each of those changes has resulted in a new edition of this book to maintain currency with the existing hardware and software directions of the system family.

Second, to help you with software buying decisions, the different types of software necessary to do "real work" are also described.

Finally, we discuss ways to apply Application Systems to improve business operations. Proper selection and use of Application Systems products is impossible unless you understand how you can use these components to fill business needs. Specific Application Systems hardware and software configurations for typical environments are offered. Many important computer automation planning issues are also discussed.

What This Book Is Not

Many computer books try to be all things to all people, covering everything from checkbook balancing to the Space Shuttle's redundant flight computer complex. This book is not a general overview of computers. It is specific to IBM's Application Systems (a broad enough subject for any single book). This book is neither a technical reference manual (IBM will sell you that) nor a guide to computer programming. It does, however, provide a good understanding of IBM's Application Systems and how to use them in the business environment.

Finally, this book does not expect you to be an engineer. Business people are typically short on time and patience as far as technical matters are concerned. Although some technical discussions are necessary, we have tried to keep these as simple and concise as possible while still conveying necessary and useful information.

How To Use This Book

Chapter 1 introduces the entire AS/400 family, including the Model 150, an AS/400 System/server priced in the range of a PC server but including full OS/400 capabilities. Three new models are introduced are introduced, plus one special- purpose derivative model. Each of the three new models offers increased flexibility in meeting the customers' needs in both hardware and software over the equivalent model being replaced. Main storage capacity and disk storage capacity in general have been increased. The AS/400 family on its largest model can support 40,000 MB of main storage and 4.29 TB of disk storage.

That flexibility comes from the capability to feature the amount of interactive performance required by the customer. The models are referred to as server models, which in their base can provide some minimum amount of interactive capability, but by adding interactive features, the processors are tuned to provide up to the full processing capabilities in an interactive environment. It is no longer necessary as a result to select between a fully interactive environment, or a specially tuned server environment for some of interactive capability. The pre-loads previously offered in the custom mixed-mode systems continue to be offered on the new server/interactively featured systems.

The AS/400 which offered features to achieve up to 99.94% availability, can be configured as a clustered group of systems, or as a logically partitioned symmetrical multi-processor system or group of systems to achieve 100% availability, which when combined with remote journal capability on an off-site system offers the capability to your processing complex to survive through natural disasters.

Another important difference is that the operating system (OS/400) is now bundled with the hardware; it is not possible to buy the hardware without getting the OS/400 operating system with it. The latter part of the chapter examines the elements (built-in database, multiprocessor architecture, etc.) that make up AS/400 computers and separate them from the competition's offerings. These elements of the AS/400 family are contrasted to those of the System/3X computers.

A section on performance and benchmarks is included to assist in comparing the AS/400 family computers against competitive computers. This section should be particularly helpful in understanding the workloads used to measure the systems and how those workloads relate to your particular business. The new processors measure performance differently. As a result, the amount of interactive performance being used simply subtracts from the total performance capability of the processor, and the remainder is completely available to the environment for client/server processing, with no other subtractions. A section was added which explains the change in IBM's method of measuring their systems to more closely reflect how the customer is using those systems.

Chapter 2 surveys the many hardware options available for Application Systems, including terminals, printers, disk expansion, and communications. Included is the network station, referred to in early literature as the Thin Client, which introduces a new concept in workstations, and pen-enabled mobile computers, including 333 MHz performance. Disk adapters are capable of compressing your data to achieve increased capacity without requiring additional hardware expense. This capability combined with Hierarchical Storage Management allows the customer to set a group of policies in place which move less frequently used data to archive state automatically. The FSIOP has been renamed as the Integrated PC Server, and the performance has been improved sufficiently to allow its use as a Windows NT Server under the covers. The largest models of the AS/400 can provide up to 16 parallel Windows NT Servers without need to be concerned about "blue screen failure." The section on I/O devices and adapters is provided primarily as a reference to help you identify and select the proper options for your Application System.

Chapter 3 describes the workings of the three types of programs necessary to do productive work with AS/400 computers: application programs, operating systems, and System Licensed Internal Code (SLIC), and continues with a discussion of application programs. Some Application Systems application programs useful to most businesses are discussed. New with this edition is a discussion of Lotus Notes, which has been split into two parts–a server portion called Domino and a client portion that retains the name Lotus Notes. Notes provides collaborative computing support while Domino runs on the Integrated PC server and also executes natively on the AS/400. Many applications have been refreshed with Operations Navigator to provide a GUI interface. OfficeVision and Job Scheduler have been improved to provide many of the functions requested by the customers. Many OfficeVision functions are migrating to Domino 5.0. We also address an emerging application area–Neural Networks–which has been moved into the Intelligent Miner product for data mining. New search algorithms are implemented to improve data mining and query performance capabilities. Industry-specific application programs are introduced with an example. Finally, the question of "prewritten" vs. "custom" application programs is addressed.

Chapter 4 continues the discussion on operating systems. First, basic operating system concepts such as "multiuser" and "interactive processing" are defined in terms of their usefulness in the business environment. Then the Application System's operating system products are described. New for this edition, Client Access/400 has been split into Client Access Family for Windows for AS/400, Client Access Express for Windows for AS/400, and Client Access Family for AS/400. A preview is provided of how DB2/400 evolves on its way to becoming a full function Universal DataBase, including complex objects, user defined types and user defined functions. Included in this chapter is a section on developing application programs from a host perspective. This is then extended to include migration of host-based applications to the client/server environment. Many of the communications functions only available previously on SNA and APPC are protocol-based networks now available on TCP/IP. Kernel threads have been added to increase performance for many of the Windows- and Lotus-based functions. An increasingly large proportion of OS/400 is threadsafe. The potential impacts to be expected upon host and client/server program migration (as a result of the emergence of object-oriented programming) are then surveyed, including an introduction to Java and frameworks.

Chapter 5 shows how specific AS/400 options and software products are used to participate in the computer communications environments commonly found in businesses. New security services for APPN and TCP/IP are discussed, as well as networks and AS/400 support for Internet services.

With the advent of the new security services discussed in Chapter 5, the emphasis of the AS/400 has been shifted to one of network computing, particularly leaning toward the electronic business (e-biz) environment. Security elements like firewalls, Internet Connection Secure Server, HTTP Server, WebServer, Cryptographic support, Certificate Management, and IBM Payment Server are positioned relative to interconnecting the AS/400 with the Internet. E-Business functions like Net.Commerce, Domino.Merchant, Domino on AS/400, Net.Data, NetQuestion, and Lotus Enterprise Integrator are discussed to help with setting up an Internet business.

Chapter 6 discusses issues related to the selection of Application Systems hardware and software for small, medium, and large businesses. Hypothetical businesses are outfitted with the appropriate Application Systems. Important topics such as user training, ergonomics, security, maintenance, leasing vs. buying, and cost justification are then discussed. In particular, AS/400 online education and security and its importance in an Internet environment has been expanded upon. Charts are provided to allow comparison of previous AS/400 system models to the current standard for measuring system performance.

To provide for reference, the appendices list (1) user groups who have significant experience with the AS/400 family, (2) the various service offerings available from IBM on the AS/400, (3) contact information for User Groups, (4) a listing of standards and standard interfaces with which AS/400 TCP/IP is compliant, and (5) screen capture shots of EZ Setup.

To help you better understand the topics covered in this book, key terms and phrases are defined and **highlighted**. These key terms are also listed in the index at the back of this book. If, while reading, you forget the definition of a key term or phrase, the index will quickly provide the page(s) on which the term was originally discussed.

Your "Members Only" Web Site

The AS/400 world changes every day. That's why there is a companion web site associated with this book. On this site you will find updates to the book and other AS/400-related resources of interest to anyone involved with the AS/400. However, you have to be a member of the "AS/400 Insiders Club" to gain access to this site.

When you purchased this book, you automatically became a member (in fact, that's the only way to join), so you now have full privileges of the AS/400 Insiders Club. To get into the "Members Only" section of the companion web site, go to the Maximum Press web site located at *http://www.maxpress.com* and follow the links to the AS/400 area. From there you will see a link to the "AS/400 Insiders Club" section. When you try to enter, you will be asked for a user ID and password. Type in the following:

- For your user ID enter: *AS/4009e*

- For your password enter: *rapid*

You will then be granted full access to the "Members Only" area. Visit the site often and enjoy the updates and resources with our compliments—and thanks again for buying the book. We ask that you not share the user ID and password for this site with anyone else.

Figure I.1. IBM System/3.

A Glance Backward at the System/3X Family

On July 30, 1969, IBM executives from the entire company joined 1200 IBMers at their plant site in Rochester, Minnesota, to announce the System/3 computer shown in Figure I.1. This system was the first computer totally developed in Rochester. Although only of historical interest today, the System/3 represented some significant advances in the technology of its time. For example, it introduced Monolithic Systems Technology, which allowed engineers to package more circuitry in a smaller space, as well as a punch card one-third of normal size that held 20 percent more information. This was the first advancement in punch-card technology in over 40 years. To celebrate the announcement of the System/3, Rochester IBMers held a dance featuring Ralph Marterie and his orchestra in a newly constructed building. The Rochester plant, which became a full IBM division in November of that year, was tasked to develop a "low-end" computer family. One System/3, fondly named "Old Reliable," ran faithfully until it was shut down in September 1973. When it was finally retired, its meter showed that it had run for 15,377.97 hours, representing more run time than any other system in existence.

The System/32, shown in Figure I.2, was the next member of the family. It was announced in January 1975 and featured direct keyboard data entry and a display that could present up to 6 rows of text 40 characters long. The System/32 had up to 32K of memory and up to 13 MB of fixed disk storage.

Figure I.2. IBM System/32.

Figure I.3. IBM System/34.

Figure I.4. IBM System/38.

Figure I.5. IBM System/36.

The System/34 computer, announced in April 1977, was the first system truly designed to manage multiple (local and remote) workstations (i.e., terminals and printers), each being up to 5000 feet away from the computer. This allowed it to perform tasks for up to eight local users simultaneously. The System/34, shown in Figure I.3, provided up to 256K of memory and 13 MB of fixed disk.

Next came the System/38, announced in October 1978. This represented a divergence from its S/3X predecessors, offering a new architecture optimized for application development productivity. The System/38, shown in Figure I.4, could support up to 32 MB of memory, 14 GB of disk storage, and 256 local workstations.

Once again, building on the architectural base of the System/34, the first System/36 was announced in May 1983 (Figure I.5). It grew to support up to 7 MB of main memory, 1.4 GB of disk storage, and 72 local workstations. Other models of the System/36 varying in processing power and capacity were announced over time. Collectively the System/3, System/32, System/34, System/36, and System/38 are known as the **System/3X** family of computers.

The last S/36 model (the 5363) was enhanced and renamed the **IBM ASEntry** system. IBM has announced its intentions to provide future enhancements to the ASEntry products. This means that they are vital to IBM's midrange product strategy, as we will see later in the book.

On June 20, 1988, IBM unveiled the AS/400 family of products. The AS/400 has close architectural ties with System/38 while in most cases providing application program compatibility with both the System/36 and the System/38. Since the original announcement of the AS/400 family, IBM has regularly announced new AS/400 hardware and software products—a trend that shows no signs of slowing.

How AS/400 Computers Differ from System/3X Computers

What characteristics make IBM AS/400 computers different from the System/3X family of computers? The answer lies in the areas of compatibility, performance, expansion capability, and usability.

The AS/400 computers offer more **compatibility** across the product line than did the System/3X computers. Two operating systems and a single architecture are used consistently across the entire AS/400 family. This means that programs and data can be freely exchanged among AS/400 systems and used without any changes. This was not possible in the System/3X family, in which different architectures and operating systems prevented the System/36 from running System/38 programs without change (and vice versa). Further, the AS/400 operating system was the first "midsize computer" operating system to participate in IBM's **Systems Application Architecture (SAA)**, which allows programs to be exchanged among PS/2s, AS/400s, and System/390s.

AS/400 computers can also run programs written for the System/3X family. Many of those written for the System/38 will need little or no change, and many of those written for the System/36 can be migrated to AS/400 systems using available tools. In fact, the AS/400 Advanced/36 allows coexistence of the System/36 SSP operating system and applications with the OS/400 operating system and applications. When coexisting, the two operating systems share a common file system and can make calls to use each other's I/O functions. This means that System/3X users can move their custom-written System/3X application programs to AS/400 computers. Also, many of the System/3X software companies have migrated their application program offerings to the AS/400 systems, allowing users to choose from a vast array of software to solve business problems. Chapter 3 looks more closely at AS/400 compatibility.

AS/400 computers can also run programs written for other computers, both from IBM and from selected competitors. (This capability is referred to as portability.)

The **performance** of a computer is the speed at which it can work. The higher the performance, the better. For example, the largest AS/400 computers offer performance several thousand times that of the largest System/38. The performance advantage of the AS/400 family is afforded primarily by a combination of faster processors, more efficient architectures, more storage, and improved disk units. With the addition of server models, performance is affected by the tuning provided within the operating system to the applications that are executing on the system. We look more closely at performance in Chapter 1.

The AS/400 computers offer more **expansion capability** to support growing needs. First, because the AS/400 computers are fully compatible from the smallest system to the largest, users can grow without the disruption of conversion that used to accompany moving from a System/36 to the larger System/38 family. In the AS/400 family, there is a much wider range of growth between the largest and smallest systems. The integrated approach with expansion towers used in the new AS/400 systems better lends itself to configuration flexibility and modular expansion than did the rack-mounted approach used in the older AS/400 B through F models or the older box approach of the System/38. The largest AS/400 systems can span several of these towers and accommodate up to 4,200 GB of disk storage in a single system, compared with the 165.4 GB of the rack-mounted F models or the 14-GB maximum of the largest System/38. Furthermore, the AS/400 system can support up to 250 communications lines, surpassing the maximum of 12 lines with the System/38.

Each AS/400 computer also offers expansion slots that can accept various controllers and adapters to add function and performance. For example, main storage can be expanded from 128 MB to 40,960 MB in the largest AS/400 computer through the addition of storage expansion adapters. As necessary, additional expansion slots can be added to the Advanced Systems by installing additional I/O card units in AS/400 towers. Chapter 2 describes many optional controllers and adapters that can be installed to add capability to AS/400 computers.

Not only do AS/400 computers offer more advanced capabilities, they are **easier to use** than comparable System/3X systems. The operating system required for normal operation comes preloaded on all systems, eliminating the tedious installation process. The user interface of this operating system conforms to IBM's **Common User Access (CUA)** method, providing online help and consistency with other SAA environments (e.g., Operating System/2 on the Personal System/2). Those used to System/3X computers will also see many similarities when interacting with the operating system for AS/400 computers. Also, most of the familiar System/3X devices (terminals, printers, etc.) can be used with the new family of computers. IBM's Electronic Customer Support offered for all AS/400 systems is another way to get help when you have a question. Every AS/400 system also comes with computer-based education programs that teach new users about many aspects of the new AS/400 computers. Some authoring tools are also available on AS/400 computers that allow you to design your own courses to meet specialized training needs.

1

What Is An AS/400 System?

This chapter provides an overview of the IBM AS/400 family of computers, covering the highlights of these systems and then moving in for a closer look at the details. The characteristics of the AS/400 computers are compared with those of the IBM System/3X family.

The IBM Application System/400 (AS/400) family of products represents IBM's newest generation of midsize business computing systems. Like their predecessors, the System/3X family, they are **multiuser** computer systems, meaning a single computer can interact with more than one user at a time. In developing the AS/400 systems, designers drew from the ease-of-use features of the System/36, combined these with the advanced architecture and productivity of the System/38, and then added new functions. In addition to the many application programs developed directly for execution on the AS/400, many of the application programs developed for the System/36 and System/38 computers can be migrated to and used on AS/400 systems by applying the migration tools available.

Many users have no concept of what equipment makes up the computer system they use daily. Fortunately, it is not necessary for them to, just as it is not necessary to understand the inner workings of a carburetor to drive a car. However, it is helpful to have a fundamental view of what general elements make up an AS/400. Figure 1.1 shows the components of a very simple AS/400 system configuration. The heart of the

Figure 1.1. Components of a simple AS/400 system.

system is the system unit, which contains the "brain" that runs the computer programs and controls all activities. People interact with the computer system through terminals (or personal computers [PCs] acting as terminals) that display computer information and allow for keyboard entry.

The terminal shown on the left side of the figure is the **system console**. The system console is a specially designated terminal used by the system operator to manage the day-to-day operations of the computer system. The other terminals are for general-purpose use. The printers shown in the figure are used to generate reports, documents, graphs, and the like. A printer can be a workstation used to fill the needs of specific user(s), or it can be shared by all users. Both terminals and printers were initially attached to the system unit via twinaxial cable (or twinax), typically laid in the building's walls or ceiling. In today's environment, the terminals (or PCs) and printers are attached through many other media including radio communications and telephone wiring.

Figure 1.2 shows the packaging used for the AS/400e server 170. This packaging is typical of the AS/400 system line in that it encompasses the primary components of the computer system including everything necessary to comprise an entry system except the terminal functions identified above. Among the elements which distinguish the system from other systems available in the mid-range marketplace are the rounded rear cover which allows it to be placed against walls, and the air intake scoops at the bottom and mid-area of the unit's front. The rounded rear cover allows air exhaust and cabling to exit from the rear. And the fact that all air intake is through the front cover allows the unit to be placed against walls and desks at either side.

Application-Centric Computing

As a result of recent releases, the AS/400 system has been transformed from a host-centric computing system to an **application-centric** computing system. This transformation has been accomplished while supporting and expanding the host-centric applications that execute on the AS/400 system. Those host-centric applications constitute the core of

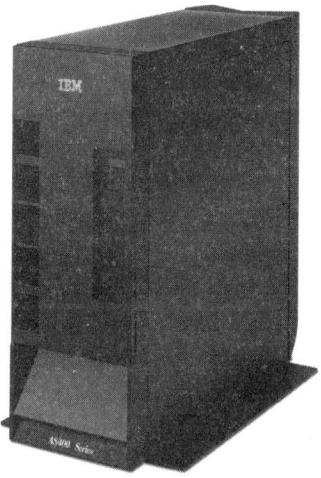

Figure 1.2. AS/400e server 170.

the 350,000 installed systems. The system configuration shown in Figure 1.1 is an example of what constitutes a **host-centric** computing system: All the computational capability resides in a centralized processor called the host, and that host is surrounded by non-intelligent terminals that provide data input to the application programs, which both reside and execute on the host.

An application-centric computing system is one that will execute and support an application's data and programs on the operating system, regardless of the operating system of origin (Windows, Macintosh, UNIX, Lotus, Java, etc.). The support may include network-centric computing systems, in which case the data and/or programs may reside on separate computing systems, some of which may be Internet servers, and the application, which is the composite of the data and program, may execute on a different system. In an application-centric computing system, the application itself may have been defined on one vendor's computing system and be executing on a different vendor's computing system.

Consider the system configuration shown in Figure 1.1. If the terminals were replaced randomly by both AS/400 systems and PCs, with the vendors of the PCs selected at random, and the terminal connection interface were replaced by a **Local Area Network (LAN)**, then the hardware portion of the application-centric paradigm would have been met. If in addition the applications to be executed within the configuration of LAN-interconnected systems could be developed on any of the systems, regardless of the vendor source, and would still execute on any other of the systems (regardless of the vendor source), then the software part of the application-centric paradigm would have been met.

Within the context of this description of application-centric computing, not only is host-centric computing included, *open systems computing, client/server computing,* and *distributed computing* are also included. The AS/400 Advanced Series achieved the transformation to an application-centric computing system by supporting all of these forms of computing system structures. Host-centric computing was defined earlier. Open systems computing, client/server computing, and distributed computing will be defined in the following paragraphs and are described in greater detail in later chapters.

The AS/400 Advanced Series achieved the transformation to an application-centric computing system by supporting all of these forms of computing system structures. Figure 1.3 illustrates the architecture implemented to achieve the open and client/server portions from what was previously a host-centric base with distributed computing.

Figure 1.3. Advanced applications architecture.

Open Systems Computing

Open systems computing has in the minds of some people come to mean UNIX. In reality, open systems computing means that applications developed on an open system will provide the two characteristics of **interoperability** and **portability**. *Interoperability* means that both programs and people can exchange information in a meaningful way. *Portability* means that it is possible to move applications, data, and users from one vendor or computer architecture to another. Together, interoperability and portability mean that an application will achieve the same results from the same data and present the users with the same interfaces at the system level—no matter what vendor's system is executing the application.

Businesses should perceive four benefits from the achievement of the open systems computing capability: freedom of choice, flexibility and change management over time, lasting value, and investment protection:

- *Freedom of choice* means that the business can select from among many vendors the hardware and software needed.

- *Flexibility and change management over time* means that businesses can recombine and redeploy their open systems applications and information technology infrastructure as business needs dictate without requiring perfect foresight. Here, they know that the application can be moved to several different platforms over its useful life.

- *Lasting value* means the business is not locked into a single vendor's hardware or software.

- *Investment protection* is provided to the business because new software and retraining are not required if the hardware base is changed.

The AS/400 has achieved open system computing by providing an open application environment, which supports interoperability and portability not only for nearly all of the other vendors' de facto standard application interfaces, but also for most UNIX applications.

Client/Server Computing Systems

Client/server computing systems are those in which applications or resources (programs, data, and sometimes both) are spread across more than one intelligent system. Usually, the client is a workstation or a PC, and the server(s) is a larger system that controls resources such as data or hardware. The outboard intelligence is called the client, and the centralized intelligence is called the server. Most of today's LAN-connected client/server computing environments include PCs or network stations and any or all of the following: file servers, fax servers, database servers, application servers, print servers, communications servers, and Internet servers.

In many of the PC-based client/server computer systems, each of the server functions is performed by a separate PC and the user's problem is one of management to keep all of this separate activity in synchronization with the application. In the AS/400, all of the server functions are integrated and come under the control of a single operating system. As a result, performance is optimized, connectivity issues that arise from the presence of multiple servers are avoided, and when more performance is needed users can easily add memory or other features to the AS/400e systems.

The AS/400e series supports over 1600 different client/server applications under the many languages that are available. A listing of abstracts from those applications is available from the Internet at this address:

http://www.software.ibm.com/solutions/isv

The client/server environment for the AS/400 has been extended with the support for Novell NetWare 4.10 on the **Integrated PC Server** (formerly called the File Server Input/Output Processor, or FSIOP). This includes file serving, print serving, and data sharing with NetWare Loadable Modules (NLMs) while preserving NetWare commands to install, configure, and control the environment.

In addition, Novell's Internet Packet Exchange (IPX) protocol is now available as a native protocol in the AS/400 suite of communications protocols. This enables AS/400 to be plugged into existing Novell networks with fewer problems and administrative changes.

Distributed Computing Systems

Distributed computing systems at first glance look like client/server computing systems, but instead of a full copy of all data and programs residing on the server, the data may be segmented and reside across many system boundaries in the network of systems, and each application program may reside on the computer at which it is normally executed.

Although this is the normal situation, the programs may be called and executed at any computer in the network. Ideally, which computer in the distributed system network of computers is actually executing the program is unknown to the user. Except in the case of some very short programs with limited data sets, the ideal has not yet been achieved in most distributed computing system networks.

AS/400 Advanced Application Architecture

Figure 1.3 illustrates the **advanced application architecture,** which was implemented on the AS/400 system to achieve the open client/server computing system capabilities described in the preceding paragraphs. The following paragraphs will introduce the layers of this architecture. Later chapters of this book will provide additional detail for the reader.

There are seven layers in the **advanced application architecture** for client/server and distributed computing. The *top layer* is the client application layer. This primarily consists of Client Access Family for Windows for AS/400 and Client Access Family for AS/400, the PC-resident offering that allows the widest variety of clients to take advantage of the AS/400 server resources. This includes support for both the Microsoft ODBC interface and the Java DBC interface at both the client and at the server, as well as **Apple's** DAL. Client operating systems supported are:

- Extended DOS

- 32-bit Windows

- Macintosh SNA*ps

- Novell NetWare 4.10 with NLM

- Microsoft Windows 3.1

- IBM Connection

- 16-bit OS2

- Windows NT

- Windows 95/98

- Windows 3.1

- Program/400 for RS/6000

- Base DOS

- UNIX (SUN or HP)

- 32-bit OS/2

The *second layer* is the server layer, which supports client and server programming tools, OS400 server applications, PC server applications, **A-OPEN** (UNIX Spec 1170) server applications, and **object-oriented** server applications. In general, this layer enables the distributed computing function, whereby the client application might also execute at the server in whole or in part. This layer in combination with the next layer down (the open application environment) enables the AS/400 to support more than 80 percent of the most commonly used commercial APIs in UNIX applications.

The fact that these server functions are equivalent to each other allows them to share data through the integrated file system including the DB2 for AS/400 relational database. This, along with Data Propagator/400, allows flat files and relational files to coexist and PC applications to readily access data, change it, and put it back again, as well as replicate it in whole or in part to a different application. Thus, legacy applications, client/server applications, and object-oriented applications can coexist in one AS/400.

Implemented within the *third layer* as part of the integrated file system are triggers, stored procedures, declarative referential integrity, two-phase commit, and long file names. These functions are available not only for the client/server and open systems interconnect file structures but for all of the file structures supported, improving the total function of the AS/400 including legacy applications.

The *fourth layer* is the integrated midware layer, which allows the AS/400 to reduce the system management headaches associated in general with both client/server computing and with distributed computing. The integrated midware layer reduces complexity in the following areas:

- Network protocols

- Database management

- Security

- Access to coded and non-coded data (open file system)

- Enablers for advanced applications such as multimedia

- Enablers for mail and directory services

This midware is integrated and tested before it is delivered on the system as part of OS/400.

Among the tools available in the midware are Systems Manager, Managed Systems Services, OS/2 Warp server, and ADSM/400. Systems Manager and Managed Systems Services allow the AS/400 to deliver new releases of PC applications to all authorized users. OS2 Warp Server for AS/400 allows the AS/400 and Novell networks to share resources such as printers and storage devices and allows central administration of the networks. And ADSM/400 allows the backup and recovery services of the AS/400 to be extended to PC users.

The *fifth layer* is the technology-independent machine interface, which allows the AS/400 to change major hardware and software components of the system without affecting your business applications. This allows the AS/400 to change the functions and hardware below this interface without causing customers to rewrite or recompile their applications.

The *sixth layer* is the System Licensed Internal Code (SLIC), now designed in C++, which runs on 64-bit microprocessors. This layer allows new hardware to be introduced without affecting the applications above the machine interface layer until those applications are ready to exploit the new functions provided.

The final layer, the *seventh layer*, is the hardware layer. In the August 1997 release of this layer integrated DASDs were continued, and a RAID (Redundant Array of Independent DASDs) capability for the MultiFunction I/O Processor (MFIOP)-attached integrated DASDs were introduced. The Integrated PC Server (IPCS) now includes a firewall function, and new systems packaging, a family of **PCI** (Portable Computer Interface) IOPs and controllers.

Because RISC is the new evolving technology for the AS/400 family main processor, before discussing the remainder of the hardware, we will spend a few paragraphs briefly explaining what RISC technology is and the PowerPC AS implementation of that technology. Then we will point out the differences from other RISC implementations necessitated by the commercial processing nature of the AS/400 family.

Why RISC?

Although additional improvements could have been achieved with the **CISC** (Complex Instruction Set Computer)-based microprocessor family, which constituted the base for all of the pre-1995 AS/400 systems, the AS/400 was moved to a **RISC** (Reduced Instruction Set Computer) base because RISC provides extended future growth, is mainstream and strategic, can be optimized for commercial usage, and offers several advantages at a complete system level. This involves more than chips—RISC also better enables an optimizing compiler and simplifies the instruction decode function.

Before discussing those driving elements, let's define CISC and RISC somewhat more fully. CISC as implemented in the IMPI (Integrated Micro Programmed Interface) microprocessor had 392 instructions 2, 4, or 6 bytes in length, including a group of 8 different complex operations. The RISC PowerPC AS (PowerPC AS is the specific implementation of the PowerPC RISC architecture implemented for the AS/400) has 250 instructions, all of which are 4 bytes in length and require only two move-assist complex operations.

The net result is that the RISC PowerPC AS allows for growth to a larger address space, improved performance from 64-bit data and instructions, more than 20 GB (gigabytes, or billion bytes) of main storage, including a larger page size (4 KB), and significant I/O growth (greater than 4-GB addressability, more I/O busses, and three times faster bus performance). What this all means is you get more processing power with RISC. That power will be needed as the computing paradigm moves toward emerging technologies such as object-oriented programming, multimedia computing, network computing, and distributed computing.

The RISC PowerPC AS technology for the AS/400 provides synergy with the remainder of IBM and is strategic to the long-term direction of the AS/400. The question was never whether the AS/400 would move to RISC, but when the move would be made. The RISC PowerPC AS was determined to be compatible with commercial applications if some things could be added, including a Tags Active mode for single-level storage, decimal assist functions, move-assist operations for fast memory management, and vectored supervisor calls.

The PowerPC AS with a wider I/O bandwidth allowed the implementation of a larger number of I/O busses, each of which could have a greater functional bandwidth. This allows systems to grow in I/O capacity commensurate with the performance capabilities of the processor and memory components.

RISC PowerPC AS Microprocessors

A microprocessor is a computer chip containing millions of microscopic transistors that work together to form the "brain" of a computer system. The internal structure of a microprocessor is called its architecture, and many different architectures are in use today. Current AS/400 systems (and other computers, such as the IBM RS/6000 family) use one or more PowerPC microprocessors as the basis for their computing engines. These microprocessors are special implementations of the PowerPC architecture, which is based on the Reduced Instruction Set Computer (RISC) concept. The idea behind RISC (pronounced "risk") is to gain a performance advantage by utilizing a simple set of instructions executed very quickly to do all work.

The PowerPC architecture enables high levels of performance through its superscalar design, using pipelining, hardwired operations, new op codes, and formats for optimal decoding and branch prediction to improve superscalar scheduling and cycle times.

The *op code* is the portion of the instruction which tells the microprocessor what operations to perform on the data to be manipulated by the instruction. *Superscalar* means that more than one instruction can be executed in a single cycle of the processor. *Pipelining* allows instructions to be processed as if they were on an assembly line. *Optimal decoding* adds a structure to the instruction layout that makes interpretation (within the microprocessor) faster. *Branch prediction* means that (during the compiling activity) potential jumps from one section of a program to another have been inspected to predict if they will be taken, in order to minimize the delay caused by the need to empty the pipeline if the branch requirements are met.

Many compiler optimization techniques have been implemented to minimize design bottlenecks while maximizing parallelism.

AS/400 PowerPC microprocessors have on-chip cache memory. These very high-speed memory areas serve as temporary storage and reduce the amount of time the microprocessor spends waiting for information to be pulled in from main storage, where access speed may be as much as 35 times slower. There are separate instruction and data cache areas to help streamline information flow through the microprocessor.

The AS/400 versions of PowerPC microprocessors (called RISC PowerPC AS microprocessors) have several unique features not found in the base PowerPC architecture (decimal support, move assist, vectored supervisory calls, tagged operations, etc.). These extensions help RISC-based AS/400 systems maintain and enhance commercial transaction performance.

Commercial computing workloads have different characteristics than engineering/scientific computing workloads (a traditional strength of RISC). The commercial environment typically has an increased number of concurrent users, longer instruction path lengths in both application code and the operating system, decreased predictability in branches, mostly fixed point arithmetic functions, and randomly organized I/O activity. These differences are illustrated in Figure 1.4.

The RISC PowerPC AS systems also have a wider I/O bandwidth, allowing for AS/400 systems with more I/O busses. This makes for AS/400 systems with greater I/O capacity, which are necessary to maintain balance with the higher levels of performance the RISC PowerPC AS microprocessors enable. The three PowerPC AS microprocessors used in current AS/400 systems are the A10 Microprocessor, the A35 Microprocessor, and the A50 Microprocessor.

Commercial Workloads	Scientific/Engineering Workloads
Many concurrent users	Few concurrent users
Longer path length over larger set of instructions	Smaller instructions working sets
More execution time in operating system code	More execution time spent in application work
Fewer loop iterations—more branches	Tight loops
Extensive manipulation of data structures through integer arithmetic and strong operations	Extensive use of floating point arithmetic
Random I/O activity	Sequential I/O activity

Figure 1.4. Commercial vs. scientific/engineering workloads.

The A10 Microprocessor

The **A10 Microprocessor** is a single-chip **CMOS** (Complementary Metal-Oxide Semiconductor) technology implementation that performs at a 77-MHz cycle rate as a pipelined superscalar design with separate fixed point, floating point, load/store, condition register, and branch units. In entry and midsize AS/400 systems, the A10 Microprocessor has about 4.7 million transistors. It can execute up to three instructions per cycle at a peak rate of 231 **Million Instructions Per Second** (MIPS). There are two on-chip caches, a 4-KB (1 **KB**, or **kilobyte**, is about 1000 bytes) instruction cache and an 8-KB data cache, and the A10 can support an optional 1-MB (1 **MB** is about 1 **million bytes**) off-chip cache. Figures 1.5 and 1.6 illustrate the interconnection paths for the memory and I/O for the various processors using the A10 Microprocessor chip as their base.

In Figure 1.5, one additional chip is used to generate the copper I/O bus used in the system unit that houses the processor, one additional chip is used to generate each pair of external optical busses used to house I/O in the external expansion towers, and the memory is driven directly by the A10 Microprocessor chip. In Figure 1.6, the I/O is driven in the same way as in Figure 1.5, but the memory bus is partitioned into two busses, each of which is supported by a separate storage control chip that manages the main storage accesses, and up to 0.5 MB of intermediate-level cache can be supported.

Figure 1.5. A10 Microprocessor I/O and main storage interconnect for entry and midrange processors.

Figure 1.6. A10 Microprocessor I/O and main storage interconnect for midrange and high-end processors.

The A35 Microprocessor

The **A35 Microprocessor** is a single-chip **CMOS** (Complementary Metal-Oxide Semiconductor) technology implementation of the RISC PowerPC AS that performs at a 125-MHz cycle rate as a pipelined superscalar design with separate fixed point, floating point, load/store, condition register, and branch units for entry-level to midsize AS/400 machines.

The A35 Microprocessor has about 4.7 million transistors. It can execute up to three instructions per cycle at a peak rate of 375 Million Instructions Per Second (MIPS). There are two on-chip caches, a 64-KB (1 KB is 1000 bytes) instruction cache and an 64-KB data cache, and the A35 can support an optional 1-MB or 4-MB (1 MB is about 1 million bytes) off-chip cache. Because the caches are separate, they can be accessed in parallel, increasing performance.

In midsize AS/400 systems, the A35 Microprocessor is connected to main storage through a storage control chip and to the I/O interfaces through a **Bus Control Adapter Logic (BCAL)** chip. The BCAL chip creates an intermediate interface from which other chips create either a PCI bus interface or an SPD bus interface. The base system unit in these systems always contains a PCI bus interface. The SPD bus is a private internal bus to which I/O adapters attach. The SPD bus is used in the high mid-range systems and the high-end systems to attach I/O. All expansion and extension units containing I/O adapter cards contain an SPD bus. V4R4 introduces an expansion unit containing a PCI bus which attaches up to 12 PCI based I/O adapters attached to three I/O processors.

In the high-end symmetrical multiprocessor system units, the main storage is again managed through storage control chips but the storage cards are arranged in either two or four banks, and the I/O interface is driven across a high-speed serial/parallel interface bus referred to as a **SCIL** (Serial Control Interface Logic) bus. The implementation of the SCIL bus allows the I/O devices to be packaged in a unit separate from the system processor/memory unit. The separate unit contains an SPD bus. The Model 730 systems do not take advantage of this possible separation. The Models 740 do use the separation to package the I/O in a separate tower.

As stated above, in high-end AS/400e systems, the I/O is driven from a SCIL bus (the SCIL bus is an ultra-high-speed serial interface), which drives up to three optical interface cards. The three optical interface cards **can connect** up to 18 optical busses and one copper bus. The copper bus connects to an I/O tower, which can be populated with disk units, tape units, and I/O interface cards. The main storage bus is partitioned into two busses, each of which is supported by a separate storage control chip (STGCTL) that manages the main storage accesses and up to 0.5 MB of intermediate-level cache.

This dual-memory bus architecture helps improve the performance of these systems. Figures 1.7, 1.8, and 1.9 illustrate the connection of the A35 Microprocessor in uni-processor, 8-way processor, and 12-way processor configurations.

The A50 Microprocessor

The A50 Microprocessor is a single-chip CMOS (Complementary Metal Oxide Semiconductor) technology implementation of the RISC PowerPC AS that performs at a 262 MHz cycle rate as a 4-way superscalar pipelined design with separate fixed point, floating point, load/store, condition register, and branch units in a single chip carrier for midsize to high-end AS/400 systems.

Figure 1.7. A35 Microprocessor/main storage and I/O interface for 2136 and 2119 Processors.

Figure 1.8. A35 Microprocessor/main storage and I/O interface for 2179, 2180, 2181, 2182, 2161, 2163, and 2165 Processors.

Figure 1.9. A35 Microprocessor/main storage and I/O interface for Processors 2239 and 2166.

The A50 Microprocessor also comes in two different multi-chip carriers that include the A50 Microprocessor and a single chip storage controller and I/O hub for the low-end AS/400 systems. The first package does not have support for an external cache and the processor operates at 200 MHz. The second package supports a 4-MB external cache and operates at about 255 MHz.

The A50 Microprocessor has about 12.7 million transistors. It can execute up to four instructions per cycle with a cycle time of 3.81 nanoseconds. There are two on-chip caches, a 64 KB (1 KB is 1,000 bytes) instruction cache and an 64 KB data cache. There is an optional external 4-way set-associative cache with a 32-byte high-speed data pumped interface which can support a 4 MB or an 8 MB off-chip cache. This cache-to-processor performance allows accessing 32 bytes at up to 262 MHz with a system bus bandwidth of 16 bytes at up to 87.3 MHz.

In low-end and midsized AS/400 systems (Figure 1.8), the A50 microprocessor is connected to main storage through a storage control chip, and to the I/O interfaces through a bus control adapter logic (BCAL) chip. The BCAL chip creates an intermediate interface from which other chips create either a PCI bus interface or an SPD bus interface. The base system unit in these systems always contains a PCI bus interface.

In the high-end symmetrical multiprocessor system units (Figure 1.9), the main storage is again managed through storage control chips but the storage cards are arranged in either two or four banks and the I/O interface is driven across a high-speed serial/parallel interface bus referred to as a SCIL (Serial Control Interface Logic) bus. The implementation of the SCIL bus allows the I/O devices to be packaged in a separate unit from the System Processor/Memory unit. The e-server model 740 uses the separation to package the I/O in a separate tower.

In the high-end AS/400, the I/O is driven from a SCIL bus (the SCIL bus is an ultra-high-speed serial interface) that drives up to three optical interface cards to which can be connected up to 18 optical busses and one copper bus. The copper bus connects to an I/O tower, which can be populated with disk units, tape units, and I/O interface cards. The main storage bus is partitioned into two busses, each of which is supported by a separate storage control chip (STGCTL) that manages the main storage accesses and up to 0.5 MB of intermediate-level cache. This dual-memory bus architecture helps improve the performance of these systems. The A35 and A50 Microprocessor card consumes three card slots.

Meet the AS/400 Family

Six basic computers form the core of the IBM AS/400e series family: the Entry Model 150, available in both general-purpose and server configurations, the Model 170 server versions with seven processor options, the three server models, 720, 730, and 740, and the custom application server 740-SB1.

The AS/400e server 150 continues to use the same packaging, and has received some additional capabilities in the software that is available. The Model 170 has a new lower performance entry point processor, and also a 2-way increased performance high-end processor.

The three server models 720, 730, and 740 provide increased server performance and a base interactive performance level of 35, 70, and 120 CPW respectively, and can be featured to support a significantly larger interactive workload.

The AS/400e server 720 reuses the packaging from the AS/400e system/server 620/S20 and those systems can be upgraded to the 720. The AS/400e server 720 offers four processors ranging from uni-processors to 4-way **SMPs** (Symmetrical Multi-Processors), and in general the interactive performance can be increased to approximately 50% of the client/server CPW performance capability.

The AS/400e server 730 reuses the packaging from the AS/400e system/server 640/S30 and those systems can be upgraded to the 730. The AS/400e server 730 offers four processors ranging from uni-processor to 8-way SMPs, and the interactive performance can be increased to the total CPW offered by the system processor.

The AS/400e server 740 reuses the packaging from the AS/400e system/server 650/S40 and those systems can be upgraded to the 740. The AS/400e server 740 offers two processors, an 8-way SMP and a 12-way SMP, and the interactive performance can be increased to the total CPW offered by the system processor.

The number of steps which may be taken from the base interactive performance to the maximum offered by a particular processor varies with the processor. In no case can the maximum client/server processor CPW performance value be exceeded when using the featured processor in interactive mode. (See paragraphs on benchmarking later in this Chapter for additional detail.)

The capability to feature the amount of interactive performance available on each of the 720, 730, and 740 servers allows them to support the ISV preload environment previously provided by the AS/400e custom mixed-mode server models S20-ISV, S30-ISV, and S40-ISV. Upgrades from the previous Custom Mixed-Mode Server models to the V4R4 7XX Servers are supported. The custom mixed-mode software packages continue to be provided by J. D. Edwards, Software Systems Associates, Intentia International's Movex V10.5, and International Business Systems (IBS), as well as others. The preload of the above business partner software packages continue to be offered on the AS/400e server 170.

The custom application server 740-SB1 is a main storage, DASD, and other-I/O-device constrained version of the 8-way and 12-way processor versions of the 740 server specifically tuned to provide high performance in the compute-intensive environment required by many multi-tiered computing environments. The 740-SB1 is intended to be used as a **SAP R3** application server to a separate second-tier server. The 740-SB1 models based on the A50 processor in both the 8-way and 12-way SMP versions cannot be distinguished from a 740 model with constrained main storage, DASD, and I/O functions.

A Closer Look at the AS/400 Family

Figure 1.10 contains a photograph of the AS/400e series family. Let us briefly look at each of these. The "e" in the AS/400e series names for these systems is intended to signify that the systems are capable of supporting the electronic business environment, which means that the user may establish a storefront on the World Wide Web and conduct business with the assurance for both the user and the customer that any and all transactions are secure and private.

System Unit Members

With this introduction to the members of the AS/400 family, we will describe in greater detail each of the system unit members in the following paragraphs.

AS/400 Advanced Entry Model 150 Specifics

The Entry Model 150 is the smallest, lowest-performing version of the AS/400 system. It is available in a general processing version and a server

Figure 1.10. AS/400 V4R4 family showing (from left) Models 740, 730, 720, 170, and 150.

version, each of which come in two configurations, entry and growth. The general processing **growth** version can attach up to 28 twinaxial workstations plus a single LAN connection on the MFIOP to support PC users. The server version can support up to about 150 PC-based clients and allows 28 interactive workstations to be attached via twinaxial cable.

Both models are available with up to 192 MB of main storage and 29.9 GB of disk storage, and can have up to 5 communications lines. The software integrated with the system includes support for improved performance, new Internet functions, new versions of Client Access Family for Windows, support for Windows NT Server, new encryption and security capabilities, and wireless capabilities for a small business. The Model 150 BasePak has been enhanced and will be discussed in greater detail in Chapter 4.

The AS/400 Advanced Entry Model 150 has been enhanced with a larger main storage capacity, a higher-capacity tape drive, a higher performance CD-ROM, an improved-performance Integrated PC Server (IPCS), and larger disk units. The Model 150 is targeted for the 2- to 20-user environment, including distributed locations and small businesses. The package, the smallest of the AS/400 systems and described in the following paragraphs, is shown in Figure 1.11.

Figure 1.11. AS/400 Advanced Entry Model 150.

Restraints on positioning the system unit against walls or desks do not apply unless the user removes the rounded rear cover. Air intake is entirely from the front, and exhaust is entirely through the rounded rear cover. The rounded rear cover allows for both cable exit and air exhaust independent of system positioning. The control panel on the front of the system unit is used by the system operator and service personnel to control the Model 150. From this panel, power can be turned on or off, the system can be initialized, and system problems can be analyzed. Many of these functions, including turning on the system power, can be performed remotely through communications lines.

The standard tape unit and CD-ROM can also be seen from the front of the system unit. The Model 150 can be plugged into a standard electrical outlet (90–140 VAC) or a high-voltage outlet (180–260 VAC) and meets "quiet office" guidelines (under 5.5 dB) for operational noise. Utility power failure protection can be added via a 9910 UPS, which will hold the system up in the presence of a utility power failure for 5 minutes while data from main storage is being written to disk. This, along with its attractive appearance, allows the Model 150 to fit easily beside a desk or in a corner.

The package includes a 12/20x CD-ROM, an 8-GB ¼-inch cartridge tape unit, one 4-GB DASD unit, and up to three 8-GB DASD units, a 64-bit PowerPC Advanced System Microprocessor, a 32-bit PowerPC-603 I/O Microprocessor, and an industry-standard 72-pin, 4-byte **Single In-line Memory Module (SIMM)** with **Error Correction Code (ECC)**, and may feature a 133-MHz Intel Pentium coprocessor (standard on the "Growth Server" version), and slots for 3 Portable Computer Interface (PCI) I/O adapters. The system is available both as a commercial processing–based unit, in which case some of the workstations must be twinax based, and as a server, in which case some of the workstations must be PCs and LAN connected, and a Communications Console must be present. A port is provided for an external UPS.

The system capacities and performance capabilities of the Model 150 are summarized in Figure 1.12. As shown in the figure, the Model 150 system has both entry- and growth-level models. The entry-level system has a constrained processor performance rating of 13.8 CPW (*constrained performance* means that the amount of memory and disk limit the performance), 64 MB of main storage, 4 GB of DASD, 1 communications line, and either a twinaxial adapter (twinaxial version), which can support up to 7 users (the 0182 Processor can support 28 workstations), or a LAN (server version), which can support up to 28 PC users. One modem is provided for support of the Establishment Communications System (ECS) connection.

The main storage of the Model 150 may be increased to 192 MB in three steps of 32 or 64 MB each, and three additional disk units may be provided for a total capacity of 29.9 GB. When the memory and disk capacity are at the maximum, the unconstrained processor performance is 27.0 **CPW** (*unconstrained performance* means that the processor is the first limit on performance). There are five PCI adapter slots. The five PCI slots may be populated with two-line communications adapters.

The Entry Model 150 is also available in a growth model, which changes the processor to have a unconstrained CPW rating of 35 with the maximum main storage and disk drives. The growth model supports up to 28 workstation addresses in addition to what is used in the three expansion slots. A software modem function is available for the growth model. The Entry Server is also available in a growth model,

Packages	Twinax Entry (0191)	Twinax Growth (0192)	Server Entry (0193)	Server Growth (0194)
Software	BasePak	BasePak	BasePak	BasePak
Performance				
Constrained CPW Rating	13.8	20.2	13.8	20.2
Unconstrained CPW Rating	27.0	35.0	27.0	35.0
Main Storage (MB) min/max	64/192	128/192	64/192	128/192
Disk Storage (GB) min/max	4,194/29.9	4,194/29.9	4,194/29.9	4.194/29.9
Tape and Internal Optional Attachments (max/system)				
¼-inch Cartridge Tape	1	1	1	1
CD-ROM	1	1	1	1
Physical Packaging				
PCI I/O Card Slots	5	5	5	5
Integrated PC Server and Bridge Card Slots	2	2	2	2
Workstation Attachents (max)				
Twinaxial Controllers	1	1	0/1	0/1
Twinaxial Devices	1/7	1/28	0 std 7 opt	0 std 28 opt
Communications Lines (max)	5	5	5	5
Integrated PC Server	0/1	0/1	0/1	1
Lan IOA	0/2	0/2	1/2	1/2
Integrated PC Server LAN (max)	2	2	2	2
MFIOP LAN (max)	1	1	1	1

Figure 1.12. Model 150 capacities chart.

which has an unconstrained performance rating of 35.0. Both growth models have a starting main storage of 128 MB.

The software provided with the Model 150 referred to as BasePak, includes OS/400, Query, Client Access, DB2/400 Query and SQL Development Toolkit, Performance Manager, and FAX Support/400. (A more detailed description of Entry Model 150 BasePak software is provided later in this book.) The hard-copy publications provided with the system have been minimized to include only system planning (backup communications), customizing environments (sign-on, passwords, etc.) and customized universal installation instructions. All other publications are delivered on a CD-ROM, and if hard-copy is desired it must be printed on the user's equipment.

AS/400e server 170 Specifics

The AS/400e server 170 is intended to fulfill the function of a department server. Seven processor options are allowed, ranging in performance from about twice the performance of the Model 150 processor to significantly overlapping the performance offered in the AS/400e server 720. It is not possible to upgrade to the Model 170 from any other model or from the Model 170 to any other model. Main storage feature cards are not customer installed; if the customer orders additional main storage, IBM will install the main storage and any other features also ordered.

Like its predecessors, the Model 170 is packaged into a small deskside unit, which is then cabled to the necessary AS/400 workstations and printers. Like the predecessor models, the processor performance within the AS/400e series models can be upgraded without having to change any other element of the system. The primary difference in the Model 170 relative to the previous system/server models is the much improved performance offered and the total I/O capacity of the systems. The **Model** 170 uses the same OS/400 operating system as the rest of the AS/400 family. This means that application programs and data on a 9406 Model 170 system can be used unchanged on larger AS/400e systems as a business grows.

All of the server models described now support up to 28 twinaxial workstations versus the 7 previously supported. With V4R4, the entry processor based system to the Model 170 e-server system set is based on the lowest performance processor. The entry processor model 170 is not capable of supporting the expansion unit and is limited in the amount of DASD and I/O devices which can be attached. Also with V4R4, the highest performance processor is a 2-way Symmetrical Multi-Processor (SMP) which can support the maximum set of features which may be assembled on a Model 170.

The AS/400e server 170 V4R2 (A35) and V4R3/V4R4 (A50) processors are differentiated from each other by the fact that the A50 processors support an increased interactive workload versus the previous A35 processors in the four lower performing versions. The next two highest performing processors in the V4R3 A50 versions significantly outperform the A35-based V4R2 versions in both client/server and to a lesser degree in interactive performance. The highest performing 2-way processor significantly overlaps the Model 720 processor performance in client/server computing, although it cannot be extended as far as the lowest performing Model 720 processor in interactive performance.

For the V4R3/V4R4 processors, the operating system for the server model was optimized for server applications (sharing resources with other computers) and was not optimized for interactive applications. The user must accept the interactive performance which is available from the particular processor selected.

The AS/400e server 170 was shown in Figure 1.2 at the beginning of this chapter. The Model 170 comes in a base unit and can be expanded by attaching a bolt-on expansion sidecar. In appearance, the Model 170 looks like a reduced height Model 720 but is slightly wider when the expansion sidecar is attached. The Model 170 comes standard with a PowerPC A50 RISC Microprocessor #2289(CPW performance rating 50.0 client/server, 15 interactive), 64 MB of main storage, a **Multi-Function I/O Processor (MFIOP)**, a 4.19-GB 3½-inch disk drive, 1/4-inch cartridge tape, a CD-ROM drive, a communications adapter, and a Local Area Network (LAN) port. The LAN port can be either Ethernet or token ring. The base system can also include a workstation adapter.

The Model 170 performance can be increased by selecting one of six processor upgrades (feature codes #2290, #2291, #2292, #2385, #2386, or #2388) with CPW performance ratings of 73, 115, 220, 460, 460, and 1090 respectively, while supporting interactive capacity of 20, 25, 30, 50, 70, and 70 respectively. Each of these processors is a uniprocessor, with the exception of the #2388 which is a 2-way SMP processor.

Processors #2292, #2385, #2386, and #2388 contain a base main storage of 256 MB. The 64 MB of base main storage supported by the #2289 base processor, the #2290 and the #2291 processors can be grown to 832 MB. The main storage with processor #2292 can grow to 1,024 MB. The main storage with processors #2385, #2386, and #2388 can be grown to 3,584 MB. The main storage expansion options used on these models attach within the processor cage so that they don't consume expansion slots.

The Model 170 base structure can house up to ten disk drives in two disk cage assemblies (one base-four drives, and one featured-six drives) for a maximum disk capacity of 175.4 GB. The #2289 processor is constrained to the base tower and as a result can only support 70.1 GB of disk capacity. It can also house one tape drive, one CD-ROM, and an operator panel. The internal tape, disk, and CD-ROM drives are all supported via an Ultra-SCSI interface. It is also possible to attach up to 228 twinaxial workstations spread across 6 controllers, 12 communications lines, and 5 LANs. A total of 3 high-speed Portable Computer Interface (PCI) adapters may be used (either ATM or 10/100 Ethernet). System capacities are summarized in Figure 1.13. With the exception of the #2289 processor, two external tape libraries, either ½-inch cartridge or 8-mm tape, and one optical library can be attached.

To achieve the maximum system capacities noted in the previous paragraph, it is necessary to attach the bolt-on system expansion unit. Processor #2289 can only support reduced capacities. The Model 170 system unit expansion also can house an additional PCI card cage, which can house up to 14 PCI cards.

The Model 170 system unit and the system unit expansion option can be individually plugged into standard electrical outlets (110–260 VAC). Base utility power failure protection is provided with an external CPM/UPS and Continuously Powered Main Storage (CPM), described later in this chapter.

AS/400e server 720 Specifics

The IBM AS/400e server 720 is packaged in a chassis that looks like the Model 170 mounted on a raised platform. The raised platform includes batteries and UPS electronics, and sometimes additional power supplies and disk unit support (depending upon the processor contained in the system).

The AS/400e server 720 can be ordered from the factory in high-availability versions (referring to the ability to continue operation in the event of component failures). The high-availability features on these models include redundant power supplies; internal battery backup with up to two days of **Continuously Powered Main Storage (CPM)**, which will be explained in a later section; concurrent maintenance of disk/tape devices; and hardware RAID-5/mirroring data protection.

The AS/400e server S20 is a desk-side system (Figure 1.14). It uses the previous Model 620 mechanical package and comes standard with a PowerPC A50 RISC Microprocessor #2061 (CPW performance rating 240 client/server, 35 interactive), 256 MB of main storage, a Multi-Function I/O Processor (MFIOP), a 4.19-GB 3½-inch disk drive, a CD-ROM drive, a communications adapter, a workstation controller, and a LAN adapter. The interactive performance can be enhanced by swapping the interactive base feature card for either a #1501 with 70

Uni-Processor Feature Number	2289	2290	2291	2292	2385	2386	2388
Relative System Performance*							
Client/Server interactive	50 / 15	73 / 20	115 / 25	220 / 30	460 / 50	460 / 70	1090 / 70
Cache Memory	NA	NA	NA	NA	4 MB	4 MB	4MB
Main Storage (MB) Min/Max	64/832	64/832	64/832	256/1024	256 /3584	256/3584	256/3584
Disk Capacity (GB) Min/Max	4.19/70.1	4.19/175.4	4.19/175.4	4.19/175.4	4.19/175.4	4.19/175.4	4.19/175.4
Communication Lines	1 to 6	1 to 12	1 to 12	1 to 12	1 to 12	1 to 12	1 to 18
IPCS (with 1 or 2 LANs)	0 to 2	0 to 2	0 to 2	0 to 2	0 to 2	0 to 2	0 to 2
LAN Ports	1 to 3	1 to 6	1 to 6	1 to 6	1 to 6	1 to 6	1 to 6
High to Speed PCI slot							
(ATM, 10/100 Ethernet)	0 to 3	0 to 3	0 to 3	0 to 3	0 to 3	0 to 3	0 to 3
Twinaxial Controllers	0 to 6	0 to 6	0 to 6	0 to 6	0 to 6	0 to 6	0 to 6
Maximum Twinaxial Workstations	68	228	228	228	228	228	228
CD-ROM	1	1	1	1	1	1	1
1/4-Inch Cartridge Tape							
(2.5, 4.0, 13, 25 GB uncompressed;							
5.0, 8.0, 26, 50 GB compressed)	1	0 to 1	0 to 1	0 to 1	0 to 1	0 to 1	0 to 1
1/2-Inch Tape 9348 3XXX							
(except 3480/3490/3490E to C10)	0	0 to 2	0 to 2	0 to 2	0 to 2	0 to 2	0 to 2
Uninterruptible Power Supply (w/CPM)	0 to 1	0 to 1	0 to 1	0 to 1	0 to 1	0 to 1	0 to 1
8mm Cartridge Tape (External)	0	0 to 2	0 to 2	0 to 2	0 to 2	0 to 2	0 to 2
Optical Libraries	0	0 to 2	0 to 2	0 to 2	0 to 2	0 to 2	0 to 2

* (Processor CPW) Unconstrained Rating

Notes: Relative system performance measurements (CPW values) are based on AS/400 environment, commercial processing workload (CPW). The CPW workload is representative of commercial applications, particularly those that do significant database processing in conjunction with journaling and commitment control. The CPW workload is measured on maximum configurations. CPW values may not be realized in all environments.

Figure 1.13. V4R4 AS/400e server 170 capacity and performance summary.

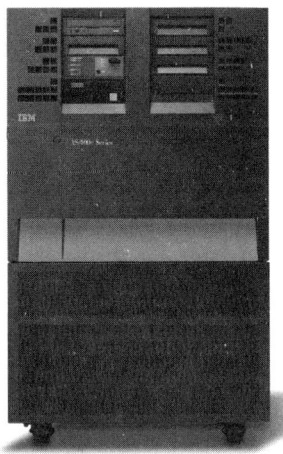

Figure 1.14. AS/400e server S20 with expansion.

CPW interactive performance, or a #1502 with 120 CPW interactive performance.

The Model 720's performance can be increased by selecting one of three processor upgrades (feature codes #2062, #2063, #2064) with CPW performance ratings of 420.0, 810.0, and 1600.0 client/server respectively, and a base interactive performance of 35 CPW. The #2062 processor interactive performance can be enhanced by swapping the base interactive feature card for increased interactive performance features cards #1501, #1502, with the aforementioned interactive performance values, or #1503 with 240 CPW interactive performance. The #2063 Processor is a 2-way Symmetrical Multi-Processor (SMP) implementation. The #2063 processor interactive performance can be enhanced by swapping the base interactive feature card for increased interactive performance features cards #1501, #1502, #1503 with the aforementioned interactive performance values, or #1504 with 560 CPW interactive performance. The #2064 is a 4-way SMP implementation. The #2064 processor interactive performance can be enhanced by swapping the base interactive feature card for increased interactive performance features cards #1501, #1502, #1503, #1504, with the aforementioned interactive performance values, or #1505 with 1050 CPW interactive performance.

The Model 720 base structure can house up to 15 disk drives in three disk cage assemblies (one base and two featured). It can also house one tape drive, one CD-ROM, an operator panel, and an 8-adapter Portable Computer Interface (PCI) I/O card cage. Up to 8,192 MB of main storage can be packaged with the 2063 and 2064 Processors. Up to 2,048 MB of main storage can be packaged with the 2061 and up to 4,096 MB of main storage can be packaged with the 2062 Processor. The main storage expansion options used on these models attach within the processor cage so that they don't consume expansion slots. Main storage must be added in matched pairs using either 32-MB or 128-MB or 256-MB DIMM storage cards. Disk Drive Capacity can be increased to 1,288 GB.

It is also possible to attach up to 2,628 twinaxial workstations, or 1,044 ASCII workstations, 128 communications lines, 32 fax lines, and 24 local area networks (LANs). Some of the Local Area Networks may be displaced by Integrated PC Servers, of which a maximum of 17 FSIOPs is allowed on a system distributed among the PCI and SPD bus capabilities. In addition, four tape libraries (either ½-inch cartridge or 8-mm tape) and 14 optical libraries can be attached. Figure 1.15 illustrates the maximum system capacities and performance capabilities for the Model 720.

To achieve the maximum system capacities, it is necessary to attach the bolt-on expansion unit, which can increase the total number of disk drives by 15, housed in three disk drive cages. The Model 720 expansion unit also can house either an additional SPD card cage or an additional PCI card cage. The 9331 SPD card cage has space for 7 SPD I/O cards, one of which is the optical bus controller, which can generate up to 4 optical busses for attachment of an additional four expansion towers. The PCI card cage in the expansion unit can house up to 14 PCI cards, among which can be two optical bus adapter cards to generate attachments for two expansion towers, which can be either storage expansion towers or I/O expansion towers. The maximum capacities of the Model 720 system can only be attained by using these expansion towers.

The Model 720 system unit can be plugged into standard high-voltage electrical outlets (180–260 VAC). Utility power failure protection is via internal battery backup and Continuously Powered Main Storage (CPM). The internal battery backup is capable of retaining main storage content for up to 24 hours using CPM. Longer periods of retention may be attained by attaching the external battery backup feature.

Attributes	2061 (Uni)	2062 (Uni)	2063 (2-way)	2064 (4-way)
Processor CPW	240	420	810	1,600
Interactive CPW				
Min/Max	35/120	35/240	35/420	35/870
Main Storage (MB)				
Min/Max	256/2,048	256/4,096	256/8,192	256/8,192
DASD Capacity (GB)				
Min/Max	4.19/1,288	4.19/1,288	4.19/1,288	4.19/1,288
Communications Lines	1 to 128	1 to 128	1 to 128	1 to 128
LAN Ports	1 to 24	1 to 24	1 to 24	1 to 24
IPCS (with 1 or 2 LANs)	1 to 17	1 to 17	1 to 17	1 to 17
Twinaxial controllers	0 to 66	0 to 66	0 to 66	0 to 66
Maximum twinaxial				
workstations	2,628	2,628	2,628	2,628
ASCII controllers	0 to 58	0 to 58	0 to 58	0 to 58
Maximum ASCII				
workstations	1,044	1,044	1,044	1,044
1/4-inch cartridge				
tape drives	0 to 17	0 to 17	0 to 17	0 to 17
1/2-inch tape				
9347				
2440/9348	0 to 4	0 to 4	0 to 4	0 to 4
3xxx	0 to 4	0 to 4	0 to 4	0 to 4
8-mm cartridge tape (external)	0 to 4	0 to 4	0 to 4	0 to 4
Diskette (8 or 5.25 inch)	0 to 2	0 to 2	0 to 2	0 to 2
Optical Libraries	0 to 14	0 to 14	0 to 14	0 to 14
Fax IOPs	0 to 32	0 to 32	0 to 32	0 to 32
Uninterruptible Power Supply	0 to 1	0 to 1	0 to 1	0 to 1
Software Tier	P10/P20	P10/P20	P20/P30	P20/P30

Figure 1.15. AS/400e server 720 performance and capacities summary.

AS/400e server 730 Specifics

The AS/400e server 730 makes up the high end of the middle range of the AS/400e series family. The Model 730 processors include the 1-way, 2-way, and 4-way processor versions of AS/400 computers using the most powerful of the A50 Microprocessors. This provides for higher performance, more users, more communications, more storage, and greater growth capability than the Model 720.

The Model 730 also includes an 8-way version of the processor. The Model 730 uses a package common with the previous Model 640 and S/30 approximately the size of the 1.6-meter rack in the previous S/30 through F 9406 models. The Model 730 uses a SCIL bus for connecting to the I/O function, the base portion of which is totally contained within the system unit tower.

The AS/400e server 730 (Figure 1.16) is a tall-tower system. The Model 730 comes standard with a PowerPC A50 RISC Microprocessor #2065(CPW performance rating 560 client/server, 70 CPW interactive), 512 MB of main storage, a Multi-Function I/O Processor (MFIOP), a 4.19-GB 3½-inch disk drive, a CD-ROM drive, a communications adapter, a workstation controller, a LAN adapter, an optic controller capable of controlling up to six optical busses, one SPD bus, and a logic cage capable of containing three additional feature cards.

The Model 730's performance can be increased by selecting one of three processor upgrades (feature codes #2066, #2067, and #2068) with

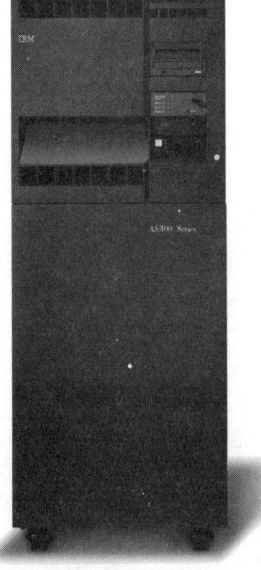

Figure 1.16. AS/400e server 730.

CPW performance ratings of 1,050, 2,000, and 2,890 respectively. The #2066, #2067, and #2068 are respectively 2-way, 4-way, and 8-way Symmetrical Multi-Processors (SMPs). Each of the above microprocessors has a base interactive performance of 70 CPW. The base interactive performance can be increased by the swapping of the base interactive feature card for one of the optional interactive feature cards.

In no case can the interactive performance exceed the client/server CPW performance value supplied by the processor. The interactive feature cards supported by the model 730 are 1507, 1508, 1509, 1510, and 1511 offering interactive performance values of 120, 240, 560, 1,050, and 2,000 respectively. With the #2065, #2066, and #2067 processors, the interactive performance can become as large as the client/server performance. The section on performance later in this chapter explains what happens when an attempt is made to get greater interactive performance than is available from the processor.

The Model 730 base structure can house up to 12 disk drives, one tape drive, one CD-ROM, an operator panel, up to 24,576 MB of main storage, and an 8-card SPD I/O card cage. Up to 18 optical busses can be generated for the attachment of expansion towers. The main storage expansion options used on these models attach within the processor cage so that they don't consume expansion slots. Main storage cards must be installed in matched pairs. Main storage card sizes available are 128, 256, 512, 1024 and 2048 MB. It is also possible to attach up to 7,000 twinaxial workstations, or 3,150 ASCII workstations, 250 communications lines, 32 fax lines, and 48 local area networks (LANs) (16 Integrated PC Servers). Twenty-two optical libraries can be attached. Whenever the second disk cage is added, the feature power supply must be added. The system capacities and performance capabilities are summarized in Figure 1.17. Maximum total disk storage capacity for the system is 2.5 Terabytes. To achieve the maximum system capacities, it is necessary to attach expansion towers to each of the 18 possible optical busses. The system maximum can contain a total of 19 busses, 18 of which are optical, and one is copper contained in the base I/O tower.

The Model 730 system unit can be plugged into standard high-voltage electrical outlets (180–260 VAC). Base utility power failure protection is provided by internal battery backup and Continuously Powered Main Storage (CPM). When the second disk cage is added, the feature power supply must also be added.

Attributes	2065 (Uni)	2066 (2-way)	2067 (4-way)	2068 (8-way)
Processor CPW	560	1,050	2,000	2,890
Interactive CPW				
Min/Max	70/560	70/1,050	70/2,000	70/2,000
Main Storage (MB)				
Min/Max	512/24,576	512/24,576	512/24,576	512/24,576
DASD Capacity (GB)				
Min/Max	4.19/2,500	4.19/2,500	4.19/2,500	4.19/2,500
Communications Lines	1 to 250	1 to 250	1 to 250	1 to 250
LAN Ports	1 to 48	1 to 48	1 to 48	1 to 48
IPCS (with 1 or 2 LANs)	1 to 16	1 to 16	1 to 16	1 to 16
Twinaxial controllers	0 to 175	0 to 175	0 to 175	0 to 175
Maximum twinaxial				
workstations	7,000	7,000	7,000	7,000
ASCII controllers	0 to 175	0 to 175	0 to 175	0 to 175
Maximum ASCII				
workstations	3,150	3,150	3,150	3,150
1/4-inch cartridge				
tape drives	0 to 17	0 to 17	0 to 17	0 to 17
1/2-inch tape				
9347	0 to 2	0 to 2	0 to 2	0 to 2
2440/9348	0 to 4	0 to 4	0 to 4	0 to 4
3xxx	0 to 8	0 to 8	0 to 8	0 to 8
8-mm cartridge tape (external)	0 to 4	0 to 4	0 to 4	0 to 4
Diskette (8 or 5.25 Inch)	0 to 2	0 to 2	0 to 2	0 to 2
Optical Libraries	0 to 22	0 to 22	0 to 22	0 to 22
Fax IOPs	0 to 32	0 to 32	0 to 32	0 to 32
Uninterruptible Power Supply	0 to 1	0 to 1	0 to 1	0 to 1
Software Tier	P10/P20	P20/P30	P30/P40	P30/P40

Figure 1.17. AS/400e server 730 capacities table.

To assist in the understanding of the discussion for the Model 730 servers, the 1-way, 2-way, and 4-way processor/memory and I/O bus connections are shown in Figures 1.18 through 1.20, respectively.

AS/400e server 740 Specifics

The AS/400e server 740 makes up the high end of the AS/400 family. The Model 740 includes 8-way and 12-way versions of A50 micropro-

Figure 1.18. AS/400e series 1-way processor/memory and I/O interconnection.

cessors. Using the A50 microprocessor provides higher performance, more users, more communications, more storage, and greater growth capability than either the Model 730 or the Model 720. The AS/400e server 740 uses a common package approximately the size of the 1.6 meter rack in the previous B through F 9406 models plus a separate I/O function tower the size of the previous Model 500 system unit. Both the processor unit and the I/O function tower operate from a 240-V line source. The I/O function tower connects to the processor unit tower by means of a new technology interface cable called SCIL (Serial Control Interface Logic), which allows a separation between these two units of up to 100 meters. The processor unit for these systems consists of a tower the same size as the total system unit in the Model 730.

The AS/400e server 740 reuses the same package as the Model 650 (Figure 1.21). It comes standard with an 8-way Symmetrical Multi-Pro-

Figure 1.19. AS/400e series 2-way processor/memory and I/O interconnection.

cessor (SMP), PowerPC A50 RISC Microprocessor #2069 (CPW performance rating 3,660.0 client/server, 120 CPW interactive), 1,024 MB of main storage, a Multi-Function I/O Processor (MFIOP), a 4.19-GB 3½-inch disk drive, a CD-ROM drive, a 6-bus-capable optical controller, a communications adapter, a workstation controller, a LAN, one SPD bus, and a logic cage capable of containing five additional feature cards and three additional 3½-inch disk units.

The Model 740 can be upgraded to a 12-way PowerPC A50 RISC Microprocessor #2070 (CPW performance rating 4,550.0 client/server, 120 interactive). The base interactive performance can be increased by

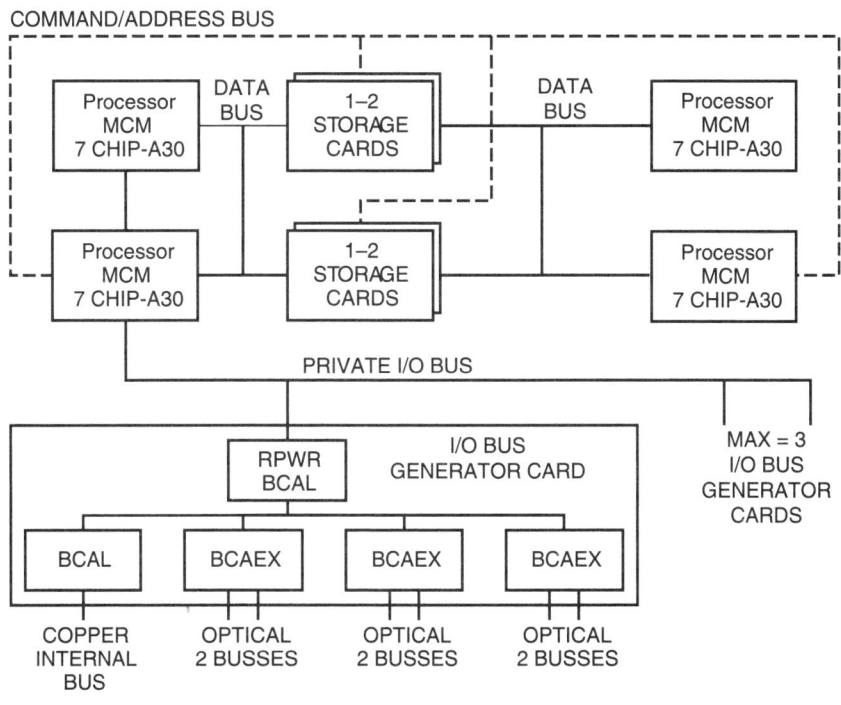

Figure 1.20. AS/400e series 4-way processor/memory and I/O interconnection.

swapping the base interactive processor function for one of the interactive feature processors #1510, #1511, #1512, or #1513 with interactive CPW value ratings of 1,050, 2,000, 3,660, or 4,550 respectively. In no case can the interactive performance value exceed the client/server performance value. The section on performance later in this chapter explains what happens when an attempt is made to get greater interactive performance than is available from the processor.

The Model 740 base structure can house up to four 3½-inch disk drives, one tape drive, one CD-ROM, an operator panel, up to a maximum of 40,960 MB of main storage in increments of four main storage cards each, and a 16-slot SPD I/O card cage. The SPD I/O card cage contains the disk units, the optical adapter cards, the MFIOP, and up to

Figure 1.21. AS/400e server 740 and e-server 740-SBI.

three feature cards. Up to 18 optical busses and two feature optical controllers for the attachment of expansion towers can be generated from the base. The main storage expansion options used on these models attach within the processor tower so that they don't consume I/O expansion slots.

Main storage must be plugged in groups of four cards. Main storage card sizes are 128, 256, 512, 1,024 and 2,048 MB. It is also possible to attach up to 7,000 twinaxial workstations, or 3,150 ASCII workstations, 300 communications lines, 32 fax lines, and 72 local area networks (LANs). Up to 36 Integrated PC Servers may be used instead of the local area networks, where a IPCS can contain two LANs. Twenty-two optical libraries can be attached. The 5052 Storage Expansion Unit may be added to the base I/O tower to increase the total number of 3½-inch disk drives to 20. A maximum disk capacity of 4.29 Terabytes is supported. The total system capacities and performance capabilities of the Model 740 are summarized in Figure 1.22. To achieve the maximum system capacities, it is necessary to attach expansion towers to each of the 18 possible optical busses. The S40 server supports up to 48 LANs with up to 12,288 PC workstations attached.

Attributes	2069 (8-way)	2070 (12-way)
Processor CPW	3,660	4,550
Interactive CPW Min/Max	120/3,660	120/4,550
Main Storage (MB) Min/Max	1,024/40,960	1,024/40,960
DASD Capacity (GB) Min/Max	4.19/4,290	4.19/4,290
Communications Lines	1 to 300	1 to 300
LAN Ports	1 to 72	1 to 72
IPCS (with 1 or 2 LANs)	1 to 16	1 to 16
Twinaxial controllers	0 to 175	0 to 175
Maximum twinaxial workstations	7,000	7,000
ASCII controllers	0 to 175	0 to 175
Maximum ASCII workstations	3,150	3,150
1/4-inch cartridge tape drives	0 to 17	0 to 17
1/2-inch tape		
9347	0 to 2	0 to 2
2440/9348	0 to 4	0 to 4
3xxx	0 to 8	0 to 8
8-mm cartridge tape (external)	0 to 4	0 to 4
Diskette (8 or 5.25 Inch)	0 to 2	0 to 2
Optical Libraries	0 to 22	0 to 22
Fax IOPs	0 to 32	0 to 32
Uninterruptible Power Supply	0 to 1	0 to 1
Software Tier	P40/P50	P40/P50

Figure 1.22. AS/400e server 740 performance and capacities summary.

The Model 740 system unit processor tower and the base I/O tower must be plugged individually into standard high-voltage electrical outlets (180-260 VAC). Base utility power failure protection is provided by internal battery backup and Continuously Powered Main Storage (CPM). The internal battery backup is capable of retaining 16 GB of main storage content using CPM for 24 hours. To extend the retention interval to 48 hours, or to support more than 16 GB of main storage, the external battery backup feature must be installed.

To accommodate users with the previous 19-inch rack-mounted equipment, the new 7X0-based models can interface compatibly with that equipment. It is also possible to perform processor performance upgrades within the new models. These models use the same OS/400 operating system as the rest of the AS/400 family. In fact, the operating system is now bundled with the hardware, which means that when one of the e-systems, whether it is used as a server or general-purpose system, is ordered, the operating system is included with that order. For previous hardware models, an operating system license was ordered separately from the hardware. For clarity, we will refer to all AS/400e servers as Application Systems. When we discuss a specific product, the specific name will be used.

Custom Mixed-Mode Servers

The custom mixed-mode servers software preload capability continues to be supported on the Models 720, 730, and 740. The customer can define the interactive workload desired to be supported by selection of the interactive workload feature. Applications software can be selected from a set of tested business partners. The applications software in general fits into an Enterprise Resource Planning environment. The following list identifies the companies whose software can be preloaded, the program name, a summary of application areas addressed by the program, and links to the program provider's Internet site. This software preload capability is also available on the AS/400e server 170.

IBM Solutions Packaging Web site: *http://www.ibm.com/as400/developer/packaging/*

SSA—BPCS Client/Server or Mixed Mode

BPCS Client/Server is a comprehensive set of integrated client/server applications that addresses the core system needs of industrial sector enterprises on a global scale. BPCS Client/Server covers Configurable Enterprise Financials applications, Supply Chain Management applications, Multi-Mode Manufacturing applications, and CIM applications, as well as Electronic Commerce applications such as EDI. BPCS Client/Server is based on SSA's proven object technology foundation that ensures that it operates identically from an end-user's perspective across any supported AS/400 server.

SSA Web site: *http://www.ssax.com*

MAPICS—MAPICS XA

MAPICS is the most widely used manufacturing software system in the world. Its modular design allows selecting from more than 40 applications to custom configure the right solution for a specific manufacturing situation.

Mapics Web site: *http://www.mapics.com*

JBA International—JBA System 21

This software contains an integrated enterprise-wide suite of supply chain applications that provide manufacturing, financial, service management, customer service, and logistics solutions with expanded functional fit for the automotive, beverage, food, and apparel and footwear sectors.

JBA Web site: *http://www.jbaworld.com*

International Business Systems—IBS - ASW

ASW covers an extensive range of functions in modules for

- Management Information
- Data Warehousing
- Sales and Distribution
- Financial Management
  - Manufacturing

IBS Web site: *http://www.ibs.se* and *http://www.ibsus.com*
San Francisco Project: *http://www.softmall.com/sf*

Intentia—the Movex System

The Movex System is a fully integrated ERP system with a high degree of functionality for manufacturers and distributors.

Intentia Web site: *http://www.intentia.com*

Baan—BaanERP

BaanERP is a suite of components including: sales, warehousing, purchasing, manufacturing, projects and service, finance, technology, and architecture. Baan is a world leader in innovative application solutions for the extended industry with over 4,000 customer sites in over 60 countries. The BaanERP solution can be preloaded on AS/400e Series (except Model 150).

Baan/400 newsletter (subscribe by emailing): *ibmbaan@us.ibm.com*
Baan Web Site: *http://www.baan.com*

Infinium—Infinium Suite for IBM AS/400

The Infinium Series for the IBM AS/400 has been designed, and optimized, for the AS/400. The Infinium Suite for AS/400 runs native to the AS/400. The Infinium Suite for AS/400 includes financial management, materials management, human resources, and process manufacturing solutions. The Infinium Suite for AS/400 includes five packages which may be ordered separately or as a suite:

- Infinium Human Resources

- Infinium Financial Management

- Infinium Materials Management

- Infinium Process Manufacturing

  - Infinium AS/400e Extensions

Infinium Web site: *http://www.infinium.com/html/as_400_products.html*

Acacia Technologies—Acacia Suite for AS/400

Acacia Technologies offers a full suite of enterprise-wide applications and tools designed to run manufacturing and distribution enterprises. These products include Enterprise Resource Planning (ERP), Warehouse Management System (WMS), Advanced Planning and Scheduling (ASP), Data Warehousing, and a variety of powerful tools. All Acacia Technologies products are designed exclusively for the AS/400 client/server platform.

Also, all current releases of Acacia products are Year 2000 compliant.
Acacia Web site: *http://www.acaciatech.com*

Lilly Software Associates—Visual Manufacturing

Visual Manufacturing is Lilly Software Associates' comprehensive ERP solution for manufacturers. Designed to accommodate jobshop, engineer-to-order, make-to-order, make-to-stock, and mixed-mode manufacturing environments, VISUAL Manufacturing provides the technology needed to improve productivity, control costs, and increase profits.
Lilly Software Associates Web site: *http://www.lillysoftware.com*

SAP-Base R/3 Package

For over two years, IBM has been delivering preloaded R/3 software to AS/400 customers all over the world. This offering provides a quick, simple start in working with SAP R/3. It provides the option to have the base R/3 application installed in a 2-tier or 3-tier configuration offering a savings of at least three fewer days of on-site install time. Upon arrival, the system is ready for consultants to begin R/3 customization and configuration.

SAP—Ready to Run R/3

Customers will find SAP's Ready to Run R/3 solution on AS/400e to be among the easiest-to-use and fastest-to-deploy, utilizing a unique selection of hardware and software management tools and support materials as part of the package. Ready-to Run R/3 offerings on AS/400e in easy-to-order packages for 25, 50, 785, 100, 150, 250, and 500 R/3 users are available as a single foot print solution eliminating the hidden multi-tier costs of competitive offerings. Predefined R/3 Users and Profiles, Operating Modes, System Maintenance and Backup Schedules and Alert Monitor threshold values are just a few of the software customization options available as part of the preload package.
SAP website: *http://www.sap.com.menu*

Custom Applications Servers

The only custom application server currently offered is the SB1, a second-tier server in a compute-intensive environment. The AS/400e custom application server SB1, as a result of its intended use in a compute-intensive environment, has a large main storage with tight restrictions on the other I/O functions available.

The Model SB1 is a tall-tower system connected by a cable to the base system unit I/O tower (similar to the Model 530 I/O tower except not bolted to the processor system unit). The mechanical package (Figure 1.21) approximates the size of the B through F model white racks and comes standard with an 8-way PowerPC A35 RISC Microprocessor (125,888 normalized FI Dialog Steps per hour at 65% CPU utilization), 4,096 MB of main storage, a Multi-Function I/O Processor (MFIOP), two 8.58-GB 3½-inch disk drives, a CD-ROM drive, a 6 bus-capable optical controller, a communications adapter, a workstation controller, a LAN, and one SPD bus.

The Model S40-SB1's performance may be increased by swapping the 8-way processor with a 12-way processor (feature code 2311) for 185,533 normalized FI Dialog Steps per hour at 65% CPU utilization. Both of the processor configurations supported on the Model S40-SB1 are Symmetrical Multi-Processors (SMPs). Additional performance can be achieved by replacing the #2310 and #2311 processors with the A50 processors available in either an 8-Way (#2312) or 12-Way (#2313) configuration to achieve 274,426.23 and 396,789.40 FI Dialog steps at 65% CPU utilization, respectively.

The Model 740-SB1 base structure can house up to four 3½-inch disk drives to achieve a maximum disk capacity of 34.35 GB to enable mirroring of the disk data, one tape drive, one CD-ROM, an operator panel, and a 16-slot SPD I/O card cage. Main storage may not be increased beyond the base 4096 MB on the #2310 and #2311 processors. The #2312 and #2313 processors accommodate 8,192 MB of main storage.

Up to 5 optical busses can be generated for the attachment of expansion towers or to attach to other processors. It is also possible to attach up to 7 twinaxial workstations, or 6 ASCII workstations, 16 communications lines, 2 fax lines, and 5 local area networks (LANs). Two optical libraries can be attached, as can one cryptographic card. The Model 740-SB1 capacities are summarized in Figure 1.23. Two I/O expansion towers may be optically attached, expanding the total number of I/O cards to 29. The Model SB1 system unit processor tower and the base I/O tower must be plugged individually into standard high-voltage electrical outlets (180–260 VAC). Base utility power failure protection is provided by internal battery backup and Continuously Powered

Processor Feature	2310	2311	2312	2313
Processor Configuration	8-way	12-way	8-way	12-way
Processor Type	A35	A35	A50	A50
Main Storage (GB)	4	4	8	8
DASD Capacity (GB)				
Base	16.7	16.7	16.7	16.7
Maximum (for mirroring)				
Communication Lines	1 to 16	1 to 16	1 to 16	1 to 16
LAN Ports	1 to 5	1 to 5	1 to 5	1 to 5
Twinaxial Controllers	0 to 1	0 to 1	0 to 1	0 to 1
Maximum Twinaxial Workstations	28	28	28	28
ASCII Controllers	0 to 2	0 to 2	0 to 2	0 to 2
0 to 2				
ASCII Devices	28	28	28	28
¼-Inch/8mm Cartridge				
Tape/CD-ROM	0 to 3	0 to 3	0 to 3	0 to 3
½-Inch Tape				
2440/9384	0 to 4	0 to 4	0 to 4	0 to 4
8-mm Cartridge Tape (External)	0 to 4	0 to 4	0 to 4	0 to 4
Diskett (8 or 5¼-Inch)	0 to 2	0 to 2	0 to 2	0 to 2
Optical Libraries	0 to 2	0 to 2	0 to 2	0 to 2
Fax IOPs	0 to 2	0 to 2	0 to 2	0 to 2
Expansion Towers	0 to 2	0 to 2	0 to 2	0 to 2

Notes: Model SB1 performance measurements when used as a SAP R/3 application server—FI Dialog Steps per hour may not be realized in all environments.

    2310 ⇒ 125,888 normalized FI Dialog Steps per hour at 65% CPU
    2311 ⇒ 185,533 normalized FI Dialog Steps per hour at 65% CPU
    2312 ⇒ 274,426.23 normalized FI Dialog Steps per hour at 65% CPU
    2313 ⇒ 396,789.40 normalized FI Dialog Steps per hour at 65% CPU

FI (financial) Dialog Steps per hour is a workload derived from SAP-defined benchmark testing. This workload calculation at 65% CPU utilization can be used to size AS/400 configurations for specific customer situations.

Results can be obtained through IBM/SAP International Competence Center in Waldorf, Germany. Additional performance data from SAP-defined benchmarks that demonstrate AS/400 scalability in a multi-tier environment can also be obtained through IBM/SAP competency centers or SAP's Web page: http://www.sap.com/

Capacities shown are for models shipped from the plant and include any prerequisite expansion.

Figure 1.23. AS/400 Custom Application e-server SB1 performance and capacities summary.

Main Storage (CPM). The internal battery backup is capable of retaining 16 GB of main storage content using CPM for 24 hours. To extend the retention interval to 48 hours, it is necessary to install the external battery backup feature.

The SB1 application server runs SAP-BaseR/3 Package and BaanERP software meeting the full range of business requirements, including financial accounting and controlling, sales and distribution, materials management, production planning, and human resources management. Information and early warning systems are also available. Business Information Warehouse can edit external and internal data to support decision-making at necessary corporate levels.

System Availability

Since their inception, the AS/400 systems have had availability as a target. The average single AS/400 system in 1997 had an availability of greater than 99.9 percent, with average unplanned outages of less than 9 hours per year. Daily reports are accumulated on greater than 87,000 AS/400 systems in the United States. These reports show that on AS/400 systems shipped since January 1996, the average interval between hardware problems is 61 months. The results indicated in the first sentence above were accomplished through a combination of hardware and software actions. The hardware and software items described below identify the actions taken by the AS/400 to achieve that availability. The five items described after the hardware and software actions, are what is available to take the AS/400 the next step to an availability of 99.99 percent.

On the *hardware* side, things like battery backup and continuously powered main storage protect against utility failures and the loss of data that could result from those failures. Redundant bulk power supplies and independent redundant local voltage regulators protect against power system failures. RAID-5, mirroring, and redundant write cache protect against data loss from disk unit failures, while concurrent maintenance allows the repair of those failures without loss of the system to your users. System Power Control Network (SPCN) turns the system and its remote components on and off at the same time and monitors the remote units to enable maintenance actions before they cause a catastrophic system failure.

From the *software* side, items like commitment control and journaling, auxiliary storage pools, system managed Access paths, save-while-active, S/R parallelism, hierarchical storage management, BRMS, and ADSM (combined with the pretesting of the integrated operating system and applications code) reduce the duration of the recovery actions needed if an outage does occur. Figure 1.24 describes the hierarchy of actions needed to achieve 100-percent availability.

The following paragraphs describe the options offered as well as the choices which the customer must make to increase the AS/400 availability. Included in the choices are capabilities like logical partitioning, multi-system coupling, data and application resiliency, clustering of systems, and disaster tolerance.

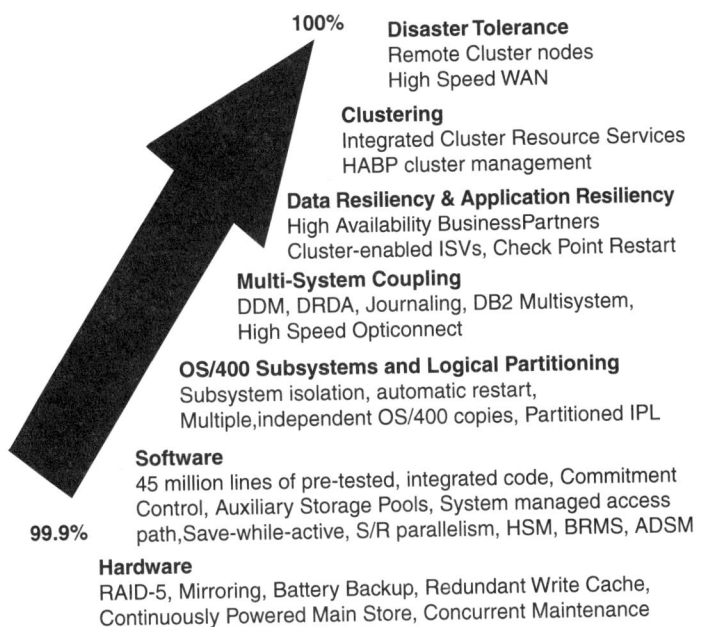

Figure 1.24. AS/400e availability solutions.

OS/400 Subsystems and Logical Partitioning

Logical partitioning is the creation of several independently functioning systems within the covers of a single system. The requirements are the presence of n-way **Symmetrical Multi-Processors (SMT)** and sufficient main storage. The primary partition requires one processor and 256 MB of main storage. Creating and managing secondary partitions is done from the primary partition. Each secondary partition requires a minimum of one processor, 64 MB of memory, an I/O processor with disk resources and its own console device.

There can be multiple secondary partitions, each with its own I/O resources assigned from the list of total system resources. No resources can be shared between partitions. An installation of a secondary partition does not impact other partitions, but an IPL of the primary partition requires an IPL of all secondary partitions. Figure 1.25 illustrates how logical partitioning might appear on a single system.

New processor and memory resources can be allocated to a secondary partition by an IPL of that partition, not the entire system. Avail-

Figure 1.25. AS/400e logical partitioning.

able I/O resources, e.g., disk, tape, and CD-ROM can then be allocated to that secondary partition without an IPL. Tape, I/O Processors, and CD-ROM devices can be switched between partitions, and can also be dedicated to individual partitions. Adequate communications resources such as LAN adapters, should be dedicated to each partition.

OS/400 is licensed once for the entire system by its normal processor group, independent of the number of partitions. V4R4 of OS/400 is the initial enabling release for logical partitioning, and must be installed on each partition. Pre-V4R4 releases are not supported for logical partitioning.

An internal virtual bus provides the option to use OptiConnect for high performance communications between partitions. OptiConnect allows applications on one partition to access the database of another partition using DDM remote SQL, although disk resources are not physically shared. So although logical partitions can be operated independently, the high speed internal bus connection between partitions enables applications having a need for multiple AS/400 application servers to access a single database server.

System values for each partition are set independently. Each partition has a different system name, and can use a different primary/secondary national language, or even be operated in different time zones. Multinational companies can centralize multi-country operations in a single location while retaining the national characteristics of each system.

The increased scalability of the AS/400 provides the opportunity for companies to consolidate multiple AS/400s into fewer, more manageable systems. **Logical Partitioning** (LPAR) in OS/400 enhances the role of the AS/400 as a consolidated server. Logical partitioning provides both the power and flexibility to address multiple systems requirements in a single machine. Logical partitioning needs to be considered for environments requiring server consolidation, business unit consolidation, mixed production and test environments, and integrated clusters.

Multi-System Coupling

Multiple AS/400 systems can be coupled using the OS/400 resources associated with Distributed Data Management (DDM), Distributed Relational Database Architecture (DRDA), Journaling, DB2 MultiSystem support for Symmetrical Multi-Processors, and high speed OptiConnect.

Data Resiliency and Application Resiliency

Data resiliency and application resiliency are being provided by the IBM high-availability business partners DataMirror, Vision Solutions, and Lakeview technology. Resilient resources are object replicated to one or more nodes of a cluster. Resilient resources are associated with a cluster Resource Group. Check point restart is a capability included within the software provided by these business partners. Also included within the business partner provided software is cluster management, data replication, and application availability tools.

There are two types of Cluster Resource Groups supported, one for **data resiliency**, and one for **application resiliency**. Data resiliency provides the capability to switch the point of access for a set of data over to a backup node which is maintaining an exact replica of that data. Application resilience provides the capability to switch an IP address, representing the application server, to a backup node and to restart the application in the event of a primary node failure.

AS/400 Continuous Availability Clustering

Continuous availability cluster solutions are designed for those customers who require access to their data and systems 365 days a year and 24 hours each and every day. The continuous availability cluster solutions can use a pair of AS/400 systems consisting of any AS/400 system or server. The systems are connected together using a high-performance data path, either optical, or ATM. Also, the systems are connected to either a local area network or a wide area network containing either terminals or Personal Computers. Figure 1.26 illustrates the system interconnection for continuous availability. Figure 1.27 illustrates the supported cluster topologies including a remote cluster node connected by a high speed wide area network through a switch.

Cluster Resource Services within the OS/400 operating system reduce the complexity of managing AS/400 clustered systems. OS/400 keeps track of data and applications for those systems. Cluster management and data resilience applications (provided by high-availability business partners) protect the customers business from unplanned and planned outages as well as site loss disasters.

Figure 1.26. System interconnect for high availability.

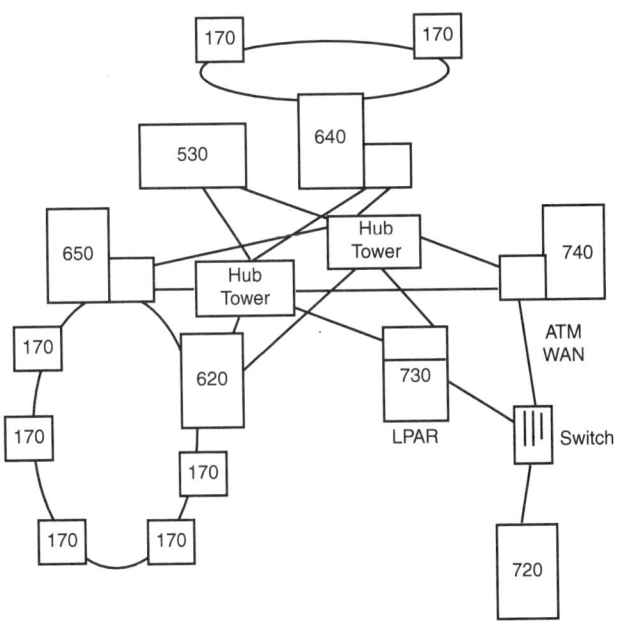

Figure 1.27. Cluster topologies supported for AS/400.

Cluster Resource Services contain an open set of APIs providing cluster facilities available to AS/400 application providers and customers to enhance application availability. These APIs allow the creation, configuration, and administration of the cluster. Systems are defined into the cluster as **cluster nodes**. Communication interface addresses are defined to form the cluster node interconnection links.

Cluster Resource Services also provide low-level facilities such as heartbeat monitoring, reliable message delivery, switch-over administration, and distributed activities. The services are built on cluster topology and messaging functions which keep track of each node in the cluster and ensure that all nodes have consistent information about the state of cluster resources. **Heartbeat monitoring** ensures the active state of each node. If the heartbeat for a node fails, the condition is reported such that the cluster can automatically fail-over to the resilient resources on the backup node.

AS/400 clusters support up to 128 nodes (instances of OS/400), using any combination of the existing OptiConnect, WAN, and LAN connectivity options to build the cluster. A single workstation (containing the continuous availability business partner cluster management application) manages all systems in the cluster. OptiConnect hardware is a connectivity method for high and mid-range models. ATM provides a high-performance connection to remote systems in a cluster. Ethernet and Token-Ring LANs can be used to connect low-end AS/400 models into a cluster.

Data resilience support for modern applications has been enhanced with the introduction of **Byte Stream File (BSF)** replication. Business partner solutions provide real time recording of changes to BSF data replication to remote systems. Transfer of changes using remote journaling protects in-flight data at the point of failure.

Disaster Tolerance

Disaster tolerance is provided by the support of remote cluster nodes as replication points for resilient data. The remote cluster nodes can be off the customer site and may even use facilities of other businesses like IBM to provide recovery mechanisms. High-speed **wide area network (WAN)** facilities like ATM are used to support the remote cluster nodes.

Disaster environments include hurricanes, tornados, floods, etc., wherein the business becomes unable to utilize its local facilities for a period of time.

A 1998 Gartner Group study compared the availability of various systems. The only systems which ranked higher than the AS/400 were systems which were clustered. The average NT Server outages were 40 times worse that the AS/400.

Continuously Powered Main Storage (CPM)

With the exception of the Entry Model 150, which uses an **Uninterruptible Power Supply (UPS)**, the AS/400e servers all use **Continuously Powered Main Storage (CPM)** to provide protection against utility failures.

It becomes impractical to provide batteries as a backup methodology for systems with up to 40 GB of main storage and expect the data resident in that storage to be dumped to the available disk storage during the life of the batteries. The required dump interval is greater than 2 hours, during which time the entire system must be kept operating, because all the facilities of the system unit are required. To counteract the impracticality of not having adequate battery or UPS availability, CPM is provided.

Here is how CPM works: After a utility power failure is detected by the power system of the system unit, a signal is sent to the operating system, which alerts the processor of an impending shutdown. The operating system allows continued operation for 45 seconds to determine if the utility failure is permanent. During the first 30 seconds, the processor executes to a place to stop at a machine interface boundary. After the 45 seconds have elapsed without utility recovery, the AS/400 system begins preparations for CPM, during which time the MFIOP assists the processor in writing internal register contents to memory. At 90 seconds the AS/400 power-off occurs. In CPM power-off, no power is supplied to any system units except main storage, which, though still powered, has switched to a low-power state in which its refresh clock is slowed way down to preserve power. The system continues in this low power state until utility power is restored.

Once utility power is restored, the system automatically powers on and begins an **Initial Program Load (IPL)** (if previously enabled by the user). Main store refresh is restored on any system power on. The operating system detects that the system was previously powered off into CPM. It then writes all changed pages from the preserved main storage to DASD and initiates a re-IPL to perform any required error recovery operations. For large main storage configurations, an external battery can be configured to extend the period of time supported under the CPM control envelope.

AS/400 Upgrades

There are two methods available for upgrading within the AS/400e series product line: upgrading within a model and upgrading through a system unit swap.

Upgrading Within a Model

This method is used if the need is for more performance or input/output device functionality and the current system is not using the maximum performance features available within that specific AS/400 model. These could be the processor, interactive processor feature, main storage size, attachable I/O device capability, or disk storage size. In this situation, within a model, performance can be upgraded by swapping processors, adding additional main storage, or adding disk storage or additional IOPs without having to swap system units. In general, the system should be upgraded within the model until those maximums are reached. This method of growth is referred to as *horizontal growth*.

Upgrading Through a System Unit Swap

Another way to upgrade within the AS/400 family is to replace the current AS/400 system unit with a more powerful model (e.g., you upgrade a Model 720 to a Model 730, or 740 by changing the system unit). This method is used if the current system is at its processor and storage maximums, or if the number of users has increased beyond the capabilities of the current model. This method would also be used if there is a need for application programs that only run on newer RISC-based AS/400 models or if you are upgrading from an older AS/400 model. This method of growth is referred to as *vertical growth*.

Upgrades Between Models

No upgrades between Models 150, 170, 720, 730, or 740 servers may be accomplished without the exchange of the system unit. You can continue to use all the same workstations, modems, etc. But if your upgrade is to a Model 730 from a model 150 or 720 it may not be possible to move any existing I/O processors. Upgrades to a model 720, 730, or 740 from a model 170 are not supported. Also, if your upgrade is to a Model 720, it will be necessary to use either the attached expansion unit with the SPD bus feature or an external 5072 System Unit Expansion Tower to accommodate your previous model's IOP features. The non-support of SPD IOPs on the Models 150, 170, or the base model 720 results in the non-support of all external DASD units, diskette drives, and non-SCSI external tape drives on these models. You cannot upgrade to or from the Model 150 without changing the system unit.

It is not possible to upgrade between a V4R2 version of the AS/400e server 170 and a V4R4 version, because a system unit swap is required. It does not make sense to upgrade between the lower three models within the two releases because the performance differences are insufficient to justify the cost of the system unit swap. Processor upgrades within the Model 170 are supported provided the processor upgrade retains the same or later processor technology model, A35 to A35, A50 to A50, or A35 to A50.

Upgrades from the older AS/400 F Models to the new AS/400e systems are fully supported with the following exceptions in devices or adapters: 9406 stage 1 B level hardware, including 5030 and 5031 I/O Card Units; early 9404 hardware, including 315-MB, 5¼-inch disk storage, 3½-inch disk storage units (feature codes 1105, 1107, and 1109), and 120-MB tape; some early stage-2 hardware, including DASD/TAPE (feature codes 2600, 2622, 2647); communications adapters (most 615X, 617X and standard ECS adapters); and LAN attachments (feature codes 2625, 2636, and 6160).

The following 9402 and 9404 hardware won't fit or work with the new system units: integrated diskette units, battery backup units, and previous release 9402/9404 Expansion Units. Main storage exchanges from the CISC Advanced System 200 and 300 sequence numbered models to the RISC Advanced System 400 and 500 sequence numbered models are not supported. No B, C, D, or E Model upgrades are supported.

Main storage exchanges from the 9404/9406 F models and the 3XX models, and from the 4XX and 5XX models are no longer supported. Appendix F identifies the recommended migration paths between older AS/400 system/server models and the new system/server models.

Performance Overview

One important aspect of a computer system is the speed at which the computer can perform work, or the performance of the computer. The higher the performance, the more work the computer can do. Many things—such as the processor, main storage, disk storage, I/O bandwidth, and program design—affect the performance of a computer system. It is difficult and often misleading to predict the overall performance of a computer system by looking at selected specifications of the individual components that make up the computer system. Although things such as disk unit seek times and raw processor speed (usually measured in Millions of Instructions Per Second, or MIPS) are important, they do not provide the whole picture in terms of overall system performance.

In addition to these considerations, in the case of the AS/400e Series computers, performance must be considered in relation to the environment in which the computer system is executing. The AS/400 may operate in a general-purpose (batch and interactive processing) environment or in a client/server environment. What makes a computer function well in one of these environments may be an inhibitor in the other environment. (A computer that has been tuned for the client/server environment will perform weakly in an interactive environment and vice versa.) As a result, different methodologies are used to measure computer performance for those different environments.

When choosing a multiuser computer system, it is important to understand that the maximum number of active users is different from the maximum number of workstations that can be attached to a system. History has shown that when the active number of users is greater than 40 percent of the maximum number of workstations allowed, there is a strong probability that some of the users will start to experience a decrease in response. The maximum number of users is not a system configuration limitation but rather a system performance limitation for the benchmark used. Therefore, if occasional users are among the user population, it is normally desirable to put more workstations on a system than can be simultaneously supported.

The **response time** of a computer system is at least as important as throughput. The satisfaction and productivity of users can be drastically affected by a computer's sluggish response after the user hits the enter key. As was mentioned earlier, response time is related to the workload on the computer system. This is not intended to imply that every workload will see sub-second response time.

The AS/400's System/36 environment allows a program originally written for a System/36 architecture to be migrated to and used on an AS/400 system. With the capability of running SSP-based programs on all AS/400 Advanced Series RISC processor-based models concurrently with the OS/400 operating system, there should no longer be any performance degradation when running old System/36 applications on an AS/400.

Benchmark Testing Overview

Benchmark testing has evolved as the best way to compare the overall performance of different computers. Benchmark testing involves loading the computer system with various programs designed to simulate a workload and then measuring how the system behaves under the load. Through this benchmark testing, all elements of the computer system come into play and the overall performance of selected computer systems can be meaningfully compared.

To perform benchmark testing, the test group must make assumptions about the kind of work being done and the behavior of the users at each workstation. For this reason, the performance measurements derived from a benchmark may vary significantly from what users will get if their business environment does not match the assumptions made in the testing. For example, word processing users typically load a system down more heavily than users performing business transactions. Therefore, a system with heavy word processing activity will usually not be able to support as many users as a system performing order entry.

However, because all assumptions are the same for all computers included in the benchmark testing, it is possible to get a good idea of the relative performance of tested computer systems. IBM has conducted benchmark testing on AS/400 systems using the CPW benchmark, which is designed to simulate a typical business workload (e.g., order entry, accounts payable, and accounts receivable).

When IBM's AS/400 group benchmarks a system, the benchmark is against a criteria which measures how that system is intended to be used. The general purpose systems like the previous model 600 and model 650, are benchmarked against their ability to support interactive users. In this context, whatever system capacity is not being used for interactive users is available for performing other workloads like client/server based file serving or print serving. Other systems like the server-based systems, are intended to provide the majority of their capabilities for the batch mode server-based functions like printing, file serving, communications serving, etc. They are benchmarked against a criteria which measures how well the systems perform in that environment.

The AS/400e solutions packaging preload environments are measured against a criteria which combines the need to get a larger number of interactive users applying a workload while still allowing a significant client/server workload. The AS/400e solutions packaging preload environments only expect to perform their function with this increased interactive workload while supporting a limited set of business partner applications.

The four charts shown in Figure 1.28 illustrate the expected performance for the described benchmark environments for different targeted systems groupings. Note the difference between the performance curves based on the AS/400e server 170 using the A35 processor and the curves for the same family using the A50 processor. The A35 processor family curves are based upon a system CPW, whereas the A50 processor family curves are based upon a processor CPW. With the introduction of the A50 processor in the model 720, 730, and 740, and the use of interactive feature cards on the processors for those systems, all of the processor performance curves track the model 170 type curve up to the maximum Processor CPW rating. The interactive performance simply subtracts what is being used from the total processor rating, and the remainder is available for client/server performance. If the processor performance capacity in either interactive or client server criteria is exceeded, a decrease in performance is the result according to the System Default Priority criteria selected. The System Default Priorities are discussed in a following paragraph.

Figure 1.28. Benchmark criteria used for measuring the persormance of the various AS/400e Series systems and servers. *(Continued on next page.)*

60 EXPLORING IBM AS/400 COMPUTERS

Figure 1.28. Benchmark criteria used for measuring the persormance of the various AS/400e Series systems and servers. *(Continued from previous page.)*

As an example, for the AS/400e 740-2069 processor, total processor CPW rating is 3660 (if the interactive feature 1511 is present, the maximum interactive performance is 2000 CPW, and a minimum client/server performance capability of 1660 CPW is available). If at any point in time, only 50% of the interactive performance is being used, then 2660 CPW is available for client/server usage. Depending upon how the job priorities are set, a big difference exists in the results.

System Default Priorities

If the system default settings are retained, initially server workload response times will increase because cycles are kept for the interactive workloads. If the interactive workload continues to increase, a point is reached where interactive response times will degrade incrementally, and finally the available CPW for server workload will decrease significantly (to where the sum of interactive workload plus server workload is less than the rated processor workload; that is, the 3660 used in the above relationships will have decreased to a value significantly lower).

Interactive Jobs Favored

If the priorities are set to favor interactive jobs, when the interactive workload exceeds the rated capability, the server workload jobs experience increased response times because the cycles are kept for the interactive jobs. The interactive response times do not degrade until the processor is saturated, and the available CPW for server workload goes to zero.

Server Jobs Favored

If the priorities are set to favor the server jobs, the interactive jobs experience increased response times because the cycles are kept for the server workload.

CPW Benchmark Test Results

In 1996, IBM introduced a new benchmark testing parametric called Commercial Processing Workload (CPW), which replaced the RAMP-C benchmark previously used. IBM chose to make the change to CPW because RAMP-C was driven by the increased performance levels of current AS/400 models and the recognition that users are now utilizing more OS/400 software function. (Contention, queuing, and journaling are examples of software functions that RAMP-C did not test.) In today's environment, IBM feels that CPW benchmarks provide a more representative result than RAMP-C.

Figure 1.29 shows the interactive CPW performance ratings of the V4R4 RISC-based models of AS/400 systems. Additional information on other benchmark results on the AS/400 and other vendors' general-purpose commercial processing systems' performance may be obtained from the Transaction Performance Council (TPC, *http://www.tpc.org*), which publishes test results on a wide variety of systems.

Symmetrical Multi-Processing (SMP)

Some of the **AS/400e** models use Symmetrical Multi-Processing (SMP), meaning they use more than one processor in a single system. (The later discussion "Hardware Architecture Overview" contains more on how multiple processors achieve this performance increase.) With SMP, the performance rating increases with each new processor added. For example, if you compare a single processor system to an SMP system with two processors of identical power, you get a performance increase of about 70%. The reason you don't get a 100% improvement is that the two system processors must spend some of their processing power coordinating activities with one another. They must also share the same main storage, I/O bus(ses), disk storage, and so on. For these reasons, adding a second system processor does not result in doubling the performance of the system. However, you do get significant performance improvements with SMP configurations. Figure 1.30 shows the performance advantage afforded by the use of 2-, 4-, and 8-way processors in the Model 730, along with 8-way (2240) and 12-way (2243) processors in the Model 740 SMP configurations.

Server Performance

Client/Server Labs measures server performance on systems for many companies, using a benchmark suite specially tailored for servers. The server environment evolved as a result of two nearly coincidental events:

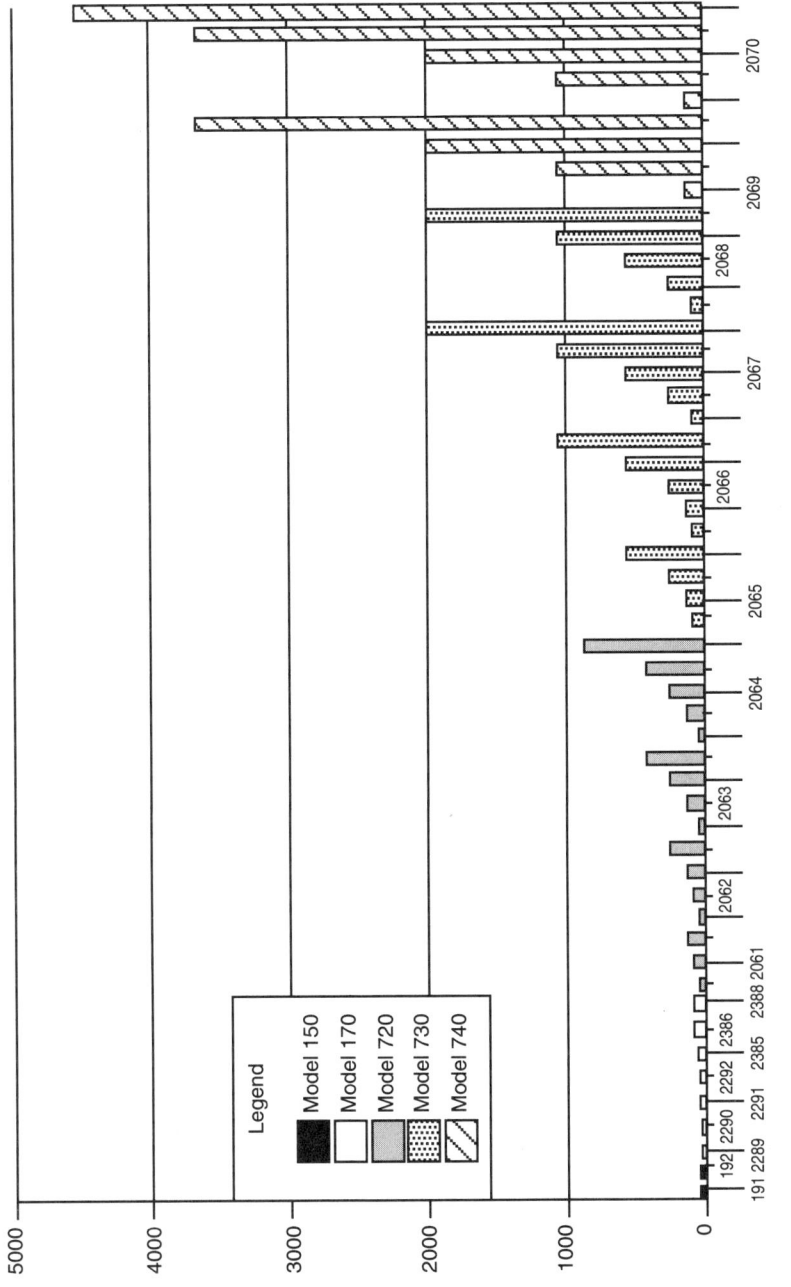

Figure 1.29. Interactive CPW values for V4R4 AS/400 systems.

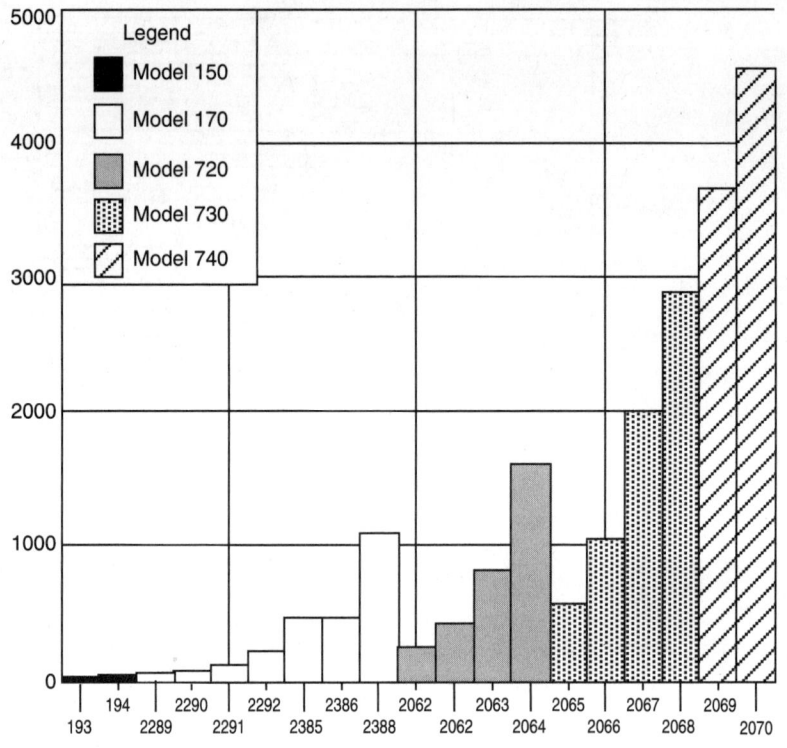

Figure 1.30. V4R4 client/server CPW values for AS/400e servers by model grouping and processor.

(1) the personal computer (PC) penetration into the generalized business world, and (2) the natural desire to share the information contained on those PCs. The PC put the power of computers into the hands of each critical individual within a business.

The need to share the results on one PC with the users on several PCs resulted in the definition of the Local Area Network (LAN). An example of an application across a LAN would be this: If one secretary at a business location reserved a conference room for 1:00 P.M. on Tuesday, other secretaries would see that the conference room was reserved (including when, and by whom). As in this example, a LAN should be used to connect together groups of users with some common interest. The first LAN to be defined was Ethernet (which eventually became IEEE 803.2), followed later by the token ring (which became IEEE 803.5). LAN definitions, speeds, and protocols proliferated that could not talk to each other until the distributed computing environment emerged, settling upon TCP/IP and APPC as the LAN access method and management structure.

The other problem of only networking PCs is that if one user wants a specific piece of information and the PC that has that information is turned off at the time the information is needed, the information cannot be accessed. Also, since PCs have limited disk storage space, individual users were asking why they should spend money and time creating a repository for data that, once created, might be of no further interest. Finally, the question of controlling access to the information on the network was begging for an answer because of privacy issues (and need-to-know basis relative to the business).

An answer that evolved was to create the client/server relationship, in which the PCs were the clients and the server was a large centralized repository of information. In this environment, the client requested either programs or data from the server, which checked the authorization of the client to receive that information and sent the data to the client. The client then processed the data and sent the results back to the server repository for long-term storage. It was found that in order to check the authorization, find the programs and data, and provide enough storage repository to be useful, the server required the processing characteristics of the client. In fact, in the case of certain long-running applications, it would be preferable to execute the application at the server and send only the results of the application to the client, who could then decide whether the data generated should reside on the server or at the client. Since the long-running application executed on the server, this freed up the client resources for execution of short-running applications during the long application's execution time.

It follows, then, that minimizing paths in the server for APPC and TCP/IP, and minimizing database search structures (via good search algorithms, improved base structures, some capability for parallel I/O processing, efficient file serving, and efficient batch processing capability) are the characteristics of a good server. The performance of the server models is shown in Figure 1.30, with the tallest column showing the server batch processing performance at Version 4 Release 4. It is no longer necessary to limit the configuration and the available application set to provide improved interactive performance as was done for the custom mixed-mode S20-ISV, S30-ISV, and S40-ISV models.

RPMark95

The Workplace Server Benchmark has been acquired and altered by Client Server Labs to become RPMark95. Client Server Labs maintains an Internet home page that, in addition to AS/400 server performance, includes data from other vendors compared to the AS/400 Server systems. Refer to this Internet address for the latest information:
http://www.cslinc.com//rpmarkrpmark.htm

Interactive Performance

The interactive performance capabilities of e-servers 720, 730, and 740 systems is established by which of the interactive feature cards is plugged into the system processors. The table in Figure 1.31 identifies the interactive features that can compatibly be plugged into each of the processors for these systems and the interactive performance associated with each feature.

Opticonnect Performance

The AS/400e server 7XX models support a high-performance optical bus connection called OptiConnect. Through this connection, AS/400 systems can be connected together and cooperate (exchange programs and data) without suffering the performance degradation typically associated with system interconnection via other methods (e.g., TCP/IP, Ethernet, or token-ring networks).

Measured performance capacity increases (1.5 to 1.7 times the performance of a single system, depending upon application efficiency) have resulted from connecting two AS/400 systems together via OptiConnect. Currently, up to 32 AS/400 systems can be connected via OptiConnect to provide loosely coupled distributed computing.

Loosely coupled computing is an environment in which data and programs are exchanged between computers over a serial communications line and the only thing shared from a hardware aspect of the systems is the communications line. The coupling is referred to as "loose"

AS/400e server 720

Feature	1500	1501	1502	1503	1504	1505
Processor						
2061	35	70	120			
2062	35	70	120	240		
2063	35	70	120	240	560	
2064	35	70	120	240	560	1050

AS/400e server 730/740

Feature	1506	1507	1508	1509	1510	1511	1512	1513
Processor								
2065	70	120	240	560				
2066	70	120	240	560	1,050			
2067	70		240	560	1,050	2,000		
2068	70		240	560	1,050	2,000		
2069		120			1,050	2,000	3,660	
2070		120			1,050	2,000	3,660	4,550

Figure 1.31. Interactive features with processor associations for 720, 730, and 740 systems.

because the potential processing occurring in the system (from which the information is being moved) is significant during the period of the transfer, and because of the problems involved as a result in keeping the information in the sharing systems synchronized.

A Closer Look

Many elements provide the functions and performance of IBM AS/400 computers. This is perhaps the appropriate place to mention that many of the concepts used in the AS/400 system were built on those of IBM's System/38 computer. This fact is a testimonial to the rich function and growth capability built into the original System/38!

The remainder of this chapter provides a closer look at the following aspects of the IBM AS/400 systems: hardware architecture. clustering technology, OptiConnect technology, main and auxiliary storage, packaging, and the fiber optic bus.

Hardware Architecture Overview

The underlying arrangement and interconnection of a computer system's electrical components is called its hardware architecture. This architecture is the fundamental structure upon which all system functions are built and has the largest effect on how the computer system will behave. A basic understanding of the AS/400 system architecture (Figure 1.32) makes it possible to compare AS/400 computers with other systems and to understand important aspects of system performance and capacity.

The core of the AS/400 computer (as in all computers) is the system processor (shown near the center of the figure). The system processor is

Figure 1.32. Block diagram of AS/400 hardware used in all PCI-based models (150, 170, 720).

the circuitry that actually executes a computer program's instructions and does all the mathematical calculations. The smallest piece of information (data) in the computer is called a **bit**. Bits are grouped into **bytes** (8 bits), **half words** (16 bits), **full words** (32 bits), and **double words** (64 bits) inside the computer. These groupings form the computer's representation of numbers, letters of the alphabet, and instructions in a program. AS/400 system processors move information around one double word (64 bits) at a time. Since much of a computer's time is spent moving information around, the double-word organization helps improve overall system performance.

Other bits inside the system processor are used to uniquely identify or address storage and input/output devices (e.g., a disk unit) within the computer system. AS/400 system processors group 64 bits together to form a unique address. This 64-bit addressing provides 18,446,744 trillion (2^{64}) unique addresses, which is more than any other IBM computer system from PCs to the largest System/390 computers. This is more than enough addresses for today's mid-size computer environment (and even for the foreseeable future). In fact, the largest AS/400 systems and servers today have just identified the capability to use 4+ trillion of those addresses. This shows the kind of growth potential inherent in the AS/400 architecture.

The "memory" or main storage (shown at the top of the figure) provides a work space for the system processor. Since much of a computer's time is spent moving information to and from main storage, the speed of main storage can be a limiting factor to the overall performance of any computer system. The speed of storage is measured by the time it takes to respond to a request to store or recall information, or the **cycle time**. The main storage cycle time for AS/400 computers varies depending on the model.

The shorter the cycle time, the better the system performance. The largest AS/400 computers can have up to 20,480 MB of main storage. The main storage in all AS/400 systems provides error detection and error correction. This main storage error detection and correction works to protect the all-important integrity of user information in the computer system.

All AS/400 system processors also use cache memory to help increase the effective cycle time of main storage. A **cache** is a small and very-high-speed memory area that sits between the processor and main storage. The idea is to keep the information most likely to be needed next in cache to avoid the time delay associated with main storage. AS/400 systems have data and instruction caches on the processor to accelerate performance when accessing information/program instructions (respectively).

Another important part of the AS/400 architecture is the **System Licensed Internal Code (SLIC)**. SLIC is a set of extremely simple instructions (never seen by the computer programmer or user) that are directly performed by the electronic circuits within the system processor. All user program instructions are automatically converted into a series of these SLIC instructions, which are then executed by the system processor.

The input/output (I/O) processors (shown at the bottom of the figure) are responsible for managing any devices attached to the AS/400 system. Each of these specialized processors has independent responsibilities and performs tasks in coordination with the system processor. A computer that has multiple processors working together with the system processor like this has a multiprocessor architecture. The advantage of having multiple processors performing work simultaneously is simply that more work can be done in a given period of time. For example, the workstation I/O processor manages the detailed processing associated with the multiple terminals and printers attached to the system, allowing the system processor to concentrate on doing more productive work for the user. The same is true of the other specialized I/O processors such as the storage I/O processor, which manages disk, diskette, and tape devices attached to the AS/400 system.

The I/O processors communicate with the system processor over an I/O **bus** (called the SPD bus), a group of wires that carry information very quickly from one area to another inside the computer system. As indicated in the figure, some AS/400 systems have a single I/O bus whereas others have multiple I/O busses. Because only one information transfer can occur on any one bus at any one time, systems with multiple busses have the advantage of allowing overlapping transfers between I/O processors and the system processor or main storage. Therefore, multiple busses contribute to the overall system performance advantages of larger AS/400 systems.

Various controllers and adapters plug into physical slots in each of the packages used to provide electrical connections to the bus. In addition to I/O processors, a service processor (shown in the upper right of the figure) is built into every AS/400. It is responsible for starting the system and constantly monitoring the health of the entire computer. It interacts with the system operator through the control panel and helps with such things as system fault isolation, error detection, and error reporting. It is the equivalent of having a built-in service person who watches over things with relentless consistency.

All AS/400 systems employ a multiprocessor architecture in that they have a system processor and multiple specialized processors (e.g., workstation and I/O processors) to handle specific tasks. However, larger AS/400 models (e.g., Models 170, 720, 730, and 740) employ multiple system processors to cooperatively execute a single copy of the operating system (OS/400), thus appearing to be a single large processor. This multiple system processor architecture is called the **N-way multiprocessor architecture** (where *N* is replaced by the number of processors), also referred to as the Symmetric Multi-Processor (SMP) architecture.

Figure 1.33 shows how *N*-way models are organized. (*Note:* All system processors share the same I/O busses, I/O processors, and main storage.) Symmetric Multi-Processors process in parallel, sharing a task list. Each processor in a symmetric multiprocessor set has its own data and instruction cache, and its own virtual storage view of the system. In the case of a query, each processor in the SMP group will process in parallel against a segment of disk storage to resolve the query. Figure 1.34 illustrates the memory and I/O connections for the 8-way and 12-way processor models.

AS/400 Clustering Technology

The AS/400 leverages the clustering capability to provide both high availability systems and to allow for horizontal growth of the AS/400 systems. The following paragraphs discuss the performance and connection characteristics provided by the Opticonnect capability for horizontal growth. Of course these characteristics apply also in the high availability connection for resilient data and resilient applications.

What Is OptiConnect/400?

OptiConnect/400 is the system-to-system interconnection fabric that allows distributed functions and applications to operate at high speed. It can be used to form a high-performance, multi-system, loosely coupled cluster.

Figure 1.33. 730 hardware architecture block diagram.

Two things differentiate OptiConnect from traditional communications-based distributed operations. The first is a system bus connection between multiple systems using high-speed fiber optic technology. The second is an I/O driver embedded in the operating system that streamlines the application access to data on a remote system.

To accomplish this, OptiConnect provides a shared bus on which systems communicate using a peer-to-peer protocol. Once OptiConnect establishes system connections on the shared bus, much of the **APPC** (Advanced Peer to Peer Communication) protocol stack is bypassed. The OptiConnect fast-path connection for database transactions provides **DDM** (Distributed Data Management) access to databases any-

Figure 1.34. 740 8-way and 12-way hardware architecture block diagram.

where in the OptiConnect cluster at a fraction of the standard communications code path. Data warehouse, DRDA, and data propagation functions can use this technology.

Traditional communication protocol overhead is too impractical for heavy workload distributed applications. To minimize latency, or the time it takes to send a message and receive a response, the protocol chosen must be efficient in the number of code steps required. To maximize bandwidth, or the amount of data that can be transferred in a unit of time, high-performance hardware must be used. The OptiConnect channel is very efficient and the best solution for both latency and bandwidth. The length of the cable affects how low latency can get. As distance increases, the speed of light becomes a limiting factor for a given bandwidth. OptiConnect is limited to 500 meters over the 1063-Mbps (megabit-per-second) link used on RISC models and 2 kilometers over the 220-Mbps link supported on CISC models.

OptiConnect/400-Enabled Functions

An OptiConnect cluster can consist of up to 14 systems with full system-to-system connectivity and up to 32 systems in complex structures where all satellite systems must communicate with one or two hub systems. Figure 1.35 illustrates the clustering of three systems through an expansion unit hub.

The OptiConnect for OS/400 software provides a streamlined communications path across the dedicated system buses. Together with the hardware the following functions can utilize the high-speed system-bus-level connections between AS/400 systems:

- All **Distributed Data Management** (DDM) operations for supported object types can run across OptiConnect, including data files, data areas, and data queues.

- All **Structured Query Language** (SQL) support provided by Distributed **Relational Database Architecture** (DRDA) will run across OptiConnect, including distributed unit of work and remote unit of work.

- DB2 Multi-system with its DB2400 support for multi-node files will run across OptiConnect, providing data warehouse functions of Query/400 support and two-phase commit.

- ObjectConnect400 will operate over OptiConnect to provide high-speed system-to-system save/restore functions.

- Standard APPC Conversations are available over OptiConnect with an OptiConnect communication controller. This allows for **System Network Architecture Distribution Services** (SNADS), display station pass-through, network printer pass-through, and other functions.

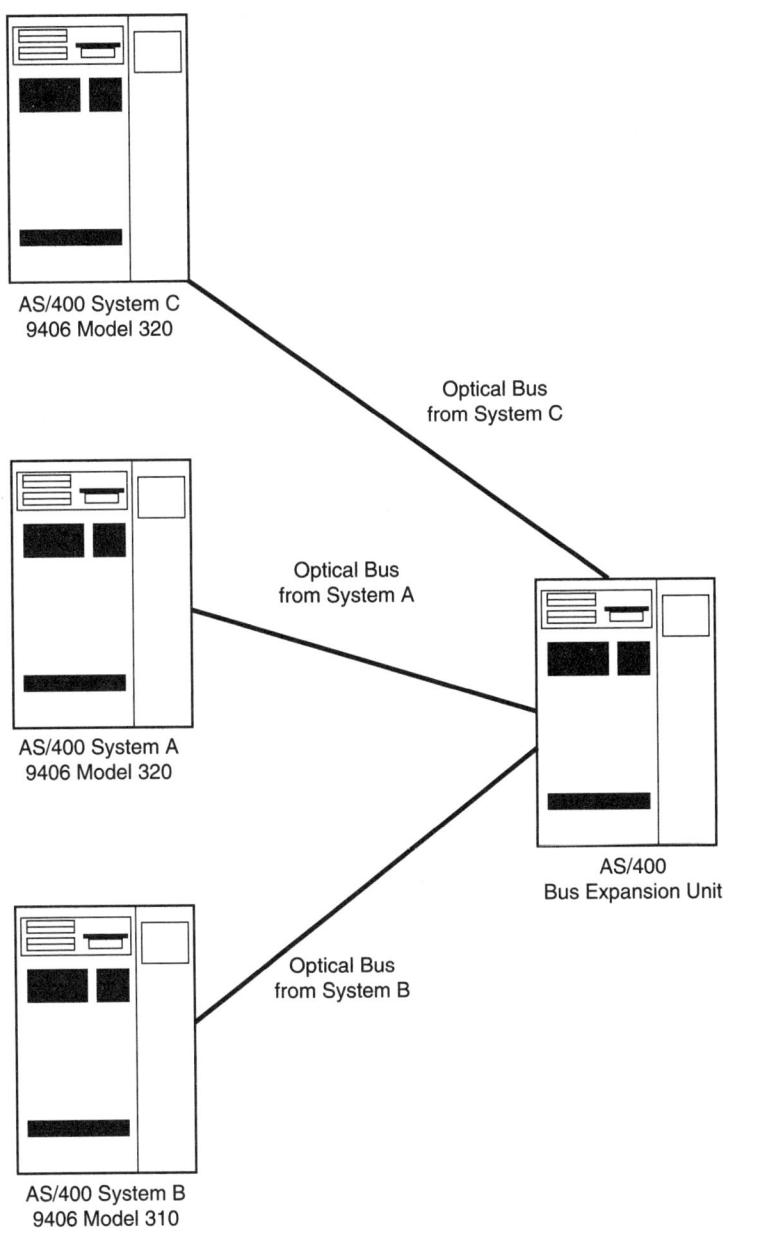

Figure 1.35. Three-system cluster with one bus given up in each system to connect to the expansion tower.

- OptiConnect has an **Application Program Interface** (API) to which business partner software packages can code.

OptiMover for OS400 is a special, low-cost PRPQ version of OptiConnect for OS/400 software. It enables non-DDM functions to utilize the OptiConnect high-speed link, allowing system-bus-level connections between AS/400 systems. PRPQ stands for **Programming Request Per Quote**. Business partner software packages written to these APIs allow customers to take advantage of this lower-priced option.

OptiConnect/400 Environment

There are two primary uses for the OptiConnect technology. *Horizontal growth* is the traditional and most popular use. Separating database operations from application workload allows multiple systems to operate as a cluster to grow computing power beyond what a single system can provide. It is important to understand that not all applications are conducive to this type of workload distribution. The horizontal growth/scalability is dependent on the database I/O intensity. The best implementation is the separation of the interactive application from the corresponding data while maintaining the batch application on the same system as the batch data. Techniques are available that transparently manage the batch job submission to the database server system.

The second use for OptiConnect technology is *high availability.* When used in conjunction with business partner applications such as those offered by Lakeview Technology and Vision Solutions, efficient high-availability solutions can be achieved. The OptiConnect technology provides the most efficient use of CPU resources to allow fast replication of data between systems.

Main Storage

The "memory" or main storage is the set of electronic circuits within an AS/400 system that provides a "workspace" for the system processor. Data and programming instructions are moved from disk storage to main storage for the programs and the processing of data. After execution or processing, modified data are moved back to main storage and kept there until no longer needed. At that point, the data are typically written back to disk storage for safekeeping.

AS/400 systems spend much time moving information between the system processor and main storage. There are two major reasons that this is so. First, all programs currently being executed by the system processor reside in main storage. Therefore, the system processor must (at some point) retrieve every instruction from main storage. Second, main storage holds the data to be acted on by the system processor. Since the information traffic between the system processor and main storage is heavy, the speed of main storage is important to overall system performance. That is why high-speed cache memory, which increases the effective speed of main storage, is included in the system design.

As we have seen, every main storage location in AS/400 main storage consists of 64 pieces of information, or bits. All information in main storage is encoded using these 64-bit groupings, called double words. In addition to the 64 bits of information, each word in main storage has several additional bits (called **check bits**) that are generated based on the value of that particular 64-bit word. In the event that one or two of the 64-bit words is somehow corrupted, the check bits notify the AS/400 computer that the error exists. If only one of the 64 bits is corrupted, as is usually the case, the check bits actually restore the corrupted bit and correct the error. This main storage error detection and correction works to protect the all-important integrity of user information in the computer system.

In earlier days of computing, the main storage size limited the amount of work a computer could manage at any one time. This limitation capped the size of programs, the number of programs that could be run concurrently, the number of users that could share the system, and so on. In modern computers a technique called virtual storage alleviates the need to squeeze all active programs and data into main storage.

Storage Management

The methods used within a computer system to manage main storage and disk storage, called the computer's storage management, are fundamental to the capabilities of the computer. Understanding the basics of storage management provides insight into one of the unique features of AS/400 computers as compared with traditional computer systems.

Figure 1.36 shows conceptually what the storage in AS/400 computers looks like. All programs and information currently being used by

Figure 1.36. AS/400 main storage and fixed disk storage.

the computer system must be contained in main storage, which resides inside the computer's system unit. Main storage is relatively expensive and responds at very high speeds (compared to disk storage) when called on to provide or store information. Because main storage loses all information when the computer system is turned off, it is called *volatile* storage.

Disk storage is less expensive but cannot provide or store information as quickly as main storage. Disk storage is said to be non-volatile because it does not lose its information when the power is turned off (or lost owing to a power failure). As a result of this non-volatility and relatively low cost, disk storage is commonly used to hold all information that must be readily available to the computer. Disk storage may reside either inside the system unit or inside a separate box cabled to the system unit (as depicted in the figure).

When the AS/400 computer is first turned on, information vital to an orderly startup and smooth operation is automatically copied from the disk to main storage. Once normal system operation is established, users can begin to do their work. During the course of this work, users will start various computer programs. As each program is started, it is copied from the disk to main storage and then executed. Depending on the work being done, the computer programs manipulate various sets of data that are also loaded from the disk as needed. It does not take long to realize that the main storage in a computer can quickly become filled up with programs and data as the system is called upon to do more and more work.

In earlier days, the main storage size limited the amount of work a computer could manage at any one time. This limitation capped the size of programs, the number of programs that could be run concurrently, the number of users that could share the system, and so on. In today's environment, a technique called virtual storage (discussed more fully in the next section) alleviates the need to squeeze all active programs and data into main storage. In computers that support virtual storage, the computer basically "fakes out" the computer programs and users and appears to have much more main storage than it actually has. (The AS/400 allows a virtual storage size of 18 million terabytes). Virtual storage therefore allows more programs, data, and users to be simultaneously active on the system than could be supported in real main storage.

Although virtual storage is a powerful system feature, the "swapping" between disk and main storage is processing overhead that can reduce the overall system performance. A little swapping does not appreciably hurt performance, but increased swapping does. When the swapping performed by a virtual storage system becomes excessive, the system is said to be "thrashing," or spending too much time swapping information between disk and main storage. Thrashing can be reduced by increasing the amount of main storage in the AS/400 system through the installation of main storage expansion options. Increasing the main storage in the system provides more room for programs and data, reducing the amount of virtual storage swapping. Thrashing can also be reduced through system management means such as rescheduling work for off-peak periods.

The virtual storage concept is implemented in many of today's computer systems to one degree or another. AS/400 systems implement their virtual storage scheme through a concept called *single-level storage*. This simply means that in AS/400 systems, no distinction is made between disk storage and main storage. All storage appears to be one homogeneous sea of main storage accessed in exactly the same way. This consistency provides for a simple and efficient virtual storage implementation that is the same for programs, data, temporary holding areas, and so forth. The simplicity of single-level storage results in a consistent and more complete virtual storage system than most other implementations.

Another difference between AS/400 storage management and that of conventional computer systems is object-oriented access. With this concept, all programs, databases, documents, and so on stored in AS/400 computers are stored as independent entities called **objects**. The AS/400's object-oriented access again provides the user and the programmer with a simple and consistent way of managing all programs and information in the system. Users can access an object by simply referring to its name. The AS/400 security system will check to make sure that the user has authorization to use the object and that it is being used properly. This is called *capability-based addressing*. The AS/400 system manages the complexities associated with the physical location and addressing of the information.

AS/400's implementation of single-level storage and capability-based addressing spreads information through various disk units in a way that optimizes storage efficiency. Objects provide consistency in the areas of security, usage, and systems management for all items stored on AS/400 systems. Objects can be organized into groups called *libraries*. A library (which is also an object) is analogous to a drawer in a file cabinet (or a subdirectory, for those familiar with PC disk management). A library might contain all programs related to the accounting function of a business to keep things organized. Because access to libraries can be restricted by the AS/400 security system, a payroll database, for example, might be kept in a library separate from other business information for security reasons.

Virtual Storage

Virtual storage is a technique for using main storage that alleviates the need to squeeze all active programs and data into main storage. As mentioned earlier, with virtual storage the computer basically "fakes out" the system, appearing to have much more main storage than it actually has. The virtual storage supported by AS/400 systems is over a whopping 18 million terabytes (TB) in size (over 18 quintillion [18,000,000,000,000,000 or 18×10^{15}] unique addresses). This 18 million TB of addressing capability is enough to keep track of the information contained on over 9 quintillion pages of single-spaced computer output—a stack of paper over 800 billion miles high that could stretch between the earth and the moon 3 million times. Virtual storage therefore allows more programs, data, and users to be simultaneously active on the system than could be supported in real main storage without virtual storage.

Virtual storage works as follows: A user tells the computer to start a word processing program. The computer first attempts to load the needed portion of the word processing program into main storage. If there is no space left in main storage, some space is made available by overwriting an inactive portion of some program or by "swapping" out some inactive data to a temporary space on the disk. The needed portion of the word processing program can then be loaded in the available space, and the user can then begin typing the memo. If the program that was overwritten or the data that were "swapped" out are again needed, they are reloaded from a disk unit to some other available main storage area. Therefore, a virtual storage computer system is constantly swapping programs and information between main storage and disk storage, robbing Peter to pay Paul and vice versa.

Virtual storage allows the maximum size program or combination of all programs and data to be limited only by the combined amount of main storage and disk storage space rather than by the amount of main storage alone. The advantage of virtual storage is that neither the programmer nor the user of any AS/400 system needs to be concerned with main storage size. The system seems to have as much main storage as needed, and they are never aware that information is constantly being swapped from main storage to disk storage and back again. This swapping is handled automatically.

Auxiliary Storage

Auxiliary storage, commonly used to keep data and program information in all computers, is an inexpensive way to retain and later access information. Information kept on auxiliary storage can be easily modified or kept unchanged over long periods of time as an archive. Because all auxiliary storage is nonvolatile, the information stored remains intact whether the computer is turned on or off. The AS/400 systems use four types of auxiliary storage: diskette, disk, optical libraries, and tape.

Diskette Storage

Diskettes are a portable magnetic storage medium that can be used to record and later retrieve computer information via a diskette unit. The diskettes consist of a flexible disk with a magnetic surface permanently enclosed in a square, protective outer jacket, as shown in Figure 1.37.

One of the primary functions of diskettes is to provide portable storage, allowing for the transfer of programs and data between computers. To this end, all similarly configured AS/400 computer systems can freely exchange programs and data via diskettes. Also, information on System/3X diskettes can be freely exchanged with a properly configured AS/400 computer.

82 EXPLORING IBM AS/400 COMPUTERS

Figure 1.37. Diskette used with application systems.

Disk Storage

Earlier in the chapter we introduced another kind of auxiliary storage used with AS/400 systems called disk storage units or **Direct Access Storage Devices (DASDs)**. These are high-capacity magnetic storage devices commonly used in all types of computers from PS/2s to large mainframe computer systems. The basic anatomy of a disk unit is shown in Figure 1.38. Disks consist of a drive mechanism with permanently installed metallic disks often called platters (because they are shaped like a dinner plate). These platters have a magnetic surface that can store information. Disk units will be described in greater detail later in this book.

Disk unit performance is important to the overall performance of a computer system in most applications. This is particularly true in virtual storage and/or multiuser environments, in which there is heavy transfer of information between disk storage and main storage.

The *performance* of a disk unit refers to the rate at which information can be located and transferred between the disk unit and the main storage. The speed at which a disk unit can position the read/write head over the proper region of the platter is the average **seek time**, usually expressed in milliseconds (1/1000 second). After the read/write head is properly positioned, the system must wait as the platter spins until the needed data begins to pass under the read/write head. The average time it takes for the platter to rotate to the proper position is called the average **latency** (also expressed in milliseconds).

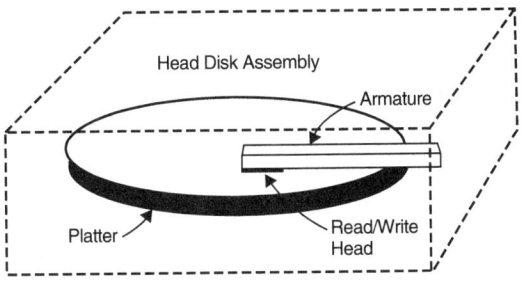

Figure 1.38. The anatomy of a disk unit.

Finally, once the read/write head is positioned and the data begin to pass by on the spinning platter, the information is transferred from the disk unit to the computer system. The speed at which this is done is called the data transfer rate and is usually expressed in **millions of bytes per second** (MBps). The shorter the average seek time and the average latency, and the higher the transfer rate, the better the performance of the disk storage subsystem and the overall computer system. Figure 1.39 shows the average seek times, average latency, and data transfer rates for some internal disk units that are provided as standard equipment on AS/400 systems.

In addition to the disk unit specifications, there are other performance considerations when configuring the disk storage subsystem of an AS/400 system. Some disk units have multiple actuators whereas others only have one. (The **actuator** is the accessing mechanism of the disk unit, which carries the read/write head and flies over the surface of the disk detecting or imprinting the magnetic bits.) Often, each actuator in a disk unit can perform independently, so the more actuators you have for a given amount of disk storage, the better the performance. In fact, choosing disk storage configurations that have more actuators for a given amount of storage can result in higher performance than selecting disk units with faster specifications but fewer actuators. This is particularly true with AS/400 systems because single-level storage tends to spread information over many areas of the disk units. This spreading of information produces more efficient operation because the actuators can all share the load, but it does emphasize the need to follow proper backup procedures.

Computer System	Standard Configuration	Fixed-Disk Devices Used	Average Seek Time	Data Transfer Rate	Latency	Number of Actuators
Advanced Entry	4194 MB 4194-MB disk unit	One 3.5-inch	8.6 ms	20 MB/sec	5.56 ms	1/drive
Advanced 36	1030 MB 1030-MB disk unit	One 3.5-inch	8.6 ms	5 MB/sec	5.56 ms	1/drive
	1960 MB 1960-MB disk unit	One 3.5-inch	8.6 ms	5 MB/sec	5.56 ms	1/drive
720, 730, 740, 170	4194 MB 4194-MB disk unit	One 3.5-inch	8.6 ms	40 MB/sec	5.56 ms	1/drive
720, 730, 740, 170 150	8580 MB 8580-MB disk unit	One 3.5-inch	8.6 ms	40 MB/sec	5.56 ms	1/drive
720, 730, 740, 170	17500 MB 17500-MB disk unit	One 3.5-inch	8.6 ms	40 MB/sec	5.56 ms	1/drive

Figure 1.39. Performance characteristics of internal fixed disks provided as a standard in AS/400 systems.

Optical Libraries

Optical libraries consist of arrays of optical disks associated with one or more optical disk read/write units. In some cases, the optical storage read/write units also have one or more conventional magnetic disk storage units associated with them to improve the write performance from a system perspective. The optical disks may be CD-ROM, WORM, or WMRM technology, each of which imposes different requirements upon the read/write unit and upon the controller within the system. CD-ROM is an abbreviation for **Compact Disk–Read Only Memory,** and the technology presents digital data in a continuous serpentine path across the surface of the optical disk. WORM is an abbreviation for **Write Once, Read Many.** This technology presents data in circumferential paths across the surface of the optical disk. Because the data will only be written once, this technology generally has the header embedded on the raw media, and a sector corresponds to the data content that can fit in the shortest circumferential track. WMRM, sometimes referred to as erasable optical disk technology, is an abbreviation for **Write Many, Read Many** and also presents data in circumferential paths across the surface of the optical disk. But because the data written at one time must be erased before new data may be written to replace it, WMRM must follow the sectoring, header, trailer, and error correction rules of magnetic disk technology, including bad track recovery and directory management.

Tape Storage

The last type of auxiliary storage to be covered is magnetic tape or simply "tape." One primary purpose of tape is to provide a backup storage medium for information on the computer's disk storage. The low cost and high recording densities inherent in tape make it ideal for archiving information. Tape is also very useful in distributing programs and transferring information from one computer system to another. Diskettes can be used for these same functions, but the higher storage capacity of tapes is preferred if you are dealing with a large amount of information. Tape storage consists of a long flexible strip coated with magnetic material and rolled on a reel or into a cartridge.

Packaging Technology

Most of the circuitry in AS/400 systems was built using IBM's version of **Very Large Scale Integration** (VLSI) technology called **Complementary Metal-Oxide Semiconductor (CMOS)**. This packaging technology builds circuits with 0.25-micron-sized elements, allowing up to 25 million high-speed transistors in a single chip. Main storage is implemented using IBM's 16-Mb and 64-Mb (16-million-bit) memory chip technology. Sixteen-megabit chips are used on all except the largest-capacity memory cards, which use 64-Mb chips to achieve an improved packaging density.

Five basic mechanical designs are used in AS/400 computer system units. The sizes range from the desk-side tower of the Model 150 to the dual tall-tower racks that house the Model 740. The system unit package contains the system processor, main storage, tape, disk units, a CD-ROM, and some number of I/O controllers.

The main storage for the A10 Microprocessor-based processors is contained on a card that measures about 7 x 3 inches and plugs directly to the processor card. Main storage for Models 170/720 is packaged on standard DIMM form factor cards. Main storage for the A50 Microprocessor-based processors for Models 730/740 is contained on separate 9 x 15-inch cards contained in a separate metal container called a book. Other circuitry is packaged on 9 x 11-inch cards that are plugged into an internal card chassis (called a cage), allowing for electrical connections to the bus. The design is modular, and the various elements can be easily added or replaced without the need for IBM service personnel.

All AS/400 systems use the cable-thru wiring scheme. Cable-thru allows multiple displays or printers (i.e., workstations) to be attached together in a daisy-chain fashion as shown in Figure 1.40. With cable-thru, it is not necessary to run a separate cable from the computer to each workstation. Instead, a single cable from the computer can be used to attach up to seven workstations over a distance of up to 5000 feet.

Figure 1.40. All applications use the cable-thru approach to attach to local workstations.

Fiber Optic Bus

The fiber optic bus design continued from the D, E, and F models permits the larger Advanced Series systems to add additional I/O busses to an AS/400 system. This allows the system to accommodate more I/O devices without loading down existing I/O busses. The fiber optic cable that attaches these additional SPD I/O busses (i.e., system unit expansion features) uses laser light rather than electrical signals to exchange information with the rest of the AS/400 system. Using light allows the additional I/O busses to operate at full speed over greater distances and eliminates the electrical interference inherent in electrical cables carrying high-speed signals. The fiber optic cables can carry light signals at a rate of 1063 Mbps. Except for the rack-mounted 5042 units, V4R2 upgrades that contain the older 266-Mbps fiber optic cables must be upgraded to the 1063-Mbps type. With these optical cables, the various towers of an AS/400 system can be located up to 100 meters apart rather than within the 12-foot limit imposed by earlier electrical I/O bus cables. Furthermore, optical cable configurations are available that will allow inter-tower distances of up to 2 kilometers in some situations.

2

Options and Peripherals

Application systems are likely to be found in many diverse environments—from fish markets to insurance companies. The activities performed by people in these environments vary widely, and so do their computing needs. Application systems can be customized to many environments by selecting the appropriate optional equipment. This includes **feature cards, internal options,** and **peripherals**. Feature cards are circuit boards containing electronics that provide some additional capacity or function(s) to application systems. They can be installed in one of the I/O expansion slots provided in all Application System computers. Peripherals are devices that attach to Application System computers, usually via a cable, and perform functions under the computer's control. This chapter covers

- Workstations
- Main Storage Expansion Options
- Auxiliary Storage Options
- Communications Options
- Other Options

Although this chapter does not provide comprehensive coverage of all the optional equipment that can be used with application systems, it does introduce the reader to many devices that are representative of those most commonly used in the business environment.

Workstations

The devices used to interact with application systems are known as **workstations**, which can be either terminals or printers. A **computer terminal** (also called a display station) is the TV-like device that converts the computer's electrical signals into light images that convey information to the user. Terminals also come equipped with a keyboard that allows the user to send information back to the computer. **Printers** are electro-mechanical devices that print the computer's electronically encoded information onto paper. If a workstation is near the computer system—for example, in the same building—it can be *locally* attached to the computer system via a cable. If the workstation is not near the computer—for example, in another state—it can be *remotely* attached over communications lines. Either way, the function provided to the workstation user is the same. Some type of workstation is required to allow the user to interact with the application systems. Many types of workstations can be used with application systems. In this chapter, we look at the following:

- InfoWindow II 3486/3487 Display Stations

- InfoWindow II 3488/3489 Modular Display Station

- Operations Console

- Personal Computer (PC) Terminal Emulation

- Retail Workstations

- Network Computer Workstations

- Printers, both impact and nonimpact

- Workstation Controllers

- Twinaxial Controllers

- ASCII Controllers

- Protocol Converters

InfoWindow II 3486/3487 Display Stations

The 3486 and 3487 Display Stations (Figure 2.1) are members of the InfoWindow II family of text-only display stations (also called terminals) for use with the application systems. The 3486 is the entry member of the InfoWindow II family of displays. It is compatible with the earlier 3476 and 3196 displays while providing some additional features. First, the 3486 supports an enhanced user interface that employs a mouse and special graphical characters (e.g., scroll bars, radio buttons, pushbuttons, check boxes, and continuous window frames) to ease the user's interaction with application programs. This enables AS/400 applications (specially written or used in conjunction with the IBM WindowTool/400 product [5798-RYF]) to provide pop-up menus and help screens popular with personal computer (PC) users.

Also provided by the 3486 is support for two display sessions and one printer, split-screen viewing of new 32 x 8 and 49 x 8 screen formats, and a built-in calculator. As with all InfoWindow II displays, the image presented on the 3486 Display screen has been improved (new character fonts, reduced flicker, etc.) to comply with emerging display-quality standards (ISO 9241 part 3).

Finally, the 3486 can support a PC-type printer (for example, an IBM Personal Printer Series II), which can be cabled directly to a port provided on the rear of the 3486. This printer can be used as a system printer, just like other printers attached to the Application System, or it can be used to print an image of whatever is on the 3486's screen. Printers supported now include laser printers such as the IBM 4019 and 4029 or the Hewlett-Packard LaserJet III.

The 3486 displays are monochrome only and have 14-inch display screens. The displays can be either green on black (BG models) or amber/gold on black (BA models). Which you choose is purely a matter of individual taste. Either version can display 24 lines of text 80 characters in length while still leaving a row at the bottom to display status mes-

Figure 2.1. InfoWindow II 3486/3487 Modular Display Station.

sages. The display comes with a tilt swivel base to allow a comfortable viewing angle. The record/play mode feature of the 3486 displays includes the ability to store up to 1500 often-used keystroke sequences that are recalled by pressing a single command key.

The display can be set up to go blank after a specified time of keyboard inactivity to protect the display's **phosphors**, which, like those used in a television, are deposited on the inside surface of the display and glow, when excited by electronic signals generated by the display station, to create an image. When a display station is left on but unattended, an image can be permanently "burned" into the phosphors. The blanking feature prevents this. A blanked image is automatically restored when any key is pressed. This feature can be adjusted through operator setup functions, as can the alarm volume, keyboard clicker volume, cursor shape, and other items.

The provided key-lock disables the keyboard and display, helping to prevent unauthorized entering or viewing of information. You also have the choice of either a 102-key keyboard (IBM Enhanced Keyboard) like those used with Personal System/2 computers or a 122-key typewriter keyboard. Either keyboard has an adjustable slope (6- or 12-degree tilt). The primary difference in keyboards is that the 122-key keyboard has more programmable function keys. The InfoWindow II 3487 Display Stations are compatible with the older InfoWindow 3477 and 3179 Display Stations. They are functionally the same as the 3486 Display Stations described earlier but offer larger display screens on all models and a color display on one model:

- 14-inch color display (HC models)

- 15-inch green-on-black display (HG models)

- 15-inch amber/gold-on-black display (HA models)

Color can be used to effectively highlight and associate information on a display, making the information clearer. Some highlighting capability is provided on most monochrome displays, but color provides additional flexibility in this area while providing a more pleasing image. The 15-inch display offers larger characters, which is especially helpful when operating the 3487 in its 27 lines of 132 characters mode. The image presented on the display screen of all InfoWindow II displays has been improved (new character fonts, reduced flicker, etc.) to comply with emerging display-quality standards (ISO 9241 part 3). Finally, an optional barcode magnetic badge reader (i.e., the 7695 Model 250) can be attached to the 3487 to allow data entry through barcodes or magnetic badges in addition to normal keyboard entry.

InfoWindow II 3488/3489 Modular Display Station

The InfoWindow II 3488 Modular Display Station (Figure 2.2) and the InfoWindow II 3489 Modular Display station embody a modular design that allows the user to attach a Personal System/2 display (any VGA or VGA-compatible display) to the 3488/3489 display logic module. That is, the user has the flexibility to customize the display station to suit his or her needs by selecting from any PC-type monitor. As user needs change, the monitor can be upgraded. Conversely, if the user moves

Display type: Personal computer display (user selected)
Features: Separate Display Logic Module

Figure 2.2. InfoWindowII 3488 Modular Display Station. Separate display logic module can be seen on the right.

up to a PC workstation, he or she can retain the monitor and use it with the PC. Functionally, the 3488 provides the same functions as the 3486/3487 Display Stations discussed earlier, including light pen, color, and mouse functions.

Operations Console

The AS/400 Operations Console allows PC workstations with Windows 32-bit operating systems to locally or remotely perform AS/400 system operations and services via an AS/400 System Console Session. AS/400 Client Access for Windows 95/NT must also be installed to allow the System Console Session.

The Operations Console is a follow-on to the AS/400 Client Access PC5250 Console function. Operations Console can be used as a System Console Session when connected to AS/400 systems running AS/400 V4R3 or later. Operations Console connects to the **MultiFunction I/O Processor (MFIOP)** through a special cable, orderable with the AS/400 hardware, at rates up to 115,200 bps (depending on the attached AS/400 model).

Operations Console also provides the ability to remotely perform System Console and Control Panel functions. To use the remote console capability, called Remote Controlling System (RCS), a Local Controlling System (LCS) must be initially set up. This requires a Windows NT 4.0 desktop to be directly attached to the AS/400 and running the Operations Console functions. The remote console also includes a Graphical Control Panel Application that allows a PC user to select AS/400 Control Panel functions from the desktop. All control panel functions are supported, including system power on, except for those reserved for onsite CE use. To use this program, another special cable which may be ordered with the AS/400 hardware, must be connected to the AS/400 Control Panel. This program can be used with AS/400e systems running OS/400 V4R1 or later.

The Operations Console is an install option of Client Access, and is packaged with both Client Access for Windows 95/NT and with EZ Setup (See Chapter 3) on the Operations Navigator CD-ROM. Operations Navigator can be enabled from Operations Console if help desk is present. This centralizes the system management functions through a single ASYNC connection to the AS/400. Developers can use a AS/400 Control Panel sockets API to write Windows 95/NT applications to do

AS/400 Control Panel functions. It is possible to remotely connect a Local Controlling System for Operations Console using the ECS modem and TCP/IP dial up. It is possible to replicate the control panel function on a Remote Console, and provide control of the AS/400 system from that console.

Personal Computer (PC) Terminal Emulation

With the proper feature card and software (e.g., Client Access Family for AS/400 for Windows or Client Access Family for AS/400), a PC (Figure 2.3), a Personal System/2, or any other vendor's PC can also be used as a terminal for application systems. In this case, the PC is said to be acting like or *emulating* a terminal. In the simplest case, the PC appears to the application systems to be like any other terminal with no special capabilities. The user can then interact with the application systems just as with any other terminal discussed so far. Further, a printer

Type:	Color/text and graphics
Features:	Local intelligence, advanced graphics
Options:	Various models, connection type

Figure 2.3. Properly configured personal computers can be used as workstations for application systems.

attached to the PC can be used both as a printer for PC application programs and as a system printer for the AS/400 application programs. Hitting a simple keystroke combination temporarily suspends terminal emulation, and the PC is changed back into a normal PC able to run the many PC programs available today.

Because the PC is a computer, not just a terminal, it has its own intelligence. It is therefore called an **intelligent workstation**. This intelligence can be used to run PC programs independent of the application systems, or it can be used to work with the application systems, and it provides for the direct interaction between PC programs and those running on application systems. This type of interaction can be done without user intervention to perform functions ranging from simply transferring a file between the PC and the application systems to more complex program-to-program communications (e.g., cooperative processing). You can also concurrently interact with multiple application systems with a single PC or sign on to a single system as more than one terminal. Chapter 6 further discusses interaction between PCs and application systems in the context of the Internet and of intranets. For more information about PCs, refer to *Exploring IBM Personal Computers, 9th Edition* (IBM document G325-0400, Maximum Press).

To simplify the ordering process for PC systems that will attach properly to the AS/400 systems, IBM has added the ValuePoint/400 to its product line of orderable systems. The ValuePoint/400 systems come with all the necessary hardware and are preloaded with Client Access Family. If you have an existing PC system that you desire to attach to an AS/400 system with an appropriate twinaxial, ASCII, or LAN interface, but not including the proper level of software, the AS/400 will detect this and automatically download the current level of Client Access Family, providing you with the selection of either the Windows 95/98/NT support or Windows 3.1/OS/2/DOS support.

Retail Workstations

Retail workstations are basically PCs with a cash drawer and with some unique characteristics added to interface with customers and sales items. Those characteristics include the ability to print receipts on a rolling tape and acknowledge receipt of checks, the ability to present to the customer and the operator the price of what is being checked out, and an interface to at least one and sometimes several forms of UPC (Universal Product Code) barcode reader. With the advent of token-ring and Ethernet local area networks (LANs) on both the PC and the AS/400e series, a method for direct connection of those workstations now exists. An illustration of a retail workstation is shown in Figure 2.4. Of course, in some situations the retail workstation is connected via wireless methods. The AS/400e series in the retail environment will be discussed in greater detail in Chapter 5.

IBM Network Station #8361

The IBM Network Station 8361 is a cross between a personal computer and a traditional non-intelligent terminal (Figure 2.5). It provides the flexibility of a personal computer and cost approaching that of a nonintelligent terminal while connecting to a local area network (LAN), and eventually to either coaxial cable or twinaxial networks. The Network Station cannot function on its own because it receives its programming from a server over a LAN.

Figure 2.4. A typical retail workstation.

98 EXPLORING IBM AS/400 COMPUTERS

Figure 2.5. The IBM Network Station.

In early publications the IBM Network Station was referred to as the Thin Client. The IBM Network Station is used with a personal computer display (VGA or higher), a mouse, and a keyboard. There is a parallel port (e.g., for connection of a printer), a serial port (e.g., for connection of a modem), and a built-in speaker. The LAN connection can be either Ethernet (8361 Model 100) or token ring (8361 Model 200) or either (8361 Model 1000).

Network Stations use a PowerPC microprocessor (the #8361 Model 1000 uses a 200 MHz version of the PowerPC microprocessor). The IBM Network Station comes standard with 8 MB of memory (expandable to 64 MB) and 1 MB of video memory expandable to 2 MB. No disk or diskette drive (or any other auxiliary storage) is used with the Network Station. All programming and data is provided to the Network Station by an AS/400 server. The IBM Network Station can be used with all existing AS/400 application programs (about 25,000 or so) and provides a new graphical Windows-like user interface (Figure 2.6). Other functions that may be downloaded include 3270 emu-

Options and Peripherals **99**

Figure 2.6. AS/400 ACXT Sample Screen, including Web Browser, Java Applets, AS/400 HTML Gateway, Remote Control Windows Apps, AIX X/Windows, 5250 Green Screen, and 3270 Green Screen.

lation, UNIX, AIX, X-terminal software, remote windows applications, Web-based applications, a Web browser, and a Java virtual machine. This allows the execution of Java applets (application programs written in the Java programming language and downloaded on demand).

The network station boots up (gets started) from any AS/400 equipped with the supporting software (program 5733-A06 for V3R2 or 5733-A07 for V3R7, or, for V4R1, Navio NC Navigator or IBM Network Station Browser). It can also boot up from other types of servers provided they have the necessary supporting software.

The Network Station Manager for AS/400 is an additional piece of software that supports the Network Station, providing central client management for the Network Stations connected to the AS/400. The NC Navigator browser supports 2-way e-mail using a POP3 server. Navigator 4 supports Real Audio and Adobe plug-ins. Encryption, cut and paste, and audio for ICA clients is supported as well as Java Virtual Machine and Just in Time Compiler with currency support (including

Eurocurrency). Lotus eSuite 2.0 has been added to the software which may be downloaded to the Network Station, and ORION will manage Network Stations running JavaOS and JavaOS for Business from Sun. A twinaxial enabled Network Station is provided for AS/400 customers wanting Network Stations but wanting to avoid rewiring for LAN attachment.

Printing Technology and Printers

Printing technologies have exploded, providing dramatically expanded choices in speed, resolution, connectivity, color, and paper handling function. The technology is important, but printing applications still drive printer decisions. Some of the key considerations are these:

- **Document Characteristics:** Electronic output documents, where the application composes the entire output page (as opposed to only variable data with preprinted forms), has greatly increased the use of electronic forms, barcoding, image and graphics, typographic fonts, and color. Preprinted forms remain a major requirement in many environments, particularly where carbon copies must be produced.

- **Printing Applications:** Where does the application reside, what output data stream is created, and where will it be printed.

- **Printer Location:** Where the printer will be located in the AS/400 computing environment, how will it communicate, and what systems and applications will be supported.

- **Relative Importance:** Where is the printing application on a scale from convenience or personal up to mission-critical. The characteristics and management required for mission-critical printing are normally significantly different from printing to a convenience printer.

- **Printing Volumes:** Printing at a speed of 60 pages per minute and higher is generally considered production printing. The

AS/400 supports individual printers capable of printing at greater than 1000 pages per minute (InfoPrint 4000 Advanced Printing System).

- **Print Window:** Usually related to print volumes, the print window refers to the time duration available for a given print application. For example, a month-end statement run may need to be done within a three-day print window.

- **Printing Costs:** Includes both costs of acquisition and operational costs.

- **Network Presentation:** What are the requirements for distributing and "presenting" the information. Should reports be electronically distributed, then viewed and (optionally) printed. Do you want to present company documents - i.e., statements - electronically to a customer?

- **Document Archival:** Do reports on business documents need to be archived for later retrieval? For example, do you need to electronically archive customer invoices or statements to be accessed on demand in a customer service application?

- **Other Factors:** Such as special forms, environmental considerations, etc. Special forms can include heavier paper stock or even plastic (i.e., credit or membership cards). There are some printers (for example, the InfoPrint 62) that can handle these kinds of forms.

Changes in document characteristics is one big change in AS/400 printer requirements. AS/400 printing has traditionally meant printing simple lines of text on twinaxially connected impact printers. Printer decisions were primarily based on speed. With electronic **documents**, anything can be printed anywhere on the page. This has transformed the role of printing with business processes. The printed document becomes part of the organizational workflow. For example,

- Bar-coded labels are scanned during order picking to automatically update shipped quantities.

- Documents with zip codes encoded in PostNet barcode are automatically routed by scanning equipment, and result in significantly lower mailing costs.

- Checks printed with MICR encoding are automatically processed.

- Payment coupons with invoice number and invoice amount encoded in barcode can be scanned upon receipt instead of being rekeyed.

- Scanned documents, such as checks or freight bills, can become part of the customer statement.

Electronic printing also means the design and quality of documents can be transformed through the use of typographic fonts, image, graphics and color. This provides for

- The elimination of preprinted forms, replacing them with applications that print the entire document on blank paper.

- The customization of documents for each customer, tailoring both design and message.

- Printed documents that are more effective and more readable, and that project a more professional corporate image.

Generally, AS/400 printed output comes from three types of applications, each with different print data streams or print languages:

- Line-at-a-time mode printing in SCS (SNA Character Set) format

- Page-mode printing in AFP (Advanced Function Printing) format

- Page-mode printing in ASCII format.

Traditional AS/400 output is lines of text and/or data in SCS printed a line at a time.

AFP applications have sophisticated electronic output, printing full pages instead of lines and using external print resources (electronic forms, fonts, images, graphics, and barcodes) in that process. Generally, these applications are created in system- and printer-independent format (AFP), then converted into printer-specific format (IPDS, or Intelligent Printer Data Stream). IPDS is termed "intelligent" because it is a two-way printing process with error recovery by page. IPDS printing is, in essence, a client/server application between the AS/00 (specifically, Print Services Facility/400) and the printer. (Refer to Chapter 4 for more details on AFP and PSF/400.)

Client, LAN, or network applications can create either line-mode or page-mode output, although most now tend to be full pages using either HP-PCL or Adobe PostScript print data streams. The AS/00 natively supports only AFP, SCS, IPDS, and line data formats. ASCII print formats, such as HP-PCL and PostScript, are supported through print transforms, or sent as is. Note that all of these print formats (plus image formats such as GIF and BMP) except HP-PCL can be sent to IPDS printers.

As the AS/400 is a multiuser computing system, the print applications tend to be line-of-business ones with significant page volumes. Client or LAN applications, on the other hand, tend to be personal and have lower volumes.

Given these different kinds of printing applications the location of the printer becomes important. To date, most AS/00 printers have been twinaxially connected directly to the system. More and more, printers are LAN-connected, and organizations would like LAN-attached printers to handle both AS/400 and LAN print jobs. With network-centric environments, more of the communication connections are TCP/IP. Attaching a printer using an IP address provides flexibility. However, the TCP/IP support for printing is limited, both in document function, and print management. In this environment, IPDS acts as a bridge to provide full application and print management function.

Printers

Printer technology breaks down into two categories, impact and nonimpact. Within each of those categories are many subclasses, and line and page printers are available in each category. Impact printers essentially are divided into wire-matrix technology and band-matrix technology. Nonimpact printers include thermal fusion, inkjet, and laser. The business decision about which technology to select, impact or nonimpact, should be driven by the types of output documents required. If the output documents must have many copies that are legally guaranteed duplications (carbon copies), then impact printers must be used. If the required output documents are predominantly letters, memos, and so on, and a diskette or copy electronically stored is sufficient to meet the legal requirements, then nonimpact printers can be used. For the majority of businesses, the documentation requirements are a mixture of the two requirements, and some combination of the two types of printers will be required.

The remainder of the discussion of printers will discuss the characteristics of the printer technology as it relates to a business environment for each major category of both the impact and nonimpact printers. Figures will be presented that identify the characteristics of some widely used IBM printers, listing at least one printer in each of the technologies. In these tables, differences in the quality of print, the available throughput, the suitability of the printer for graphics output, and the external interface to the printer will be identified.

Impact Printers

Impact printers fit into two broad categories: wire-matrix and band printers. Band printers consist of straight alphanumeric band printers and band matrix printers. As mentioned earlier, the decision to use an impact printer should be driven by the need to produce carbon copies (documents of this type are commonly referred to as continuous forms). Five carbon copies are normally considered a maximum, after which the quality of the print deteriorates so badly that it may not be readable. In general, impact printers are noisy and, because of the force involved, have been found to require a greater frequency of repair than nonimpact printers.

As a result of the noise, impact printers should be located where they will disturb the fewest people. (See Chapter 4 for a detailed positioning of printing and electronic documents in the AS/400 environment.) Impact printers normally use pin-fed continuous forms. Impact printers can also handle non-text print elements such as barcodes, electronic forms, fonts and image.

Wire-Matrix Technology

Wire-matrix printers come in 9-wire and 18-wire formats. They produce documents by selectively firing magnetic hammers against the wires, which impact a print ribbon interposed between the wires and the document as the print head is scanned across the page. In general, the 9-wire printers produce a near-letter-quality document, whereas an 18-wire printer produces a letter-quality document. The wire-matrix printers produce good graphics output in black and white, but because the number of colors available in a ribbon is limited, the production of color is generally limited to three colors: black, red, and green, and little shade of gray differentiation.

The available throughput varies from 60 to 700 characters per second, which correlates to 1 to 14 pages per minute. Graphical resolution varies from about 144 pels vertical by 240 pels horizontal for the 9-wire printers to 360 pels vertical by 360 pels horizontal for the 18-wire printers. Multiple fonts may be printed with relative ease with the wire-matrix technology printers. A pel is the number of dots which can be placed within a dimension of one inch either vertical or horizontal.

A new printer technology is the multiform printer. The IBM 4247 Multiform Printer supports up to two continuous form inputs and up to four cut-sheet form inputs. This provides the capability to combine printing applications and printers. For example, an IBM 4247 Multiform Printer can be set up with preprinted invoice forms in one continuous input, label stock for barcode labels in the other continuous input, and plain paper (for customer letters) in a cut sheet input.

Band Printers

As mentioned earlier, band printers fit into two categories: the strict alphanumeric and expanded character set type, and the band-matrix type. The strict alphanumeric band printers produce letter-quality documents, but can do no graphics printing. The printer has a band with the characters that can be printed impregnated on it, a print ribbon is between the band and the document to be printed, and a set of hammers is moved across the document's surface. The band is moved in one direction at a very high speed, the hammers are moved across the document, and when a character to be printed is aligned with a hammer, the hammer is fired and drives the band into the ribbon, impressing the character onto the document. A 48-character band has four copies of each character on the band and four hammers, which are moved across the 80 or 132 possible print positions. A 128-character band has two character sets on the band for the same printer.

The throughput of the printer depends upon how fast the band is moving, how many characters constitute the print set, how many hammers there are, and how fast the hammers move across the paper. Some printers move the hammers at a fixed rate after every possible character has been optioned to that print position, some move their hammers when all have fired at the character for that print position, and some have a hammer for every print position, in which case when the hammers have all fired the line is complete and the document is moved. Character band printers can output documents at from 365 to 2200 lines per minute, which correlates to 7 to 67 pages per minute.

Shuttle-matrix printers (e.g., the 6408 and 6412) can produce limited graphics and near-letter-quality documents. Rather than using a band with all characters impregnated on it, shuttle-matrix printers use a shuttle that contains all the components necessary to make up a complete character. Each hammer must fire several times for each character position to form a full character from the components resident on the band. As a result, shuttle-matrix printers are typically slower than strict alphanumeric band printers. Also, the quality of the characters produced by shuttle-matrix printers is not quite as good as those produced by strict alphanumeric band printers because of fly-time variations, variations in belt speed, and the stretching/shrinking of the belt due to hammer impact. Shuttle-matrix printers produce documents at a rate of 475 to 1200 lines per minute, which correlates to about 10 to 24 pages per minute. Both of the band impact printers have the same difficulty as the matrix printer in producing multiple colors, and for the same reason ribbon colors are limited. To change fonts, the band/shuttle must be changed. To change pitch, the band/shuttle must be changed as must the hammer movement distance.

The shuttle-matrix printers can produce limited graphics and near-letter-quality documents. Instead of having the *characters* impregnated on it, the shuttle has the *components* that make up a character impregnated on it. Each hammer must fire several times for each character position to form a full character from the components. Shuttle-matrix printers produce documents at a rate of 500 to 1400 lines per minute, which correlates to 10 to 42 pages per minute. The 6400-series printers can print in multiple fonts, pitches and lines per inch spacing under program control. Figure 2.7 shows a comparison and summary of the characteristics of various impact printer workstations available for the AS/400 System. Figure 2.8 shows a #4230 Wire Matrix Printer, and Figure 2.9 shows a #6400 band matrix printer.

	4230 Matrix Printer	4232/4247 Matrix Printer	6252/6262 Impact Writer	6408/6412 Line Matrix Printer
Type	Near letter quality	Near letter quality	Letter quality	Near letter quality
Technology	9-wire dot matrix	9/18-wire dot matrix	Character band	Band matrix
Throughput Pages/min.	375–600 cps 1–16 ppm	200–700 700 cps 4–14 ppm	800–2200 lpm 24–67 ppm	500–1400 lpm 15–42 ppm
Graphics Resolution	144 pels vert. × 240 pels horiz.	144 pels × 144 pels 4–8 colors	N/A	144 x144 pels
Paper Handling	Continuous forms to 13.2"	Continuous forms to 13.2" +/ cutsheet	Continuous forms	Continuous forms
Data Stream Support	IPDS/ASCII/ APA/SCS	IPDS/AFP/ APA/SCS	SCS/ASCII	IPDS/SCS/ ASCII
Interface	Parallel or Twinax Serial	Parallel or Serial, Twinax, token-ring, ethernet	Twinaxial/ Serial, Parallel	Twinaxial/ Parallel (PC)/ token-ring/ ethernet
Desktop/Floor	Desktop	Desktop	Floor	Floor/Desktop

Figure 2.7. AS/400 impact printer summary comparison (ppm, pages per minute; cps, characters per second; lpm, lines per minute).

Figure 2.8. IBM 4230 wire matrix printer.

Figure 2.9. IBM 6400 band matrix printer.

Non-impact Printers

Two categories of non-impact printers are commonly used with AS/400 systems: inkjet and laser. Both kinds produce high-quality documents on individual cut sheets of paper and support multiple type styles and fonts.

Inkjet printers (e.g. the 4076 ExecJet II) print by moving a set of nozzles (from which ink can be sprayed) across the surface of the paper while the paper is moved perpendicularly to the nozzle motion. Documents produced are of letter quality. In fact, the quality of inkjet printing has improved so much that it now competes with the quality of laser printers. Multiple colors of ink can be used, and the ink can be mixed to produce essentially any shade of any color. Graphics can be produced with a resolution of 600 by 600 pels or greater. Printing speed ranges from 83 to 400 characters per second, which correlates to 1 to 8 pages per minute.

Laser printers (e.g. Network Printers 12, 17, 24, 4303 Network Color, 3170 Infocol 70, InfoPrint 60 and InfoPrint 4000) are used for everything from desktop publishing to production printing and use one of several variations on the same basic technique. They uses a laser to charge the surface of a drum with the image of the desired page. Toner particles attach to the drum and are then deposited on the paper as it comes in contact with the drum. This technology is called Laser EP (for ElectroPhotographic). Most new printers are in this category, and are addressing desktop production for industrial strength printing, even over TCP/IP networks. Included in the latest set of network printers are the InfoPrint 60, InfoPrint 62, and InfoPrint 4000, the characteristics of some of which are shown in Figure 2.10 (which provides a comparison and summary of some nonimpact printers available for the AS/400).

As is shown in this table, laser resolutions (measured by the number of dots per inch deposited on the paper to compose the image) are much higher than those of impact printers. Laser printers have the highest throughput of the non-impact printer types. Laser printers provide throughput from 5 to over 1000 pages per minute. They provide better print quality and are less noisy than impact printers. Figures 2.11, 2.12, and 2.13 show photographs of these printers. The InfoPrint 62 uses a new technology called cold fusion printing, which enables printing on a wide variety of media, such as plastic and paper to 80 lbs, and labels.

Laser printers are offered across a very broad spectrum, supporting applications from desktop to production printing and all points in be-

	4076 ExecJet II Printers	Network 12 Network 17 Network 24	Network Color	Infocolor 70	3160/3900 Infoprint Printers
Type	Letter quality	Letter quality	Letter quality	Letter quality	Letter quality
Technology	Inkjet	Laser/EP	ColorLaser	ColorLaser	Laser/EP
Throughput Pages/min. (ppm)	3	12-24	3 color, 12 mono	70	700
Graphics Resolution	600 pels × 300 pels	600 dots/ inch (dpi)	600 dpi	600 dpi	240 IPDS, 600 ASCII
Paper Handling	Cut sheet	Cut sheet	Cut sheet	Cut sheet	3160 cut sheet, 3900 fan fold paper
Data Stream Support	PPDS/APA	IPDS/ PostScript/ PCL	Postscript	IPDS, PostScript	IPDS, PostScript, PCL
Interface	Serial	Twinax serial, parallel, token-ring, ethernet	Serial, parallel, ethernet or token-ring	Token-ring, ethernet	Token-ring, ethernet, channel
Desktop/ Floor	Desktop	Desktop/ floor	Floor	Floor	Floor

Figure 2.10. AS/400 nonimpact printer comparison and summary.

tween. As applications increase in print volume, it becomes more critical to evaluate how the AS/400 interacts with and manages printing. For example, AS/400 AFP (Advanced Function Printing) applications can yield performance advantages because of an efficient data stream and efficient management of print resources (such as electronic forms and images). IPDS applications also provide full page-level error recov-

Options and Peripherals **111**

Figure 2.11. IBM InfoPrint 60 laser EP network printer.

Figure 2.12. IBM InfoPrint 62 cold fusion EP printer.

ery. This is less important if printing a two-page spreadsheet, but critical if printing invoices at 60 pages per minute or statements at 1002 pages per minute.

A new laser printer technology is the shared network printer. These printers can connect simultaneously to multiple servers (i.e., AS/400

Figure 2.13. IBM InfoPrint 4000 laser EP printer.

and LAN) and can automatically handle print jobs in any "language" (such as SCS, IPDS, PostScript, and HP-PCL). (These "languages" are described in Chapter 4 under "Advanced Function Printing.") The IBM 3130 Advanced Printer and the IBM Network Printer Family, and the IBM InfoPrint distributed printers are examples of shared network printers. These printers can switch automatically between different servers, and offer new controls over each print writer session.

Laser printers provide throughput of from 5 to over 1000 pages per minute with the best print quality of any of the technologies discussed and also are quieter than any of the other printers in this section.

Workstation Controllers

To attach any local workstation to an Application System computer system, the proper **workstation controller** must be installed in the computer's system unit or an expansion unit. (*Note:* Remote workstations are attached through communications lines, not through a workstation controller.) The workstation controller is a microprocessor-controlled intermediary between the workstation and the Application System processor. The workstation controller receives keystrokes from the workstation and sends back formatted views of screens for display on the terminal of the workstation. Managing the workstation traffic (e.g., keystrokes) leaves the system processor in the Application System computer free to run user application programs. The result of this multiprocessor architecture, as was discussed in Chapter 1, is that the AS/400 system is able to do more work in a given amount of time. Two types of workstation controllers can be used with AS/400 computers: twinaxial workstation controllers and ASCII workstation controllers.

Twinaxial Workstation Controllers

Twinaxial workstation controllers are the most commonly used type of controller. They allow the attachment of the most popular workstations (including all terminals and printers discussed in this book). The controller itself is cabled to a box that provides twinaxial connectors. One end of a twinaxial cable is attached to one of the connectors, called a port, on the box. The other end of the cable can be attached to up to seven local workstations in a daisy-chain fashion over a distance of up to 5000 feet (this was illustrated at the end of the last chapter in Figure 1.55). This daisy-chain feature is called **cable-thru** and greatly simplifies the wiring needed to connect workstations to an AS/400 system. Information moves through the twinaxial cable at over a million bits per second (bps), allowing for fast information flow.

The Entry Model 150 can support 7 twinaxial terminals in the entry version and 28 twinaxial terminals in the growth version. The LAN versions can support a maximum of 28 twinaxial terminals. Base twinaxial support provides for up to 28 local workstations (any mix of terminals and printers) daisy-chained over 4 ports (up to 7 workstations per port). Feature 2722 provides 8 twinaxial ports with up to 40 active workstations. And by using the Portable Computer Interface (PCI) adapters, the SPD bus-attached 6050 Twinaxial Workstation Controller, and the 6180 Twinaxial Workstation Adapter (connecting 40 workstations for each instance of usage), up to 2628 workstations can be attached to a Model 720. A 9176 or 9177 Client Access Console can also be attached to base LAN machines.

The AS/400e server 730 and the AS/400e server 740 come standard with a twinaxial workstation controller or an ASCII workstation controller. The twinaxial workstation controller for the 9406 provides 8 ports that can support a total of 40 workstations (no more than 7 on any one port). By adding optional 6050 Twinaxial Workstation Controllers, Model 730 and Model 740 can support up to 7000 twinaxially attached workstations over 175 workstation controllers.

For all AS/400e series twinaxial workstation connections, a 20-foot cable is attached between the controller and an external box that provides the 8 port connectors. This external box is designed to be mounted on the floor, wall, or tabletop. From 1 to 175 twinaxial workstation controllers can be installed in a single AS/400 9406 system for attaching those workstations.

ASCII Workstation Controllers

Although twinaxial workstations are preferred with AS/400 systems, the systems can also support low-cost American Standard Code for Information Interchange (ASCII) terminals and printers. ASCII workstations transfer information at a slower rate (maximum of 38,400 bits per second [bps]) than twinaxial workstations (1 million bps). However, an ASCII workstation controller is useful if you already have a significant investment in ASCII terminals and printers, because it allows you to use them with an AS/400 system.

There is no ASCII workstation controller for either AS/400 Advanced Entry Model 150, or for the AS/400e Model 170 in its server versions. The AS/400e server 720 is only capable of attaching ASCII terminals if the SPD bus system unit expansion or optically connected expansion towers are present. The AS/400e server 730 and 740 are capable of accepting ASCII workstation support in the base system unit. Base ASCII workstation support (feature code 9171) can be selected for inclusion in the standard configuration of any of the last identified systems. The 9171 ASCII workstation controller is able to support up to 12 workstations (6 terminals and 6 printers) over 6 ASCII ports. Actually, 1 terminal or 1 printer is cabled directly to each of the 6 ports—making for 6 devices.

To get to the base ASCII support's configuration maximum of 12 ASCII devices, you must directly cable 6 ASCII terminals to the 6 ASCII ports and then attach 1 printer to each terminal, totaling 12 devices. Adding the 6142 ASCII 12-Port Workstation Attachment adds 12 more ASCII ports for a total of 18. This allows 18 ASCII devices (any combination of terminals and printers) to be directly attached to the AS/400e system 6XX/SXX. Although this also allows up to 36 ASCII devices to be attached (18 terminals and 18 printers cabled to the terminals), 18 simultaneously active ASCII devices are the maximum number supported on a base ASCII attachment. The server systems identified earlier are capable of supporting only the base ASCII attachment. No expansion of ASCII terminals beyond the base is allowed.

To attach more ASCII workstations to e-systems that are not server systems, you can install one or more optional 6141 ASCII Workstation Controllers, each of which will add 6 ASCII ports to the system. For further expansion and more flexibility, you can add a 6142 ASCII 12-Port Workstation Attachment to each 6141 ASCII Workstation Controller. By adding a 6142 ASCII 12-Port Workstation Attachment to a 6141 ASCII Workstation Controller, you go from 6 ports capable of supporting 6 ASCII terminals and 6 ASCII printers to 18 ports capable of supporting 18 ASCII workstations (any combination of terminals and printers). The Model 720 can have up to 58 ASCII workstation controllers, each equipped with an ASCII 12-port workstation attachment, which provides for up to 1044 ASCII workstations.

As with the Model 720, Model 730 and Model 740 include support for twinaxial or ASCII workstations in their standard configuration. For those who choose ASCII support, a 6141 ASCII Workstation Controller is included in the standard configuration. In this standard ASCII workstation configuration, you can have up to 12 workstations attached to a system (6 terminals and 6 printers) over 6 ports.

Again, 1 terminal or 1 printer is cabled directly to each of the 6 ports, making for 6 devices. To get to the standard configuration's maximum of 18 ASCII devices, you must add the 6142 ASCII 12-Port Workstation Attachment. Since 18 is also the maximum number of workstations that an ASCII workstation controller can handle, you get 1 port for each device and thus the flexibility to attach any combination of terminals and printers. The Model 730 and Model 740 support up to 175 ASCII workstation controllers. If each ASCII workstation controller is equipped with an ASCII 12-port workstation attachment, you can have 3150 ASCII workstations attached to each of these systems.

LAN-Connected Terminals

Additional workstations may be attached to the local area networks (LANs) supported by these systems. These terminals must be intelligent terminals, including personal computers, network stations, or retail terminals. Each LAN can support up to 256 terminal addresses. The Model 150 with 2 LANs can attach 512 intelligent terminals, either personal computers or network stations. The Model 170 with up to six LAN ports can attach 1536 intelligent terminals. The Model 720 can attach 6144 intelligent terminals through 24 LANs. The Model 730 can attach 12,288 intelligent terminals through 48 LANs. The Model 740 can attach 18,432 terminals through 72 LAN connections. The Model S40-SB1 can attach 1280 intelligent terminals through 5 LANs.

Protocol Converters

Whether a workstation is attached locally or remotely, it must speak the same "language" or **workstation protocol** as the computer system and its programs. You should be aware of (but not necessarily understand) three workstation protocols: 5250 protocol, 3270 protocol, and ASCII protocol.

The **5250 protocol** is the set of rules used by workstations designed specifically for use with Application System computers as well as earlier System/36 and System/38 computers. The 5250 protocol and twinaxial cable can be considered the "native tongue" of IBM's application systems. The protocol gets its name from the 5250 family of workstations designed for the System/3X family.

The **3270 protocol** is the set of rules used by workstations designed specifically for use with IBM's larger System/390 family of mainframe computers. This protocol gets its name from the 3270 family of workstations designed for the System/390 computers. Finally, the **ASCII protocol** is the set of rules used by a wide variety of devices (including terminals and printers) made for the computers of many different computer manufacturers.

If the user wishes to attach a workstation using a workstation protocol different from that being used by the AS/400 computer system, a **protocol converter** is required. This is a stand-alone device that accepts information from a workstation using the workstation protocol and converts that information to the desired workstation protocol being used by the computer system. The protocol converter can be thought of as a "translator" that sits between the workstation and the computer.

There are many situations in which a user might need a protocol converter (for example, the user has a workstation that uses the 3270 protocol attached to a S/390 Computer System. Alternatively, a user might be switching from a computer that primarily uses an ASCII workstation to application systems. With a protocol converter, the investment in ASCII terminals could be preserved by using them with the application systems. However, the ASCII workstation controller is the preferred way of attaching ASCII devices to AS/400 systems. With protocol conversion native to the AS/400 via the MultiProtocol Transporting Network Architecture, external protocol converters are no longer necessary to attach ASCII or 3270 workstations. Those who already possess protocol converters may still use them with the AS/400.

Main Storage Expansion Options

Nothing seems to grow faster than the computer user's appetite for main storage. Several different options allow the user to expand the main storage in AS/400 computers. However, because of technical differences inside the systems, main storage expansion options are not necessarily interchangeable between the different Application System models.

Model 150 Main Storage Capacities

The AS/400 Model 150 comes standard with 64 MB of main storage in the entry version and 128 MB in the growth version. That base main storage may be expanded by adding either one or two additional 64-MB DIMM modules (3110) or 32-MB DIMM modules (3182) until a maximum total main storage capacity of 192 MB is achieved. (The DIMM Module is an industry standard for packaging silicon storage devices.) The range of main storage sizes for the 9401 Model 150 is shown in Figure 2.14. All main storage plugs into the processor card and uses no I/O slot capability.

AS/400e server 170 Main Storage Expansion Options

The e-server 170 supports the 32-MB, 128-MB, and 256-MB DIMM packages. The e-server 170 systems with processors #2289, #2290, and #2291 start with the 64 MB made up of a single pair of 32-MB DIMM cards and can grow to 832 MB by adding one pair of 128-MB DIMM

118 EXPLORING IBM AS/400 COMPUTERS

Figure 2.14. AS/400e server 150 main storage sizes.

cards and one pair of 256-MB DIMM cards. The base 32-MB DIMM cards continues to be used. A total of 6 DIMM storage cards is supported. Only one pair of 256-MB DIMM cards is supported.

The e-server 170 systems with processor #2292 starts with one pair of 128-MB DIMM cards for 256 MB, and can grow to 1024 MB by adding a pair of 256-MB DIMM cards plus a second pair of 128-MB DIMM cards. A total of 6 DIMM storage cards is supported. Only one pair of 256-MB DIMM cards is supported.

The e-server 170 systems with processors #2385, #2386, and #2388 start with a 256-MB base main storage and can grow to 3.584 GB by populating the available 14-DIMM positions. The main storage must be installed in matched pairs. A total of 14 main storage slots are available. The maximum main storage can only be attained if all main storage slots are populated with 256-MB DIMM cards.

In all cases, in the above main storage configurations, the main storage must be populated with matching pairs of the same part number DIMM card. Figure 2.15 illustrates the range of options available in main storage size defined by the processor present in the Model 170 systems.

Figure 2.15. AS/400e server 170 main storage size options (by processor).

AS/400e server 720 Main Storage Expansion Options

All e-server 720 systems come standard with 256 MB of main storage built from two 128-MB DIMM cards. Depending on the processor option selected, the main storage can be increased to 2048 MB, 4096 MB, or 8192 MB. In addition to the 128-MB DIMM cards, 32-MB DIMM cards and 256-MB DIMM cards are supported.

Processor #2061 supports a total of 14 main storage slots, a maximum of 6 of which may be populated with 256-MB DIMM cards. The remaining 8 slots must be populated with 32-MB DIMM cards to achieve the maximum of 2048 MB.

Processor #2062 supports a total of 30 main storage slots, a maximum of 14 of which can be populated with 256-MB DIMM cards. The remaining slots 16 slots must be populated with 32-MB cards to attain the system maximum of 4096 MB.

Processors #2063 and #2064 support a total of 48 main storage slots, a maximum of 30 of which can be populated with 256-MB DIMM cards. The remaining 18 slots must be populated with 32-MB DIMM cards to achieve the maximum of 8192 MB. Figure 2.16 illustrates the

120 EXPLORING IBM AS/400 COMPUTERS

Figure 2.16. AS/400e server 720 main storage size options (by processor).

range of options available in main storage size defined by the processor present in e-server 720 systems.

AS/400e server 730 Main Storage Expansion Options

The e server 730 has two base and ten feature main storage slots for the #2065, #2066, and #2067 processors, and four base and 8 feature main storage slots for the #2068 processor. Main storage cards are available in 256 MB, 512 MB, 1024 MB, and 2048 MB sizes. For the 2065, 2066, and the 2067 processors, main storage cards must be installed in pairs of equal capacity cards up to a capacity of 16,384 MB. Above 16,384 MB, main storage features must be installed in quads of main storage cards of equal capacity. Base main storage for these processors is composed of a pair of 256-MB cards, and maximum main storage is 24,576 MB.

For processor 2068, main storage features must be installed in quads of equal capacity cards. The base main storage for the #2068 processor is composed of a quad of 256-MB cards.

Figure 2.17 shows the possible main storage configurations available in e server 730 systems.

Options and Peripherals **121**

Figure 2.17. AS/400e server 730 main storage size options (by processor).

AS/400e server 740 Main Storage Expansion

AS/400e server 740 systems come standard with 1024 MB of main storage composed of four main storage slots and 16 main storage expansion slots. Main storage cards are added in groups of four identical cards. The base factory built system has 1024 MB from using four 256-MB cards. The maximum 40,960 MB can only be achieved by replacing the base 256-MB cards with 2048-MB cards plus adding sixteen 2048-MB main storage #3193 feature cards.

Other main storage sizes can be achieved by installing 128-MB (#3189), 256-MB (#3190), 512-MB (#3191), or 1024-MB (#3192) main storage expansion cards in the available slots (again installed in sets of four identical cards). Figure 2.18 illustrates the achievable main storage sizes for these systems.

Auxiliary Storage Options

As was shown in Chapter 1, there are five basic types of auxiliary storage devices used with application systems:

Figure 2.18. AS/400e server 740 main storage size options (by processor).

- Diskettes
- Disk units
- CD-ROM
- Tape
- Optical

Let us now look at the specific auxiliary storage options available for the application systems.

Diskette Storage

Diskette storage is commonly used by many different types of computer systems. It provides a convenient way to transfer small amounts of information between systems. Although diskettes can also be used for making backup copies of the information stored on disk units, they lack the storage capacity to be effective for this, particularly for larger disk units. AS/400 systems do not come standard with any diskette storage, but several options allow the user to have diskette storage on AS/400 systems.

Diskettes consist of a flexible circular magnetic medium enclosed in a square package. Diskettes are manually inserted into a diskette unit that spins them inside the jacket. The read/write head inside the diskette unit makes contact with the spinning disk much as a record player's needle contacts a record. As the disk spins, the head magnetically reads and writes information on the disk's surface. All AS/400e systems can be configured with diskette units that allow them to use diskettes either 5¼ inches or 8 inches in diameter (or both). Either type of diskette can hold up to 1.2 MB (million bytes) of information. (*Note:* The Entry system supports a 5¼-inch diskette drive option, but IBM does not offer an 8-inch diskette drive option for that system.)

9331 Model 11 and 9331 Model 12 Diskette Units

Either the 5¼-inch diskette unit 9331 Model 012 or the 8-inch diskette unit 9331 Model 011 can be externally attached to most AS/400 systems (except the Models 150, 170) using a 6146 Diskette Adapter. This adapter attaches to the internal 2624 Tape Control Unit. Alternately, some (mostly older) AS/400 systems attach these diskette units via the 6112 Diskette Controller. The combination of adapter and diskette unit is useful for moving information between similarly equipped AS/400 systems, AS/Entry 9402 Y10 systems, or earlier System/36 and System/38 computers. However, this diskette unit is not compatible with the 5¼-inch diskettes used by IBM personal computers. Figure 2.19 shows the 9331 Model 12 5¼-inch diskette unit.

Disk Storage Overview

Disk storage provides the non-volatile (not erased when power is turned off) long-term storage for the programs and data used on a regular basis. It composes the second level in the hierarchy of storage of AS/400 systems (main storage is the first). The function of disk storage is to hold information that must be readily available to the computer system yet preserved when power is turned off. It is used to store the operating system, application programs, and data.

Figure 2.19. The 9331 5¼-inch diskette unit for the AS/400e models.

Disk storage is provided by disk storage units (also called a Direct Access Storage Devices or DASD) that store information on the surface of one or more platters (metal disks shaped like a dinner plate). The platters spin at a very high constant speed while the built-in read/write head records or detects information on the platter's surface. The arm that positions the read/write head is called the *actuator*. Unlike diskettes, the read/write heads in disk units never actually touch the platter's magnetic surface but are positioned extremely close to that surface. All AS/400 systems support many different disk unit configurations. Disk unit performance is very important to the overall performance of a computer system.

Each disk unit attaches to the computer through control circuitry contained within the units of the system. This function might be provided by the Multi-Function Input/Output Processor (MFIOP) provided with the AS/400 systems or an optional disk adapter card that is often necessary to support disk storage beyond that provided as standard with the AS/400 system.

All new AS/400 disk adapters perform hardware disk **compression**. The data is dynamically compressed/decompressed by the disk controller, independent of the system processor. The average compression ratio achieved is twice, with four times attainable. The compression is limited to user ASPs (Application Storage Pools) and is performed at the disk arm level. RAID-5 and mirroring of data continue to be supported in the compressed environment. Disk drives supported include only those with 1, 2, 4, 8, or 17.54 GB capacities. The hardware disk compression is performed by the disk controller, independent of the system processor.

Figure 2.20 lists the various disk units used with AS/400 systems, and Figure 2.21 summarizes the maximum combinations of disk unit controllers by system model.

The following paragraphs describe the disk storage expansion options for the following AS/400 models:

- Integrated Hardware Disk Compression

- AS/400e server 150 Disk Options

- AS/400e server 170 Disk Options

- AS/400e 720 Disk Options

- AS/400e 730 Disk Options

- AS/400e 740 Disk Options

- AS/400e custom application server S40-SB1

- Disk Adapters

Integrated Hardware Disk Compression

Integrated hardware disk compression allows user files to be compressed by an average of two to three times, conserving disk space for the user who is reluctant to purchase additional disk units. When operating with compressed data, your performance may be slower than it would be if the data were not compressed. Compression and decompression are achieved completely within the data flow of the hardware of the disk controllers and does not involve the AS/400 system processor. Disk compression is available for all of the AS/400e internal disk units including the 17.54 GB disk units.

The overhead of compression/decompression and the variations in the length of data written to disk cause the performance of com-

Disks

Feature #	Description	CEC	5052	5055	5057	5058	5082	5083
1602	Single Disk Unit Kit (1.03GB)	X	X(1)		X(1)	X(1)		
1603	Single Disk Unit Kit (1.96GB)	X	X(1)		X(1)	X(1)		
6605	1.03 GB Disk Unit /A	X	X	X	X	X	X	X
6606	1.96 GB Disk Unit /A	X	X	X	X	X	X	X
6607	4.19 GB Disk Unit /A	X	X	X	X	X	X	X
6650	Additional Disk Unit /A (1.96 GB)	X	X	X	X	X	X	X
6652	Additional Disk Unit /A (1.03 GB)	X	X	X	X	X	X	X
6713	8.58 GB Disk Unit	X(2)	X(3)	X(2)	X(2)	X(2)	X(3)	X(2)
6906	8.58 GB Disk Unit	X(2)	X(3)	X(2)	X(2)	X(2)	X(3)	X(2)
6907	1.96 GB Disk Unit	X(2)	X(3)	X(2)	X(2)	X(2)	X(3)	X(2)
7607	Optional Disk Unit (4.19 GB)	X	X	X	X	X	X	X
7713	Optional Base 8.58 GB Disk Unit	X(2)	X(3)	X(2)	X(2)	X(2)	X(3)	X(2)
8713	Optional base 8.58 GB Disk Unit	X(2)	X(3)	X(2)	X(2)	X(2)	X(3)	X(2)
6714	Optional Feature 17.54 GB disk Unit	X(6)	X(3)	X(2)	X(2)	X(2)	X(3)	X(2)
8714	Optional Base 17.54 GB disk Unit	X(5)	X(3)	X(2)	X(2)	X(2)	X(3)	X(2)
6824	Optional Feature 17.54 GB disk Unit	X(7)	X(3)	X(2)	X(2)	X(2)	X(3)	X(2)
8824	Optional Base 17.54 GB disk Unit	X(4)	X(3)	X(2)	X(2)	X(2)	X(3)	X(2)
9606	Base Disk Unit (1.96 GB)	X	X	X	X	X	X	X
9907	Base 4.19 GB Disk Unit	X(2)	X(3)	X(2)	X(2)	X(2)	X(3)	X(2)

Storage Expansion Units and Towers

Notes:
(1) Single byte disk units cannot be placed into slots K8 through K16
(2) For best performance use with Ultra-SCSI disk unit controller
(3) No Ultra-SCSI when attached to this storage expansion unit
(4) Optional base disk unit for Models 600/620/S10/S20/170/720
(5) Optional base disk unit for Models 640/650/S30/S40/170/730/740
(6) Optional feature disk unit for Models 500/510/530/620/640/650/S20/S30/S40/S0S/170/720/730/740
(7) Optional feature disk unit for Models 600/620/S10/S20/170

Figure 2.20. Disk units compatible with Version 4 Release 4.

Usage	Features	170	720	730	740	740-SB1
External	6500 + 6501		20	36	36	0
Internal SPD	6502 + 6530 + 6512 + 6532 + 6533		9	37	37	1
Total SPD Int/Ext			20	37	37	1
Internal PCI	2726 + 9728 + 2740 + 2741	1	2			

Figure 2.21. Maximum combinations of disk unit controllers by system model.

pressed disk in most cases to be slower than uncompressed high-performance disk units. Depending upon the characteristics of the data, and its interaction with the LZ1 compression algorithm, capacity gains will vary. Historically, LZ1 compression algorithms achieve an average of three times compression ratio. The disk capacity gains from disk compression are not included in the maximum AS/400 model disk capacity limits. Users need to decide if the capacity gains resulting from compression are acceptable trade-offs against the increased recovery times. LZ1 compression has been used for tape devices over the last 10 years.

Compressed disks have the same disk subsystem availability options as uncompressed disks, with no additional restrictions (RAID-5, mirroring). Disk compression is supported only in user auxiliary storage pools. The user selects which disk arms to compress via a Disk Manager screen. Disk capacity screens reflect the projected disk capacity and the percent used. Except for performance, the existence of disk compression is transparent to applications.

Disk compression is intended to be used in the context of Hierarchical Storage Management (see Chapter 4), as part of a total storage management strategy including high performance disk, compressed disk, and tape automation. Controllers that support Hardware Data compression include: #6533 RAID Disk Unit Controller, #2741 PCI RAID Disk Unit Controller, and #9754 SPD Multi-Function I/O Processor.

To be used in the 7XX systems, the disk units listed in Figure 2.20 may have to be packaged in either a tray or a carrier.

Entry Model 150 Disk Options

The Model 150 system units come standard with 4.19 GB of disk storage mounted inside the system unit. The 4.194-GB of storage provided by the 3.5-inch disk unit (feature code 6907) can be expanded by adding up to three additional disk units, each with an additional capacity of either 4.19 GB or 8.58 GB, to achieve a total maximum capacity of 29.9 GB.

Model 170 Disk Options

AS/400e server 170 come standard with a 3½-inch 4,194-MB disk unit in the system unit. To expand disk storage in these systems, three more disk units can be added to the base or six disk units can be added if the expansion feature is present. The compatible disk units are 3.5-inch devices with capacities of 4.19 GB, 8.58 GB, or 17.54 GB.

To attain the maximum disk storage capacity for this model of 175.4 GB, all ten available disk slots must be populated with the 17.54 disk unit. To perform this addition, the bolt-on expansion side-car must be added. Disk data protection can be invoked using either data mirroring or RAID 5. All disks are connected to the multi-function I/O processor (MFIOP) using an Ultra SCSI interface. All internal disk units listed for this model in Figure 2.20 are placed in a carrier tray to enable the drives to be concurrently maintained.

AS/400e server 720 Disk Options

AS/400e server 720 comes standard with a 3½-inch 4,194-MB disk unit that resides in one of the five spaces available for disk storage in the system unit. The standard 4194-MB disk unit can be replaced with an optional 8580-MB disk unit (#7713) or an optional 17,540-MB disk unit (#6714), and up to four additional disk units can be added in the base system unit without modification.

All system units regardless of processor type can accept a feature disk expansion cage (#7128) into which five more disk units can be plugged. AS/400e server systems with processors #2062, #2063, or #2064 can have a third disk expansion cage #7128 in the power compartment.

On 720 based systems, up to 15 additional disk units may be added to these systems by means of the bolt-on #9364 System Expansion Unit. Further, the 5052 Storage Expansion Unit can be used to add another

16 disk units. Additional disk units may be added by optical connection to either #5064 SPD System Expansion towers or to the #5065 PCI System Expansion Tower.

Up to 15 additional disk units can be added to 720 systems through the #5064 System Expansion Unit. An additional 16 disk units can be added to the 720 by adding the #5081 Storage Expansion Towers, to which may be added the 5068 Storage Expansion Units.

Up to 45 additional disk units can be added to 720 based systems through the #5065 PCI Expansion Tower. Each group of 15 disk units must be supported by a #2748 Disk Unit Adapter, and one of the disk slots must be given up for the #4331 Solid State Disk unit which provides a 1.6 GB-Cache front store for the supported disk units. Expansion beyond 15 disk units requires the specification of the #5101 disk expansion unit.

Multiple storage expansion towers and storage expansion units may be added to 720 systems until a total disk storage capacity of 1288 GB is reached.

Disk units used with 720 systems may be Ultra-SCSI, Ultra2-SCSI, or 1-byte Fast or Fast and Wide SCSI compatible. Figure 2.20 lists the compatible disk units that may be used with these systems. All internal disk units listed for this model in Figure 2.20 are placed in a carrier tray to enable the drives to be concurrently maintained.

All of the system unit disks are driven from the Multi-Function I/O Processor (MFIOP) with an Ultra-SCSI interface if the devices used can support the performance. These disk units may be concurrently maintained; that is, the units may be unplugged and re-plugged while the system continues to operate with no physical damage to either the disk units or the system (with no data loss if either data mirroring or RAID-5 has been enabled).

AS/400e server 730 Disk Options

AS/400e server 730 come standard with 4194-MB of disk storage provided by a 3½-inch disk unit (feature code #6907), which takes up one of the four spaces available for disk storage in the system unit. This disk unit may be replaced with the 8.580-GB 3½-inch disk unit (#6713) or with the 17.54-GB 3½-inch disk unit (#6714).

An additional eight disk storage units may be added by installing two #5055 Disk Cages inside the system unit. An additional eight storage units may be added by including a #5058 Storage Expansion Unit on the top of the system unit.

Additional disk units may be added by optical connection to either 5082/5083 SPD Storage Expansion towers or to the #5065 PCI System Expansion Tower. Up to 15 additional disk units can be added to 730 systems through the #5082/5083 Storage Expansion Unit. An additional 16 disk units can be added to each 5082/5083 by adding 5068 Storage Expansion Units.

Up to 45 additional disk units can be added to 720 based systems through the #5065 PCI Expansion Tower. Each group of 15 disk units must be supported by a #2748 Disk Unit Adapter, and one of the disk slots must be given up for the #4331 Solid State Disk unit which provides a 1.6 GB Cache front store for the supported disk units. Expansion beyond 15 disk units requires the specification of the #5101 disk expansion unit.

All disk storage in the 730 system units is Ultra-SCSI compatible and is attached to the Multi-Function I/O Processor (MFIOP). Supported disk storage units are listed in Figure 2.20. All internal disk units listed for this model in Figure 2.20 are placed in a carrier to enable the drives to be concurrently maintained.

The disk units in the system unit may be concurrently maintained if data mirroring or RAID-5 have been enabled. That is, these disk units may be unplugged and re-plugged while the system continues to operate with no physical damage to either the units or the system and no data loss. Multiple storage expansion towers and storage expansion units may be added to 730 systems until a total disk storage capacity of 2,500 GB is reached.

AS/400e server 740 Disk Options

AS/400e server 740 comes standard with 4194-MB of disk storage. The standard disk storage is made up of one 4,194-MB 3½-inch disk unit (feature code #6907) that takes one of the four spaces available for disk storage in the I/O tower of the system unit. The 4,194-MB disk unit may be replaced with the 8.580-GB 3½-inch disk unit (#6713) or with the 17.54-GB 3½-inch disk unit (#6714).

An additional 16 disk storage units may be added by including a #5058 Storage Expansion Unit on the top of the I/O tower of the system unit. More disk units can be added to the system by connecting a #5082 Storage Expansion Tower and a corresponding #5058 Storage Expansion Unit. Each #5058 Storage Expansion Unit supports up to 16 additional disk units.

The exception to this maximum disk storage capacity is the Model SB1, which has a disk storage capacity range of 16.77 GB to 34.35 GB.

All disk storage on 740 systems is Ultra-SCSI compatible and is attached to the Multi-Function I/O Processor (MFIOP). Supported disk storage units are listed in Figure 2.20. All internal disk units listed for this model in Figure 2.20 are placed in a carrier tray to enable the drives to be concurrently maintained. The disk units in the system unit may be concurrently maintained if data mirroring or RAID-5 have been enabled. That is, these disk units may be unplugged and re-plugged while the system continues to operate with no physical damage to either the units or the system and no data loss. Storage expansion towers and storage expansion units may continue to be added until a maximum disk unit capacity of 4,290 GB is achieved.

Model SB1 Disk Options

AS/400e custom application server SB1 comes standard with 4,194 MB of disk storage. The standard disk storage is made up of one 4,194-MB 3½-inch disk unit (feature code #6907) that takes one of the four spaces available for disk storage in the I/O tower of the system unit. The 4,194-MB disk unit may be replaced with the 8.580-GB 3½-inch disk unit (#6713) or with the 17.54-GB 3½-inch disk unit (#6714).

An additional 3 disk storage units may be added to a maximum disk storage of 34.35 GB. Of this maximum, 16.77 GB must be used to mirror the base 16.77 GB of disk storage.

All disk storage on Model SB1 systems is Ultra-SCSI compatible and is attached to the Multi-Function I/O Processor (MFIOP). Supported disk storage units are listed in Figure 2.20. All internal disk units listed for this model in Figure 2.20 are placed in a carrier tray to enable the drives to be concurrently maintained. The disk units in the system unit may be concurrently maintained if data mirroring or RAID-5 have been enabled. That is, these disk units may be unplugged and re-plugged while the system continues to operate with no physical damage to either the units or the system and no data loss.

Model 2100 Versatile Storage DataServer

The Model 2100 Versatile Storage DataServer is intended as an enabler for server consolidation. The Model 2100 can be concurrently attached to up to 16 separate systems, with its 2.1 terabytes of data space partitioned dynamically among those systems. The Ultra SCSI differential interface allows data to be moved both to and from the 2100 at up to 40 MB/sec.

The interface can also support Fast and Wide SCSI at a reduced performance of 20 MB/sec. The 2100 internally is fully redundant if fewer than eight different systems are interfacing to it and can use both RAID-5 and mirroring to protect against a disk failure causing a loss of data. Internally there are cross connections to send operations to either of the redundant systems or SSA ports.

Dynamic sparing is provided to allow the using systems to continue operating until a convenient maintenance period occurs. The storage space can be partitioned into logical volumes of various sizes which can be defined at installation time, and are independent of the operating systems using the partitions. The partitioning scheme supports the concurrent attachment of heterogenous platforms such as Hewlett Packard, Sun, Compaq, and the IBM RS/6000, Netfinity, or AS/400. Access to a partition may be shared among similar servers (e.g., NT to NT, AIX to AIX, etc.), providing a single database for multiple servers. In the case of data consolidation, the data integrity must be provided by the use of lock management functions within the data base manager or application. The systems administrator is provided with a RS232 modem interface into the 2100, which allows dynamic repartitioning of the space among the systems attached, as needed.

In the case of the AS/400, it is only possible to utilize the Model 2100 to a capacity of 1099.5 GB because the only defined attachment card is the 6501 External Disk Controller which uses a Fast and Wide SCSI interface limiting the addressable storage volume. The data stored is not sharable between AS/400 systems because the partitioning schemes supported are incompatible with the AS/400 single level store concepts. The 2100 device is slower than the internal disk units. One area of interest for AS/400 is the large cache available (512 MB to 6 GB), which can make certain operations requiring fast read access viable.

AS/400 Disk Adapters

Disk adapters provide the circuitry necessary to transfer information between any attached disk units and the AS/400 main storage. These disk adapters (also called **Input/Output Processors** or **IOPs**) have their own computing power used to lessen the burden on the AS/400's main processor(s) when it comes to moving information to and from disk units.

A **Multi-Function I/O Processor** or **MFIOP** (9751) is provided with every AS/400 system and fills the role of disk adapter for the disk unit(s) that come as standard equipment (and for up to 19 additional disk units). The MFIOP supports two data protection algorithms called **data mirroring** and **RAID-5**. These data protection algorithms insure that in the case of a disk unit failure, no data is lost.

The #9754 MultiFunction I/O Processor provides everything the #9751 is capable of plus hardware data compression.

The PCI base MultiFunction I/O Processor (MFIOP) supports three low-speed PCI cards slots, one high-speed PCI card slot used for the base system disk controller, and also drives one Integrated PC server. The PCI base MFIOP supports the following IOAs in its high-speed PCI slot:

- #2726 PCI Disk Unit Controller
- #2740 PCI Disk Unit Controller
- #2741 PCI Disk Unit Controller
- #9728 Base PCI Disk Unit Controller

The MFIOP supports one of the two base PCI cards in its low-speed PCI card slot:

- #9720 PCI WAN/Twinaxial IOA
- #9721 PCI Two-Line WAN IOA
- #9745 PCI Two-Line WAN IOA (Model 720 only)

The MFIOP supports the following IOAs in its two other low-speed PCI slots:

- #2720 PCI WAN/Twinaxial IOA
- #2721 PCI WAN/Twinaxial IOA
- #2722 Twinaxial Workstation IOA
- #2723 PCI Ethernet IOA

- #2724 PCI 16/4-MBPS Token-Ring IOA

- #2745 PCI Two-Line WAN IOA

- #2746 PCI Twinaxial IOA

- 9723 PCI Ethernet IOA

- #9724 PCI 16/4 Mbps Token-Ring IOA (servers only)

In the latter two low-speed slots, one of the following combinations of adapters are supported by the MFIOP:

- One or two non LAN IOAs in any combination

- One LAN and one other card.

When a **PCI Integrated PC Server** is installed in its assigned slot including the bridge card, twinaxial adapter cards are not allowed in the first low-speed slot above, and LAN cards are not allowed in either of the above low-speed slots.

The #6501 is a disk controller which can attach external differential fast and wide SCSI devices either tape or disk. The primary device which will be attached using the #6501 is an external tape device, but could also include the Model #2100 Versatile Storage DataServer.

The #6502 Disk Unit Controller for RAID is an integrated disk storage controller with a 2-MB write cache to support internally attached disk units. Like the MFIOP, this disk adapter provides RAID-5 protection for internal disk units installed in the storage expansion units (#5052, #5082, or #7117). Alternately, disk units attached through this adapter (and not in a RAID-5 array) can be mirrored.

The #6512 Disk Unit Controller for RAID is available for use as a disk storage controller. The #6512 provides an increased write-cache size (4 MB) and a faster microprocessor than the #6502.

The #2726 Disk Unit Controller is a PCI-bus-compatible disk adapter. The 2726 operates from the MFIOP as a controller for the disk devices. Both RAID-5 and data mirroring are supported. The #2726 can control up to 20 disk units of the types supported on a 40-MB Ultra-SCSI interface.

The #2748 PCI RAID Disk Unit Controller is an Ultra2 SCSI controller with a 26 MB write-cache that provides RAID-5 protection and compression for internal disk units. 4.19, 8.58, and 17.54 GB disk units can be compressed. The #2748 can control Ultra2, Ultra and Fast Wide SCSI disk units. In addition to providing RAID-5 protection for disks, the #2748 can also provide high-performance controller functions when disks are protected by system mirroring. The #2748 requires V4R4 or later operating system. A maximum of 15 drives are supported on a #2748 controller. A minimum of four drives of the same capacity are needed for a valid RAID-5 array, with a maximum of four arrays per controller. A maximum of 10 drives are allowed per array. When in the system unit, the #2748 also supports CD-ROM, DVD-RAM, and internal tape units. In an expansion tower, the #2748 can support up to three internal tape units, CD-ROM, and DVD-RAM. The #2748 requires a high speed PCI card slot.

When fewer than five disk units are installed and RAID-5 is not desired, the #9728 Disk I/O Adapter can be used. This adapter is a PCI adapter that attaches to a MFIOP or to the MIKADO controller (the MFIOP for the PCI-bus-based systems).

Those needing to attach 9337 disk units to AS/400 9406 systems can use the #6500/#6501 Disk Controller. This adapter consumes one I/O slot and uses the Small Computer System Interface (SCSI), which transfers information at an instantaneous rate of 5 Mbps.

The #6532 is among the fastest SPD bus disk controller. This disk adapter supports 20 disk storage units and supports both data mirroring and RAID-5 data protection. It uses an Ultra-SCSI interface to communicate with disk units.

The #6533 RAID Disk Unit Controller is the newest and fastest disk/tape controller that interfaces to internal disk and tape devices through Ultra-SCSI and provides RAID-5 protection and includes a 4-MB write cache. Hardware Data Compression is also supported by this adapter. In addition to Ultra-SCSI, Fast and Wide, and Fast and Narrow SCSI devices may be controlled. The #6533 also can control disks protected by system mirroring or disks with no protection. The #6533 controller is disk compression enabled and can control a maximum of 20 drives. When placed in a system expansion unit (#5064/#9364), the #6533 can also support up to three internal tapes in addition to the 16 drives. The #6533 controls disk units installed in the #5058 Storage Expansion Units and #5083 Storage Expansion Towers, and can also control disk units installed in the #5052 Storage Expansion Unit and #5082 Storage Expansion Tower. When controlling disk units installed in the #5052 or #5082, the speed is limited to Fast and Wide or Fast and Narrow performance. For additional information on RAID-5 and System Mirroring see Chapter 4.

The #2740 PCI RAID Disk Unit Controller is an Ultra-SCSI disk and tape/CD-ROM controller including a 4-MB write cache that provides RAID-5 protection for internal disk units. The #2740 PCI RAID Disk Unit Controller works with Ultra, Fast and Wide, and Fast and Narrow SCSI disk and tape units installed in the base system unit. In addition to providing RAID-5 protection, the #2740 also works with disks protected by system mirroring or disks with no protection. The #2740 controller supports a maximum of 10 drives, plus one tape and one CD-ROM when installed in the system unit.

The #2741 PCI RAID Disk Unit Controller is a disk/tape controller that interfaces through Ultra-SCSI to drives, provides RAID-5 protection, and includes a 4-MB write cache. In addition to Ultra-SCSI, Fast and Wide and Fast and Narrow SCSI devices may be controlled. The #2741 also can control disks protected by system mirroring or disks with no protection. The #2741 controller is hardware compression enabled and can control a maximum of 15 drives.

The controller can also support one tape unit and one CD-ROM when placed in a system unit. When placed in a system expansion unit (#5064/#9364), the #2741 can also support up to three internal tapes in addition to the 15 drives. One high-speed PCI card slot is required in any unit where the #2741 is to be placed. For additional detail on RAID and system mirroring see Chapter 4. Figure 2.21 shows the number of disk controllers supported by AS/400e system models.

Tape Storage

Computer systems are woven deeply into today's businesses and usually become the core of day-to-day operations. The information stored on the computer is itself a valuable asset and must be protected like any other asset. Magnetic tape storage provides a cost-effective and efficient means of backing up the information on the disk units of computer systems. Magnetic tape storage is the third tier of hierarchical storage in an AS/400 system, and is used for long-term storage of information. In general, the frequency of access to information on tape storage is significantly reduced as compared to the access frequency for information stored on disk.

A tape unit reads and writes information on the tape much as a cassette recorder records and plays music on audio cassette tapes, but the recording quality is much higher and the format employed is very different. In either case, the tape unit runs the tape across the read/write head, which is in contact with the tape surface. Electrical impulses in the read/write head are used to transfer information to and from the tape surface. Tape storage units are able to store very large amounts of data in a relatively small area. Data stored on a tape storage unit is somewhat immune from damage by external effects, but because the writing and reading methodology involves small magnetic fields, large magnetic fields in the vicinity of the tape storage will destroy the data. Tape storage is the slowest performing of the auxiliary storage methods but with compression techniques holds the most data at the lowest cost.

The following paragraphs provide a summary of both the internal and external tape units used with AS/400 systems. The tape units are connected to AS/400 systems through control circuitry located on tape I/O processors.

Internal Tape Units

Here we take a look at some of the internal tape units commonly used with AS/400e series systems.

2.5-GB ¼-Inch Cartridge Tape Unit

The 2.5-GB ¼-Inch Cartridge Tape Unit (#6380) reads and writes a ¼-inch tape cartridge capable of holding up to 2.5 GB of uncompressed information (up to 5 GB if compressed). It supports sustained data transfers at a rate of up to 300 KBps when connected across a SCSI-2 interface. The 2.5-GB ¼-Inch Cartridge Tape Unit can read and write the 120-MB, 525-MB, and 1.2-GB tape cartridges used by the 120-MB, 525-MB, and 1.2-GB ¼-Inch Cartridge Tape Units (thus facilitating the transfer of programs and data between different AS/400 systems). It attaches to the MultiFunction I/O Processor (MFIOP) provided as standard in AS/400 system units.

4-GB ¼-Inch Cartridge Tape Unit (#6382)

The #6382 reads and writes a ¼-inch tape cartridge capable of holding up to 4 GB of uncompressed information (up to 8 GB if compressed). It supports sustained data transfers at a rate of up to 380 KBps when connected across a SCSI-2 interface. The #6382 can read and write the 120-MB, 525-MB, 1.2 GB, and 2.5-GB tape cartridges used by the 120-MB, 525-MB, 1.2 GB, and 2.5-GB ¼-Inch cartridge tape units (facilitating the transfer of programs and data between different AS/400 systems). It attaches to the MultiFunction I/O Processor (MFIOP) provided as standard in AS/400 system units.

13-GB ¼-Inch Cartridge Tape Unit

The 13-GB ¼-Inch Cartridge Tape Unit (#6485) increases the performance and capacity of the ¼-Inch Cartridge (QIC) technology when the new QIC-5010 format is used to read or write data cartridges. The result is that the unattended save capacity for one QIC cartridge is increased while the save time required is reduced. Maximum direct capacity is 13 GB; compacted capacity is 26 GB. The effective data rate is 1.5 MBps direct and 3 MBps compacted. The tape drive can be mounted in either the system unit or the expansion unit. Read/write compatibility is provided for all supported AS/400 (QIC) tape formats. Attachment is via an Internal Tape Controller (#6513) using a 2-byte-wide Fast SCSI interface.

7-GB 8-mm Cartridge Tape Unit

The #6490 is a helical-scan, high-capacity, streaming internal tape drive that is an option on all AS/400 system models. (Note: the external version of this tape drive is the #7208). The sustained data transfer rate is 500 KBps. The tape unit includes data compression hardware using an adaptation of IBM's Improved Data Recording Capability (IDRC) algorithm. It provides an effective capacity of 14 GB per cartridge and an effective transfer rate of 1 MBps, depending on the type of data transferred. Hardware Data Compression (HDC) is also supported. This unit uses the same medium as the #7208 models 2 and 12. Full interchange of data is supported with the #7208 models 2 and 12 and the associated systems.

External Tape Units

Here we will look at some external tape drives commonly used with AS/400 systems. External tape units are stand-alone devices that attach to AS/400 systems through a tape I/O processor using either a differential SCSI interface or a 370 Channel interface. Figure 2.22 lists some external tape units commonly used with AS/400 systems and provides some basic information about each. The table of contents offers links to more detailed descriptions of the devices listed in the table.

OS/400 V4R2 supports #3490E-FXX tape drives in F-mode. F-mode is a configuration option of the tape drive that provides the following new functions:

- 18-track write allows interchange and software distribution with previous-generation #3480 tape drives.

- The USEOPTBLK parameter is enabled for save/restore commands to increase the performance of the tape drive.

- Random mode for random selection of tape cartridges from the auto cartridge loader is supported.

Tape Libraries

The **IBM Magstar MP 3575 Tape library Dataserver** can connect to a single or to multiple hosts using homogeneous or heterogeneous systems. It can be configured to control up to six different control paths with simultaneous support for a maximum of 3 virtual libraries. The Tape Library uses the 3570 Model C1A tape unit identified in Figure 2.22. The typical drive load to ready time is 6.7 seconds, with an average search time of 8 seconds, and a cartridge move time of less than 4 seconds when a new cartridge is needed. The tape library is available in native data capacities of 300 GB, 600 GB, 900 GB, 1.2 TB, and 1.6 TB. Using 3:1 compression results in tripling the native capacities. Five different models are available, with the largest model supporting six of the 3570 tape units, and 324 tape cartridges arranged in 6 different loaders. The 3570 C1A tape unit is IBM's most reliable tape unit.

Tape Unit Type	Interface	Number Models	System Models	Capacity GB w/o Compression	Autoloader Size Tape Cartridge	Interface Speed Burst Sustained	Compression/ Type
6365 Tape Unit	Differential SCSI	1	P03	0.840	NA	3.0 MB /300 KBps	HDC
7208 Tape Unit	Differential SCSI	5	600, S10, 620, S20, 640, S30, 650, S40, 436	2.3-14	NA	500 KBps	IOP-IDRC 2× Compaction
3570 Tape Unit	Differential SCSI	2 w-w/o split mode	600, S10, 620, S20, 640, S30, 650, S40, 436	5	10/20	3.5 MBps	3× Compaction
9427 Tape Library	Differential SCSI	1	600, S10, 620, S20, 640, S30, 650, S40, 436	14	20	500KBps	2× Compaction
9348 Tape Unit	Differential SCSI	2	600, S10, 620, S20, 640, S30, 650, S40, 436		NA	781 KBps	HDC
3490E Tape Unit	Differential SCSI	3	600, S10, 620, S20, 640, S30, 650, S40, 436	0.8	7	20 Mbps/ 3.0 MBps	IDRC -3×
3494 Tape Library	Differential SCSI	5	600, S10, 620, S20 640, S30, 650, S40 436	0.8	210-304020	MBps/ 3.0MBps	IDRC-3×

Figure 2.22. External tape units used with AS/400 systems (includes tape unit/library device type, interface used, supported tape unit models, supporting AS/400 models, capacity of base media, autoloader support and capacity, interface performance, and compression).

AS/400 Optical Storage Overview

For large volumes of information that is not needed frequently but must be immediately available when it is needed, **optical disk storage** should be considered. Unlike magnetic disks, which records information with magnetic fields, optical disks use plastic disks coated with a thin reflective alloy material and housed in a cartridge case. Information is stored on the plastic disk by either burning holes into the reflective surface with a laser beam (ablative), or by using the laser to heat the reflective alloy layer to a liquid state and then changing its reflective properties by means of a magnet (magneto-optic). This type of storage provides for extremely high data recording densities, which makes for relatively inexpensive storage. However, today's optical disk technology is slower than magnetic disk storage.

CD-ROM is an abbreviation for **Compact Disk–Read Only Memory**. CD-ROM drives read information permanently stored on **compact disks (CDs)**. AS/400 systems come standard with a CD-ROM drive.

WORM is an abbreviation for **Write Once, Read Many**. This technology stores information by using a laser to burn microscopic holes in the reflective surface of a CD. The information can then be read back by the same laser beam (at a lower power). Once the surface is burned, it can be read as often as needed. However, because this surface cannot be "unburned," no other information can be written to that particular portion of the optical disk.

WMRM, sometimes referred to as erasable optical disk technology, is an abbreviation for **Write Many, Read Many**. With this technology, information can be written, erased, and rewritten.

Optical libraries are devices that consist of arrays of optical disks associated with one or more optical disk read/write units. In some cases, the optical disk read/write units also have one or more conventional magnetic disk storage units associated with them to improve the write performance of the library system. The optical disks used may employ CD-ROM, WORM, or WMRM technologies.

CD-ROM

CD-ROM is an abbreviation for Compact Disk-Read Only Memory. CD-ROM drives are auxiliary storage devices that store and read information on the surface of an optical disk using laser light. This technique allows a large amount of data to be stored in a small physical space. Performance of the CD-ROM devices is faster than 4-mm and 8-mm tape storage but slower than disk storage and 1/4 inch and ½ inch tape storage. In addition, the data is less subject to damage due to outside influences such as magnetic fields and temperature extremes than is data stored on these other devices.

A 650-MB 12/20 CD-ROM drive is included in all AS/400 models. The 12 refers to the inner diameter read performance of the CD-ROM, the 20 to its outer diameter read performance. The CD-ROM drive is used for distribution of OS/400 and other licensed program products. It can also be used as an alternate **IPL (Initial Program Load)** device. It attaches to the Multi-Function I/O Processor (MFIOP) provided with every AS/400 system and supports transfer rates of 1800 Kbps for the inner diameter, and 3,000 Kbps for the outer diameter. The CD-ROM is also used for the distribution of software by many independent software vendors and for use by application programs directly through the HFS API (which is a native OS/400 application programming interface).

The #3995 Optical Library

The #3995 Optical Library family of products can be used to store large volumes of information using optical storage technology. These devices are in a self-contained box that rests on the floor near the computer system. There are five models of the #3995 that can be directly attached to an AS/400 system to provide storage capacity ranging from 104 to 1,342 GB (unformatted capacity). There are also #3995 models that attach directly to LANs and so can be used with AS/400 systems in a LAN environment.

Each optical disk cartridge used in a #3995 library can hold from 650 million to 5200 million bytes of information depending on the cartridge type. Magneto-optic WMRM and both ablative and continuous composite WORM recording technologies are supported in a single optical library.

The 3995 attaches to an AS/400 system through the Removable Media Device Attachment feature (#2621), PCI Magnetic Media Controller (#2729), and Magnetic Media controller (#6534). Also needed is either the Optical Library DataServer Support/400 program (#5799-XBW for OS/400 V3R2) or Group PTF 99087 for OS/400 V3R6. This support has been absorbed into OS/400 for releases V3R7 and later. This program provides a programming interface for application programs to use when accessing information stored in the #3995. That is, the application program must be specially written to take advantage of the #3995 or else the information stored in 3995 will be unavailable to the application program.

The #3995 Optical Library can attach to the AS/400e systems using either the #2729 PCI External Tape Controller, or the #6534 Magnetic Media Controller

Auxiliary Storage Controllers

Tape adapters provide the circuitry necessary to transfer information between any attached tape units and the AS/400 main storage. These tape adapters (also called **input/output processors** or **IOPs**) have their own computing power used to lessen the burden on the AS/400's main processor(s) when it comes to moving information to and from tape units.

A **Multi-Function I/O Processor** or **MFIOP** (#9751) on AS/400e server 730 and 740 fills the role of tape adapter with the help of the attached tape/disk controller. This tape adapter allows you to have up to four internal tape units in the system unit or three internal tape unit and a CD-ROM drive (in addition to disk units). Figure 2.23 lists some tape I/O processors and their characteristics.

Communications Options

With the emergence of the Internet and the intranets driven by local area networks (LANs), businesses are placing increasing emphasis on computer communications. The full range of communications options is supported by AS/400 application systems. Connections to the Internet are established using **Wide Area Network (WAN)** protocols and controllers/adapters with modem connections to the pervasive telephone network and finally to an Internet Service Provider. Wide area networks are also used to connect computers together for different branches of the same business corporate entity. (One example is that IBM, like many other companies, has divisions located in many states that are connected together by wide area networks.) Wide area network controllers also

144 EXPLORING IBM AS/400 COMPUTERS

I/O Processor #	I/O Adapter	System PCI/SPD	Device Models	Int/ext Tapes Interface	Device Set Supported
9751 (MFIOP)	2726 PCI	170,720	Ultra SCSI	Internal	6481, 6485, 6490
	9728 PCI	170,720	Ultra SCSI	Internal	6481, 6485, 6490
6501	SPD	730,740, 436	Differential SCSI	External	9337-XXX, 3490E-XXX, 3570-CXX, 3590-B1X
2621	SPD	720 expand, 730, 740	Fast SCSI	Internal	2440, 5032, 3995-XXX, 7208-XXX, 9348-00X, 9427-21X
2644	SPD	(720 w/9331 Expand), 730,740	S370 Channel	External	3422-XXX, 3430-XXX, 3480-XXX, 3490-XXX, 3490E-XXX
2748	PCI	170, 720, PCI Expansion Tower	Ultra2 SCSI	Internal	6425, 4425, 6430, 4430, 1349, 1350, 1355, 1360, 4483, 4486
2729	PCI	720, 170	Differential SCSI	External	3490E-XXX, 3570-CXX, 3590-B1X, 7208-XXX, 9348-00X, 9427-21X, 3995-CXX
2624	SPD	720 w/9331 expand, 730, 740, 436	Fast SCSI	Internal	1379, 1380, 6380, 6390
6513	SPD	720 w/9331 Expand	Fast-Wide SCSI	Internal	1379, 1380, 6380, 6390, 6481, 6485, 6490
6534	SPD	730, 740	Ultra SCSI	External	3490E-XXX, 3570-BXX, 3590-BIX, 7208-XXX, 9348-00X, 9427-21X, 3995-CXX

Figure 2.23. Disk and tape I/O processors, the supporting systems, the interface provided, and the device types which may be attached.

serve the function of connecting remote workstations, and the adapters connect the system console in some user-defined system configurations.

Intranet connections are established using local area network protocols and controllers/adapters to an appropriately wired network of personal computers or network computers and specially adapted network stations such as shared network printers. An **intranet** is a name for a local area network–connected system grouping that has in addition an external connection to the Internet. Not all LANs are intranets. The number of communications lines and local area networks supported by the Application System Series is identified in the system specifics for each particular model.

The following paragraphs are both a communications tutorial and an overview of some communications feature cards available for IBM's application systems. These **feature cards** may be complete communications subsystems, providing the communications controller and the necessary adapter on a single card. The controller circuitry may also be on a separate card designed to accommodate one of several different communications adapter cards, depending on the requirements. Though this chapter does not provide a total list of all available communication options, it does discuss representative options that fit the most common business needs. (Also in Chapters 4 and 5 you will learn more about the communications software structures supported on the AS/400 family.) Since configuration limitations govern which and how communications options can be used together in a single system, before configuring your system be sure and seek the assistance of IBM or an authorized dealer.

The AS/400 and Local Area Networks

A **local area network** (LAN) consists of a group of computers connected to a high-speed communications system that spans a confined region (i.e., a single building or campus). Computers of all sizes (personal computers to mainframes) can participate in a single local area network. The computers participating in a LAN can exchange information (programs and data) and share resources (for instance, disk storage and printers). AS/400 systems can fully participate in several types of LANs including Ethernet, token ring, FDDI, and wireless. In fact, a single AS/400 system can participate in several different LANs at the same time (see Figure 2.24 for system maximums). The AS/400 server models have been optimized to offer or "serve" resources to other computers in

AS/400e server Model Number	150	436	170	720	730	740	740-SB1
Maximum number of LANs (other than wireless) allowed by system model	3	4	3	16	32	48	5
Maximum number of wireless LANs allowed by system model	0	0	1	3	3	3	3
Maximum number of Integrated PC Server IOP's allowed by system models	1	0	1	16	16	16	2

Figure 2.24. System limits on various local area network types.

a LAN environment. There is also an integrated PC server that makes the AS/400 an efficient server in a PC LAN environment.

Ethernet

Probably the most popular local area network is the Ethernet LAN (IEEE 802.3). With Ethernet, each computer is attached as a tap off a common cable or bus. For this reason, Ethernet is called a **bus-wired network**. Thus, an Ethernet LAN is a party line on which all computers can transmit a message for all other computers to hear. Every computer has equal access to the cable and can send a message at any time without warning. To ensure that only one computer transmits at a time, there is a protocol (called **Carrier Sense Multiple Access/Collision Detect (CSMA/CD)** that each connection or node follows to transmit a message. This is the same protocol used in telephone conversations, where, for instance, only one person can speak at a time or neither is clearly understood. One party waits for the other to finish before beginning to speak. Thus, the phone line only carries one party's voice at a time, and the message is clear. This is the "CSMA" part of CSMA/CD.

The "CD" part of the protocol handles the times when two nodes start transmission simultaneously. To understand this part of the protocol, think of what happens during a telephone conversation when two people begin talking at the same time. Typically, both stop talking and begin again a few moments later, hoping that this time one begins sooner than the other. This is equivalent to what CSMA/CD does. If two (or more) nodes begin transmitting at the same time, the messages "collide" on the network. The nodes monitor for such a collision, and when one is detected all nodes stop transmitting and begin again after a pause of random length. Usually, one node will begin its retransmission before the other, thus gaining control of the network.

Ethernet adapters are available with either an SPD bus interface or a PCI bus interface. SPD bus Ethernet adapters consume one of the AS/400 SPD bus slots, or one of the card slots on the MFIOP or 2810 LAN/WAN IOP, or one of the card slots on the Integrated PC Server. PCI bus Ethernet adapters consume one of the PCI slots allocated to the MFIOP or the 2809 PCI LANWAN/Workstation IOP. PCI Ethernet adapters take one of three PCI slots assigned to a PCI controller, and if the 2838 PCI 100/10-Mbps Ethernet IOA is identified for system usage, the specific slot is defined to be a high-speed slot, only one of which exists on each PCI controller. Figure 2.25 summarizes the Ethernet controllers and adapters, the performance of each adapter, and whether it attaches to an SPD or a PCI bus.

Controller/Adapter	Performance	SD/PCI Bus or Attaches to
2629 LAN/WAN/Workstation IOP		SPD
9751 Multi-Function IOP		SPD
2810 LAN/WAN/Workstation IOP		SPD
6616 Integrated PC Server		SPD
2851 PCI Integrated PC Server		PCI
2809 LAN/WAN/Workstation IOP		PCI
6181 Ethernet IEEE 802.3 IOA	Mbps/10 Mbps	2629, 6616, or 9715 controllers
2838 PCI 100/10-Mbps Ethernet IOA	10 Mbps/100 Mbps	PCI
2723 PCI Ethernet IOA	1 Mbps/10 Mbps	PCI, 2851 2809, MFIOP

Figure 2.25. Summary of Ethernet controllers and adapters.

Token-Ring Local Area Networks

The token ring is an IBM-developed local area network able to move information at speeds of either 4 or 16 Mbps, depending on the version. The participating computers (called **nodes**) are connected through a ring-shaped wiring scheme depicted in Figure 2.26. In addition to the token-ring methodology described, a faster, more flexible technology called ATM (Asynchronous Transfer Mode) of token-ring-based LAN communications will be described.

The protocol used by the token-ring local area network is called the **token passing protocol**. With this protocol, *packets* of information are passed around the ring from node to node in a continuous circle. These packets are called **message frames** (see Figure 2.27). A unique frame called a **token frame** controls access to the ring. When a node receives a

Figure 2.26. The basic structure of a token-ring network.

Figure 2.27. Token-passing protocol used on IBM token-ring networks.

frame, the node checks to see if it is a message or a token frame. If it is a message frame, the node examines the destination address to see if the message is intended for that node. If the message is not intended for that node, the message frame is passed on unchanged to the next node in the ring. If the frame received by a node is a token frame, the node knows that the network is idle and that it may send a message frame if it has information to transfer. After it sends a message frame, the node then sends a token frame to indicate that the ring is again inactive and ready to carry information.

All AS/400 systems can participate in a token-ring network if an appropriate token-ring network adapter is added. One such adapter is the #6149 Token-Ring Adapter, which attaches to the #2629 LAN/WAN/Workstation IOP.

The #2724 PCI 164-Mbps Token-Ring IOA performs a function identical to that of the #6149 Token-Ring Adapter except that instead of attaching to a #2629 IOP, it attaches to the #2809 PCI LAN/WAN/Workstation IOP. The SPD bus and the PCI bus are explained in "Hardware Architecture Overview" in Chapter 1.

FDDI LANs

Fiber Distributed Data Interface (FDDI) networks are high-speed (100-Mbps) local area networks. These networks use fiber optic or twisted-pair cable to move information at a rate of 100 Mbps between the participating computer systems (nodes). Using light signals transmitted through the fiber optic cable, FDDI networks can move information more quickly and with greater immunity from electrical interference than can electrical LANs. The protocol used on FDDI networks is an enhanced version of the token-passing protocol used by the IBM token-ring network.

All AS/400 systems with the appropriate adapter can participate in FDDI networks. For FDDI networks using fiber optic cable, the AS/400 must be equipped with a #2618 Fiber Distributed Data Interface Adapter. For FDDI networks constructed from shielded twisted pair, the AS/400 must be equipped with the 2665 Shielded Twisted-Pair Distributed Data Interface. The #2665 **Shielded Twisted-Pair Distributed Data Interface** is often referred to as SDDI.

Integrated PC Server

The **Integrated PC Server** (IPCS), along with supporting AS/400 software, provides a **high-performance file server** for a local area network. That is, personal computers (running Windows, OS/2, or DOS) can freely and efficiently access AS/400 disk storage. The same file system can also be accessed by AS/400 host application programs and can provide LAN communications to AS/400 application programs using TCP/IP and APPN.

The fastest area of expansion is the successful marriage of the AS/400 and **Windows NT** on the Integrated PC Server. In this case the user purchases Microsoft certified Windows NT through a Microsoft reseller, including service for the software package. Up to 16 separate Windows NT servers can exist on a single AS/400e server 740. Each of the Windows NT servers is independent of the other, but can share the AS/400 disk, tape and CD-ROM facilities. The operations which support the Windows NT environment use integrated AS/400 operations and user administration. Support will be provided for multiple Windows NT releases including NT 5.0 when is arrives. Windows NT messages can be sent to AS/400 operators. The AS/400 provides simplified and more flexible drive mapping and the keyboard language can be set during NT install. The client storage space drive lettering matches the Windows NT drive numbering. Windows NT reliability is improved through the AS/400's ability to mirror the NT event log to an AS/400 message queue or job. During the Windows NT install process, it is possible to specify the type of Windows NT **event log** entries to be sent to an AS/400 **message queue**. The administrator can specify the drive sizes for the windows NT operating system. The AS/400 administrator can submit windows NT commands directly to the NT IPCS from the AS/400 with output returned to a joblog, IFS, or spool file. The administrator need not switch back and forth between the two systems. Tape backup utilities written for Windows NT can backup data to the AS/400 tape drive.

Also available to run on the IPCS is **Novell NetWare** 4.10 or 4.11. This integration allows the AS/400 disk to be used for **NetWare file serving**, enabling consolidation of AS/400 and NetWare servers into a single hardware platform. The IPCS usage as a file server for generating local area networks is expected to decrease in proportion to the volume of IPCS based networks used for supporting Windows NT.

Lotus Notes/Domino is also supported on the IPCS. **Domino** is an application development environment that includes facilities to support and enable workflow applications, electronic mail, document data storage and replication, and an integrated address book. It includes administration support allowing users to share, track, store, access, and view data of any type in Notes databases. It is expected that long-term users will migrate from the Integrated PC Server support for the Lotus Notes/Domino environment to the **Domino for AS/400** support.

AS/400 **NetServer** is preloaded as part of OS/400 at no additional charge, and OS/400 provides a single point of software maintenance. There is no NT Server license, installation, configuration, or maintenance involved. NetServer uses the AS/400 processor, disk, and LAN adapters, and user data is protected by AS/400 RAID-5 and mirroring. NetServer is managed with Operations Navigator providing simple, consistent graphical administration and operations. Users connect to NetServer using Windows Network Neighborhood using standard AS/400 user profiles and security. Figure 2.28 illustrates the interconnections for two separate Local Area Networks functioning from a single IPCS. With NetServer, users do not require Client Access to perform native file and print sharing for PC clients. Automatic translation from ASCII to EBCDIC and back is performed.

The IPCS also has the ability to act as the **firewall** processor for an AS/400, isolating the AS/400 and any intranet users from the Internet. This isolation hides the users and AS/400 addressing from the Internet while allowing visibility of the Internet addressing to the users and AS/400 (as well as allowing e-mail and other Internet functions to pass through).

The maximum number of IPCS features that may be installed on the AS/400 is 16 on an AS/400e system 740 , but if the system maximum number of LANs is less than 4, the maximum number of IPCS features is that lesser number. The maximum is the aggregate number of all LANs. A two-port IPCS is counted as 2 LANs against the system maximum. Two card slots are required for the IPCS feature.

The IPCS features require the support of OS/400 Version 3 Release 1.0 or later. Each IPCS feature may also require one or more of the following licensed programs:

- OS/2 Warp Server for AS/400 (#5769-XZ1)

- Integration of Lotus Notes option for V3R2 (#5763-SS1)

- Integration of Lotus Notes option for V3R7 (#5716-SS1)

- Integration for Netware option for V3R2 (#5763-SS1)

- Integration for Netware option for V3R7 (#5716-SS1)

- OS/400 Option 29 - Integration for NT

There are four models of the IPCS: #6618, #6617, #2854, and #6616. In PCI bus-based systems, the #2851 or if a model 170 e-server system,

Options and Peripherals **153**

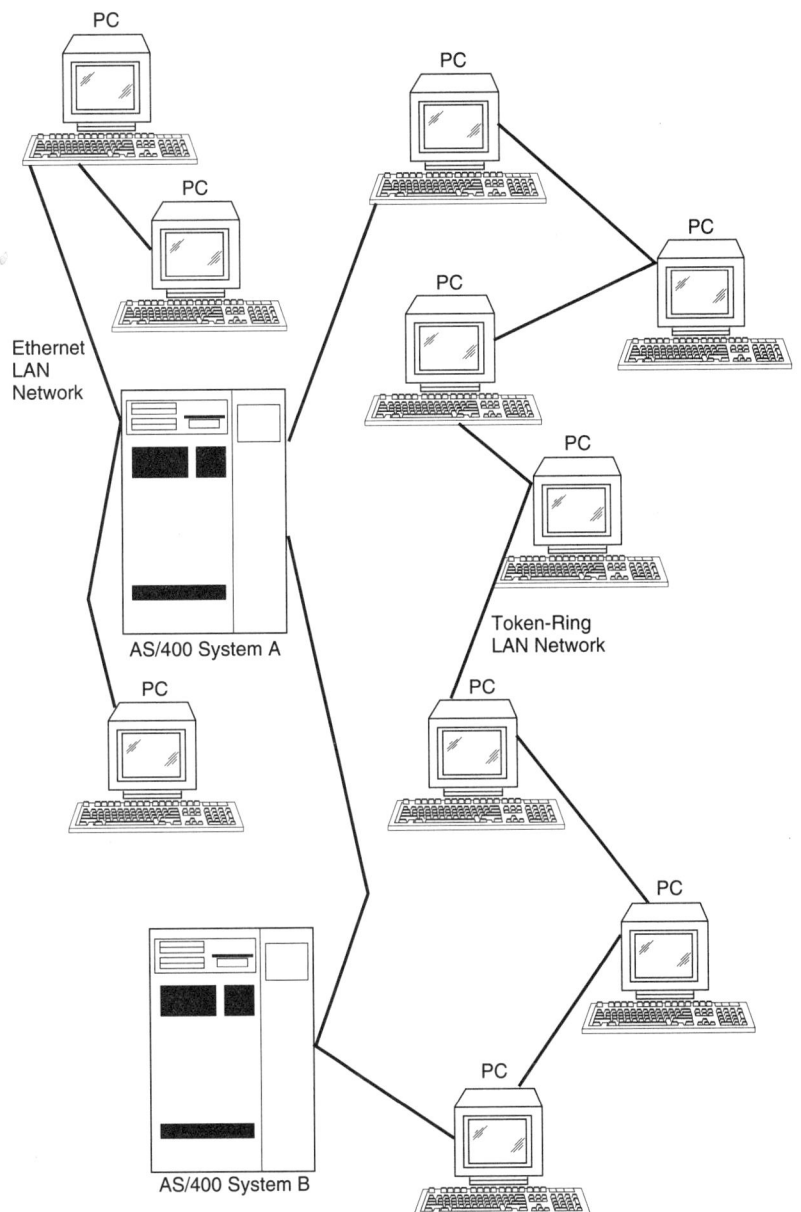

NOTES:
System A is a 9406 Model 720 with a dual-port FSIOP.
System B is a 9406 Model 170 with a single-port FSIOP.

Figure 2.28. Integrated PC server Local Area Networks with AS/400 servers.

the #2857 IPCS could be used instead of the #2854 model. Each of these versions of the IPCS have equivalent functions but a different physical format (to accommodate the model with which it is to be used). Each IPCS is a personal computer built on an adapter that can be installed inside an AS/400 system unit. It includes a microprocessor, four DIMM main memory slots (affording up to 1024 MB of memory), and two communications adapter slots into which can be plugged either Ethernet or token-ring adapters.

The OS/400 from V4R2 and forward also supplies Native AS/400 support for Windows Network Neighborhood (sometimes referred to as SMB Server or AS/400 NetServer). This provides a fully integrated file serving environment with only one system to manage, and (along with supporting AS/400 software) provides a high-performance file server for a local area network. That is, personal computers (running Windows, OS/2, or DOS) can freely and efficiently access AS/400 disk storage. The same file system can also be accessed by AS/400 host application programs and can provide LAN communications to AS/400 application programs using TCP/IP and APPN.

Integrated PC Server (#6616)

The **Integrated PC Server (IPCS)** (#6166), previously called the File Server Input/Output Processor (FSIOP), is basically a personal computer built on an adapter that can be installed inside an AS/400 system unit. It includes a microprocessor (e.g., a Pentium 166 MHz), two or four main memory slots (affording up to 256 or 512 MB of memory), and two communications adapter slots into which can be plugged either Ethernet or token-ring adapters.

The #6616 Integrated PC Server does not have adequate hardware function to support the Windows NT server requirements.

The Integrated PC Server (#6617)

The #6617 has an Intel Pentium Pro 200 MHz microprocessor and can accept one of each type or two of either LAN adapter. With the increased performance processor, the #6617 can perform as a Windows NT Server using a combination of Microsoft NT Terminal Server and Citrix WinFrame to allow personal productivity applications such as SmartSuite. Database integration is accomplished through the Client Access ODBC driver. Full BackOffice certification has been achieved.

The #6617 supports the same IOAs as the PCI Integrated PC Server (#2854), and if running the NT operating system, requires the same cable, keyboard/mouse, and display support as the #2854. In the above, where 2854 is stated, the function could as well be also performed by the #2851, or the #2857.

#6618 Integrated NetFinity Server for AS/400

The #6618 IntegratedNetFinity Server contains a 333 MHz Pentium II processor, 4 main storage slots, and 3 LAN IOA slots. Each memory card slot can contain either a 32-MB, a 128-MB, or a 256-MB memory card for a total main storage capacity ranging from 32 MB to 1024 MB. One memory card is required. The LAN IOA slots can contain PCI token-ring IOAs, PCI Ethernet IOAs, or PCI 100/10 Mbps Ethernet IOAs. All three PCI slots can be used for NetFinity server functions. Two of the three PCI slots can support native AS/400 functions. The #6618 requires three IOP slots.

When supporting Windows NT, the system drive for the Integrated PC Server can be configured as large as 8 GB. The Windows NT Integrated PC Server disk drives no longer are required to be a part of the system ASP providing the user with greater control of their disk drives. An option now exists which enables the administrator to control starting the communications when the AS/400 is sharing the LAN adapter with Windows NT Server. This allows the administrator to bring up the Windows NT Server but restrict the communications into the server

PCI Integrated PC Servers (#2865)

The PCI integrated PC Server (#2865) contains a 333 MHz Pentium Pro processor, 4 main storage slots, and 2 LAN IOA slots. This adapter requires two reserved PCI card positions, one for the processor card and the second for a bridge card to interface the processor to the system. The feature comes with a special cable that translates the connector on the back of the bridge card to an industry standard keyboard, mouse, serial and parallel connectors. Each memory card slot can contain either a 32-MB, a 128-MB, or a 256-MB memory card for a total main storage capacity ranging from 32 MB to 1024 MB. One memory card is required.

When supporting Windows NT, the system drive for the Integrated PC Server can be configured as large as 8 GB. The Windows NT Integrated PC Server disk drives no longer are required to be a part of the system ASP providing the user with greater control of their disk drives. An option now exists which enables the administrator to control starting the communications when the AS/400 is sharing the LAN adapter with Windows NT Server. This allows the administrator to bring up the Windows NT Server but restrict the communications into the server.

PCI Integrated PC Servers (#2854, #2851, and #2857)

The listed PCI Integrated PC Servers each include a 200 MHz Pentium Pro processor, four main storage card slots, and two LAN IOA positions. The adapter requires two reserved PCI card positions, one for the processor card and the second for a bridge card to interface the processor to the system. A special cable converts the connector on the card to industry-standard keyboard, mouse, serial, and parallel connectors.

The memory card slots can be populated with either 32-MB memory cards (#2861) or 128-MB memory cards (#2862) to achieve a main storage range of 32 MB to 512 MB. At least one of the memory cards must be present.

Each LAN IOA slot can contain a PCI token-ring IOA, a PCI Ethernet IOA, or the 100/10-Mbps Ethernet IOA. The PCI Integrated PC Server (#2854) can support two IOAs in any combination, with a maximum of one 100/10-Mbps Ethernet IOA. The features for the LAN IOAs come from the following list:

- PCI Ethernet IOA (#2723)

- PCI 16/4-Mbps Token-Ring IOA (#2724)

- PCI 100/10-Mbps Ethernet IOA (#2838)

- Base PCI Ethernet IOA (#9723)

- Base PCI 16/4-Mbps Token-Ring IOA (#9724)

- Base PCI 100/10-Mbps Ethernet IOA (#9838)

If the Windows NT operating system is to be run on the #2854, #2851, #2857 or #6617, then the IPCS Extension Cable for NT (#3025) is required. The IPCS Keyboard/Mouse for NT (#1700) is the default in the United States, and the #6546-002 display is recommended in the United States. IBM's Web site at *http://www.as400.ibm.com* contains a list of supported displays, keyboards, and mice. If the OS/2 operating system is to be run on the #2854, then the cable, mouse, and display features are not recommended.

The software functions of 5769-SS1 Option 29 are the same for Windows NT whether the IPCS function is implemented with the #6616, #6617, the #2851, #2854, or the #2857. This includes Windows NT Terminal Server, Back Office certification, Internal TCP/IP LAN, firewall, etc.

Product Preview

IBM continues to invest in the AS/400 Integrated PC Server (IPCS) line of products for Windows NT Server and a fully integrated AS/400 Firewall, both of which are enhanced in V4R3. OS/400 Integration with Windows NT Server is enhanced with V4R3 to provide support of multiple Windows NT Server releases. This enhancement prepares the AS/400 IPCS to run Windows NT Server 5.0, which is expected to be made available by Microsoft in 1999. IBM's support for Windows NT 5.0 on the AS/400 IPCS is subject to completion of Microsoft's product certification.

Statement of Direction

In a future release of OS/400, IBM intends to continue to enhance both the Intel processors and memory capabilities of the AS/400 Integrated PC Server (IPCS). Customers using OS/2 Warp Server for AS/400 and Novell Netware 4.11 on the AS/400 IPCS will be supported with their current capabilities until January 31, 2001; however, these products will not be enhanced.

It is recommended that customers running Lotus Domino on the AS/400 IPCS plan to migrate to the Domino for AS/400 product to take advantage of its enhanced capability, reliability, and integration. V4R3 is the last release of OS/400 that will support running domino on the IPCS.

Asynchronous Transfer Mode (ATM)

ATM brings 155-Mbps performance to your local area networks. In addition, ATM can run over fiber, coax pairs, twisted-pair, and token-ring wiring. ATM can carry voice, audio, and multimedia over the same network, as well as provide video service. Functions such as remote save/restore work with the streaming functions of ATM, even in the presence of burst-mode network traffic. ATM allows remote clustering, remote journaling, and hot backup sites to become faster and more effective, providing for new kinds of data-intensive applications such as storing medical imaging, online real estate viewings, and just-in-time education. With ATM, the low latency of point-to-point (PPP), cell-based communication enables more effective **On-Line Transaction Processing (OLTP)**, resulting in more effective file serving. The selection of which ATM adapter to use depends upon the pre-existing wiring of your facility. Six different ATM connection adapters are offered for AS/400 systems.

- *PCI 25-Mbps UTP ATM (2811)*. The PCI 25-Mbps UTP (Unshielded Twisted-Pair) ATM adapter allows the AS/400 to be attached using unshielded twisted-pair category 3 cabling. The 2811 should be considered when speeds of 25 Mbps are adequate and distances are less than 100 meters.

- *PCI 34-Mbps Coax E3 ATM (2819)*. The PCI 34-Mbps Coax E3 ATM card should be considered to allow the AS/400 to connect into an ATM network using coax cabling and the E3 interface. The 2819 should be considered when coax cabling and a 34-Mbps data transfer rate are adequate, and distances are less than 1000 meters.

- *PCI 45-Mbps Coax T3DS3 ATM (2812)*. The PCI 45-Mbps Coax PCI card allows the AS/400 to be attached into an ATM network using coax cabling and the T3DS3 interface. The 2812 should be considered when 45 Mbps is adequate for data transfer and distances are less than 1000 meters.

- *PCI 155-Mbps UTP OC3 ATM (2815)*. The PCI 155-Mbps UTP OC3 ATM card (2815) attaches into an ATM network using the UTP-5 interface and will be used where 155-Mbps speeds are required over distances of less than 100 meters. This interface can connect both to local area switches and directly to service provider equipment.

- *PCI 155-Mbps MMF ATM (2816)*. The PCI 155-Mbps MMF ATM (2816) card attaches the AS/400 into an ATM network using the Multi-Mode Fiber (MMF) 62.5-micron interface. This interface can connect both to local area switches and directly to service provider equipment. The 2815 will be used where speeds of 155 Mbps are needed over distances of less than 2 km.

- *PCI 155-Mbps SMF OC3 ATM (2818)*. The PCI 155-Mbps SMF OC3 ATM card (2818) attaches the AS/400 into an ATM network using the Single-Mode Fiber (SMF) 9-micron interface. This interface is primarily intended for direct connection to service provider equipment but can be used for local area switches. The 2818 will be used where 155-Mbps speeds are required over distances of from 16 km to 40 km.

Wireless Local Area Networks

The wireless network is a type of local area network that allows participating computer systems to communicate over radio waves. This can be useful in situations where users roam the building or campus with portable computing devices or where wiring is expensive or impossible. Where the computing resource and device layouts change periodically, the AS/400 Wireless LAN Adapter can provide a solution. Figure 2.29 illustrates a wireless LAN network with two wireless repeaters connecting a simple network of three computers.

An AS/400 wireless LAN is enabled in one of two ways. For Version 4 systems, IBM Wireless Connection (5798-TBW) provides the system support to enable wireless repeater devices (**access points**) to be attached to an existing AS/400 token-ring or Ethernet LAN connection. Intelligent LAN-based devices (i.e., PCs) and portable transaction computers are supported in this environment. For Version 3 systems, an AS/400 wireless LAN adapter I/O attachment processor (feature codes 2663 and 2668) is necessary to provide the workstation controller support for portable transaction computers. Access points can be attached to an existing AS/400 token-ring or Ethernet LAN, or to an RS-485 port on the wireless LAN adapter. Wireless Connection is a TCP/IP sockets based server connecting real time, 5250 mobile devices with the AS/400. Wireless connection supports multiple instances of itself on the same AS/400 system, allowing large users to consolidate smaller AS/400 systems into one or more larger AS/400 data centers.

The 2668 Wireless LAN Adapter uses direct-sequence, spread-spectrum radio, operating in the 2.4- to 2.4835-GHz band. Operation in the United States does not require a license from the **Federal Communications Commission (FCC)**. The 2668 Wireless LAN Adapter comes

Figure 2.29. AS/400 wireless LAN with wireless repeaters.

with an antenna and a cable for connecting the antenna to the adapter. The area of coverage may be extended beyond the coverage provided by the antenna attached to the adapter by adding AS/400 wireless LAN access points to the network via either an Ethernet or token-ring LAN backbone, or an RS-485 (unshielded, twisted-pair-wired) backbone. In addition, access points may be connected without wires, acting as wireless repeaters. Each adapter or access point generates one cell of coverage area. Networks are designed by creating overlapping cells to ensure consistent coverage of the area desired.

The AS/400 2668 Wireless LAN Adapter allows transparent seamless movement of data and messages from cell to cell while maintaining a continuous host session. It operates with existing application software interfaces. Existing 5250 and LAN-oriented applications can use the AS/400 2668 Wireless LAN Adapter without change, and it supports the AS/400 family of wireless LAN and data collection devices. The AS/400 2668 Wireless LAN Adapter also operates with the DATASPAN 2.4-GHz family of products from the Telxon Corporation.

The raw bit rate for the AS/400 2668 Wireless LAN Adapter is configurable to 1 or 2 Mbps, shared by all active devices in the network. The range covered by one cell in most office environments is from 100 to 300 feet in all directions, depending on the building structure, antenna type, and antenna placement. Outdoors, with a clear line of sight between specialized antennas, a range of up to 3 miles may be achieved.

With Version 4 Release 1, it no longer is necessary to purchase either of these adapters because software is now able to use any local area network (Ethernet or token ring) to which an antenna attachment has been attached to communicate with your wireless devices. This is discussed in greater detail in Chapter 4. Figures 2.30 and 2.31 illustrate some of the devices that may be used with the AS/400 when operating in a wireless environment.

Wide Area Networks (WANs)

A wide area network (WAN) is a group of computers connected to a communications system. It is called a "wide area" network to indicate that the computers participating in the network need not be geographically confined to a particular building or campus (as is the case with a

LAN). WANs can provide a connection between two computers located across town from one another or between hundreds of computers across global distances.

To participate in a WAN, the AS/400 system must have the proper programming (which is included in the OS/400 operating system) and be equipped with the proper electrical **interface**. The term "interface" refers collectively to the connector, electrical voltage levels, connector pin functions, and so on, that are provided for the physical attachment to a communications line.

Just as there are different rules of grammar and punctuation in English, French, and other languages, there are different rules for various types of computer communications. In computer communications, a set of rules is called a **communications protocol**. The protocols of most interest for our purposes are async, bisync, SDLC, X.25, and IDLC. Each of these different protocols is supported by OS/400 and has the

Figure 2.30. Wireless computers and access points.

Figure 2.31. Pen-based computer example.

same basic goal of moving information from one place to another efficiently and reliably. And each has advantages and disadvantages. The one you use will depend on your requirements in the areas of transmission speed, cost, and compatibility with the other device(s) in the network. At all times, however, each device using a given communications line must be using the same protocol.

Some popular electrical interfaces used with WANs are 232/V.24, V.35, V.36, X.21, and ISDN interfaces. While it is not necessary to understand exactly what these cryptic names mean, it is important to understand that there are different types of interfaces necessary to support different types of WANs. The interface may be provided by a separate adapter card working with a communications controller card, or it may be built onto the same card with the communications controller circuitry. Now let's look at some specific communications adapters for the AS/400 family.

Six-Line Communications Controller (2629)

The 2629 Six-Line Communications Controller is a specialized computer on a card (IO processor) that can handle the traffic of up to six independent communications lines. It requires a separately purchased interface adapter for each line. The adapters that can be used with the 2629 Six-Line Communications Controller include the following:

The 2699 Two-Line WAN IOA is a multi-protocol I/O adapter. The adapter is programmed by the cables which are attached to a particular line protocol. The 2699 Two-Line WAN IOA can interface to communications lines using Async, BSC, SDLC, X.25, PPP, or Frame Relay. Several physical interfaces (EIA 232V.24, V.35, V.36, and X.21) are also supported based upon the cable used. The cables that configure the line protocol are listed in Figure 2.32.

Other adapters are as follows: A 6149 or 9249 16/4-Mbps/Token-Ring IOA (for token-ring LANs); an Ethernet IEEE 802.3 IOA (for Ethernet LANs; feature codes 6181 or 9381); or the 6180 or 9280 Twinaxial Workstation IOA (for the attachment of workstations).

ISDN Basic Rate Interface Adapter

The 2065 Integrated Services Digital Network (ISDN) Basic Rate Interface Adapter provides an interface to the communications line compatible with the ISDN standards. ISDN is becoming prevalent in Europe and Japan and beginning to become more available in the United States. Like X.21, ISDN uses a digital interface to transfer information, improving the overall efficiency of the information transfer and eliminating the need for a conversion to traditional analog communications. Each ISDN basic rate interface adapter supports two 64,000-bps "streams of information" over an ISDN communications link (full duplex). Each of these streams of information is called a B Channel. In addition, each ISDN basic rate interface adapter supports one 16,000-bps stream of information, called a **D Channel**, over that same ISDN communications link. Up to two ISDN Basic Rate Interface Adapters can be used with every 2629 Six-Line Communications Controller, but no other adapters may be used with that 2623 Six-Line Communications Controller. The ISDN adapter supports the ISDN Data Link Control (IDLC) protocol for communications over ISDN lines. A maximum of two ISDN adapters are supported per 2629 Six-Line Communications Controller.

Adapter Feature Code	Cable Feature Code	Description
2699 Two-Line WAN IOA	0330	V.24/EIA232 20-ft cable
	0331	V.24/EIA232 50-ft cable
	0332	V.24/EIA232 20-ft Enhanced cable
	0333	V.24/EIA232 50-ft Enhanced cable
	0334	V.24/EIA232 80-ft Enhanced cable
	0335	V.36/EIA449 20-ft cable
	0336	V.36/EIA449 50-ft cable
	0337	V.36/EIA449 150-ft cable
	0338	V.35 20-ft cable
	0339	V.35 50-ft cable
	0340	V.35 80-ft cable
	0341	X.21 20-ft cable
	0342	X.21 50-ft cable
2720 PCI/WAN/Twinaxial IOA and 2721 PCI/WAN IOA	0348	V.24/EIA232 20-ft PCI cable
	0349	V.24/EIA232 50-ft PCI cable
	0350	V.24/EIA232 20-ft Enhanced PCI cable
	0351	V.24/EIA232 50-ft Enhanced PCI cable
	0352	V.24/EIA232 80-ft Enhanced PCI cable
	0353	V.36/EIA449 20-ft PCI cable
	0354	V.36/EIA449 50-ft PCI cable
	0355	V.36/EIA449 150-Ft PCI cable
	0356	V.35 20-ft PCI cable
	0357	V.35 50-ft PCI cable
	0358	V.35 80-ft PCI cable
	0359	X.21 20-ft PCI cable
	0360	X.21 50-ft PCI cable
9720 BASE /PCI/WAN/ TWINAXIAL IOA	0348	V.24/EIA232 20-ft PCI cable
	0349	V.24/EIA232 50-ft PCI cable
	0351	V.24/EIA232 50-ft Enhanced PCI cable
	0352	V.24/EIA232 80-ft Enhanced PCI cable
9721 Base/Two-Line/ WAN IOA	0348	V.24/EIA232 20-ft PCI cable
	0349	V.24/EIA232 50-ft PCI cable
	0350	V.24/EIA232 20-ft Enhanced PCI cable
	0351	V.24/EIA232 50-ft Enhanced PCI cable
	0352	V.24/EIA232 80-ft Enhanced PCI cable

Figure 2.32. Configuration cables for various adapters to support various protocols.

The Async Protocol

The **Async** (short for *async*hronous) protocol is a low-speed, low-cost communications method commonly used by many devices. With Async, individual bytes of information are transmitted (one byte at a time) with no fixed relationship between bytes. Figure 2.33 shows one way a byte might be packaged before it is sent over an Async communications line. The start bit tells the receiving end that information is coming down the line. The user's data follows the start bit. The parity bit is used by the receiving end to check for transmission errors in the user's data. Finally, the stop bit signifies the end of the transmission of the character. This is just one example of how information might be transmitted over an Async line. The user can select other organizations—including eight user data bits, no parity bits, and two stop bits. These different organizations exist primarily because of the many types of equipment that have used this protocol over the years. The specific organization used must be established at both ends of the communications link before communications can begin.

The Bisync Protocol

The **Bisync** protocol (short for *bi*nary *sync*hronous communications, or BSC) is a byte synchronous protocol. The "synchronous" in "Bisync" means that a special character preceding the information synchronizes the receiver with the incoming information. This synchronization allows many bytes of information to be sent as a single block, in contrast to the asynchronous protocol, in which a single byte is sent at a time. The ability to send blocks of characters makes Bisync more efficient

Figure 2.33 Example of Async protocol data organization.

than the asynchronous protocol. Bisync is an older communications protocol used by terminals and other equipment to exchange information with many different types of computers, including IBM's System/360, System/370, and System/390 mainframes. As a result of its past popularity, many of today's computer systems still use this protocol.

The SDLC Protocol

The **Synchronous Data Link Control (SDLC)** is a bit synchronous protocol. The use of SDLC allows the sending of any data without the use of transparency. As with Bisync, SDLC is a synchronous communications protocol. However, SDLC is a more flexible protocol that is part of IBM's **Systems Network Architecture (SNA)**. SNA is a set of communications standards published by IBM and used as a road map to ensure that compatible communications are provided for current and future computer systems and software. SNA is discussed further in Chapter 6.

The X.25 Protocol

The **X.25 protocol** is an industry standard used in packet-switched networks available to the public today. Although more traditional communications networks are based on **analog** or voice-type communications signals, packet-switched networks use **digital** or computer-like communications signals. Each packet is then sent to its destination elsewhere in the network through the most economical and available route. Because each packet is routed in the most efficient way, overall information flow is improved over conventional techniques. The X.25 protocol is fully supported in IBM's Systems Network Architecture and also supports TCP/IP and other protocols.

The IDLC Protocol

The IDLC protocol is similar to SDLC, except that with IDLC the other computer need not wait to be **polled** by the computer in charge of the network, as it is with the SDLC protocol. Instead, both computers have an equal ability to transmit messages to and receive messages from each other. The IDLC protocol is used by the AS/400 to communicate over an **Integrated Services Digital Network (ISDN)**, a type of digital network that fits more naturally with computer communications than do the traditional analog communications used with telephone networks.

Currently more popular in Europe and Japan, ISDN communications services are starting to become more common in the United States. Computers attach to an ISDN with a digital connection, eliminating the need for the conversion to analog signals. There are different levels of ISDN service, which correspond to different transmission speeds. AS/400 systems can currently participate in the slower or **basic rate** of ISDN service. Even though this is the slowest ISDN service level, information is transferred at up to 64,000 bps per B channel with two B channels per adapter.

Frame Relay

A frame-relay network is a high-performance version of an X.25 network. Connections through the network are "permanent" and are labeled by a DLCI (Data Link Connection Identifier). The AS/400 uses LAN protocols over the frame-relay network. Essentially, frame relay provides a way to transport LAN traffic over a WAN. Frame relay is supported on the AS/400 via the SPD bus-attached 2666 High-Speed Communications IOP, the SPD bus-attached 2629 LAN/WAN/Workstation IOP with a 2699 Two-Line WAN IOA, and the PCI-attached 2809 PCI LAN/WAN/Workstation IOP with a 2721 PCI Two-Line WAN IOA installed.

Integrated FAX Adapters

In some previous releases of the AS/400 systems, when a fax connection was required, the user had to connect to a PS/2 or some other personal computer system to obtain a fax connection for receiving or sending data to remote fax locations over the telephone network. The 2664 Integrated FAX Adapter plugs directly into the AS/400 Models 730 and 740. The 2664 Integrated FAX Adapter significantly reduces the cost and overhead of using fax on the AS/400. The 2664 Integrated FAX Adapter consists of a single-card-width book that plugs into the AS/400 logic card assembly and to a telephone line. Additional detail about the use of the 2664 FAX Adapter is provided in "Facsimile Support/400" in Chapter 3. Two ports are provided capable of transmission and receipt of facsimile data to or from a group 3-capable fax machine, an AS/400, or a PC with appropriately programmed fax adapters.

PCI fax access cards (#2750, #2751, #2752, 2753, and#2761) allow sending and receiving faxes using the analog and digital connections under Facsimile support for AS/400. The file fax command allows the filing of received faxes as Class F TIFF objects. Faxes can be viewed using viewing products like are provided with Lotus Domino, and SAP AL Viewer.

Modems

A **modem** converts computer information into communications signals and transmits them over telephone lines (i.e., it *mod*ulates the computer information). A modem at the receiving end then converts the telephone line signals back into computer information (i.e., it *dem*odulates the telephone line signal). The term "modem" then derives from the terms "*mod*ulate" and "*dem*odulate." Computers need modems because telephone lines were originally designed to carry electronically encoded voice messages from one point to another. The telephone converts the speaker's voice into electronic signals suitable for phone line transmission. Although the information in a computer is already electronically encoded, it is not in a form that can be transmitted over standard phone lines. For this reason, a device is needed to convert the electronically encoded computer information into electronic signals suitable for telephone line transmission. A modem can be thought of as a telephone for a computer. Just as both parties need their own telephones to hold a conversation, both computers must have their own modems to transfer information over the phone lines. Modems are often used in the construction of wide area networks (WANs). Figure 2.34 lists some representative modems commonly used with AS/400 systems. Figure 2.35 shows the 7855 Modem and Figure 2.36 shows the 5822 Digital Service Unit/Channel Service Unit.

Integrated Analog Modem #2761

The #2761 is the first in a family of PCI IOAs based on DSP technology and allows the modem function to be integrated into the IOA itself and supports multiple analog modem ports (8). The #2761 runs the following protocols without the need of an external modem:

- SLIP/PPP

- Multilink PPP

- X.25

Modem Type Number	Interface Line	Data Rate -bps	Line Type	Full/Half Duplex	Auto-Call Support	Features
5853	V.24/EIA232	2,400	Switched	Full	Yes	Self-Test Data Rate Tuning
786X	V.24/EIA232	4,800/ 19,200	Leased	Full	No	SNBU, Self-Test, LPDA, Data Multiplex, Data Rate Tune
7855	V.24/EIA232	9600	Leased, Switched	Full	Yes, Switched	SNBU, Data Compression, Data Rate Tune,
7852	V.24/EIA232 Data/Fax	33,600/ 14,400	Leased, Switched	Half	Yes, Switched	SNBU, Password Protect, Synch/Async Switching
5822 DSU/CSU	V.24/EIA232 or V.35	56000	Leased, Switched	Half	NA	Complies with Bell Pub 62310/ Digital Data or Service Networks, Point to Point or Multi-Drop

Switched Line typically means a standard voice-grade telephone line. Necessary connections are made when the user dials a phone number and terminated when the user hangs up.

Leased Line means a telephone line maintains a predefined communications link (no phone number need be dialed).

Switched Network Backup Unit (SNBU) denotes the capability of a modem to automatically fall back to a switched phone line connection if the leased line normally used deteriorates to an unusable quality.

Figure 2.34. Characteristics of some representative modems commonly used with AS/400 systems.

- SDLC

The AS/400 perceives the #2761 as a single I/O Adapter with eight individual line resources available. The #2761 requires V4/R4 and an available PCI slot.

Figure 2.35. The 7855 modem.

Figure 2.36. The 5822 Digital Service Unit/Channel Service Unit.

Remote Workstation Controllers and Lines

An earlier section, "Wide Area Networks (WANs)," discussed attaching application systems to communications lines. This section discusses **remote workstation controllers,** the devices needed at the remote workstation end of the communications link. These devices perform basically the same function as the local workstation controllers. Remote workstation controllers are cabled directly to workstations and manage the workstation traffic for the computer system. The difference is that remote workstation controllers attach to the computer via a communications line and modems, as opposed to a local workstation controller, which is a card installed directly in the computer. Remote workstation controllers allow terminals and printers to be located at remote locations, giving distant users access to the application systems. Figure 2.37 illustrates a 5394 Remote Workstation Controller and Figure 2.38 illustrates one methodology for workstations to be attached to an AS/400 using a remote workstation controller. Two models of remote workstation controllers are used with the AS/400, the 5394 Remote Workstation Controller and the 5494 Remote Workstation Controller.

5394 Remote Workstation Controller

The 5394 Remote Workstation Controller functions include local screen printing, enhanced keyboard, reversed video, and file transfer through the Client Access Family for AS/400. The 5394 can support up to 16 workstations using twinax cable and cable-thru technology. The communications interface is either EIA 232/V.24 at up to 19,200 bps, or X.21 with SDLC at up to 64,000 bps.

5494 Remote Workstation Controller

The 5494 Remote Workstation Controller can do everything the 5394 could do plus it can attach 56 twinaxial workstations over four ports. In

Figure 2.37. The 5394 Remote Workstation Controller.

addition to standard twinaxial connections to workstations, the 5494 can connect directly to an Ethernet, token-ring, or wireless LAN at the remote site. This allows, for example, a token-ring network of PCs to access a remote AS/400 system. Alternately, the 5494 Model 002 could be attached to from one to five AS/400 systems over a token-ring network and twinaxially attached to the users' workstations. Only one token-ring network attachment is allowed per 5494, and the total number of workstations supported cannot exceed 80 (up to 56 twinaxially attached and the rest token-ring network-attached devices). The 5494 also supports the 5250 data stream extensions, which enable interaction with some application programs (specially written or used in conjunction with the IBM WindowTool/400 product [5798-RYF]) using a mouse and spe-

Figure 2.38. Remote workstations can be attached to an Application System through remote workstation controller.s

cial graphical items (e.g., pop-up windows, scroll bars, radio buttons, pushbuttons, check boxes, and continuous window frames).

Power and Packaging Options

Figure 2.39 lists the power and packaging features for the various AS/400e systems and identifies which of the systems accept the particular feature and the function performed by the feature on that particular system.

UPS for Models 150 and 170

An **Uninterruptible Power Supply (UPS)** significantly improves system uptime by minimizing the impact from power fluctuations and outages. The Models 150, 170, and 436 support an external UPS (#9910). UPSs are available in two capacities: 660 VA and 1.3 KVA. The UPS offers continuous no-break power, a keypad and digital display with 15 programmable operation functions and alarm set points, and brownout boost to save battery run time.

In the case of the Model 170, two special CPM/UPS devices are offered, one at 800 VA and the other at 1000–1400 VA. The higher rated unit output VA capability depends upon the input voltage range. Contact IBM sales personnel if interested in this particular unit.

AS/400e series Packaging Expansion Features

The following sections discuss the expansion features available for the AS/400e series models 7XX.

System Unit Expansion (5064/9364)

The #5064/#9364 System Unit Expansion is a bolt-on expansion unit that can expand the I/O function of the Model 720 system unit. The basic expansion unit contains a five-slot 3½-inch disk unit cage, a 650-watt power supply with space for redundant power supplies for both the expansion unit and the system unit, and either a 6-card #9331 SPD bus card cage, or a 14-slot #9329 PCI card cage. The function can be

Options and Peripherals **175**

Feature Code	720	730	740
9364/5064	System Unit expansion		
9331 SPD Cage	SPD Card Cage		
9329 PCI Cage	PCI Card Cage		
7128 DASD Cage	DASD Expansion Unit		
7130 Cage	Tape Expansion CAGE		
5143 Power Supply	Pre-Req for #5052 Storage Expansion Unit Redundant Power Supply		
5153 Power Supply			
5052	Storage Expansion Unit	Storage Expansion Unit	Storage Expansion Unit
5055		Storage Expansion Cage (4 disk units)	Storage Expansion Cage
5058	Storage Expansion Unit	Storage Expansion Unit	Storage Expansion Unit
5073/5072 I/O Card Expansion	1063 Mbps System Expansion Tower	1063 Mbps System Expansion Tower	1063 Mbps System Expansion Tower
5083/5082 Disk Expansion	1063 Mbps DASD Expansion Tower	1063 Mbps DASD Expansion Tower	1063 Mbps DASD Expansion Tower
2686 Optical Link Processor	266 Mbps Optic Link Card (not recommended)	266 Mbps Optic Link Card (not recommended)	266 Mbps Optic Link Card (not recommended)
2688 Optical Link Processor	1063 Mbps Optical Link Card	1063 Mbps Optical Link Card	1063 Mbps Optical Link Card
2695 Optical Link Adapter		System Unit feature	System Unit feature
2688 Optical Link Processor	Plugs on 2674 </= 3	Plugs on 2674 </= 3	Plugs on 2674 </= 3

Figure 2.39. Power and packaging feature matrix for Advanced Series 7XX systems.

expanded by the addition of two 3½-Inch Disk Unit Cages (#7128) and a 3-slot 5¼-Inch Tape Unit Cage (#7130).

1063 Mbps PCI Expansion Tower #5065

The PCI Expansion Tower (#5065) is used on models that can attach additional I/O towers for adding up to 445 disks, up to 12 PCI IOAs and 2 removable media units. The #5065 includes a 1063 Mbps optical bus card, an optical cable, 12 PCI IOA slots, space for 45 disk units sized as 3.5 inch devices, space for 2 internal tape or DVD units, 1 battery backup unit, N+1 redundant/hot swap power supplies without local regulation, and one #2824 PCI LAN/WAN/Workstation IOP. The 12 IOA slots are in 3 groups of 4 slots. Each group of 4 slots is supported by a #2824 PCI LAN/WAN/Workstation IOP. In each group of 4 slots, 2 slots are high speed slots and 2 slots are low speed slots.

The 45 disk positions are in groups of 5 disk units, with each group of 5 disk units supported on a separate SCSI bus from a #2748 Disk Unit Adapter. Each #2748 has three SCSI buses and is capable of supporting up tEo 15 disk units. The #5065 can package from zero to three #2748 Disk Unit Adapters and each adapter must be installed in a PCI SCSI card slot. The #2781 PCI Magnetic Media Controller may also be installed in the PCI SCSI card slots to support external tape devices. Figure 2.40 identifies the card plugging arrangement for the #5065 PCI Expansion Tower. The base tower can support the first 15 disk units, when holding 16 or more disk units, the 5101 disk unit expansion for 30 disks is required.

SPD Bus Card Cage (#9331)

The #9331 SPD Bus Card Cage allows six SPD bus I/O cards to be plugged into the 5064 System Expansion Unit. The remaining card cage slot is reserved for an 2688 Optical Link Card used to attach up to four additional 5073 System Expansion Units or 5082 Storage Expansion Units to the system unit.

PCI Card Cage (#9329)

The #9329 PCI Card Cage allows 14 PCI adapters plus two Optical Link Cards. The remainder of the PCI cage card slots are used by logical

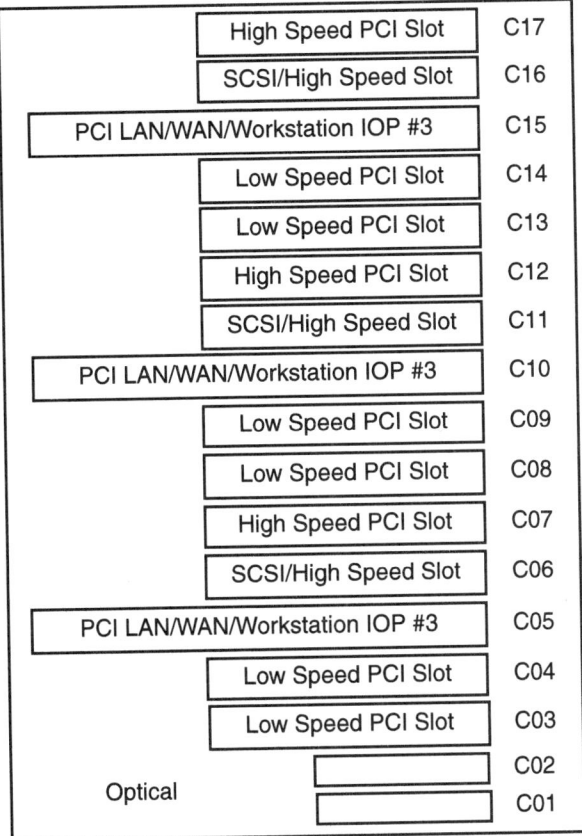

Figure 2.40. Card layout for PCI expansion tower.

controllers, which manage the activity of the PCI cards inserted in the other slots. Some of these 14 slots are for high-performance PCI adapters, and some are restricted to slow performance adapters.

3½-Inch Disk Unit Cage (#7128)

The 3½-Inch Disk Unit Cage can accept any five of the disk units listed under "Disk Storage." The interface within the disk unit cage is Ultra-SCSI, but may drive Fast and Wide SCSI or Fast and Narrow SCSI devices.

5¼-Inch Tape Unit Cage (#7130)

The 5¼-Inch Tape Unit Cage can accept any three of the tape units listed under "Internal Tape Storage." The interface within the tape unit cage is Ultra-SCSI, but may drive Fast and Wide SCSI or Fast and Narrow SCSI devices.

Storage Expansion Unit (#5058)

The #5058 Storage Expansion Unit mounts on the top of the #5073/#5083 Bus Expansion Towers for all Advanced Series 7XX models. The #5058 Storage Expansion Unit provides the capability to mount up to sixteen 3½-inch disk storage units.

System Expansion Tower (#5073)

The #5073 System Expansion Tower has four compartments for additional tape storage. In addition to tape storage, the #5073 System Expansion Tower provides 13 additional I/O expansion slots and can feature a #5058 Storage Expansion Unit on the top. The #5073 provides base power and redundant power for the tape units and the I/O expansion slots, and, when featured with the #5058 Storage Expansion Unit, both cooling and power for up to sixteen 3½-inch disk units. The #5073 uses a 1063-Mbps optical interface to connect to the system unit.

Storage Expansion Tower (#5083)

The #5083 Storage Expansion Tower provides for up to 16 internal disk units. An additional 16 disk units may be added with the #5058 Storage Expansion Unit for a total of 32 disk units. The #5083 Storage Expansion Tower uses a 1063-Mbps interface. The #5083 Storage Expansion Tower and the #5073 System Expansion Tower have the same appearance and are illustrated in Figure 2.41.

Advanced Series Base Optical Bus Adapter (#2696)

The #2696 Base Optical Bus Adapter is required on any Advanced Series Model 720, 730, and 740. The #2696 Base Optical Bus Adapter generates both the copper bus internal to the system and up to six optical busses for attachment of bus or storage expansion towers. The #2696 can accept a maximum of three #2686 and/or #2688 Optical Link Processors.

Advanced Series #2686 Optical Link Processor (266 Mbps)

Each #2686 Optical Link Processor can attach two busses and up to two bus or storage expansion towers. Three cables are required to attach two towers; two cables are required to attach one tower. The towers are connected in a ring with the system unit. The #2686 Optical Link Processor executes at 266 Mbps. Any mixture of #2686 and #2688

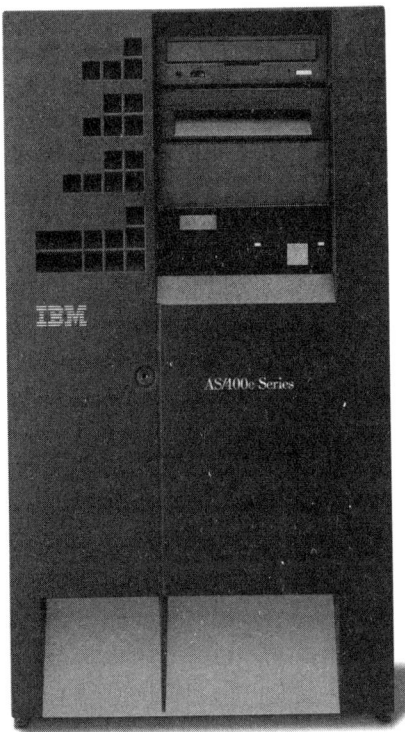

Figure 2.41. Disk Storage Expansion Unit for AS/400 Advanced Series 3XX/5XX mounted on a system unit.

Optical Link Processors may exist on an optical bus adapter as long as the total is not greater than three.

Advanced Series Optical Link Processor (#2688)

Each #2688 Optical Link Processor can attach two busses and up to two bus or storage expansion towers. Three cables are required to attach two towers; two cables are required to attach one tower. The towers are connected in a ring with the system unit. The #2688 Optical Link Processor executes at 1063 Mbps. Any mixture of #2686 and #2688 Optical Link Processors may exist on an optical bus adapter as long as the total is not greater than three. The #2688 Optical Link Processor may only attach to a #2695 or #2696 Optical Bus Adapter.

Other Adapter Options

This section contains a group of attachments, either cards or other system elements which do not group with any of the other categories of devices and adapters.

Cryptographic Processors

Data encryption is required to support many financial institutions, to support e-business transactions on the Internet, and to securely exchange data on a worldwide basis. A maximum of 3 cryptographic functions is supported on any single system.

Cryptographic Processors (#2620/2628)

The 2620/2628 Cryptographic Processor helps improve the security of an AS/400 system by encoding information using cryptographic techniques (ANSI Data Encryption Standard [DES]). That is, AS/400-resident information can be scrambled via encryption keys, making it meaningless to anyone except those who have the key. This capability is particularly beneficial where valuable AS/400 information might be exposed to unauthorized access via a communications network like the Internet.

The 4754 Security Interface Unit (SIU) is an optional device that attaches to the cryptographic processor and allows the user to enter cryptography keys by sliding a personal security card through a reader. The 2620 Cryptographic Processor is restricted to use in the United States and Canada. Outside the United States and Canada, the 2628 Cryptographic Processor must be used. The 2628 uses a lower-precision algorithm.

Product Preview PCI Cryptographic IOA (#4800)

The #4800 PCI Cryptographic IOA is a half-length PC form factor PCI adapter which offers rich cryptography functions. The adapter securely stores the cryptographic keys. Bulk data encryption on the adapter is performed at 12 MBps. The #4800 is available worldwide. The level of cryptographic function provided is determined by software which is downloaded to the adapter. The #4800 is supported under the #2824 in any PCI slot.

0059 Transition Data Link

The 0059 Transition Data Link is used to ease the transition from System/36 or System/38 to AS/400. The 0059 is a stand-alone device that allows a S/3X to be attached to an AS/400 through local workstation controllers, as shown in Figure 2.42. This physical connection, along with the System/36 or System/38 migration aids and OS/400 allows the operator to efficiently transfer information from one system to the other at twinaxial cable speeds (with a raw data rate of over 1 million bps). This provides an alternative to using the time-consuming and error-prone diskette or tape method of transferring information between systems.

The 0059 may be the only alternative for information transfer if the two systems are not configured with compatible tape or diskette devices. Local workstations can also be attached to the 0059, allowing them to access either system from a single terminal. The users hit a simple keystroke sequence to switch from one system to the other. Printers attached to the 0059, however, must be dedicated to one system or the other. The 0059 attaches to one workstation controller port on each system, providing seven addresses from each system. These seven addresses can be dedicated to information transfer between systems, work-

Figure 2.42. Example of a 0059 transition data link configuration.

station support, or any combination of the two. Usually, the more addresses assigned to transferring information between the two systems, the higher the transfer rate.

Terminal Multiconnector and Telephone Twisted-Pair Adapter

The most common way to attach local workstations to application systems is through twinaxial cable. The 5299 Terminal Multiconnector and Telephone Twisted-Pair Adapter (TTPA) shown in Figure 2.43 provides a wiring alternative. With TTPA, unused telephone twisted-pair wiring is used. That may already be installed in the building, as long as it conforms to IBM Type 3 Media specifications. This reduces wiring costs at the expense of the maximum distance allowable from the computer or remote workstation controller to any workstation. With twinaxial cable this distance is 5000 feet, with the less expensive twisted-pair it is 1000 feet. The 5299 provides 10 telephone connectors that are used to attach up to seven workstations and one computer system (two connectors are used for problem determination procedures). The 5299/TTPA connections can coexist with twinaxially attached workstations on other ports of the computer system. The 5299 and TTPA do not require power to operate.

Figure 2.43. The 5299 Terminal Multiconnector and Telephone Twisted-Pair Adapter.

3

AS/400 Software

The previous chapters closely examined the system units and optional equipment of the Application Systems. This chapter begins the discussion of how that hardware is put to work, namely, the all-important **software**. Software is a general term for the many programs that execute in computers. It is software that harnesses the Application Systems' computational power and allows you to perform many diverse and useful tasks. The chapter begins by introducing you to the software structure used by the AS/400 and continues with a discussion of the kinds of software used to actually perform useful work with Application Systems. The three general categories of software along with the job each performs are discussed. Then, AS/400's compatibility with software written for System/3X computers is discussed, followed by a group of programs that fit into the applications category, but are useful across a wide spectrum of businesses.

AS/400 Software Architecture Overview

A computer system is divided into two functional categories, software and hardware. Hardware is the part of the computer system that provides some form of tactile feedback like hardness when you touch it and is recognizable as rectangular or oblong in shape when you look at it. Software is the part of the computing system that executes the work on the system. Software is programs. The model of software that constitutes the programs that execute on the AS/400 systems is divided into three segments, application programs, operating system programs, and SLIC programs. Figure 3.1 illustrates the layered structure relationship of the three segments. The user's view of application systems is illustrated by the arrows at the top of the figure. That is, the user sees mostly the application programs which are being executed, with barely a glimpse at the operating system functioning behind the scenes (what the user perceives is governed by the methodology provided by the operating system).

Application programs (the shaded area in Figure 3.2) constitute the work that is desired to be performed on the computer. Those application programs range from a relatively straightforward function such as payroll (an individual's hours worked are multiplied by a pay rate, appropriate taxes are subtracted and retained, and finally a check is printed out for the individual) to data mining (which looks for subtle relationships in information accumulated indirectly).

The **operating systems** layer in our model is shown shaded in Figure 3.3 directly below the application programming layer. The operating

Figure 3.1. Conceptual software model of the Application System's basic software structure. The three layers of the software model work together (and with the hardware) to perform useful work for the user.

186 EXPLORING IBM AS/400 COMPUTERS

Figure 3.2. The application program software layer of the model. The application program defines the particular tasks the computer is performing for the user.

Figure 3.3. The operating system software layer of the model. The operating system provides the environment in which the application program(s) run.

systems layer interfaces directly to the application programs and performs tasks for the application under control of the application. Application programs rely on the operating system to perform many of the detailed housekeeping tasks associated with the internal workings of the computer. The operating system provides the environment in which applications execute. Operating systems accept commands directly from the user to do such things as copying files and changing passwords. The operating system must also manage the system variables used for tailoring the major types of objects supported by the system, such as programs, files, and communication protocols, and provide national language support. The details of operating systems are discussed in greater detail in Chapter 4, which is devoted to AS/400 operating systems. The integrated nature and the rich set of functions of the AS/400 operating system (OS/400) is among the things that make the AS/400 different from other midrange computers.

The third and final layer of software in the software model (the shaded area in Figure 3.4) is called the **System Licensed Internal Code**

Figure 3.4. The SLIC software layer of the model. SLIC directly controls the hardware elements of the application systems and shields application programs and the operating system from hardware details.

(SLIC) layer. SLIC in many ways is considered as part of the hardware because it instructs the hardware directly what to do for the software. Unlike application programs or operating systems, SLIC is used only by other programs. SLIC never interacts directly with the user or programmer and exists only to help application programs and the operating system perform their tasks. SLIC instructions help hide the hardware specifics from the application programs, making application-program compatibility possible across a wide range of hardware.

System Licensed Internal Code and some of its interfaces to the hardware and operating system are part of the **Technology Independent Machine Interface** which has enabled the AS/400 to continuously improve the hardware and operating system while maintaining compatibility to the applications set.

In the following paragraphs the use of SLIC in the AS/400 is explained in more detail, and then the factors that differentiate the AS/400 and other computer software layers are described in "How the AS/400's Software Layers are Different." How the layers interact with each other is described in "How the Layers Work Together." AS/400 software compatibility with System S/3X programs is then identified in "AS/400 Software Compatibility—Will S/3X Programs Work?" AS/400 software compatibility through CISC and RISC hardware evolutions is discussed in "Inside AS/400 Compatibility." Finally, "Applications Architecture" addresses the areas of program portability, program interaction, and standard user interface. After the introduction to application program architecture, the remainder of the chapter is devoted to describing the characteristics and attributes of selected prewritten applications and comparing those applications versus custom applications.

System Licensed Internal Code (SLIC)

System Licensed Internal Code (SLIC) is the third layer of the software model. The set of SLIC instructions in AS/400 computers is embedded deeply within the computer system and is considered to be part of the computing machine itself rather than part of a program running on the machine. Unlike application programs or operating systems, SLIC is used only by other programs. It is the particularly rich SLIC layer in AS/400 that helps set its architecture apart from those of more conventional computers. The built-in database, single-level storage, object-oriented architecture, and other AS/400 features described in "Hardware Architecture Overview" in Chapter 1 are all designed into the SLIC layer of AS/400, making them part of the machine itself. This results in highly efficient, consistent, and easy-to-use implementations of these functions.

SLIC is a set of extremely simple instructions (never seen by the computer programmer or user) that are directly performed by the electronic circuits within the system processor. All user program instructions are automatically converted into a series of these SLIC instructions, which are then executed by the system processor. The portion of the instruction cache used for SLIC is dynamic and movable within the instruction cache space. In any case, because there are more SLIC instructions than can fit in the **Instruction cache (I-cache)**, some must reside in the slower main storage area. All SLIC instructions in the I-cache will execute in one I-cache cycle time, or the time it takes the I-cache to respond to the system processor's request for the SLIC instruction. Because all actions of the system processor are dictated by SLIC instructions, the system processor runs in lockstep with the I-cache cycles. When needed, SLIC instructions are in the slower main storage and the system processor is delayed, reducing the overall system performance. The larger I-cache area provided in the AS/400 computers holds more of the SLIC instructions, thus contributing to higher system performance.

How the AS/400's Software Layers Are Different

One of the basic differences between AS/400 and traditional computer systems can be seen by examining the software layers. Figure 3.5 shows the three software layers of our model (application, operating system, and SLIC) in a little more detail. The figure shows the traditional software layers side by side with those of the AS/400. The first thing to notice is the difference between where the various software functions reside in the layers. In the traditional system, functions such as security, database, and communications reside in the operating system layer (which is usually made up of a collection of separately purchased operating system products). With this traditional approach, each operating system product must be installed and maintained separately. This is why a highly skilled individual called a **systems programmer** is needed to support this kind of system.

Figure 3.5. The AS/400's software architecture differs from that of more traditional systems. Implementing more function in the SLIC layer and providing a one-piece operating system results in improved efficiency, consistency, and simplicity.

With the AS/400 approach, much of the basic database, security, and other functions are built into the SLIC layer. Because SLIC implementations are in general more efficient (by nature of their "closeness" to the hardware), overall system performance is improved. The operating system for the AS/400 (OS/400) provides all its functions in a single product. This eliminates the need for the operator to install, tailor, and manage the multiple operating system components in traditional operating systems and make sure that each works with the others as new versions are shipped at different times. The price you pay for this simplicity is that you get all OS/400 functions whether you need them or not, whereas the user of traditional systems can select only the traditional operating system components needed at a given time (of course the user is now responsible for ensuring that these selected components work properly together.)

Another basic difference lies in the way a programmer properly "sees" the systems. With the traditional system, system functions such as database management or security reside in the operating system and therefore can be modified by a systems programmer. This gives the systems programmer more flexibility in customizing the computer system at the expense of more complexity. With the AS/400, ease of use and efficiency are gained at the price of some flexibility. For example, because the database functions are built into the SLIC instructions, they cannot be modified. If programmers want to change how the database is managed, there are some things they simply cannot do. In a traditional system environment, the database functions are not part of the operating system but are purchased as a separate component, such as Oracle, Sybase, or Informix. Thus, there's a choice with other systems that is not available in OS/400.

How the Layers Work Together

To appreciate how the three software layers work together in performing tasks for the user, we'll trace a typical series of events of a computer session. Let's set the stage by beginning with Figure 3.6, where a salesperson is using a word processing program to type a memo to a prospective customer. The word processing application program has finished processing the most recent set of keystrokes and instructs the operating system to provide the next set of keystrokes when they are available. To comply with the request, the operating system asks the SLIC instructions to provide the next set of keystrokes when available.

Now that the stage is set, see what happens as the salesperson types the next line in the letter. When the salesperson holds down the Shift key and presses the T key on the keyboard, the terminal sends the **scan code** corresponding to each key over the twinaxial cable to the workstation controller in the AS/400. The workstation controller receives the scan code and translates it into its intended meaning. Because the workstation controller knows that the Shift key has been pressed and not released, the scan code associated with the T is translated into the letter T. Next, the workstation controller stores the T in a buffer area and echoes the T to the workstation, where it appears on the display.

192 EXPLORING IBM AS/400 COMPUTERS

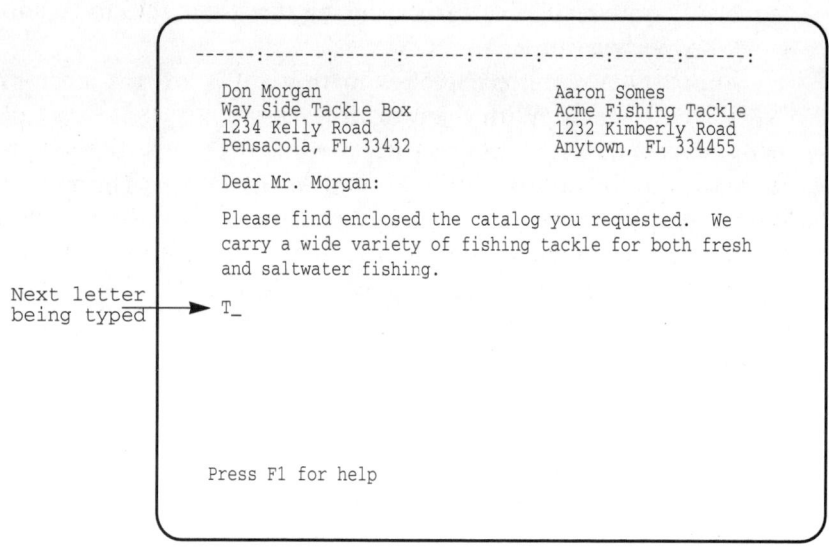

Figure 3.6. A salesperson is typing a memo using a word processing application program. The salesperson has just pressed the T key on the keyboard while also depressing the Shift key.

Notice that the workstation controller manages this entire transaction independent of the main processor or any of the software layers. This is typical of the multiprocessor architecture, which allows the main processor to concentrate on the user's application program rather than managing workstation traffic. In fact, the workstation controller will continue to manage all interaction with the salesperson's terminal until the salesperson presses the Enter key at the end of the line. The scan code associated with the Enter key signals the workstation controller to interrupt the main processor and notify it that new information is ready for use.

Here is where the software layers of our model come into play. First the SLIC verifies that all went well in receiving the information; then it notifies the operating system that the information is correct, ready, and waiting for use. The operating system makes the information available to the application program and then reactivates the application program, which was dormant and waiting for the next keystroke. The application program processes the information as necessary, instructs the operating system to wait for the next keystroke, and the whole thing starts all over again.

For simplicity, we have glossed over many of the detailed steps that the computer must perform simply to process a series of keystrokes. As complicated as this process may be, computers easily perform these steps in small fractions of a second. Similar but more complicated cooperation among the three software layers occurs for most functions performed by the computer, such as reading or writing a file on a disk and communicating with other computers.

Software Compatibility

In the following sections, we will build on the discussion of software layers to explain compatibility issues of the AS/400 Application System. We will delve into making your system backwards-compatible with prior systems and introduce you to how programming code is written.

AS/400 Software Compatibility—Will S/3X Programs Work?

Before the introduction of the AS/400, the System/3X computer family was the most widely used business computing system in the world. As a result, a wide variety of application programs had been developed for those computers. The flexibility afforded by virtue of this large and diverse software base allowed System/3X computers to fill many different needs. Of course, this tremendous choice of available programs did not exist when the original System/3X computers were first announced. It took the independent efforts of a great many people over many years to develop the large software base that exists today for System/3X. To capitalize on that software base, software compatibility was a primary objective in the design of AS/400 computers. That is, most programs written for the System/3X family will either run directly on or can be easily migrated to AS/400 computers.

It is important to understand that of the three software layers in our software model, compatibility with programs in the application program layer is the most important. Why? First, application programs typically represent the primary share of a user's software investment. Being forced to abandon an application program because of incompatibilities may also make the user throw away whatever data and training/experience have accumulated with the application program—both of which can be substantial. Some users have developed custom application programs at considerable cost in development time and money. Incompatibility at the application program level would render these programs virtually useless. Last, and perhaps most important, application layer compatibility allows AS/400 Application Systems users access to the thousands of application programs that have been developed for System/3X computers.

What about the operating system and SLIC layers? Maintaining compatibility with earlier System/3X operating systems software is not as important for several reasons. Operating systems typically represent only a small fraction of the user's software investment. The AS/400 maintained the S/38 machine interface (also referred to as the technology-independent machine interface) layer through the development of the AS/400, CISC, and RISC transitions, even though the microcode under that layer was allowed to change to accommodate the new hardware.

Further, a new operating system is usually necessary to allow the users to have access to the new features of the computer system not considered by the programmers of the old operating system. In 1996, the AS/400 announced the capability for concurrent execution of System/36 SSP-compatible applications with OS/400 on all models of the AS/400. In 1994, AS/400 Advanced System 36 Model 236 was announced, offering direct execution of System/36 application programs. In 1995, coexistence and concurrent execution of OS/400 and SSP application programs on the Advanced 36 Model 436 was announced. Of course the user is automatically supplied with a new SLIC layer that fully supports the hardware with every AS/400 system.

Inside AS/400 Compatibility

To understand AS/400 compatibility you must understand something about how software is typically written. First, a programmer writes a program's instructions or **code** using a **programming language** (e.g., COBOL or RPG), which is basically a library of computer instructions from which a programmer may choose to write programs. The list of programming language instructions is called **source code**. To run the program on a computer, the source code instructions must be converted into instructions a computer can understand. This conversion process is called **compiling** the program. When source code is compiled, the result, called **object code**, can be directly executed by the computer hardware. In addition to programming languages, the programmer can use predefined lists of operating system commands to do things like start programs and present menus. These predefined lists are called **procedures**. With this background, let us look at how AS/400 provides compatibility with System/3X programs.

Programs written for System/38 computers, in general, are *object-code-compatible* with AS/400 systems. That is, you can take the object code for a program written for a System/38, load it on an AS/400, and run the program. This is possible because of AS/400's **System/38 environment**, which makes the AS/400 system look like a System/38 to the application program. Furthermore, most of the operating system commands used on the System/38 are the same as those used on AS/400. For this reason, System/38 procedures will also run with little or no change.

Programs written for the System/36 are supported on AS/400 through the **SSP operating system**. SLIC has an emulation that looks at every instruction from the S/36—operating system, utilities, compilers, and applications—and executes the correct sequence of AS/400 instructions. Regardless of basic differences between the architectures of the AS/400 Systems and the System/36, AS/400 systems are now object code compatible with System/36 application programs. There is no longer any need for a programmer to make any changes in the application program source code. Simply load the System/36 object code on an AS/400 without recompiling. The program can then be run under AS/400's SSP operating system. On all RISC-based systems, SSP programs (even with Assembler code embedded) will execute with the performance improvements provided by the RISC environment. OS/400 Version 4 Release 2 is provided with every AS/400 system unit purchased. SSP can only be obtained with a separate license for its use.

Applications Architecture

In the early 1990s IBM had a project called SAA (**Systems Application Architecture**). The project's goals were to accomplish portability, interoperability, and user interface compatibility. All of IBM's system development locations were involved, and the rules to achieve the three objectives were established. The SAA project is no longer in existence, but the AS/400 system developers continue to follow the rules. As a result, the AS/400 is a leader in providing programs that meet SAA requirements for the support of object-oriented programming, multimedia, client/server, and intranet/Internet computing.

Program Portability

Portability means that an application program can easily be migrated across family boundaries (e.g., from an AS/400 to a System/390 mainframe) with only minor changes. This allows the user to migrate any application programs to larger (or smaller) computers as business needs change. Plus, the same application program can be used on multiple types of computers that may be found in a single business, bringing common function to all users. Another advantage of program portability is that programmers who follow the conventions established by SAA can offer their programs to users of computers in all three families. This gives users a wider variety of programs from which to choose.

EZ Setup provides a graphical user interface for guiding the new AS/400 user through the process of getting his system functioning for the first time. An **EZ Setup Wizard** leads the user through the steps needed to get the system functioning and customized for the business. The Wizard simplifies the initial setup tasks and reduces the setup time. It also configures local access or the **Operations Console**, performs initial NetServer configuration for Client Access, and launches Operations Navigator. EZ-Setup can auto-start attached servers. Appendix D is a compilation of the screens seen by the operator during the EZ-Setup activity. Among the areas of assistance provided by EZ-Setup are:

- Installing Client Access for Windows 95/NT base functions and Operations Navigator on a PC with a 32 bit Window Operating System

- Connecting the PC to an AS/400 system

- Setting the AS/400 system name, date, time, and security values

- Creating AS/400 security and system operator profiles

- Defining LAN connections for token-ring, Ethernet, and IPCS adapters

- Defining TCP/IP interfaces, starting TCP/IP and host servers

- Creating shortcuts to AS/400, Technical Studio, service home pages, and installing the Netscape browser

- Launching the Welcome Center

Welcome Center

Users can quickly go from "out-of-box" to a basic operating state, by means of a browser-based information tool called Welcome Center. Welcome Center guides users through installation and configuration of a new AS/400 system. The Welcome Center is tailored to users familiar with a PC Windows interface, but new to the AS/400 interface. Information is layered to provide as much or as little information as needed. The information is divided into:

- **Customize for your Business.** Here, users can choose additional setup tasks appropriate to their environment. EZ-Setup users are automatically brought to this section if they elect to launch Welcome Center.

- **Guided Setup.** These are the steps needed to manually perform the same tasks that EZ-Setup can perform automatically.

- **What's Next.** This includes directions on other areas a user may want to explore.

The **companion programs** EZ-Setup and Welcome Center are shipped on a CD-ROM. These programs run on a PC with the Windows 95, 98, or NT operating system and require **Operations Console** software to be installed. The PC must be connected to the AS/400 system via the Operations Console Cable.

Program Interaction

By following the communications conventions, one program can communicate directly with another program running on a different computer system. The programs in different families of computers in a network can cooperate directly with one another with little or no user assistance. This relieves the user of having to control the interaction between various computer systems and provides for a sophisticated computer environment.

Standard User Interface

It takes time for a user to learn to use a given application program. Not only must the basic function provided be understood (for instance, spreadsheet or database), the user must also learn the details of interacting with the user interface of a specific program. This includes function key definitions, how to select a menu item, call up help information, and so on. The Systems Application Architecture has defined standards for these items and other interface elements called **Common User Access (CUA)**. The goal of these user interface standards is to allow for transfer of learning, ease of learning, and ease of use across programs for all major computer families.

Application Programs

The software architecture overview described how three basic software layers in an Application System cooperate to perform useful work for the user. A layered model was used to illustrate the software architecture. This section concentrates on the top layer of the model—application programs. It is the application programs that "apply" the Application Systems' computational power to a particular business task.

IBM has created some naming conventions for AS/400 applications to distinguish those that execute on the preceding CISC-based systems from those that execute on RISC-based systems. The intention is that the CISC-based applications will always execute on the RISC-based systems, but eventually some programs will be written for the RISC-based systems that will not execute on the CISC-based systems. Thus, when you see an application with "/400" in the name (e.g., Ultimedia/400), it will execute on both RISC- and CISC-based systems. However, when you see an application with "for OS/400" in the name (e.g., Ultimedia for OS/400), it will only be guaranteed to execute on the RISC-based systems.

Some businesses use application programs designed, written, and sold by other companies. These are called **prewritten** application programs. Compatible programs include those written by IBM, those written by IBM Business Partners, IBM AS/400 Client Series, and those written by general software vendors. The programs written by software vendors are supported on the AS/400 under Client Access/400 and execute on AS/400 client systems, not originally on AS/400. Examples of Client Access/400–supported programs will be discussed in Chapter 4.

Other companies choose to design and write their own **custom** application programs or use a combination of prewritten and custom application programs. The remainder of this chapter looks at both application program alternatives. Some prewritten application programs are discussed, but by no means does this chapter provide a complete consumers' guide to all prewritten software for AS/400. Comprehensive coverage of the many business application program products available today would fill many books, which would be obsolete by the time they were published.

This chapter helps the reader to make more informed purchasing decisions and gives examples of the kinds of things available from prewritten application programs. In the last part of the chapter, we briefly look at custom software alternatives.

Can Prewritten Programs Fit the Bill?

Today's **prewritten application programs range** from simple programs that concentrate on a very specific task to powerful and very complex groups of programs designed to work together. They perform many functions—as diverse as the environments in which computers are found today. Many prewritten application programs are useful in most business environments (for example, **word processing** and **accounting**). These are known as **cross-industry** application programs because they are not specific to any particular industry segment. Other prewritten applications address the specialized needs of a particular industry (e.g., manufacturing or utilities). These are called **industry-specific** application programs. As a rule, the application programs written by IBM fit into a cross-industry category as opposed to an industry-specific category. The applications programs in the IBM AS/400 Client Series written by IBM business partners tend as a group to fit more readily into an industry-specific grouping set. In both cases, there are exceptions.

Cross-Industry Application Programs

Examples of popular available application programs written by IBM include the following AS/400 programs:

- OfficeVision/400
- AFP PrintSuite for AS/400
- AnyMail/400
- Query/400
- Encoded Vector Indexing
- AS/400 Business Graphics Utility
- ImagePlus/400
- Facsimile Support/400
- CallPath/400
- Ultimedia System Facilities (multimedia)
- Ultimedia Business Conferencing/400 (multimedia)
- Job Scheduler/400
- Lotus Notes/Domino
- Data Warehousing
- Data Mining

Brief descriptions of the functions of the listed application programs are now provided.

OfficeVision for AS/400

There are many time-consuming and labor-intensive activities involved in simply conducting business in a typical office environment—for example, generating/distributing documents, sending/reading notes, and scheduling/attending meetings. The **Office Vision for AS/400** (5763-WP1 for Version 3 Release 1 [CISC], and 5769-WP1 for Version 4 Release 1 [RISC]) application program for AS/400 systems is designed to streamline these types of activities, improving the overall operation of the office and thus of the business in general. Figure 3.7 shows an example of a simple OfficeVision for AS/400 environment. The AS/400 system is running OfficeVision for AS/400—and display stations, printers, and personal computers (PCs) are attached. Any user of any display station or PC can access the functions offered by OfficeVision for AS/400.

Figure 3.7. Example of an OfficeVision for AS/400 environment.

OfficeVision for AS/400 also supports Lotus Notes 4.5 client access to the mail, directory, and calendar services of the AS/400.

The various functions provided by OfficeVision for AS/400 can all be accessed by selecting the appropriate series of icon options. This icon-driven approach makes OfficeVision for AS/400 easier to use. More experienced OfficeVision for AS/400 word processing users can bypass the icons by entering commands at the bottom of the screen. This allows the more experienced user to go more quickly to the desired function within OfficeVision for AS/400. Figure 3.8 illustrates the main menu for OfficeVision for AS/400.

Now let's look at the functions provided by OfficeVision for AS/400. The new client/server versions of AS/400 extend OfficeVision for AS/400 functions beyond the boundaries of a single AS/400. That is, most of the calendar functions can be performed on a remote calendar as though it were local. This includes printing a remote calendar on a local printer,

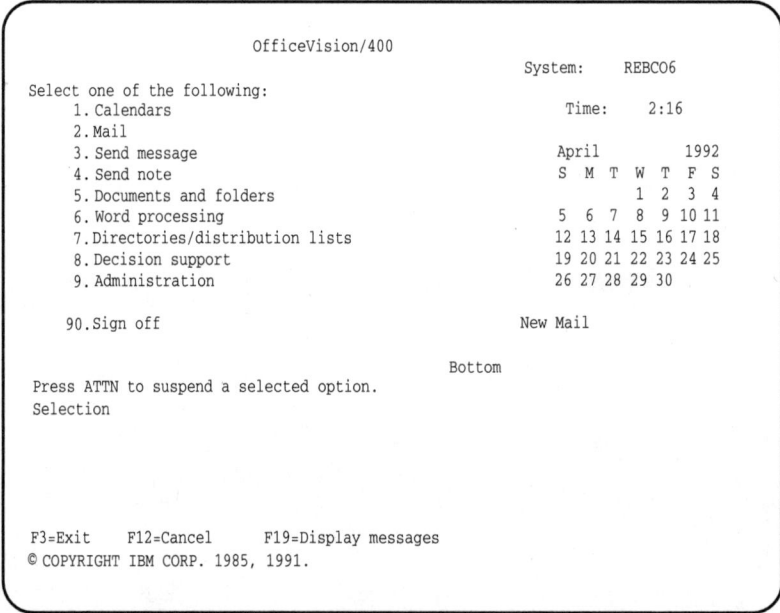

Figure 3.8. OfficeVision for AS/400 main menu (functions can be accessed through menus or commands).

support for the industry standards on electronic mail (TCP/IP SMTP/MIME), providing extended application interface capability such as exits to call an alternate program (for instance, a fax application), and providing an alternate administration program (for integrating programs).

OfficeVision for AS/400 has a graphical user interface and is designed for business professionals who manage a variety of appointments, projects, and people on a daily basis. This easily customizable software program combines the desktop personal productivity tools of a Windows-based **Personal Information Manager (PIM)** with the features and flexibility of IBM OfficeVision for AS/400. Through an intuitive graphical user interface, you can access host OfficeVision for AS/400 functions (e.g., electronic mail, document processing and management, calendar services, and information storage) from your PC.

The following list provides a thumbnail sketch of OfficeVision/400 functions:

- *Calendar Management.* An electronic version of a personal appointment book with group scheduling capability does for time management what word processing and electronic mail do for business correspondence. Calendars on the Notes client hard drive and AS/400 are synchronized. Figure 3.9 illustrates the OfficeVision calendar function.

- *Electronic Mail.* Electronic versions of written communications range from a hand-delivered note to a colleague down the hall to complex documents express-mailed across global distances. When electronic mail is received, the user can store, print, reply to, or forward the mail with a few keystrokes. Mail is sent to AS/400 user IDs and downloaded to the Notes client. Figure 3.10 illustrates the OfficeVision screen for sending an electronic message.

- *Document Management.* A document library function allows management of the large number of documents typically associated with the office environment. Documents in the document library are stored in folders with other related documents. The AS/400 security system limits document access to those authorized by the document author. Figure 3.11 shows the OfficeVision folder management screen.

204 EXPLORING IBM AS/400 COMPUTERS

```
                              Weekly Calendar
   8a
   ............          _____   Calendar......   STRAND RECO6
   MON                   TUE .........A WED .........A THU .........A FRI
   04/06/92              04/07/92      04/08/92        04/09/92        04/10/92
   8a                    8a            8:00a.....E  3  8a              8a
   _____         _____   VACATION DAY    _____ _____
   9a                    9a            LYNN BACK UP    9:00a.....M  4  9:00a.....M  6
   _____         _____   _____ STAFF MEETING   STAFF MEETING
   10:00a....E  1        10a           _____ 10a             10a
   CUSTOMER              _____   _____ _____ _____
   REQUESTS              11a           _____ 11a             11a
   _____         _____   _____ _____ _____
   12n                   12n           _____ 12n             12n
   _____         _____   _____ _____ _____
   1p                    1:00p.....E 2 _____ 1:00p.....E  5  1p
   _____         EQUIPMENT     _____ PERFORMANCE     _____
   2p                    REQUIREMENTS  _____ SPECIFICATION   2p
   _____         J.D. CONT.    _____ H09Q18          _____
   3p                    _____   _____ _____ 3p
   _____         _____   _____ _____ _____
   4p[                              5:00p           500:p          5:00p

   F3=Exit              F4=Prompt       F6=Add item       F=9Display item
   F10=Change item      F12=Cancel      F16=Remove item   F24=More keys
```

Figure 3.9. Screen from OfficeVision for AS/400's calendar function.

```
                              Send Message
   Type message.
        Todd, I need your report today on the sales results for the last quarter.
   Debbie


   Type distribution list and/or addressees, press F10 to send.
         Distribution list ........  _____ _____  F4 for list

   -----Addresses-----
   User ID   Address    Description
   TJS       RCHTOWN
   ADMIN     LOCAL
   _____   _____
   _____   _____
   _____   _____
   _____   _____
   _____   _____
                                                                   More. . .
   F3=Exit      F4=Prompt    F5=Refresh    F9=Attach memo slip    F10=Send
   F12=Cancel   F13=Change defaults   F18=Sort by user id    F19=Display messages
```

Figure 3.10. Screen used to send an electronic message to another user.

- *Word Processing.* Documents can be created and edited, including changing, inserting, moving, copying, and deleting text. Text can be underlined, highlighted, and centered on a page. With the Language Dictionaries/400 program (5738-DCT), various proofreading capabilities can automatically check for spelling errors against multiple dictionaries and make corrections. Figure 3.12 shows the screen used in OfficeVision to search for particular words or phrases in a word processing environment, and Figure 3.13 shows the screen used to create documents in that environment.

- *Word Processing Enhancements.* It is also possible to completely replace the OfficeVision word processing function with *WordPerfect* for the AS/400. Images, graphics, tables, charts, may all be imported and embedded in documents created in OfficeVision for AS/400 word processing.

```
                      Work with Documents in Folders

   Folder ....  STRAND
   POSITION TO .......  _____   Starting characters

   Type Options (and Document), press enter.
      1=Create      2=Revise      3=Copy        4=Delete        5=View
      6=Print       7=Rename      8=Details     9=Print options 10=Send
      11=Spell      12=File remote 13=Paginate  14=Authority

   Opt Document      Document Description         Revised      Type

   __ _____
      LETTER           Practice Letter           04/08/92     RFTAS400




                                                                    Bottom
   F3=Exit      F4=Prompt    F5=Refresh   F10=Search for document
   F11=Display names only    F12=Cancel   F13=End search    F24=More keys
```

Figure 3.11. OfficeVision for AS/400 documents are organized into folders conceptually like those in filing cabinets.

EXPLORING IBM AS/400 COMPUTERS

```
                        Specify Document Text Criteria

     Document list description.............:  SAMPLE

     Language............................:  ENU   US English

     Type seach criteria, press F10 to start search.
        AND: +    OR:  |


                                                    AND/
     Phrases                                         OR      Exact     Synonym
     Monthly * report                                 ±       N          N
     1992                                             -       N          N
     _____         -       N          N
     _____         -       N          N
     _____         -       N          N
     _____         -       N          N
     _____         -       N          N
                                                                      More. . .

     F3=Exit      F10=Start search    F11=Specify document details criteria
     F12=Cancel   F16=AND all phrases F17=OR all phrases  F24=More keys
```

Figure 3.12. Screen used to search for a document by specifying words to look for within the text of the documents.

```
     LETTER P:12                    Edit                  pg:1     Ln:7
     <2...T:...T3...T:...T4...T:...T5...Tv...T6...T:...T7...T:...T8...T:.
     ..T9
     Today's office activities can be divided into four major categories-
     business communications, administrative services, decision support
     and business applications. IBM recognizes this reality, and IBM
     office software is designed accordingly.

     IBM office software programs are designed to work with each other.
     This enables you to access information from an application in one
     program, such as a spreadsheet, incorporate it into another applica-
     tion, then distribute the document electronically to all branch
     office locations.




     F1=Copy        F7=Window        F14=Get option       F20=Change formats
     F2=Move        F8=Reset         F15=Table/Columns    F21=Nondisplay keys
     F3=Exit/Save   F9=Instructions  F16=Adjust/Paginate  F22=Spell functions
     F4=Find char   F11=Hyphenate    F17=Function         F23=Word spell aid
```

Figure 3.13. Screen used to create documents in OfficeVision for AS/400.

- *Contextual Help.* This is provided by pressing the Help key. **Hypertext links** are also provided in the *word processing* help text.

- *Directory Management.* Personal directories, distribution lists, and the system directory may all be managed with OfficeVision for AS/400. In a network of AS/400 systems running OfficeVision for AS/400, the system directory of one AS/400 can be **shadowed** on all other AS/400 systems. Nicknames and distribution lists can be downloaded to the Notes client. Figure 3.14 shows an example of a personal phone directory in OfficeVision.

- *Internet Addressing.* This function is provided by an alternate mail addressing panel into which either an Internet address or a regular OfficeVision for AS/400 address can be entered. The addressing panel will accept any Internet address. Distribution

```
                    Specify Personal Directory Criteria

   Type choice, press Enter

   Personal directory.............:  EXAMPLEDIR      Name, F4 for List

   Description....................:  IBM-Supplied Example Telephone Directory

   Type search criteria, press Enter.
        Last name .........   _____      Blank=All
        First name ........   _____            Blank=All
        Street address ....   _____  Blank=All
        Postal code .......   _____            Blank=All
        Area code .........   ___                   Blank=All
        Phone number ......   _____            Blank=All




   F3=Exit       F4=Prompt         F5=Refresh         F6=Add entries
   F11=Change entries    F12=Cancel    F13=More tasks    F19=Display messages
```

Figure 3.14. Example of a personal phone directory using the directory function in OfficeVision for AS/400.

lists may also be entered using this panel. Figure 3.15 illustrates the appearance of this panel. PostNet Bar Code is also supported, enabling the business to take advantage of the Post Office discounts offered when zip codes are printed in the PostNet Bar Code on mailing envelopes.

In addition to the functions that are built into OfficeVision for AS/400, the capability to bring in additional functions is included. Up to ten user options are allowed on the main menu. The OfficeVision for AS/400 offers a decision support path to some separately purchased program products such as Query/400, JustMail for AS/400, and the AS/400 Business Graphics Utility. Another OfficeVision for AS/400 capability is to provide a path to functions defined by programmers employed by your company. Finally, OfficeVision for AS/400 provides an application programming interface that allows other programs to interact directly with OfficeVision for AS/400. This type of program-to-program interaction

```
                                    Send Note
         Type mailing information, press F6 to type note.

         Subject ..............  _____
                                 _____
         Reference ............  _____
                                 _____
         Type distribution list and/or adresses, press F10 to send.
              Distribution list .........._____   _____   F4 for list
              ------------------------Addresses-------------------------
         Type nickname, user ID address, or internet address. One per line.
         BertM wlkas33 _____
         masie@vnet.IBM.com_____
         Langes@WLKAS33.DFW.IBM.COM_____
         MYRONA WLKAS19_____
         Bill_____
         _____
         _____
                                                                More....
         F3=Exit    F6=Type Note    F9=Attach memo slip    F10=Send    F11=Change details
         F12=Cancel    F13=Change send instructions    F14=Specify list    F24=More
```

Figure 3.15. Internet addressing mixed with local intranet addressing.

allows a programmer to add custom programs that cooperate with OfficeVision for AS/400 while shielding the user from the complexities of the interaction.

OfficeVision JustMail for AS/400 (5798-TBT)

OfficeVision JustMail for AS/400 (5798-TBT) can help provide the critical information a business needs when and where the business needs it. Like OfficeVision for AS/400, JustMail for AS/400 supports Lotus Notes 4.5 clients. JustMail for AS/400 is an entry-level mail system that allows business professionals to create, address, and transmit electronic mail worldwide. JustMail for AS/400 allows the AS/400 users to share and communicate messages, notes, documents, and PC files through a network. If the business needs to create and revise documents, customers can activate their favorite *word processing editor* and call it from the JustMail for AS/400 application enabler. JustMail for AS/400 uses the wide variety of communications protocols available on the AS/400 for mail exchange between IBM and non-IBM systems, public networks, and PC LANs.

JustMail for AS/400 supports Internet addressing through a mail addressing panel into which an Internet address or an OfficeVision for AS/400 address is entered. Any Internet address can be used without having a corresponding address in the system. Distribution lists may also be entered using this panel. JustMail for AS/400 also supports PostNet Bar Codes, allowing a business to take advantage of Post Office discounts for printing barcoded zip codes on mail envelopes.

AFP PrintSuite for AS/400 AFP

AFP PrintSuite for AS/400 is a family of application programs for transforming traditional line-mode printing to full-page documents and reports. Providing an output that blends application data with a variety of fonts, images, text, graphics, and barcoding. Although the standard interface to AFP document function is with DDS and external printer files, in some situations a different approach is required. For example, you may want to change the format of your invoice without making changes to the line-of-business invoicing program. The AFP PrintSuite products (with the exception of AFP Toolbox) enable application-independent document formatting. The intention is to apply the AS/400 print model to the network by managing AS/400 and network pages, and using IPDS to provide industrial strength printing over TCP/IP.

PrintSuite includes the following four separately orderable document formatting applications:

Advanced Print Utility (APU)

Advanced Print Utility (APU) is an interactive end-user system that transforms existing application output into advanced electronic documents. No application changes are required because APU works from the output spool file created by the application. Through a AS/400 user interface, a new document is built. The new document can incorporate electronic forms, images, fonts, barcodes, text, and other elements. The existing output data is brought up visually, so placement of each element on the page can be changed and the existing application data can conditionally determine page layout and the copies produced. This all-new production system has been enhanced to include outline fonts and enhanced field mapping. Once the document design is complete, the new application can be put into production using the APU monitor. The APU output monitor is a complete production subsystem that controls how APU applications (or any print application for that matter) are produced and managed, including user exits, queue control, and distribution logic. As an example, different copies of a single document (an invoice) can be automatically routed to different queues.

Page Printer Formatting Aid (PPFA)

Page Printer Formatting Aid (PPFA) is a compiler that converts AFP print formatting resources (page definitions and form definitions) from source to object format. Page and form definitions are standard AFP resources that control how line-mode application output (called **line data**) is mapped to a page. Once these definitions are created and specified in the printer file, existing application output is dynamically changed. Recent enhancements include finishing, Double Byte Character Sets (DBCS), outline fonts, and relative positioning. When the application is next run, it creates full pages of AFP output, not lines of SNA character sets. With page and form definitions, existing applications can be dynamically changed without changes to the application program.

AFP Toolbox

AFP Toolbox allows full control over the AFP print data stream, using an object programming interface. The AFP Toolbox consists of a set of C and **C++ objects**, functions, and callable **Application Program Interfaces (API's)** that can be used to format complex printed electronic output. Two application areas in which AFP Toolbox is particularly useful are (1) when each page is tailored to the data contained on that page and (2) when applications have a standard interface to output, allowing the addition of enhanced output characteristics in one place. It is also possible to embed a scanned image into a document, or create a standard AFP "print driver" for a series of applications. The AFP Toolbox APIs enable a developer to code these document characteristics at a high level and have the appropriate AFP structure fields automatically created.

SAP R/3 AFP Print

SAP R/3 AFP Print provides AFP print support for SAP R/3 applications. Basic support enables R/3 reports to be printed on IPDS printers. Extended support enables enhancement of existing R/3 output (for example, an invoice) with electronic forms, typographic fonts, and images. SAP R/3 AFP Print is built into R/3 print processing for maximum efficiency.

AnyMail/400 and POP3

The AnyMail framework for mail in OS/400 embeds open network access, OfficeVision/400 directory, store-and-forward service, and customization options, giving the user a complete mail service offering. Through the directory users can keep track of the location of the people with whom they wish to exchange mail. The directory information can automatically connect one user's system to any of the open networks that cannot connect to the Internet—ARPA, Internet, CompuServe, America Online, Prodigy, and so on.

In addition to the open network connection capability, AnyMail can also bridge between local area networks and can be customized to match the security and multimedia functions that are desired. If the Fax for AS/400 product is installed and fax connections have been set up correctly, it is possible to send any document directly from your print spooler out on fax.

Multimedia content can be included in e-mail, which previously only included text. This means that images, video clips, and binary attachments such as spreadsheets and word processor documents can accompany e-mail. This support is compatible with the **Internet mail protocol (MIME)** and with the OfficeVision/400. These functions only work from an intelligent workstation such as a PC, not from non-programmable terminals such as the 5250 workstation.

Post Office Protocol, Version 3 (POP3) is the Internet client/server protocol that allows e-mail to be delivered temporarily to a post office server when the final destination client is not available or logged onto the post office server. POP3 mail is the **SMTP/MIME** format. The POP3 server is built as an extension on the AnyMail framework described earlier. POP3 allows a server to behave as if the destination for e-mail isn't a client but a server that receives mail on behalf of the client. The POP3 protocol then defines how a client will interact with its POP3 post office server. POP3 protocols allow a client to identify its POP3 post office on a server. The client can then ask about the mail stored there, request that the server deliver the mail, and allow the deletion of any unwanted mail. When a POP3 mail client logs onto a POP3 server, the user doesn't actually see the POP3 protocol being used. Usually POP3 retrieves all the e-mail received since the last time the client logged on. User clients supported by POP3 and AnyMail/400 include Windows 95 CC:Mail Release 7, Lotus cc:Mail, all versions of Eudora, OS/2 Warp's UltiMail Lite, all versions of Netscape 2.0, Windows 95 Microsoft Exchange, and Macintosh Claris Em@iler.

Query/400

To manage a business is to make many decisions based on the information available. Since computer systems manage the information of the business, it makes sense that the computer system should provide the management information necessary to make good business decisions. AS/400 database files organize vast amounts of business information. Since too much information can be as bad as not enough, the business problem is to find what information is necessary. Query/400 (5769-QU1) is designed to help summarize and sift through the information in

AS/400 databases. Query/400 can be started either from an OfficeVision for AS/400 menu (with appropriate function keys) or by issuing a command on any AS/400 command line.

To get the information wanted from an AS/400 database in the form desired, a **query** must be used. A query provides the *blueprint* specifying which information will be retrieved from the database and how it will be presented. Figure 3.16 shows the main menu for a query to a telephone directory database, and Figure 3.17 shows the report resulting from a query. Users can create their own queries by answering a series of questions presented on the screen. Since no programming experience is required for this, users' dependence on programmers is reduced, allowing the computer system to become a more flexible tool. However, users do need to learn some simple steps to create a query.

Depending on motivation and sophistication, users may or may not wish to create their own queries. If need be, a programmer can create a library of commonly used queries for users. Once the query is defined, it can be saved in the system, allowing any authorized user to generate the query report at any time by issuing a single command. The results of a

```
QUERY                              Query

Select one of the following:

        1. Work with queries
        2. Run an existing query
        3. Delete a query

       20. Files
       21. Office tasks




Selection or command
===> _____
     _____

F3=Exit         F4=Prompt      F12=Previous

[ ]
```

Figure 3.16. Main menu for a query to a telephone database.

```
NAME            STREETADDR        CITY              STATE   ZIPCODE

Susan P Ganters  987 Abbey Hwy    Mushroom Manor    OR      67891

Perry C Swenson  19821 Metro Hwy  St. Paul          OR      67891

Matt F Thomas    961 S 19th Ave   Piney Island      OR      67898
```

Figure 3.17. Report resulting from a user query to a telephone database.

query can be displayed on a terminal's display, printed on a printer, or saved in a new database file. The information can be merged into documents using OfficeVision/400 or the DisplayWrite word processing program (used on Personal System/2 computers). Query/400 can be used on any AS/400 database defined using the Interactive Data Definition Utility (IDDU), Data Description Specification (DDS), or Structured Query Language (SQL), all discussed in the section on OS/400. A version of Query/400 called **Query/36** is available for Advanced 36 SSP-based systems.

Encoded Vector Indexing

Encoded Vector Indexes are a new type of index that significantly improves query performance. Encoded Vector Indexing is an enhanced form of bit-mapped indexing, and can be used to build bit-mapped indexes on the fly. The **Encoded Vector Index (EVI)** keeps track of the distinct values that can be found in the key column, but instead of having a separate bit array for each distinct value, it assigns a code (1, 2, or 4 bytes) to each distinct key value.

The part of the EVI that maintains the translation from the key value to code is called the **symbol table**. The second sub-object of an EVI is the **vector**. The vector is an array in which the subscript of each array element represents the relative record number of a row; and the value contained in each element is the code for the value contained in the indexed column of that row. Figure 3.18 illustrates a symbol table and a vector. Encoded Vector Indexes provide accurate statistics for cost-based query optimization. The Encoded Vector Index is 1/16 the size of the old (RTREE) indexes. Bitmap indexes can be built up to ten times faster. The reduction in size allows more indexes to reside in main storage. Query performance is improved. Accurate statistics allow quicker and more intelligent query optimization. And Encoded Vector indexes provide protection from the "run-away" query.

Encoded Vector Indices can only be used for statistics and selection (not for ordering), can only be created through SQL, and cannot be journaled. The Encoded Vector Indices access path cannot be saved in V4R3, and the EVI logical file can only be opened in the arrival sequence, and has no data writes. Encoded Vector Indices can cause inserts or updates to fail if a new distinct key value is inserted and the distinct key value is exceeded for the EVI. EVI's are automatically rebuilt (refreshed) when distinct key count limits are near. For EVI's only,

Symbol Table

Value	Code	Count
Small	"X00"	2
Medium	"X01"	2
Large	"X02"	2
Ext Lg	"X03"	4

Where xx identifies the hex value of the code item

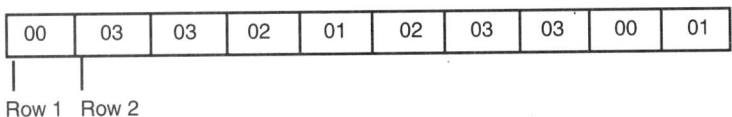

Row 1 Row 2

Create Encoded Vector Index i1 on t1(c1) with four distinct values

Figure 3.18. Illustration of a symbol table and a vector when using Encoded Vector Indices.

it is possible to display index types, distinct key counts, and overflow counts. The SQL Create Index statement is the only way to create an encoded vector access path. An encoded access path cannot be saved to a release prior to V4R3. "Star Schema" join support has been added to allow EVI's to be used to implement join queries for improved performance.

AS/400 Business Graphics Utility

Humans have always drawn images to present and interpret information. Images are native to humans and thus are both enjoyable and powerful communication devices. The greater the amount of information to be conveyed, the greater the need for graphic representations. It is therefore not surprising that business relies heavily on images to convey information to customers, employees, management, and so on. With the increased use of computers, it is also not surprising that computer-generated images (called **computer graphics**) are common in today's business environment. The AS/400 Business Graphics Utility (BGU) (5716-DS1) provides Application System users with a tool to construct a computer image. The BGU provides straightforward menus and contextual online help text. This, along with the exercises and tutorials provided in the "BGU User's Guide," allows nonprogrammers to create and use computer graphics.

This is how you create graphics with BGU. First, through a series of menus (or commands for more experienced users), the appearance and format of the desired image are defined. Next, the type of image (pie graph, bar graph, line graph, surface graph, histogram, Venn diagram, or text chart) is selected. Font style, size, color, and position are also selected. Once the format and appearance of the graphic image are defined, the data is input to the graph. The data can be provided by specifying a database file (containing the data) or by keying in the data from a keyboard. After the data have been placed into the graph format by either means, BGU can display the image in black and white or color on a graphic workstation such as a PS/2.

Because data are input separately from designing the graph format, the same BGU graph format can be used over and over again with different versions of the data. The chart management facility of BGU allows you to manage (copy, rename, etc.) your BGU graphics library. The data can be modified and then immediately regraphed to perform a "what-if" type of analysis. Images can also be printed on a plotter or graphics printer (e.g., a 4076 ExecJet II printer) or stored on the system using the **Graphics Data Format (GDF)**. As a GDF file, the image can be integrated into OfficeVision for AS/400 documents and applications as well as be used by other GDF-compatible computer systems (e.g., System/390).

Although there were BGU versions for the System/36 and System/38 computers, AS/400 BGU has been enhanced in the areas of GDF support, database input, number of chart types and fonts, and so forth. Most of the graphic images created with BGU/36 (5716-BGU) can be migrated to AS/400 BGU through available migration aids. System/38 BGU graphics easily migrate to AS/400 BGU through available migration aids.

ImagePlus/400

Surely computers have become the preferred way of collecting, managing, and distributing information in business today. However, a lot of paper is still circulating in offices because much of the day-to-day information needed to support business cannot be encoded in traditional computer systems. Examples of such information are *signed documents, photographs,* and documents that contain *both text and drawings.* Because of this **hard-to-manage information**, many highly computerized businesses still have to resort to the manual methods of doing business that have been with us since before the advent of computers. They must still deal with rows of filing cabinets, overflowing in-baskets, envelopes, stamps, mail delays, wastebaskets, couriers, and folders. Often, handling this hard-to-manage information creates bottlenecks in an office's productivity and can significantly delay the entire business cycle. Advances in computer performance and optical storage technology have resulted in products, such as IBM's ImagePlus systems, to handle this hard-to-manage information.

ImagePlus/400 is a family of hardware and software products designed to capture, store, and manipulate images. An **image** is an electronic photograph of a document that is stored inside a computer. Any type of document can be captured inside a computer system as an image. ImagePlus facilitates the office changeover from a paper system to an electronic image system. That is, ImagePlus does for hard-to-manage documents what word processing did for standard letters and reports.

To understand the concepts, let's trace some hard-to-manage documents through a hypothetical insurance company using ImagePlus. The ImagePlus example that follows is an insurance claim for Mr. Lowrey (a customer) for hurricane damage to his home. For this example, Mr. Lowrey's claim for repair of damage will be processed.

Figure 3.19 shows the ImagePlus system used by our insurance company to process claims. First, the insurance company receives three estimates from various contractors for the repair of Mr. Lowrey's home. Since these are signed estimates with handwritten notes and include photographs of the damage, they fall into the category of hard-to-manage documents. The documents are first sent to the operator of the **scanning** workstation to prepare an image of each estimate document in the computer. The scanning workstation consists of a Personal System/2 running the PS/2 ImagePlus workstation program and an image scanner

Figure 3.19. An example ImagePlus system.

plus a printer. The scanner is similar to a copy machine, but rather than producing a duplicate image on another sheet of paper, the scanner electronically produces a duplicate image in the PS/2's memory. The extra-wide 8508 monochrome display allows the user to view an image on one side of the screen and enter textual information (e.g., name, address, phone number, account number, and date the case was opened) on the other.

Once the image is in the PS/2, it is compressed to conserve disk space. The images are sent to the AS/400 via Client Access/400 over the interconnecting LAN, using the communications capabilities of Client Access/400. They are stored in a shared folder on an AS/400 disk unit. Then the ImagePlus/400 Workfolder Application Facility/400 (5733-055), which is specially written to use the facilities of the ImagePlus system, takes over. The Workfolder Application Facility uses the AS/400's built-in database functions to index the stored images. This indexing associates the images with Mr. Lowrey's account number and other pertinent information to facilitate the quick retrieval of the images; that is, all information related to Mr. Lowrey's claim is linked together inside the computer system, in an electronic workfolder called a **case**.

Another thing the Workfolder Application Facility does is to place a copy of the images on the 3995 Optical Library DataServer, which is described in Chapter 2. In our example, the Workfolder Application Facility allows the claims supervisor to prioritize Mr. Lowrey's case with the other active cases and assign the case to a claims processor who is using a **viewing** workstation. There is no need for a scanner or a printer at the viewing workstation. The claims processor using the viewing workstation can now view all of the information associated with Mr. Lowrey's case. During the processing of Mr. Lowrey's claim, the claims processor can take actions such as suspending the case while waiting for additional information, suspending the case for a specified number of days, or completing the processing and closing the case.

Since the information about Mr. Lowrey's case is all in order, the claims processor completes the necessary processing and closes the case. Selected information about Mr. Lowrey's case is sent to the computer located at corporate headquarters. For now, the images pertaining to Mr. Lowrey's case are removed from the AS/400's fixed disk, freeing space for other active cases. But the 3995 Optical Library DataServer keeps a permanent record on optical disk for audit purposes. Later, if some of Mr. Lowrey's case images are needed, they can be recalled from the 3995 Optical Library DataServer. They can be displayed on a viewing workstation as before, or they can be sent to a printing workstation if hard copies are required—for external correspondence. This is one example of an ImagePlus environment.

A very important point about the whole ImagePlus system architecture is that it is designed to accommodate other application programs. That is, any programmer can write an application program that uses image capture, manipulation, storage, indexing, and printing functions provided by the Application Programming Interfaces (APIs), found in the Workfolder Application Facility/400 (5733-055). Here is an example of how different business environments are accomodated: a real estate office can capture photographs of the exterior and interior of the houses that are for sale and store them in an ImagePlus system. Then, via computer images, a real estate agent can essentially "walk" prospective buyers through the house before they ever leave the real estate office, saving everyone a lot of time. This is just the beginning. Image processing is in its infancy, but it will clearly play a role of increasing importance in businesses of the future.

The ImagePlus Visual Info for AS/400 is becoming more closely integrated with *EDMSuite*, including an advanced workflow feature as a graphical building tool. The modular structure provides more customer options with improvements for both the client and server in document security application and development. A single search can be defined to investigate multiple document repositories.

Facsimile Support/400

Facsimile Support/400 (5798-TBY), is a program for AS/400 systems that may either use the 2664 Integrated FAX Adapter, described in Chapter 2, or operate in conjunction with PCs and other programs and provides basic support for sending and receiving facsimiles (faxing). Support is present for sending or receiving single- and double-byte character set fonts, compressed image objects, uncompressed image objects, and barcode objects. Figure 3.20 shows a simple setup that can be used to send and receive faxes. In our example setup, a 2664 Integrated FAX Adapter is attached to a standard telephone line (or more than one). The 2664 Integrated FAX Adapter is used to control the communications between the AS/400 and any of the millions of fax machines in the world that conform to the industry-standard Group 3 Facsimile Ser-

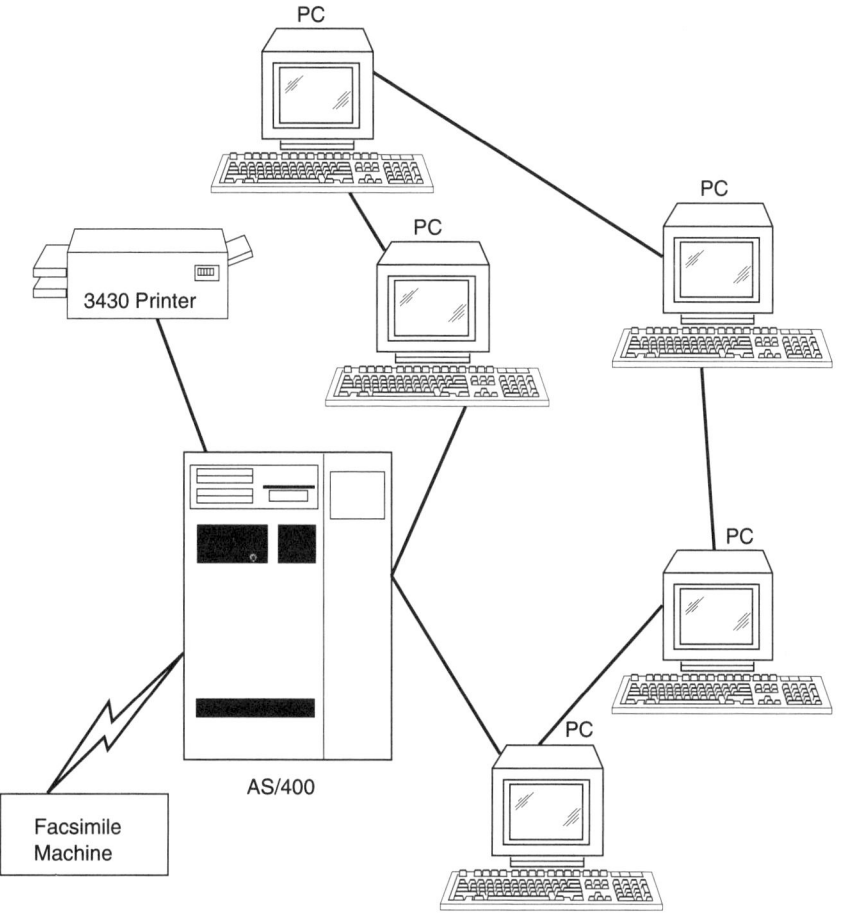

Figure 3.20. Facsimile Support/400 allows fax machines to be used as remote printers and scanners for the AS/400 system.

vice. A complete menu interface is available to support the fax environment. That menu interface is called Enhanced Services.

Facsimile Support/400 can also be used without the 2664 Integrated FAX adapter. A PC with an IBM fax concentrator or GammaLink fax adapter could also be used to send and receive faxes if attached to the AS/400 via a token-ring network, an Ethernet network, or a 2699 Two-Line WAN IOA using a twinax cable. The other PCs and terminals are general-purpose personal computer workstations used as AS/400 workstations attached to the AS/400. With either of these setups, all of the other fax machines in the world appear to the AS/400 system to be printers, so anything that the user in our example could print, that user can now send to any fax machine, together with a cover sheet generated by Facsimile Support/400.

Alternately, the user could request that the AS/400 system automatically send the fax after business hours, when the phone charges are less expensive. When someone sends the user a fax, it is received over the phone lines by the 2664 Integrated FAX Adapter. The fax is then transferred to the AS/400, where it can be stored in a document folder, displayed on a graphics-capable workstation or 3489 InfoWindow II Display, or printed on any printer supporting the compressed image function of Advanced Function Printing (e.g., a 3816 Printer). In addition to providing this basic fax support, **Command Language (CL)** commands can be embedded in programs to allow programmers to incorporate fax functions in their application programs.

Facsimile Support (5798-TBY) also provides support for Windows NT clients for AnyMail integration of facsimile activity and inbound routing of faxes to clients on an intranet. It is possible to print to fax through the Client Access AFP print driver in Windows NT using Client Access for Windows 95/NT for AS/400, as well as to browse the Facsimile Support/400 phonebook databases. It is possible to customize cover pages and attach level-one PostScript, GIF, TIFF, and BMP mail attachments.

CallPath/400

CallPath/400 (5716-CP3) is a programmers' tool for the AS/400 that allows programmers to write applications that *coordinate a business's telephone system* with application programs. For example, application programs can be written to automatically sequence through and dial a list of potential customers, making the telemarketing staff more productive. In another example, a CallPath/400 application program could be written to identify a caller by phone number (using the calling line identification service offered by the phone company) and automatically pull up that customer's information to the operator's display. If the call needs to be transferred to another extension, the user can simultaneously transfer the telephone call along with the screen of customer information to the telephone and workstation of the other employee with a few keystrokes.

It is important to understand that CallPath/400 by itself cannot perform these functions. CallPath/400 is a program that is basically an extension to the OS/400 operating system, to make it easier to write application programs that interact with telephone equipment. For this reason, CallPath/400 is really an enabler rather than an application program. An **enabler** is a program that provides services to application programs to make the programmer's life easier and to provide an insulation layer to help maintain application program compatibility as hardware and software evolve. That is, CallPath/400 is a tool for the programmer who wishes to write an application program that conforms to IBM's **CallPath services architecture**. This architecture is IBM's stated long-term direction for coordinating application programs and telephone equipment.

Multimedia

In the discussion of the Workfolder Application Facility/400 (5733-055) in ImagePlus/400, the ability to embed photographs into an insurance industry report using the capabilities of ImagePlus/400 was described. In this section we will describe the ability to combine visual images with audible commentary and video feedback in presentations and other business activities. (In the insurance example, customer or client testimonials and videos of wind damage might be included.) This can all be done over the Internet between branches and the home office of the insurance company. No other multimedia system uses PC multimedia, in which the PC is the client and the AS/400 is the server, each platform doing what it does best. The AS/400 runs the applications, database, and communications, and the PC delivers the multimedia. All of the processing impacts are on the PC.

A sample multimedia configuration is shown in Figure 3.21. Among the characteristics that make this a multimedia configuration are the mixture of media, analog/digital communications, optical/DASD storage devices, local and remote connections, and networking of the workstations. It is of further significance to the multimedia characteristic that the connection capabilities provide nearly equivalent performance for both the locally connected devices and the remotely connected devices. The AS/400 in this environment provides security, system management (SystemView System Manager for AS/400 [5769-SM1]), ease of use, networking, and object/database management, including shared repositories.

224 EXPLORING IBM AS/400 COMPUTERS

Figure 3.21. An AS/400 multimedia system configuration.

The performance and ability of Ultimedia to handle applications is improved with the addition of **Complex Objects** (LOBs), user defined functions and user defined types, to DB2 for AS/400 .

Client Access Ultimedia Tools for AS/400

Client Access Ultimedia Tools for AS/400 (5716-US1) is an enabler product that allows users to enable their applications with multimedia. It requires Client Access/400 and supports both OS/2 (2.11 or higher) and Windows (3.1 or higher) clients. The workstations in a multimedia environment are at the minimum PS/2s or equivalent with a minimum of 8 MB of main storage and one or more of the following: audio adapter, motion video adapter, audio speakers, and/or CD-ROM drive. Figure 3.22 shows the software interface between the AS/400 function and the intelligent workstation (PC) function. Effectively the workstation handles the capture and presentation of the objects of the multimedia session while the AS/400 performs the manipulation of the objects and manages the network (taking care of the security and storage of the objects)

Ultimedia Business Conferencing/400

To assist in illustrating the functions of the Ultimedia Business Conferencing for AS/400 (5716-UB1), our example will be a medical clinic networked with an associated hospital, as shown in Figure 3.23. The doctors in the clinic are concerned about a heart patient who has completed an ultrasound test. The ultrasound test was videotaped, and

Figure 3.22. AS/400 multimedia software interface.

Figure 3.23. AS/400 configuration support for business conferencing.

the sound of the blood movement was superimposed on the videotape. The videotape is played back through the *Picturetel* to combine the video, audio, and blood-pressure/heart-rate data on a single path. The AS/400 captures all of this information, ties it into the patient's record (a shared folder), stores the information on the optical storage library for future retrieval, and networks the information to the connected PCs.

The information is presented simultaneously on both PCs, one at the clinic and one at the hospital. The doctors confer about the images seen and the sounds recorded during the test by talking to their PCs essentially as they would over a telephone. The conversations are captured by the AS/400 and made a permanent part of the patient records. With Ultimedia Business Conferencing/400, these events took place: the conference was scheduled by the AS/400 for each doctor and the Picturetel, the needed patient information was identified to make the conference useful, and a set of minutes was produced about the conference. The minutes were then dispatched to each doctor's PC, where they became part of the doctor's records.

IBM Job Scheduler/400

IBM Job Scheduler for AS/400 (5769-JS1) facilitates unattended operations, resulting in improved efficiency and accuracy in managing batch applications. This works by providing a multisystem full-function job scheduler and control of the report distribution system. Scheduling functions include:

- Automation
- Batch job stream management
- Forward planning and production forecasting
- Full calendaring of operations
- Dependency scheduling

Any batch-capable function can now be scheduled. The job scheduling can occur on a single system or across a network consisting of multiple systems. Job Scheduler/400 includes a set of additional functions, consisting of the following:

- Job reporting
- Repetitive distribution
- Capturing job streams as they are submitted
- Passing job parameters via Local Data Areas (LDAs)
- Operator notification via paging support

Jobs can be scheduled either via calendar functions or by dependency functions. The calendar scheduling functions include

Multiple processing schedules per day or multiple holiday calendars

- Individual calendars

- A hierarchy of calendars

- Fiscal calendars

- Full audit trails of processing activity

Examples of control methods for how jobs can be run include daily, by a calendar, by date, by day, once, at the end of the month, by minute, based on a number of days, by sequence, the first week of the month, the last week of the month, and based on job dependencies. These provide **batch job stream management**.

Jobs can be sequenced to run based on three types of dependencies:

- *Completion of previous jobs.* Jobs or groups of jobs that depend on each other can be set up (for example, a payroll job can be set up to run only after preceding dependent payroll jobs have been processed). The jobs can be run in parallel or serially based on user definitions.

- *Other job activity or lack of activity.* You can define a list of jobs that cannot be active when the specified job is to be submitted; the job will be delayed until all the jobs in the list are inactive.

- *General object dependencies.* A list of object dependencies used to control jobs can be defined (for instance, a central site receiving payroll information from a remote site). You can also define the condition that an object must not exist before a job will run.

Job Scheduler/400 can also track the completion history of jobs and complete a log of the activities that went into processing the job. The completion history is a job-by-job log of when Job Scheduler/400 last ran, how long it took, and what the results were. It presents a detailed history of Job Scheduler/400 activities including changes to the job schedule, job processing, and the starting and ending times for the Scheduler.

Job Scheduler/400 also provides reports of applications, calendars, command lists, dependencies, distribution recipients, job histories, job lists, library lists, logs, parameters, and schedules, and can automatically distribute reports and their associated spool files to users wherever they are located. This thereby provides the functions of job reporting, repetitive distribution, and the capture of existing job streams as they are submitted.

Automation means that Job Scheduler/400 can assist by adding to the list of managed jobs those jobs normally submitted through other application software packages. With proper placement of a special command, Job Scheduler/400 will capture the parameters and values associated with those jobs and automatically add them to the job list. Administration by function and specific job scheduling authority is allowed using the flexible security support of the OS/400. The combination of being able to control the job sequencing and the reports to be received as a result provides for **forward planning and production forecasting**. The ability to schedule jobs by the calendar functions provided and the logs that result from the execution of those jobs yields **full calendaring of batch operations**. As the job parameters are captured into a local data area of the database files, they can be passed between networked systems acting as peers using **Distributed Data Management (DDM)**. This is what is meant by passing job parameters via **Local Data Areas (LDAs)**. Finally, Job Scheduler/400 allows a pager message to be sent to a user upon completion of a job, which results in **operator notification** via **paging support**. Multiple pager messages can exist on the system to be sent to different users based on normal or abnormal completion of jobs.

IBM Job Scheduler can schedule a dependent job and can copy jobs to another AS/400 system. A calendar can be used with most schedule codes to schedule a job, and there is also member-level object dependency. A formula can be used to perform date manipulation, such as setting a value to be "today's date plus 57 days."

Commands can be run from a job in restricted state using a console monitor, including a view to show the different types of dependencies that exist for a job; and a status value can inform you when a job is waiting on a dependency. If you are submitting a job, parameters are present to allow you to override checking dependencies and to update dependency flags when the job is completed. The days of the week can be used for report distributing to determine when a recipient receives a report, and the spooled file can be removed when reports have been distributed. Job Scheduler has a Graphical User Interface (GUI) to define and refine complex job automation schedules, improving the ease with which job schedules can be managed across systems in groups.

Data Warehousing

Data warehousing is an emerging concept for applying information technology to solve business problems. Estimates are that over 90% of the Fortune 2000 businesses had in place some form of data warehouse before the end of 1996. Data warehousing consists of a set of hardware and software components that analyze the massive amounts of data that companies are storing to improve business decisions. That data used to operate the business includes a wealth of knowledge and may be a partially wasted asset. Data warehousing applied properly can make it possible to do the following:

- Understand business trends

- Improve forecasting decisions

- Bring better/more timely products to market

- Analyze daily sales information

- Speed decisions that can affect a company's performance

Data warehousing concepts define *operational data* and *informational data.* **Operational data** is the data that runs a business. This data is typically stored, retrieved, and updated by the **Online Transactional Processing (OLTP)** system. An OLTP system may be a reservations system, an accounting application, or an order entry application. Operational data is typically stored in a relational database, but it can be stored in legacy hierarchical or flat file formats. Characteristics of operational data include the following:

- Updated often and through online transactions

- Not historical data (not more than 3 to 6 months old)

- Optimized for transaction processing

- Normalized in the relational database for easy update, maintenance, and integrity.

Informational data is stored in formats that make analysis easiest. Analysis can be:

- Decision support (queries)

- Report generation

- Executive information systems

- In-depth statistical analysis

Informational data is created from the operational data within a business. Informational data makes up a data warehouse. Informational data is summarized operational data, denormalized and replicated, infrequently updated from operational systems, optimized for decision support applications, possibly "read only" (no updates allowed), and stored on separate systems, reducing the impact on operational systems.

Transformation or propagation tools are used to build the informational database, during which, data may be moved from multiple operational systems and manipulated into a format appropriate for the warehouse. This may:

- Create new fields derived from existing operational data

- Summarize data to the most appropriate level needed for analysis

- Denormalize the data for performance purposes

- Cleanse the data to ensure that integrity is preserved.

To **cleanse** the data means to ensure the integrity of data when it is loaded into the warehouse. For example, if data were pulled from two operational systems that use different field names for the same data, cleansing techniques would ensure that the data fields conform to the warehouse definition upon loading.

Here is one situation in which a transformation is needed: A retail outlet's database contains every detail about every purchase in the form of operational data. That database contains the answers to the following questions:

- What items were purchased?

- At which store did the transaction take place?

- How was it paid for?

- Who was the consumer?

Because the data is stored in a format appropriate for recording of these transactions, querying this data to analyze it can be a time-consuming effort and can adversely affect the performance of the transactional system.

Here is another example: A business analyst tracking sales may want to review data collected from every store by product to forecast inventories, determine profit margins, or track revenues compared with the previous year. The ability to generate summary-level informational data from the operational data provides the performance benefits the analyst can take advantage of to quickly view the trends and problem areas affecting the business.

Relational databases store data in a two-dimensional format, or *data structure*: tables of data represented by rows and columns. Multidimensional data structures provide additional dimensions. Multidimensional data structures provide a way to analyze data stored in the warehouse, resulting in fast response times when dealing with different levels of data common in a decision support environment. Answers to business questions can be determined by slicing and dicing through the data, or by drilling down or rolling up to different hierarchical levels. The structure of the data can be changed as the business changes. In a **relational database system**, multidimensional analysis can be achieved through specific database designs, (e.g., a series of indexed summary tables, or through hypercubes or multicubes). Cube approaches can be described as an extension of the spreadsheet model, that is, storing aggregate values in cells of a multidimensional spreadsheet.

On-Line Analytical Processing (OLAP) products are multidimensional analysis tools that store data using these data structures. **Data**

marts contain informational data that is departmentalized, tailored to the needs of specific departmental work groups, and characterized by small size, generally less than 10 GB. **Metadata** is information about the data warehouse and the data contained in that data warehouse, and is composed of two parts, *technical data* and *business data*. **Technical data** contains descriptions of the operational database and the data warehouse. The warehouse administrator uses technical data to maintain the warehouse so as to know where all of the data is coming from. **Business data** helps locate information in the data warehouse without knowing the base implementation of the database. Business data information is presented in business terms instead of the terms the programmer used when the database was built and provides information about how recent the data is, which operational database the information came from, and how reliable the data is.

Business *intelligence software* refers to the tools used to analyze data, and consists of **Decision Support Systems (DSS), Executive Information Systems (EIS)**, and data mining tools. DSS tools allow the building of ad hoc queries and generate reports. EIS combine decision support with extended analysis capabilities and access to outside resources. **Data mining** tools allow automation of the analysis of data to find patterns or rules used to tailor business operations. The tools are easy to use and graphically oriented, with point and click functionality.

Data Mining

Data mining is the search for relationships and segmentation in the data in the data warehouse. *Discovery-driven data mining* is the finding of new relationships and segmentation that are totally unexpected. IBM's newest product in this area, Intelligent Miner (5733-IM1), provides a framework for using all of IBM's current and emerging data mining techniques. Intelligent Miner is scalable, flexible, and open—integrating components and extracting data from many environments, including all DB2 for AS/400 relational database family products. It provides client support for Windows, Windows NT, and AIX.

Intelligent Miner is designed for business users, not data analysts, offering the derivation of new, comprehensible information through predictive modeling, database segmentation, link analysis, and deviation detection using data-mining techniques. Figure 3.24 illustrates the functions and layers of the construct for Data Mining. What makes the

Figure 3.24. Data mining constructs.

AS/400 with its OS/400 operating system a good server on which to perform data warehousing and data mining? The five requirements of a data warehouse server are performance, capacity, scalability, open interfaces, and multiple data structures. Intelligent Miner has increased its functionality through support for a full range of statistical functions including correlations, factor analysis, linear regression, univariate curves, and bivariate statistics. The existing mining techniques have been optimized, and one mining technique, net value prediction, has been added.

Performance

The database server must be capable of supporting the user's performance expectations during analysis. Many warehouses contain over 100 GB of data, with very complex analysis tasks being executed against the database. Parallel computing technologies become quite important when dealing with this large a size.

The AS/400 at the single-system level supports parallel computing, using its DASD I/O processors on the DB2 for AS/400 database and Symmetrical MultiProcessing (SMP), which can apply the resources of up to 12 processors cooperatively for a single job/query. In addition, with Opticonnect up to 128 nodes (where a node is an instance of OS/400) can be connected in a loosely coupled relationship.

The power of all 128 nodes can be brought to bear both in containing the warehouse size and in performing the analysis required. DB2 Multisystem must be installed to support the loosely coupled technology.

Capacity

The capacity of the server and hardware must be enough to store your entire data warehouse. Data warehouses may be partitioned or split across multiple systems, but the server must support a data view that hides the data physically location. Again the Opticonnect capability comes into play providing 32 times the maximum disk storage on a single server (4.29 TB) along with DDM (Distributed Data Management) and DB2 Multisystem.

Scalability

The typical data warehouse starts out at the data mart level serving a department, and grows over time to an enterprise-wide warehouse. The AS/400 is scalable from a minimum of 4.196 GB of DASD space on the entry model 150 to up to (4.29 TB) on a model 740, to the previously described 32 processing systems cooperatively interconnected with Opticonnect.

Open Interfaces

Open interfaces are needed to support the analysis tools required to extract the information a business needs. Locking itself into proprietary interfaces could cause a business to incur major expenses to support new analysis tools as the business changes. AS/400 supports both IBM-supplied solutions like DataPropagator Relational Capture and Apply for OS/400, which moves data from DB2 regardless of what type of system it resides upon, and products from vendors such as Information Builders Inc., Oracle, ExecuSoft, Sybase, Praxis, DataMirror, and so on. Usability has been improved through the addition of a Java user interface, a sequence builder, an Expert Use mode, task guides, and a progress indicator.

Multiple Data Structures

Multiple data structures, both relational and multidimensional, must be supported. Multidimensional data structures are supported by database designs such as star-schema using the DB2 for OS/400 architecture or by products from IBM business partners such as AMIS/400 from CAP Gemini, MIT/400 from SAMAC, and the suite of data access products, including ESSBASE/400 from ShowCase Corp.

Intelligent Miner has been extended to include text analysis tools (clustering, classification, feature extraction) by using an advanced search engine and providing Web access tools.

Data Mining Example

One example of how data mining can help business was the discovery of an unsuspected relationship between young men with small children who enjoyed football, beer, Thursday nights, and diapers. If these young men went to the store on Thursday night during football season to buy diapers for their young children, they would also would stop at the beer display and pick up some beer to drink during that weekend's games. If a brand of diapers was located on the same aisle, the young men would pick up whatever brand of diapers it was, regardless of price. Needless to say, the retailers located the most profitable brand of diapers on the same aisle as the beer.

Collaborative Computing

Collaborative computing is an environment in which many users require the coordination of multiple actions toward the accomplishment of a common goal. Programs that enable the achievement of that coordination are known collectively as **groupware**. Groupware applications help organizations communicate, collaborate, and coordinate strategic business processes both within and beyond the boundaries of the business to achieve improved business results. Examples of groupware are Lotus Notes and Domino. Lotus Notes 5.0 supports the client functions, and Domino 5.0 supports server functions. Domino for AS/400 is described in Chapter 5 with regard to its use for e-commerce and network computing capabilities. Lotus Notes 5.0 client functions support:

- Advanced client/server e-mail

- Direct Web browsing, Web agents, and off-line access to Web pages

- Calendaring and scheduling for personal calendaring, task management, and group scheduling

- Support for mobile workers

- Bundling and integration with Netscape Navigator and Microsoft Internet Explorer

- Optional, high-performance Lotus components.

Domino 5.0 Server Powered by Notes provides:

- HTTP Web Server accessed using a standard Web browser

- Calendaring and scheduling with freetime search and interoperability

- SMTP-MTA (Simple Mail Transfer Protocol-Message Transfer Agent) providing mail coexistence between Notes Mail and OfficeVision mail (OfficeVision for AS/400)

- Support for Internet standards, including SMTP/MIME, X.400, JAVA, Netscape plug-ins, ActiveX, POP3, HTTP, HTML, MAPI, SNMP, SSL, and CGI

- Integration with corporate data, including AS/400 data via DataPropagator/400 (5716-DP1).

Lotus Notes provides a work environment centered on people as individuals, teams, and organizations. It is the leading client/server platform for developing and deploying groupware applications. In communications, Lotus Notes Rich Text E-Mail includes images, video, audio, spreadsheets, and graphs, as well as a wide range of protocols. Remote employees can review and edit the same document, and each team member sees the others' comments highlighted in a different font and color, helping to enable effective *collaboration*. Coordination is achieved by the management of the workflow among a dynamic task force.

Notes 5.0 and Domino 5.0 are supported on the Pentium version of the AS/400 Integrated PC Server (6617). With the RISC models, a CD-ROM provides for installation of the Integrated PC Server. For the CISC-based models, the CD-ROM installation requires Client Access/400 to install Notes 5.0 Domino on the Pentium Integrated PC Server (IPCS). AS/400e server Model 150 with the Integrated PC Server does not receive a complementary copy of Lotus Notes client and Domino Server code. All other orders for Integrated PC Server include AS/400 Integration BasePak for Lotus Notes, which includes one copy of the Domino Server software and one copy of the Lotus Notes client software in addition to the installation software. Also available is AS/400 Integration Enhanced Pak for Lotus Notes (providing database integration support between DB2 for AS/400 and Lotus Notes) and advanced backup and recovery options using Adstar Distributed Storage Manager for AS/400.

Lotus Notes

Lotus Notes uses a **Rapid Application Development (RAD)** environment to deliver its capabilities. The RAD environment employs a range of skills from user-created views to agents, formulas, macros, LotusScript, and C++ APIs for the professional developer. Lotus Notes also uses a *document-centric* database management system, in which each database can include the full range of text combined with Notes Access Control Lists to ensure appropriate security (Notes includes RSA encryption for high-sensitivity information). There is also an *integrated messaging system,* in which anything you can see or hear in Notes can be mailed over a wide range of supported protocols.

Lotus Notes replication functionality sets it apart from other groupware products by providing the following features:

- Notes Database Management System (DBMS) allows for on-demand or automatic scheduled synchronization of geographically separate copies of a database. Efficiency is achieved by only updating new and changed documents or fields, and updating is accomplished in the background.

- Notes DBMS distributes information via the Internet, thus having no concern for geography. TCP/IP, LAN connections, SLIPs, and

PPP aid in this effort, and Notes manages data authentication and encryption. (TCP/IP, SLIP, and PPP are Internet protocols.)

- Notes DBMS allows a user located remotely to use the same data as an office co-worker

- Each *Integrated PC Server* (IPCS) can support up to 200 concurrent users. Up to 8 Notes servers can be consolidated in AS/400 CISC-based systems, and up to 16 Notes servers can be consolidated on AS/400 RISC-based systems.

IBM offers two AS/400 integration packs for Lotus Notes: The AS/400 Integration BasePak for Lotus Notes allows the Integrated PC Server to act as a LAN adapter, providing software to install Notes on the Integrated PC Server. It also includes one copy each of Lotus Notes R4 server and a full application development client license. The AS/400 Integration BasePak for Lotus Notes also includes server administration, the ability to add Notes users via the AS/400, the ability to exchange mail between OfficeVision for AS/400 and Notes Mail, and shadowing of the AS/400 SDD (System Distribution Directory) to the Notes Name and Address book.

With the availability within Notes of SMTP-MTA (Message Transfer Agent) and POP3, AS/400 Notes users can communicate with a wide variety of other mail clients. Even non-programmable terminals have interoperability, as they will receive the text and attachments as storable, forwardable PC files.

The Integrated PC Server supports existing Notes database functions, including replication and compression. DB2/400 data can be imported to Notes databases. Options are available for shadowing DB2/400 data into Notes as either a full or an incremental refresh. An optional user exit program allows Notes updates to DB2/400. Web Navigator allows Notes clients to simply click wherever they want to go. *Web Publisher*, a separate Lotus product, allows for batch conversions of Notes-created documents to *HTML*.

Lotus Enterprise Integrator (NotesPump)

Lotus Enterprise Integrator previously known as **NotesPump** is a Lotus product that allows data transfer automation between heterogeneous data sources including Notes, DB2, Oracle, Sybase, and many 32-bit

ODBC-compliant databases. The Lotus Enterprise Integrator for AS/400 program includes all applicable functions supported in the Lotus Enterprise Integrator 2.5 release. A variety of data transfer requests are allowed by Lotus Enterprise Integrator, including:

- Query and transfer of a results set to a different target data source

- Replication of data between two dissimilar (or similar) data sources

- Propagation of data from the DB2 program to a Lotus Enterprise Integrator program target using the IBM DataPropagator program activity

- Polling for a condition and a scheduled transfer when the condition is met

- Archiving data based on condition or timestamp

- Accessing data in real time using a Domino application and a Lotus Enterprise Integrator program-support back-end (relational) database.

The initiation of these transfer activities can be scheduled, event driven, or executed ad hoc, and administration is performed from the Lotus Enterprise Integrator Administration Notes database. Synchronization of data authorizations between DB2/400 and Notes databases is an additional activity between the AS/400 system and the Lotus Enterprise Integrator program.

Customized data transfer requests can be written in addition to the Lotus Enterprise Integrator predetermined activities to provide additional data transfer control or manipulation. These customizations use the Lotus Enterprise Integrator program extensions to LotusScript and the Lotus Enterprise Integrator C's APIs. The Lotus Enterprise Integrator Administrator database can be used to select data source views and fields, and Web clients can be enabled to submit Lotus Enterprise Integrator program activities from any browser.

Additional information can be found at:

- http://www2.lotus.com/services/notesua.nsf

- *http://www.edge.lotus.com*

Client Series and Application Development Programs

In September 1992, IBM initiated the IBM AS/400 Application Development Program to facilitate the selection of a full array of high-level languages, CASE, and object-oriented development tools offered by a variety of third-party vendors. This business partners program was later expanded to include products developed for the client/server environment.

The AS/400 Application Development Program identifies independent software vendors providing advanced application development tools to the AS/400 marketplace. The AD Program provides a means to select vendors with quality tools and identify those tools through the use of a unique "AS/400 Application Development" emblem (shown in Figure 3.25).

The AS/400 Client Series is an exclusive set of applications recommended for use in the AS/400 client/server environments. The applications can come from either IBM or independent software vendors. After qualifying for the series, applications can be identified by the "AS/400 Client Series" emblem (shown in Figure 3.26). IBM also supplies a CD-ROM including this information. Additional detail on Client Series products can be found on this Internet address:
http://www. softmall.ibm.com/as400.

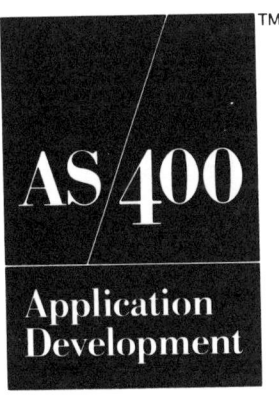

Figure 3.25. AS/400 Application Development emblem.

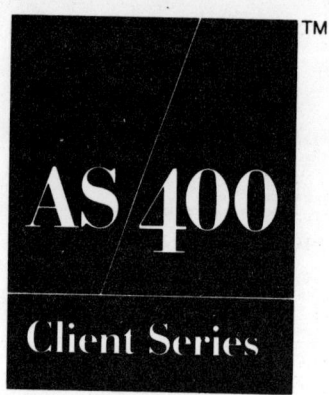

Figure 3.26. AS/400 Client Series emblem.

Industry-Specific Application Programs

The cross-industry application programs discussed up to this point are of a highly general nature, able to fill the common needs found in even the most diverse business environments. They were designed to be as general as possible to cover the largest market possible—sort of the "all things to all people" approach. For example, the OfficeVision for AS/400 office application program might be used to fill the needs of a department store in one instance and a legal office in the next. In most cases, a business also has some needs that are more specialized to its particular industry. Therefore, another type of prewritten application program, called an **industry-specific** application program, may be desirable. As the term "industry-specific" implies, this type of application program is specially designed to address the needs of a well-defined business category. A real estate office has application-program needs that differ from those of a dental practice. Each would benefit by an appropriate prewritten yet highly specialized industry-specific application program.

Many software companies have put a great deal of effort into developing industry-specific programs for the System/3X computers. Since AS/400 systems can run many of these programs as well as those specially written for the AS/400, highly specific business/professional environments can be addressed. There are industry-specific applications designed for manufacturing companies, insurance companies, real estate offices, medical practices, construction companies, law practices, churches, and so on. These programs are often **modular**, meaning that they are really several different programs designed to work closely together. Each program or module can be used individually or share information with the others. Modular programs allow you to select only the modules you need, reducing costs for those not needing "the works."

An example of a modular, industry-specific application program is IBM's **Manufacturing Accounting and Production Information Control System/DataBase (MAPICS/DB)**. MAPICS/DB is designed to meet a wide variety of needs for manufacturing (e.g., a furniture manufacturer) and process companies (e.g., a gasoline refiner). It consists of 17 separate programs or modules, each providing specific functions. They can be broken down into three areas:

- Order processing and accounting

- Advanced manufacturing

- Process

The order processing and accounting modules of MAPICS/DB meet basic business needs in the areas of general ledger, accounts payable, accounts receivable, order entry, purchasing, and so on. Many of these modules are really very general in nature, allowing them to fit very well in manufacturing or nonmanufacturing companies. The advanced manufacturing MAPICS/DB modules focus on the manufacturing flow through the plant. They help manage the bills of materials of products, monitor in-process inventory, balance work center loads, track labor, cost jobs, and schedule production. These modules are designed specifically for manufacturers and would be of little use to a legal office, for example. Finally, the process MAPICS/DB modules fill the very specialized needs of the process companies. This includes dealing with recipes, batch quantities, yield calculations, and batch/lot tracking.

In addition to the basic MAPICS/DB modules, other companies have produced companion programs that work with MAPICS/DB to provide additional functions. These types of "add-on" program offerings are very common when dealing with the more popular industry-specific application programs. MAPICS/DB is just one example of an industry-specific application program. Hundreds of software companies have written thousands of industry-specific application programs, and new application programs are appearing almost daily. Before custom software, discussed next, is purchased, industry-specific software should be carefully considered.

Custom Application Programs

Prewritten application programs fit many needs. They are comparably inexpensive, flexible, and convenient tools. In some cases, however, users may find that the fit of their application program to the way the business operates needs to be that of a tight glove. This is especially true in environments in which the application systems are needed to perform highly unusual and specific tasks or there is a need to conform to existing company procedures. In these cases, it's better to develop custom application programs written to the user's exact specifications.

Custom application programs are designed and written by programmers employed by the company or by consultants contracted for just that purpose. In either case, the basic development steps are the same. First, a software specification is developed that describes the actions of each program, and the specific interface is projected for the input and output of the program. Then a preliminary version of the program is written that demonstrates the final program. This preliminary version is evaluated by the user, and the specification is altered to reflect any needed changes. Last, the final program and user manuals are written and put in place at the user's location. Typically, user training will be provided by the developer and any problems will be ironed out.

Once the user accepts the program, the software has to be supported: Users will need a place to go when they have questions not addressed by the manuals. Support also includes making necessary changes to the application program, which the changing business environment will often require. This kind of ongoing support is critical to the success of any computer automation project.

Most of the time, custom application program development is more expensive and time-consuming than the prewritten application program approach. In many environments, however, this additional expense and time can be recovered by the increased productivity that can result from custom applications that precisely fit the needs of the environment. An additional benefit of custom application programs is their ability to change as a company changes. Getting major modifications to prewritten application programs may be difficult or impossible.

The AS/400 functions and programming tools including the basic architecture of AS/400 systems makes for a very productive program development environment. The built-in database and single-level storage provide high-level structures and consistency. According to IBM, this, along with the programming tools available for AS/400, can increase programmer productivity by about 3 to 1 over that of the System/36. Custom application programs used with System/36 and System/38 computers can be run on the AS/400 through the use of appropriate migration tools. In Chapter 4, the following are considered:

- "Application Development Facilities" discusses some of the AS/400 tools and Integrated Language Environment (ILE), which assists in the development of custom application programs.

- "Emerging Application Development Environments" describes C++ object- oriented programming.

- "Emerging Applications Environments" describes Frameworks, Java, and Open Doc application environments.

Before leaving custom application programs, we should discuss the use of existing applications for the new system purchaser or migrating system purchaser. Most system purchasers have a set of programs that were fine for the centralized system they are moving from. They now must choose to maintain that environment or move into a client/server computing environment. This is particularly true if the business has invested in some PC systems that need to be networked with a host system as a server. In addition to Frameworks, Java, and Open Doc, "Emerging Applications Environments" in Chapter 4 identifies the choices the system purchaser has, related to older programs migrating to a client/server environment.

4

Operating Systems

Few areas in information processing create more confusion and apprehension than the operating system. This chapter is designed to help remove some of the mystery associated with the operating systems used with Application Systems and make you familiar with operating system topics such as interactive processing and multiuser capabilities and how these concepts apply to the business environment. You will also be introduced to the concepts of client/server environment, network computing, including the client/server variations called Internet computing and intranet computing, and how this type of computing differs from interactive processing, as well as the special characteristics imposed upon the client and the server to support these emerging types of computing.

The two AS/400 operating systems, SSP and OS/400, will be discussed, including when each should be used and when both might be used. The object technology languages C++ and Java are discussed, and the San Francisco frameworks objectives and Open Doc standards are positioned. The Application Development Facilities supported by the AS/400 operating system are functionally outlined, and the programming language environments for that development are described. A perspective is provided on SystemView tools for managing the AS/400 resources and the resources of other connected computers and peripheral equipment.

Operating System Products

Application Systems use one of two operating systems. The Advanced 36 computers use the IBM System Support Program (SSP) originally developed for System/36 computers. All models of the AS/400 systems exclusively use the IBM Operating System/400 (OS/400). This section provides an overview of both operating systems and then looks more closely at OS/400.

Introduction to Operating System Concepts

The operating system provides the necessary interface that allows the user and application programs to interact with computers. The user interacts directly with the operating system's user interface to manage files on a disk, start application programs, print files, and so on. The operating system performs those tasks that all applications must perform, providing a uniform, consistent method for accomplishing those tasks. The operating system also performs tasks directly under the control of application programs without any user assistance. The application program initiates tasks by directly interacting with the operating system through the **Application Program Interface (API)**.

This is simply a set of operating system commands that can be issued directly by the application program. The API simplifies the job of the application programmer because it is not necessary to become involved with the details of hardware interaction. Further, when an application uses the API, it is shielded from changes in the computer hardware as new computers are developed. The operating system can be changed to support new computer hardware while preserving the API unchanged, allowing application programs to run on the new computer. To understand the job of the operating system, it is necessary to understand two basic concepts:

- Batch vs. interactive processing

- Multiuser and multiapplication

The AS/400 uses an integrated operating system, either SSP or OS/400 or both SSP and OS/400. Unlike a personal computer (PC), in which the operating system comes in pieces—Windows, Paradox, Internet support, Communications support, etc.—the OS/400 operating system comes with all essential pieces and the user need not be concerned with whether the interfaces will operate properly together. IBM has done extensive testing on the system to ensure that those interfaces operate properly. The disadvantages of the integrated approach are that the user must take OS/400 as an entity, and it is not possible to tune the operating system to suit the user's desires.

Batch vs. Interactive Processing

To understand the concepts of batch and interactive processing, consider an analogy between the postal service and the telephone. If you wish to ask a distant friend some questions, you can either write a letter or phone. With the first option you gather all your thoughts, put them on paper, and put the letter in a mailbox. A few days later (assuming your friend is responsive) you go to your mailbox and get the responses to your questions in the form of a document. This is analogous to batch processing with a computer: You request the computer to answer some question(s) or perform some task(s). Some time later (from minutes to days) you go to the printer and get the computer's responses in the form of a report.

In the early days of computing, batch processing was the only alternative for computer interaction. Batch processing continues today, and many jobs are still handled this way. As an example, a remote branch of a company quite often has the hours worked by the employees keyed in during the day, stores the information (accumulates it in a database) until the lower telephone rate evening hours, and then sends the data to the computer system located at the company central office. The data is then processed, and the checks are printed and mailed to the remote location for distribution to the employees.

Moving back to our analogy, at times you cannot simply write down your list of questions in a letter because some of the questions will depend on answers to one or more initial questions. In this case, you must either send several letters back and forth or call your friend to discuss the questions. Calling is preferable if you need an answer to your question in a hurry. Having a dialogue with your friend over the phone would be analogous to interactive processing on a computer. With interactive processing, you have a dialogue with the computer system from a terminal: You type in questions or requests and the computer immediately responds. The primary advantage of interactive processing is that the user gets an immediate response, which is required in many business applications (e.g., airline reservations and a retail checkout lane). Interactive processing was developed after batch processing and is now widely used in most business environments.

Some business applications of computers use a combination of batch and interactive processing. For example, a payroll clerk might type information from time cards into a computer terminal in a dialogue style (interactive processing). Once all time cards are entered and verified to be correct, the clerk may issue a command to the terminal that tells the computer to print all checks (a batch job). The clerk would later get the checks from the printer. The operating systems of Application Systems support both batch ad interactive processing.

What Are Multiuser and Multi-application Computer Systems?

A multiuser computer system exists when the hardware and software of a single computer system can be shared by two or more users simultaneously. For contrast, personal computers (PCs) contain hardware and software that are designed to interact with one user at a time and thus are called single-user computer systems. There are two categories of multi-user systems, multi-user–single task, and multi-user-multi-task. The multi-user–single task systems have not been seen since the early days of computers, and as the name implies, many users performing exactly the same application used the system at the same time. Airline scheduling systems are examples of this type system. It was not required that the users operate in synchronization. In a multi-user multi-tasking system, each of the users can be using a different application. Regardless of the definition, in a multi-user computer system, from two to many hundreds of computer terminals are attached to a single computer. Each terminal used in this manner is referred to as a **Non-Programmable Terminal (NPT)**.

Personal computers emulating 5250 data streams when attached to AS/400 systems are in reality being used as non-programmable terminals because their internal intelligence is not being exploited to perform any part of the computing task other than serving as a repository for data. Each terminal provides its user with a "window" into the computer system and allows the user to perform tasks independent of all other users. Although the single computer system is being used simultaneously by many users, users are usually unaware of the activities of other users and seem to have their own computer system. However, a user may see the computer "slow down" (increase response time) as more and more users sign on to the computer and start doing work.

There are advantages in a multiuser computer system versus a single-user computer system. Because the computer system hardware and programs are simultaneously shared by many users, no one is standing in line waiting for a turn on the computer. Everyone (assuming enough terminals are attached) has access to the computer whenever it is needed to do a job. Other advantages offered by a multiuser system are in the areas of security, accounting, backup/recovery, and the like. Chapter 6 discusses the pros and cons of multiuser systems versus single-user systems and local area networks. As seen in the OS/400 executive overview, the operating systems used with Application Systems support a full multiuser environment.

Multi-application (also called multitasking) means the ability, provided by some operating systems, to switch between two or more independent application programs from a single workstation. The opposite of multi-application is single-application, which means that the computer user must finish using one program before another can be started. The operating systems for all Application Systems support a multi-application environment, just like an office environment in which workers are often interrupted in the middle of one task to perform another. This multi-application capability of operating systems is particularly useful in that it allows the user to easily switch back and forth between several simultaneously resident application programs as interruptions occur. This means that the many users connected via terminals do not all have to be executing the same application, yet all appear to be receiving the same service simultaneously.

OS/400 in the Client/Server Environment?

The client/server environment is further described later in this chapter. Here, the changes to the operating system of the AS/400 system are identified. Those changes are dealt with in greater detail in the discussion of the operating system and of the various elements of the operating system that evolved to support the changes. ODBC was added to achieve that support, new communications structures were added, and the relational database structure was modified to what became called an integrated file system, supporting data streaming, triggers, stored procedures, declarative referential integrity, two-phase commit, and long field names. These functions were added as basic to the integrated file system and as a result apply to all of the file systems supported on the AS/400 system, not only those that apply to client/server and open systems environments.

The new communications methodologies that were added support local area networks and packet-switched networks. These new methodologies evolved because the communications structures that were in place to support the small data content (typically less than 2000 characters at a time) of the Non-Programmable Terminal (NPT) type of device were inadequate to support the larger information transfers (typically in the range of 10,000 to several million characters at a time) needed for the transfer of applications and full computing data needed by the intelligent clients.

The server started out having the single function of providing files to the clients, but, over time, the functions of the server have expanded to include security control of the data, database control and management, networking, application frameworks, and systems management. In the sections dealing with OS/400, database control and management, application frameworks, network file systems, remote file systems, and systems management are discussed. Internet and intranet are discussed in Chapter 5. Security is discussed from the aspect of Internet and intranet requirements, and from a total systems management perspective under "Security" in Chapter 6.

Network computing using Internet and intranet connections changes the view of client/server computing. The specific view perceived depends upon if you are resident on the Internet, on an intranet, or on the connection system between the two networks. The Internet is a series of interconnected servers between which the users (clients) bounce as they perform computing activities. Clients may be connected to an intranet and sharing an Internet server connection.

The intranet user is a Internet client when connected to the Internet through an Internet Connection Server. Two intranet users whose only logical and physical connection is through the Internet may ping-pong from client status to server status if allowed to share resources directly.

SSP—An Executive Overview

The **System Support Program** (5716-SSP), commonly called **SSP**, was the operating system originally offered for IBM System/36 computers. Because of the popularity of that computer family, SSP has become widely used in the business community. As a result, many application programs were developed for SSP and the System/36 by many different software companies. As the System/36 computers evolved, SSP was revised to support the enhancements in the computer hardware. Although each new version of SSP provided additional functions, compatibility with earlier application programs was maintained. SSP is the operating system used on the Advanced 36 systems and provides full compatibility with earlier System/36 computers. It consists of a set of programs designed to perform many diverse hardware "housekeeping" tasks under the control of either the computer user or an application program. Tasks performed by SSP include managing multiple users, providing security, managing the flow of batch and interactive jobs through the system, sending information to a printer, and so forth.

After users sign on to an Advanced 36, they can see SSP's main help menu, shown in Figure 4.1. From this menu, the user has two methods of initiating SSP tasks. More experienced users will issue SSP commands (called **Operation Control Language [OCL]**) at the SSP command line. OCL allows quick access to all SSP functions. Groups of OCL statements can be stored as a procedure and thereby executed by a single command. Less experienced users can step through a series of menus to perform operating system tasks. Although this method is not as fast as using OCL commands, the user is prompted at every step, which is easier for novices. These menus, along with online (computer-based) help text, reduce the number of publications needed to operate the system. SSP contains over 2000 screens of online help text similar to that shown in Figure 4.2. If users get stuck while performing some operating system task, they can press the Help key. SSP's help facility then presents users with textual information concerning the operation in question.

In addition to performing tasks under direct control of the user, SSP can perform tasks under direct control of an application program. A user can issue SSP commands through keyboard entries. Application programs issue SSP commands through the SSP **Application Program Interface (API)**. This is a defined protocol for passing information and requests directly between the application program and SSP with no user

```
                              MAIN
                      Main System/36 help menu

         Select one of the following:

                1. Display a user menu
                2. Perform general system activities
                3. Use and control printer, diskettes, or tape
                4. Work with files, libraries, or folders
                5. Use programming languages and utilities
                6. Communicate with another system or user
                7. Define the system and its users
                8. Use problem determination and service
                9. Use office products
               10. Sign off the system




         Cmd3-Previous menu    Cmd7-End   Cmd12-How to use help    Home-Sign on menu
         Ready for option number of command
                                                          COPR IBM Corp. 1985
```

Figure 4.1. The main Help menu presented by the SSP operating systems used on the AS/400 Advanced 36.

interaction required. It is the job of the operating system to provide for communications. SSP comes standard with the basic communications facilities to support remote workstations. Separately ordered extensions to SSP, such as the SSP communications feature and the 3270 device emulation feature, add communications functions such as asynchronous communications support and communications with S/390 computers. Other optional SSP add-ons include the tape support feature and the System/36 Utilities. The tape support feature allows a tape backup device to be attached. The System/36 Utilities are a package of programs designed to aid the programmer in writing application programs.

The SSP can coexist with the OS/400 operating system in any Advanced Series model. The Advanced 36 Model 436 is the only model on which the SSP may exist by itself without OS/400. Up to three copies of the SSP operating system are capable of cooperative processing with the OS/400 operating system on systems with adequate memory and disk capacity. In those systems on which cooperative processing is imple-

```
How to Use Help                    Introduction

This tutorial describes how to use the help support provided with the system.
It is divided into the selections listed below. Select the option number for
the item you wish to display and press the Enter key. From the first display
shown you can view the next display by pressing the Roll Up key. To view a
previous page in this tutorial, press the Roll Down key. To use the Roll
keys, you must press and hold down one of the shift keys, and then press one
of the Roll keys.

Select one of the following:

        1. The command and function keys you can use
        2. How to use help menus
        3. How to use help procedure and control command displays

Option:


Cmd3-Return to previous menu    Cmd7-End tutorial
                                                    COPR IBM Corp. 1983
```

Figure 4.2. Examples of SSP's Help text, presented in response to pressing the Help key.

mented, the OS/400 operating system has overall control and the SSP operating system can make calls for OS/400 I/O resources to perform functions and execute across I/O interfaces that the SSP would not normally be capable of doing because the support code was never written within the SSP itself.

OS/400—An Executive Overview

Operating System/400 (5769-SS1), commonly called OS/400 Version 4, is a multiuser operating system exclusively used with all AS/400 computer systems. It works closely with the System Licensed Internal Code (SLIC) instructions in AS/400 systems to implement the database, security, single-level storage, and so on that are basic to AS/400 architecture. OS/400 represents a divergence from the more traditional operating systems used with the earlier System/36 computers. Like SSP, OS/400 is a set of programs that perform housekeeping tasks based on requests from both users and application programs. Any AS/400 user can load and switch between multiple batch or interactive tasks, each protected from disruption by other tasks or users. Unlike SSP, however, OS/400 participated in the Systems Application Architecture (SAA) activity described in "Applications Architecture" in Chapter 3. OS/400 provides a platform for the development of new application programs in an environment consistent with the Systems Application Architecture.

The environment for application development has changed from the host-centric focus prevalent at the time of the definition of SAA to an application-centric one. During the evolution from host-centric computing to client/server computing, the name SAA has been dropped by IBM even though the principles of SAA (interoperability and communication between IBM-produced systems independent of the intended marketplace for those systems or the location within IBM that produced the system) have been continued. For example, OS/400 along with the Client Access/400 extension to OS/400 provides the first step in supporting the distributed relational database.

Although OS/400 offers the user complex and sophisticated features, many things have been done to make OS/400 easier to use. One of the ease-of-use enhancements is the uniting of the AS/400 and the Windows 95/Windows NT 4.0 desktop to provide a new graphical interface for users who are familiar with the Windows interface. Other OS/400 items that directly address ease of use include automatic configuration of devices and table-driven customization.

Extensive help and online (computer-based) documentation is provided to reduce the need to go to reference manuals when the user needs more information. Online education using CD-ROMs is built into OS/400 (see "Education" in Chapter 6 for additional details on CD-ROM education programs), allowing users to learn how to use the system while sitting in front of their terminal.

In addition to performing tasks under the direct control of the user, OS/400 performs tasks under direct control of an application program, which issues OS/400 commands through the OS/400. There is a defined protocol for passing information directly between the application program and OS/400 with no user interaction required. Often, OS/400 subsequently calls on the routines of the SLIC instructions to effect the desired action. This interaction between the different software layers was discussed in "AS/400 Software Architecture Overview" in Chapter 3.

OS/400 provides multiple application programming interfaces to maintain compatibility with programs written for System/36, System/38, and of course AS/400. The AS/400 application programming interface provides some new capabilities not found in earlier operating systems, such as the structured query language method of dealing with databases. If a user gets stuck on some operating system screen, pressing the Help key causes some help text to appear on the screen. The particular help text shown depends on where the cursor was on the screen when the Help key was pressed; that is, the text will address the particular item at which the cursor was positioned. This is called contextual help.

Extensive database and communications support allows AS/400 to manage large amounts of information and participate in many communications configurations. Available application development tools improve the productivity of programmers for those writing their own custom application programs. For current users of System/36 or System/38 systems, the AS/400 uses SSP and will run System/38 object code.

A Closer Look at OS/400

The previous section provided an overview of OS/400. Even though OS/400 is fairly easy to use, it has many complex features and functions. A complete description of these features would require a separate book. However, the remainder of this chapter looks briefly at some of the most important topics and the impact upon those topics as a result of the movement to the client/server, networking, and open environments:

- Integrated File System

- Database Support

- Communications Support

- Systems Management Features

- Application Development Facilities

- Integrated Language Environment (ILE)
- Open Standards–Based Interoperability
- System/3X Compatibility
- Emerging Object-Oriented Languages
- Emerging Application Development Environments
- Software Solution Packages

Integrated File System

The Integrated File System of OS/400 provides a consistent structure for manipulating all the types of information (i.e. file types) stored in an AS/400 system (see Figure 4.3). That is, it provides a consistent structure and interface (for users and application programs) for accessing traditional data base files, libraries, folders, documents, and so on, as

Figure 4.3. OS/400 integrated file system structure.

well as increasingly important information types such as images, audio, and video.

Support is provided for:

- Stream files which can contain long continuous strings of data (examples, the text of a document or the long string of data representing a scanned image).

- CICS files which are popular on the IBM S/390 computer family.

- A hierarchical directory structure (similar to that of UNIX and OS/2) that allows objects to be organized like fruit on the branches of a tree. An object is accessed by specifying the path through the directories to the object.

- A common interface that allows users and application programs to access all information not only the stream files but also database files, documents, and other objects stored in the AS/400 system.

- The Network File System (NFS) and the Remote File System (RFS) which are popular in UNIX environments.

The Integrated File System enhances the data management capabilities of OS/400 to better support emerging and future forms of information processing (e.g., client/server, open systems, and multimedia). The benefits provided by the integrated file system include:

- Fast access to AS/400 data, especially for applications using the PC file server (shared folder) facilities.

- More efficient handling of the increasingly important types of stream data, such as images, audio, and video.

- A file system and directory base for supporting UNIX-based open system standards such as POSIX and XPG. This file and directory structure also provides a familiar environment for users of UNIX and PC operating systems such as DOS and OS/2.

- The ability to handle information (such as record-oriented database files, UNIX-based stream files, and file serving) through separate file systems or manage it through a common interface, depending on user needs.

- Also PC users can take better advantage of the graphical user interface. For example, OS/2 users can use the OS/2 graphical tools to operate on AS/400 stream files and other objects in the same way as they operate on files stored on their PCs.

- Provides continuity of object names and associated object information across national languages. This support ensures that individual characters remain the same when switching from the code page of one language to the code page of another language.

OS/400 contains a file system that connects the AS/400 to a Windows NT domain as a client. The new file system is named QNTC and uses standard POSIX API's to provide access from the Integrated File system. The transport mechanisms to the new file system use industry standard protocols NetBios and TCP/IP.

Messaging protocols between the Integrated File System and QNTC are the industry standard CIFS and SMB. Through its access to data stored within the Windows NT domain, the AS/400 becomes a mechanism for distribution of applications and data. Any AS/400 application that can use data as formatted on the Windows NT Server can use the file system, such as Java applications. Access is allowed to data on both stand-alone Windows NT Servers and the AS/400 Windows NT application processor. Support is provided for Windows NT 4.0. The total number of active Application Storage Pools (ASP's) supported has been increased from 16 to 64.

Stream Files

To better understand stream files, it is useful to compare them with AS/400 database files. A database file is record oriented: It has predefined subdivisions consisting of one or more fields that have specific characteristics, such as length and data type. A stream file is simply a file containing a continuous stream of data. Documents stored in AS/400 folders are stream files. Other examples of stream files are PC files and the files in UNIX systems. Figure 4.4 illustrates the difference between record-oriented database and stream files. The different structure of stream files and record-oriented files affects how an application is writ-

Stream Files

Now is the time for all good men to come to the aid of their country. The quick brown fox caught the wily rabbit. Peter Piper picked a peck of pickled peppers. A peck of pickled peppers Peter Piper picked.

Record-Oriented Database File

Robert	1710 1st Ave. N.E.	Orion II	52345	**Record 1**
Richard	1735 1st Ave. N.E.	Orion II	52345	**Record 2**
Rachel	1777 1st Ave. N.E.	Orion II	52345	**Record 3**
⋮	⋮	⋮	⋮	
Peter	1959 1st Ave. N.E.	Orion II	52345	**Record n**

Figure 4.4. Stream file structure vs. record-oriented file structure.

ten to interact with them and where each type of file is best used in an application. A record-oriented file, for example, is well suited for storing customer statistics, such as name, address, and account balance, because these predefined fields can be individually accessed and manipulated using the extensive programming facilities of the AS/400. A stream file is better suited for storing information such as a customer's picture, which is composed of a continuous string of bits representing variations in color. Stream files are particularly well suited for storing strings of data such as the text of a document, images, audio, and video.

Integrated File System Support

From the perspective of structures and rules, the OS/400 support for accessing database files and various other object types through libraries can be thought of as a file system and is called QSYS.LIB. Similarly, the

OS/400 support for accessing stream files is a separate file system, called QDLS. Other file systems supported under the integrated file system include the following:

- **Root**: the "root" file system is designed to take full advantage of the stream file support and hierarchical directory structure of the integrated file system, and it has the characteristics of the DOS and OS2 file systems.

- **QOPENSYS**: the open systems file system is designed to be compatible with UNIX-based open system standards, such as POSIX and XPG. It is stream file oriented and supports case-sensitive object names.

- **QLANSrv**: the LAN server file system provides access to the same directories and files as are accessed through the OS/2 Warp Server licensed program. It allows users of the PC file server (shared folders) and AS/400 applications to use the same data as OS/2 Warp Server (5769-XZ1) clients. OS2 Warp Server will run applications that do not require Graphical User Interface (GUI) interaction. OS/2 Warp Server increases save/restore performance and provides printer serving capability and TCP/IP support including NetBIOS over TCP/IP, and LAN to LAN print capability.

Users and application programs can interact with any of the file systems through a common integrated file system interface. This interface is optimized for input/output of stream data in contrast to the record input/output provided through the data management interfaces. A set of user facilities (commands, menus, and displays) and Application Program Interfaces (APIs) is provided for interacting with the file systems through this common interface. As stated earlier in this chapter, triggers, stored procedures, declarative referential integrity, two-phase commit, and long field names are supported under all file forms and therefore improve DB2 for AS/400 as well as CICS/400.

The Integrated File System can support a large Address space up to one terabyte which can be used for heap storage, shared memory and memory mapped files. In addition to the large address space, the IFS can support stream files up to 256 GB in size in the root (/), qOpenSys, and user-defined file systems. Threadsafe integrated file system API interfaces can access objects in the following file systems in a multithreaded job:

- QSYS.LIB

- QOPT

- QLANSrv

DB2 Query Manager and SQL Development Kit

The DB2 Query Manager and SQL Development Kit for AS/400 (previously called SQL/400) provides: an interactive query and report writing interface, as well as precompilers and tools to assist in writing Structured Query Language (SQL) application programs in high-level programming languages. Once created, the applications and queries can be restored and run on other systems that do not have this product installed. An SQL Development Kit for relational database uses programming languages such as C, RPG, COBOL, PL/I, and REXX.

The interactive query interfaces, Query Manager and Interactive SQL, are provided for users to generate queries and reports, and for programmers to test complex SQL statements. The DB2 Query Manager and SQL Development Kit is a member of the DB2 family of products. The DB2 database manager function is integrated into OS/400 software and AS/400 hardware and includes all the support necessary for applications and queries that use SQL to run on the AS/400.

The DB2 Query Manager and SQL Development Kit for AS/400 provides portable database applications that conform to the standards ANSI X3.135.1992, ISO 9075-1992, and FIPS 127-2 within its SQL implementation, allowing portable database applications to be written in popular programming languages. Support is also included for the Integrated Language Environment (ILE) compilers. Runtime support for the programming languages is provided directly by the DB2 for AS/400 database manager. The user can specify page headings and footings, the order, width, and indenting for any column, page breaks, and column summary information. The SQL precompilers support host variable types for **Large OBjects (LOBs)** allowing programs that use embedded SQL to work with LOB data types in SQL programs.

Data editing capabilities are also provided. They allow users to update and add data to local and remote DB2 for AS/400 tables without additional application programs. Additional user profile support is also provided, allowing administrators to tailor defaults, limits, and privileges for each user.

SQL Development Kit

The SQL Development Kit provides facilities for processing embedded SQL statements in high level programming languages and includes a prompt-driven interface for testing and running SQL statements. By conforming to industry-standard Structured Query Language, the SQL implementation for OS/400 allows the definition of, manipulation of, query of, and control of access to AS/400 data, working with both AS/400 files and SQL tables. A SQL precompiler for C++ allows application developers to write applications using C++ and embedded SQL.

Support is provided for the following DB2 for AS/400 functions: embedded static; dynamic; and extended dynamic SQL declarative referential integrity; stored procedures; triggers; two-phase commit transaction management; and explain functions that conform with IBM SQL Version 1, ANSI X3.135.1992, ISO 9075-1992, and FIPS 127-2 SQL.

Network File System (NFS)

The internal structure of the integrated file system is shown in Figure 4.5. There are five components to that file system structure. The QOPT **PFS (Physical File System)** is there to support both CD-ROM and optical libraries. The user-defined physical file system supports long-named objects, as well as allows the user to identify specific groupings of hardware to belong to particular auxiliary storage pools. The NFS Server and NFS Client PFSs are UNIX specific and will be discussed further in the following paragraphs. QNetWare Client PFS is there to support the needs of an Internet set of clients.

The NFS Server and NFS Client communicate using **Remote Program Calls (RPCs)**. The NFS Client is a physical file system that implements the AS/400 Virtual File System architecture. The NFS Client provides seamless access to remote files for local applications. The remote files could be on a remote UNIX machine, the AIX IOP, or any machine that is running an NFS Server. The Network File System con-

Figure 4.5. Integrated file system international structure.

tains both a **lock manager** and a **system monitor**. The design of the system between the server and the client is a **stateless design** (one in which after completion of the current activity it is impossible to go back to a previous activity, because there is no coherent tracking of separate activities), so changes made at the client cannot be acquired at the server until the data stream is received at the server. Therefore, the server *locks* all data that has been sent to the client until received back from the client. The server monitor keeps track of the state of the systems in the network.

Remote File System

The AS/400 Remote File System allows users to share access to devices such as optical libraries or Integrated PC Controllers (FSIOPs) among AS/400s, manage a network from a single AS/400, share data in a homogeneous AS/400 network, and get data from multiple AS/400 systems with one connection from a PC. The Remote File System allows an AS/400 to act as a client to other AS/400s to allow access, using the Integrated File System commands, to any object on those AS/400 systems. It can only talk to other AS/400 systems, and Client Access can use this connection to access data on those other AS/400 systems. It is possible to chain system connections this way, but you must pay a propagation delay penalty. The connections can be across TCP/IP, APPC, or both. Functions not supported across these connections include multiple entities like authorization lists and group profiles, extended attributes and byte locking, and save/restore functions. Also, all users share the same connection to the remote system, and symbolic links can be traversed but not created.

Client for Windows NT File System

The client for Windows NT File System provides the AS/400 access to the NT Files in the Windows NT File system via the AS/400 Integrated File System. TCP/IP transports are used to communicate with any NT Server in the domain. Connections can be made to NT on the IPCS and standalone NT Servers. The AS/400 can be used as a management control point for distributing applications. Any AS/400 application that can use data formatted on the NT Server has access to that data. If NT data needs backup, NT Backup must be used.

Advanced Function Presentation

Advanced Function Presentation (AFP) comprises a document architecture, a printer dialog and datastream, and a process for fully system-managed printing. As a document architecture, AFP is known as **MODCA-P, or Mixed Object Document Content Architecture-Presentation**. As the name implies, AFP defines pages of output that mix all of the elements normally found in organizational documents—text in typographic fonts, electronic forms graphics, images, lines, boxes, and bar codes. The AFP datastream consists of a series of structured fields that implement all of these elements. AFP output can be created on the AS/400 using printer file keywords, DDS, Advanced Print Utility (APU), page and form definitions, AFP Utilities (AFP/U), and AFP Toolbox, as well as many third-party applications.

Once a print application is enabled using AFP, many complementary applications can work with the electronic output that is produced, including Client Access/400 AFP Viewer, which provides fully graphical document viewing as well as fax and printing services. Any AFP output can be faxed using Facsimile Support/400. AFP documents can be indexed, archived, retrieved, reprinted, and faxed using OnDemand for AS/400, which now includes the OnDemand client, and Internet document support.

Increasingly, organization documents are not immediately printed, but are distributed electronically. For example, a customer may retrieve their statements electyronically using a Web browser. Monthly sales reports are produced electronically and indexed for retrieval. They can then be viewed and optionally, printed in whole or in part as required.

AFP is also an interactive printer datastream called **IPDS (Intelligent Printer Data Stream)**. This datastream is similar to the AFP datastream but is built (on the fly) specific to the destination printer in order to facilitate the interactive dialog between the AS/400 system (specifically Print Services Facility/400, or PSF/400) and the printer. AFP, SCS, line data, and ASCII files are transformed into IPDS prior to printing in order to support this dialog. The Print Services Facilities/400 now include Page Printer Formatting Aid (PPFA), DDS, performance, transform, and archiving enhancements.

The two-way function of IPDS is a key component in AFP's system-managed printing process. The process includes document services, printer services, and print process management. *Document services* include identifying and automatically downloading externally referenced document resources such as overlays, images (page segments), and fonts to the IPDS printer. *Printer services* include monitoring printer resources and memory. Finally, the entire printing *process is managed* page by page to ensure that each spooled file is printed completely and accurately. Error conditions at the printer are monitored, and full error recovery is enabled at the AS/400.

The system-managed printing process with IPDS takes on added significance in a network TCP/IP environment. Placing printers within the network and attaching them with an IP connection provides great flexibility. However, TCP/IP print support is very limited—essentially a one-way send of the print file. The AFP printing process and bi-directionality of IPDS provides a bridge across this type of connection. The result is the same application (i.e., document capabilities) function and print management as that supported with twinax-attached printers.

DB2 for AS/400

To efficiently interact with large amounts of information, it is necessary to organize that information in some uniform way. For example, the information in a telephone book is organized into an alphabetical list of names, addresses, and telephone numbers. Computers also provide a tool for storing information in an organized software structure called a database. Almost any kind of information (e.g., a department store's inventory, a library's books, personnel records, digitized sound effects, medical records, scanned images of houses, etc.) can be stored within a computer database.

All AS/400 systems come with built-in database functions, called DB2 for AS/400, as part of OS/400. The fact that DB2 for AS/400 is built into the operating system means that the database functions come pre-loaded, fully integrated with the rest of the system components, and thoroughly tested. This integration also means that each enhancement to the operating system enriches the database environment.

Over 35,000 commercially available AS/400 application solutions take advantage of the power, flexibility, and ease of use of the DB2 for AS/400 database manager. These applications are written for a wide range of industries and users, ranging from small businesses with basic accounting needs to large corporations with complex computing environments.

One important aspect of DB2 for AS/400 is the ability to define the database structure independently. That is, the database definition does not reside "inside" any specific application program. The data is therefore said to be externally described, meaning the definition "lives" inside DB2 for AS/400 and in that respect leads an existence independent from any of the application programs that use it. This is a subtle but important point, because it improves the consistency and thus the maintainability of application programs. Now the programmer has one source for all information pertaining to the database structure and how application programs use the database.

Another important feature of DB2 for AS/400 is the support for logical files. Up to now we have been dealing with real or physical database files, which are groupings of information inside a computer. The concept of logical files allows a programmer to change the appearance of the physical database to better suit individual needs without creating a separate physical database with duplicate data, which causes synchronization problems.

Both **Open DataBase Connection (ODBC)** and **Structured Query Language (SQL)** are supported for accessing the database. **Data striping** is used to improve the performance of reads and writes to the database. DB2 for AS/400 has been enabled to become a partitioned database with its tables spread across the multiple system nodes, using either user-defined ranges or hash partitioning, but still presenting a single table view to the application, which operates in support of the potential interconnection of 32 loosely coupled systems using Opticonnect/400. A database monitor tracks events inside the database and provides the information about those events to the administrator.

Among the functions in place to support Symmetrical Multi-Processing (SMP) are: parallel table scan, parallel index scan, parallel hash join, parallel hash group by, parallel index build, parallel data load, parallel index ANDing/ORing of dynamic bit maps, parallel index maintenance, and parallel encoded vector indexes. Parallel Data Load has been PTFed back to earlier releases.

The data loader utility enables loading of data exported from other data servers, such as Oracle and Sybase into DB2/400. The data load function is separated into multiple processes that run in parallel when used on multiprocessor systems with the DB2/SMP feature. This feature makes large databases load much faster. When importing logical files, constraints and triggers are maintained. It is suggested that the constraints and triggers be removed when loading and added again after the loading is complete. For importing, the user can supply field and record delimiters or a field definition file that contains information on how DB2/400 should interpret the flat file.

Customers can specify and control parallel keyed access path maintenance for database files, similar to the support for parallel keyed access path builds and rebuilds. The DB2 SMP feature is required to support this parallel access path maintenance function.

OS/400 users can also leverage Distributed Data Management (DDM) functions in DB2 for AS/400 to access databases on distant AS/400 computers or other types of computers.

Queries executed against the DB2 for AS/400 database items see improved performance when executed on a system with more than one processor because the query workload is evenly distributed across the processors within the system, a process called **symmetric multiprocessing**. The DB2 SMP feature is required to support this parallel query function.

DB2/400 has been enabled for Internet application serving, which allows immediate use of existing data on the Internet to or from a terminal no matter where in the world the terminal is located, provided the usage meets the security requirements to use the Web server and has an appropriate Web browser. The results of a query are returned to your Web browser as an HTML document. Figure 4.6 illustrates how

Figure 4.6. DB2 for AS/400 Internet-style application development environment.

the Internet connection to DB2 for AS/400 parallels the AS/400 generalized support for client/server computing.

The Data Propagator Relational Capture and Apply product enables easy management of DB2-family distributed databases containing local copies of master databases by providing automatic update support for the **shadow** copies and the capability to replicate entire copies of a file.

DB2/400 supports the data warehousing aspect of business intelligence by providing Dynamic bit map indexing, remote journal capability, a parallel data loader, the ability to build indexes in parallel, support for tables up to half a terabyte in size, and Data Propagator Version 2.

DB2/400 continues to improve its support for standards by becoming 100% compliant to SQL Entry definitions, using SQL stored procedures, and managing a system wide SQL statement cache. Operations Navigator has been enhanced, and connectivity has been improved with the addition of JDBC, Active X, and OLE/DB, along with DRDA and native TCP/IP support. DB2/400 can manage a scalar subset in UPDATE, a subquery directed to DB2 Multisystem, and supports the ALTER table instruction. Encoded Vector Indexing has been added to improve database query performance. The Optimizer continues to be improved with the addition of a query performance tuner and a memory-based performance monitor.

When queries are grouped for a large number of queries, the "hash group by" algorithm provides improved performance. Also the performance can be improved by grouping MIN and MAX functions with a suitable index to determine the minimum and maximum value of a query. The hash joint algorithm implements subqueries that result in improved performance. Complex business intelligence queries can be written without the use of views by using derived tables and common table expression support. The use of expressions is also supported in Group By and Order By operations. The system administrator can set query specific options (query time limit and query degree) in a source file used by PC applications.

Product Preview—DB2-Universal DataBase Support

There are 6 Universal **characteristics** which a database must contain before it is qualified to be classified as a Universal Database. Those **universal characteristics** are universal access, universal application, universal extensibility, universal scalability, universal availability, and universal management. Figure 4.7 positions the DB2/400 database in regard to the six base requirements for a universal database, where bold items are those in place prior to V4R4, underlined items are those added by V4R4, and light type items are those which will be supplied in the near future.

Complex Object Support

The AS/400 with **Complex Object Support** which includes Large Object (LOBs) support can store and manipulate data fields that are much larger than the previous record limit of 32 Kbytes. An AS/400 record with LOB fields can hold up to 15 Megabytes of data. With the LOB support, the AS/400 database becomes a platform for building applications that hold new data such as large text, image, and audio. This provides database access to large data as well as database control of this data. With LOB support, combined with User Defined Types and User Defined Functions, it is possible to build imaging, large text and audio functions into object oriented database applications.

Figure 4.7. DB2/400 Universal DB Support.

Datalink Data Types

The **DataLink** data type is a basic building block for extending the data that can be stored in database files. The basic idea behind the DataLink is that the actual data stored in the column is only a pointer to the object. The object can be anything, an image file, a voice recording, a text file, etc. The method used for resolving to the object is to store a **Uniform Resource Locator (URL)**. This means that a row in a table can be used to contain information about the object in traditional data types, and the object itself can be referenced using the DataLink data type. A user can use SQL scalar functions to get back the path to the object and the size of the object. As an example, deleting a row will sever the relationship to the object referenced by the Datalink, but the object itself might not be deleted.

User Defined Types

User Defined Types are derived from existing types (e.g., predefined types like integer or character). Users are allowed to create their own types, which supports strong typing and creating different user defined functions for different types. With User Defined Types, users are allowed to call a function for each row of a result set, and return some value based on the user defined type that was input to the function.

User Defined Functions

SQL is made more extensible by letting users define their own functions which may be used within SQL itself. Time is saved in re-using common building blocks designed to meet a specific need. **User Defined Functions** are a building block to support database extenders (extensions to support rich text and multimedia search and manipulation) currently supported on a Universal DataBase (UDB).

The Universal Database including the latter four items will be delivered by means of an EnhancePak in the fourth quarter of 1999. At that time the database will be renamed to some variation of DB2 Universal Database for AS/400.

Built-In Database

Deeply embedded in the architecture and operating system of AS/400 computers lies the support for the development and manipulation of a relational database structure. In a relational database, each piece of information is "related" to the others using a simple tabular structure. This provides great flexibility when defining the database and using the information it contains. Inside the AS/400's database, information is stored as records and fields. Do not be intimidated by the words. This is exactly how the information in a phone book is structured. Figure 4.8 shows an example of a telephone book listing and the corresponding relational database structure found in an AS/400 computer. The phone book itself is analogous to a set of information or a database.

The telephone example is explained in greater detail in the next section. "Relational Database—Telephone Book," which follows this section. The database example defines externally described data, and the independent structure of the database. The second example, "Rela-

Figure 4.8. Information in a database is organized much like the information in a telephone book.

tional Database—Physical and Logical Files," about a business called Atole Enterprises, explains the difference between physical and logical files. The example then explains how logical files in relational databases can eliminate redundancy in data records by providing different views of the same physical file. The third example, "Relational Database—Concurrency and Lock Management," explains the problems that can arise when logical files are replaced by multiple physical files with redundant fields.

There are ways to keep multiple copies of information up to date on computer systems without logical files, but if the examples are extended to a real business environment with many different clerks, many different programs undergoing changes, and many different types of databases, managing the problem of multiple physical files becomes time-consuming and difficult. With the logical file approach, there is no data redundancy problem to manage. These examples illustrate how logical database files can be used to provide the user with the information needed in the way that it is needed. Other logical database file structures are possible with the AS/400 computer, which can, for example, pull together selected information from multiple (up to 32) physical database files into a single logical file. This further expands the ability to deliver the right information to the various users without duplicating information in different databases. Through the AS/400 "built-in" database, users have access to information, the security and integrity of the data is protected, and programmer productivity is improved.

Telephone Book

The telephone book provides us with a method of illustrating what a relational database is, allows us to describe how such a database works with a different view for different users, enables us to define how logical files relate to the different users views, provides a capability to present a perspective of data security and data integrity, and then demonstrates one problem set associated with multiple physical databases. The information about one person in the phone book would be analogous to a record. The record contains the information for a given entry, and all other records contain similar information about their respective entries. (An employee's record contains all of the pertinent information about that employee regardless of the number of fields needed.) In this case, a record contains the name, address, and phone number of the person. Each one of these three items is analogous to a field. For example, in a relational data base, the address part of a phone book entry is called the "address field."

Manually looking up information in a phone book is time-consuming and quickly becomes fatiguing. The same is true for manually manipulating any large body of information. Once information is entered into a database, its retrieval by the computer is quick and easy. What does the built-in database capability of the AS/400 have to offer? In AS/400 computers the database structure is defined independently from user programs, the data in the database is available to all user programs for analysis, report generation, update, and so on, but the database definition does not reside in a user's programs. The data is therefore said to be externally described, meaning no single user's program on the system describes the structure or content of the database. Instead, the definition "lives" inside the AS/400's built-in database system and in that respect is independent from any one program. This is an important point, because it improves the consistency and thus the maintainability of application programs. Now the programmer has one source for all information pertaining to the database structure and how application programs use the database. Externally described data contribute to improved programmer productivity because the database will fit itself to the application program rather than the application program fitting itself to the database.

The examples in "Relational Database—Physical and Logical Files" and "Relational Database—Concurrency and Lock Management" use simple database structures. In the sections on data warehousing and data mining in Chapter 3, multidimensional database structures are mentioned. Those more complex logical database file structures are possible with the AS/400 computer, which can, for example, pull together selected information from multiple (up to 32) physical database files into a single logical file. This further expands the ability to deliver the right information to the various users without duplicating information in different databases.

Physical and Logical Files

Another important feature of AS/400 database support is the support for logical files. The telephone book example deals with real, or physical, database files, which are groupings of information inside a computer. The concept of logical files allows a system administrator to change the appearance of the physical database to better suit individual needs. For example, suppose there is a personnel database on an AS/400 computer for a fictitious company named Atole Enterprises. The organization of the personnel information is shown in Figure 4.9.

This physical database file contains all personnel information and was described externally to any user programs. A clerk (Jim) has the job of keeping an up-to-date mailing list of all employees for the company magazine, but to protect employees' privacy, Jim must not have access to the wage information that is part of the physical database file. To

	Name	Address	Phone	Wages	SS#	Date of Hire	Marital Status
Record 1							
Record 2							
Record 3							
Record 4							
Record 5							
Record 6							
Record 7							
Record 8							
⋮							
Record X							

Figure 4.9. Physical database containing personnel information.

meet these needs, a logical database file is defined that contains no information but only a "view" of the physical database that meets Jim's needs. The logical database file restricts Jim's view of the physical database file to only the information he needs. Furthermore, since Jim looks up employees by name, this is the key field defined in his logical database file. He is able to access the information by alphabetical order of employee name (his key field) rather than by the order in which the names actually appear in the physical database file. Jim's logical database file structure is shown in Figure 4.10.

Another logical database file for a different clerk (Nancy) exists using the same physical data. Nancy tracks employee service anniversaries. Her logical database file structure is shown in Figure 4.11. Nancy looks up employees by their date of hire, so this is the key field in her logical database file. Only the fields needed to do her job are made available to Nancy. As the needs of Atole change, many logical database files can be defined to meet the different employees' needs without affecting any other user or the physical database file. The restrictions

Jim's Logical Database
(Key)
Name   Address

	Name	Address	Phone	Wages	SS#	Hire date	Marital status
Record 1							
Record 2							
Record 3							
Record 4							
Record 5							
Record 6							
Record 7							
Record 8							
Record X							

Figure 4.10. Jim's logical database provides a "view" of the physical database needed to perform his job.

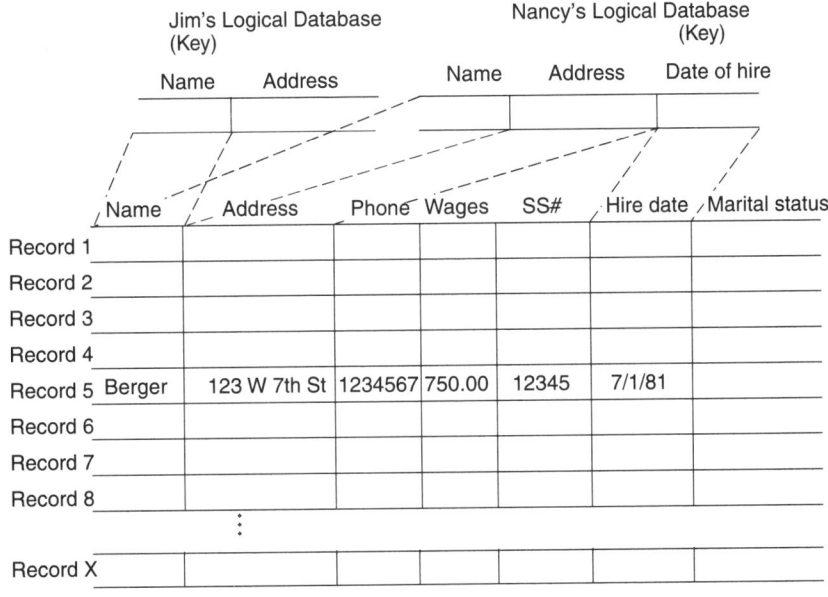

Figure 4.11. Multiple logical databases can be constructed, providing different views of the same physical database.

provided by unique views for different users/user groups inherently guarantees data security and data integrity. Also, within any particular view, fields may be further identified as read only for additional data integrity. Users are allowed to view and change data contained in the fields to which they have authorization to make changes.

This example illustrates how multiple users can use a single copy of a physical database to do completely different jobs. Without logical files, multiple physical databases would have to be kept in the computer system, wasting space. The Atole Enterprises example is extended in Relational Databases—Concurrency and Lock Management to illustrate the problems of data concurrency and lock management across multiple physical databases containing redundant data.

Concurrency and Lock Management

Figure 4.12 illustrates a situation at fictitious Atole Enterprises that can occur when multiple databases contain redundant information. The fig-

Jim's Database		Nancy's Database			Payroll Database					
Name	Address	Name	Address	Hire Date	Name	Address	Phone	Wages	SS	Hire Date
Berger	333 E 7th St	Berger	333 E 7th St	7/1/81	Berger	333 E 7th St	1234567	750.00	23422	7/1/81
⋮		⋮			⋮					
Physical Database #1		Physical Database #2			Physical Database #3					

Figure 4.12. Without logical database views, multiple physical databases would be necessary, wasting space, compromising data integrity, and complicating processing.

ure shows three different databases (one for Jim, one for Nancy, and one for payroll), each of which contains name and address fields for Atole Enterprises employees. In addition to wasting space because of the redundancy, other problems are associated with having multiple physical databases. For example, one morning Jim receives notice that an employee (Mr. Berger) has a new mailing address and Jim promptly updates the database. Later that same morning, Nancy searches for that month's service anniversaries and finds that the month is Mr. Berger's seventh anniversary with the company. She checks his address and sends him an anniversary card.

Without the logical file approach, in which Jim and Nancy share one physical copy of the data, Mr. Berger's card would be sent to the old address. With the logical database of the AS/400 computers, as soon as Jim updates Mr. Berger's address it is available to Nancy, and Mr. Berger gets his card on time. The problem solved by the single physical file with multiple logical views is one of concurrency (synchronization); that is, when multiple physical files exist with redundant data defined across those physical files, an update to a redundant field in one of those files makes it different from the identical field in the other physical files. One alternative solution is to maintain a cross-reference file that identifies all of the redundant fields of each of the physical files and an application program that updates the redundant fields of the other physical files when any of the fields receives a change.

A second problem that arises from the concurrency problem is lock management. Lock management becomes a problem because once the computer knows that a redundant field has received a change, the computer must prohibit processing with those fields of the physical files containing old data because either this will cause erroneous results or, as in our example, the information will be sent to the wrong location. To prevent that processing, the computer system locks those fields until update processing has completed. If a program has started that uses a locked field, it must be backed out of the computing system or put into a suspended state.

The illustration selected is a simple one because the data that changed was entered by an individual, but consider the problem when the redundant field is changed under control of an application program, with other application programs referencing that field for processing information. With multiple physical files with redundant fields, situations have arisen in which the entire computing system became deadlocked because the total resources of the computer were tied up and the update program could not gain access to the resources to execute to resolve the lock situations. Lock management programs are very complex programs. Lock management is also a problem when redundancy occurs over distributed databases on distributed systems.

There are ways to keep multiple copies of information up to date on computer systems without logical files, but if our example is extended to a real business environment with many different clerks, many different programs undergoing changes, and many different types of databases, managing the problem becomes time-consuming and difficult. With the logical file approach, there is no data redundancy problem to manage. This example illustrates one method of using logical database files to provide the user with the information needed in the way that it is needed.

Distributed Data Management

In a networked system environment, the Distributed Data Management (DDM) function of OS/400 allows an AS/400 user to access data on a remote AS/400 as if the data were located on the local AS/400 system.

With distributed data management, the user need not know which computer system has the needed data. If the needed database resides on a different AS/400 located elsewhere in the communications network, DDM will automatically get the information for the user.

Distributed Data Management has always allowed distributed database activity with remote AS/400 systems, but there was no support for interacting with any compatible databases on other computer systems (e.g., IBM's ES/9000 line of computers). Enhancements in the Distributed Data Management function of OS/400 include full support of the Distributed Relational Database Algorithm (DRDA). One element of Distributed Data Management's support for DRDA is called the remote unit of work. This allows an AS/400 application program to include compatible System Query Language (SQL) statements that interact with data residing on another compatible database on a distant computer system. That is, the user now has access to the data stored on other computer systems (e.g., an IBM ES/9000 computer system with an SQL/DS database). The user can interact with multiple remote databases during a single database transaction

DB2 for OS/400—An Overview

DB2 for AS/400 (DB2/400) is a relational database supporting large physical file structures, built on a records/fields structure, supporting multiple views, logical views, and read-only fields, and incorporating access-level security and data integrity.

Among the more popular database supported by OS/400 is DB2. Triggers, stored procedures, declarative referential integrity, two-phase commit, and long field names are supported under all file forms and therefore improve DB2/400 as well as CICS/400. The DB2/400 capability provides support for:

- ANSI X3.135.1992, ISO 9075-1992, and FIPS 127-2

- Structured Query Language (SQL)

- IBM's Distributed Relational Database Architecture (DRDA)

- Distributed Unit of Work—Application Directed

- Microsoft's Open Database Connection (ODBC)

- Java DataBase Connection (JDBC)

- Apple's Data Access Language

Parallel index building capability is added to DB2 Symmetric Multi-Processing (SMP) for AS/400, extending the SMP capabilities to utilize multiple processors during the creation or rebuilding of indices.

DB2 for OS/400

DB2 for AS/400 performs all the functions described in the examples used to introduce relational database concepts: multiple physical databases within a single database structure each of which contains records, fields, and some relationship; and multiple views for each physical database within the structure. Since there is no redundancy, there is no reason for concerns about concurrency and lock management. Both Open DataBase Connection (ODBC) and System Query Language (SQL) are supported for accessing the database, including SQL indexes, run SQL, and the new object types LOB and DATALINKS described earlier in this chapter.

DB2 for AS/400 has been enabled to become a partitioned database with its tables spread across the multiple system nodes, using either user-defined ranges or hash partitioning, but still presenting a single table view to the application, which operates in support of the potential interconnection of 32 loosely coupled systems using Opticonnect/400. DB2 Multisystem for AS/400 is a separately priced option for OS/400. The data partitioning does not allow ranges, although the user can specify where the hash result of individual values should reside. The main benefits of multi-system are high-end growth and greater processing power. A query issued against a distributed file will be submitted in parallel to all applicable systems in the node group, resulting in all the systems working on the query in parallel, and inside each system the query is also running in parallel. A database monitor tracks events inside the database and provides the information about those events to the administrator.

Queries executed against the DB2 for AS/400 database items see improved performance when executed on a system with more than one processor because the query workload is evenly distributed across the processors within the system, a process called symmetric multiprocessing. The results of a query are returned to your Web browser as an HTML document.

DataPropagator Relational Capture and Apply

The Data Propagator Relational Capture and Apply for AS/400 product enables easy management of DB2-family distributed databases containing local copies of master databases by providing automatic update support for the shadow copies and the capability to replicate entire copies of a file. DataPropagator Relational Capture and Apply can update source tables and replicated tables. The latest version supports both the Version 1 and Version 2 architectures, and includes a Graphical User Interface (GUI) control center. The Data Propagator Relational Capture and Apply product takes advantage of the remote journaling function to run the capture process at the remote journal location, which off-loads the capture process overhead from the production system. The apply process no longer needs to connect to the production system for differential refresh because the staging tables reside locally instead of on the production system. A new exit program allows automatic deletion of source file journal receivers that are no longer needed by the capture process. The product is compatible with all Version 4 releases.

Open DataBase Connection (ODBC)

Open DataBase Connection is a Microsoft-provided Application Program Interface specification for database access, the objective of which is to provide interoperability between applications and databases without writing database-specific code in the application. This definition sounds very similar to the program independence objective identified for the relational database in "Relational Database—Telephone Book." DB2 for AS/400 supports Open DataBase Connection. As a result, applications such as Net.Connection that use DB2 may exchange data with other applications that use ODBC. The SQL Call Level Interface is compatible with ODBC, allowing an application to be written on a PC using ODBC and then be ported to run on the AS/400 directly. ODBC is also supported by Client Access Family for Windows and Client Access Family.

Java DataBase Connection (JDBC)

The Java DataBase Connection provides the same capabilities for Net.Data as ODBC provides, including the capability for applications written in Java to access applications that use ODBC and as a result to access DB2 applications. The JDBC 2.0 API includes Scrollable result sets. Scrollable result sets allow more flexibility in processing of result sets by providing both forward and backward movement through the contents. In addition, relative and absolute positioning is allowed. As an example it is possible to move to the fourth row in a scrollable result set directly, or to move directly to the third row following the current row, providing that row exists. Result sets can be directly updatable.

An application can submit multiple update statements (insert, update, delete) in a single request to the database providing an increase in performance when a large number of update statements need execution.

Support exists for storing persistent Java objects as well as for binary large objects and structured types. Additional improvements have been made in synchronization, exception handling, method calls, generated code loop handling, field access in objects, and garbage collection; the results of which can be seen in performance and scaling of systems.

Data Striping

IBM improved the performance and capacity of DB2 for AS/400 by automatically striping all writes to the data files upon which the data will be stored. (A database file consists of many blocks of information. These blocks are randomly spread/striped across multiple devices. A single DASD device can store multiple blocks from a single file—most likely the multiple blocks for a file on a device are *not* logically contiguous.) This spreading across multiple DASD devices allows the data to be accessed in parallel. The result is a significant performance improvement because the data can be brought into main storage in parallel, instead of serially. This is made possible because the multiple I/O Processors (IOPs), supporting disk units on the AS/400 system, pre-process the data on writes and reads to improve access time.

Partitioned Database

To better serve users who have implemented or are considering implementing the loosely coupled structure of systems allowed by the

Opticonnect/400 capability of interconnecting up to 32 systems optically, DB2 for AS/400 has been enabled to become a partitioned database with its tables spread across the multiple system nodes. Spreading the tables across many nodes by using either user-defined ranges or hash partitioning, still presents a single table view to the application. This can apply the power of 384 processors (if all of the processors are 12-way symmetric multi-processors, all working in parallel) to a query. This **massively parallel database** supports parallel insert, update, and delete while allowing the DB2 for AS/400 database size to grow from a previous single system maximum of 1,546 GB up to a maximum loosely coupled parallel database limit of 49.47 TB. Symmetric Multi-Processing (SMP) is supported with the optional DB2 Symmetric Multi-Processing for AS/400, which provides parallelism in index builds and queries. SMP uses parallel table scan, parallel index scan, parallel hash join, parallel hash group by, and parallel index build algorithms.

The response time of queries executed in a symmetric multiprocessor environment resolve themselves more quickly because the power of all of the distributed processors is applied in parallel against the distributed database. This is particularly applicable when performing *data mining* against a *data warehouse*.

Database Monitor

A database monitor has been added to DB2 for AS/400. The database monitor provides information about what the database is doing, such as how many temporary indexes have been created, which information people are using the most, how many queries have exceeded a specified time limit, and which queries are using the most system resources. The data from the monitor is collected at the job or system level. The monitor provides all information from either a debug or print sequence plus the following:

- System and job name

- SQL statement and sub-select number

- Start and end time stamp

- Estimated processing time

- Total rows in file queried

- Number of rows selected

- Estimated number of rows selected

- Estimated number of joined rows

- Key fields for advised index

- Total optimization time

- Join method

- Join type and others

Database Management

A single program can use any combination of old (System/3X) functions and new AS/400 functions. This allows maximum flexibility for new database application programs and added capabilities when modifying System/3X application programs that have been migrated to AS/400. Furthermore, different application programs can simultaneously use different methods to access the same database files without interfering with one another. Although OS/400 provides the programmer/user with many ways to "get at" database information, other functions are necessary to make a complete database management system. In a typical database environment, many different users are constantly making changes to the information in the database. These changes are called **database transactions**. To maintain the accuracy or data integrity of the information in the database at all times, OS/400 plays the role of a traffic director.

First, OS/400 prevents two people from simultaneously updating the same information. Without this protection, the integrity of the database is at risk. For example, two travel agents making a reservation for their respective customers simultaneously call up the same seat in an airliner. Both reservationists see the seat as available. The first reservationist reserves the seat for Mr. Jones and posts that change to the database. The second reservationist, who still sees the seat as available, reserves the seat for Ms. Smith and posts this change to the database, overwriting Mr. Jones's reservation. Neither reservationist knows that an error has been introduced! That is a **data integrity** problem. Although this may seem to be an unlikely series of events, if it can happen it will, particularly in very active database environments in which many thousands of transactions are generated every hour. OS/400 prevents two people from updating the same database information. This is called **record level locking**.

Other improvements have been made. As an example, deleted database records are automatically reused, eliminating the need to execute the physical file command to recover unused disk storage space, and support is provided for variable-length fields—a new data type for the AS/400.

DCE Base Services/400

Distributed Compute Environment (DCE) Base Services/400 is based on the Open Software foundation (OSF) DCE Version 1.2.2. The code provided by OSF for DCE has been enhanced to provide the look and feel of AS/400 with support for AS/400 messages, menus, prompts, and help text. Improved reliability, availability, and serviceability of the DCE code are provided to make it consistent with other AS/400 products.

DCE uses **Remote Procedure Call (RPC)** as a model for implementing communications between a client and a server, in which the client side runs on one machine and makes a request for service, and the server side runs on another machine in the network and fulfills the service request. RPC extends the model of the local procedure call into the open environment and the distributed computing environment.

The RPC facility includes an application development tool and a run-time library. When developing a DCE application, an application developer defines a RPC interface between the client application and the server application. DCE uses the DCE **interface definition language (IDL)** to define this interface. The application development tool contains an IDL compiler that compiles the customer's interface definitions into portable C-language source code. The IDL-generated source code can be compiled with the customer's application code using the ILE-C compiler and can be linked to the DCE run-time library to form the distributed application.

RPC helps hide the complexities of the distributed environment from the application programmer and the user. RPC is integrated with the DCE cell directory service and the DCE security service, enabling the client application to transparently find the location of the server and have secure communications. The DCE cell directory services act as a centralized location for storing information about the resources in the distributed system. The name of an object can be looked up and information can be retrieved about the object. Distributed systems objects include the users, the systems, and the resources associated with the systems.

A single distributed directory service is created. There is no need to maintain local copies of information about distributed resources. The directory service provides a logically centralized physically distributed place to store information. The directory can accommodate all the distributed resources in an enterprise, is scalable to any size, and can grow as the distributed system grows.

The cell directory service manages a database of information about the resources in a group of systems that work together, called a **DCE cell.** The size and content of a DCE cell can be defined by the users to best suit their needs. An application uses the cell directory client function to query the directory when information is needed about the location of a resource with which the application needs to communicate.

When the directory structure is in place, a remote procedure can be referred to by a unique identifier, such as its name, by an application programmer. When it is queried, the directory returns the address location of that remote procedure to the application. The programmer does not have to hard code any addresses in a program, providing greater flexibility in the placement of logic and data in the network.

A cell directory server must be configured in the cell to use the DCE cell directory client function. This directory server can reside on any system that implements the OSF DCE cell directory server, such as RS/6000, System/390, AS/400, or Windows NT. The cell directory client function of DCE Base Services/400 is supported by a Cell Directory Server as defined by OSF DCE 1.2.2.

DCE security service ensures that clients and servers are trusted by each other by supporting an authentication service in the open distributed environment. Authentication of clients and servers by the DCE security service prevents unauthorized use of distributed resources by supporting an access control facility. The DCE security service ensures data integrity and data privacy.

The authentication mechanism used by the DCE security service is based on the Massachusetts Institute of Technology (MIT) Kerberos authentication technology. The client and server are authenticated or securely identified to each other by a third party security server. As a result:

- Users no longer need to be explicitly defined to every physical system that they need to access in the distributed environment, eliminating administrative overhead because a user or resource need only be defined to the security server once. Only one password needs to be remembered per user.

- DCE security protects the server from clients that are imposters and protects the clients from servers that are imposters, vs. security systems that only protect the intelligence at the host or server end.

- Like directory services, security has a logically central, physically distributed database for users, because of the single logical structure, changes need only be made in one place.

- A user can access all the DCE resources of the distributed system, by once logging on to a DCE system.

Once a protected session between a client and a server is established, the client can access the resources of the server using security policies to control that access. Different security policies can be set up between each client/server pair.

Data integrity verification is based on a checksum generated by DCE security to ensure that data was not tampered with during transmission. The Data Encryption Standard (DES) algorithm is used by the DCE security service to protect data privacy. The data privacy facilities are offered as the DCE DES library routines. U.S. Government import/export laws and regulations regarding "full" DES products affect this product because it enables encryption.

Once a DCE security server is configured in a cell, the DCE security client function can be used. The security server can be configured on any system that implements the OSF DCE security server.

Distributed Time Services periodically synchronize the clocks on the different nodes in a distributed network, and keep the distributed time in each node synchronized with coordinated universal time (UTC). The synchronization is needed because many distributed applications need to ascertain the order of events, compute the interval between events, and schedule events independent of where the events occurred. The DCE time server must be configured in the DCE cell and can reside on any system that implements OSF DCE time services. DCE base Services/400 implements the distributed time clerk function.

DCE for AS/400 enables and protects current investments, provides increased productivity, and grows incrementally with a business. Computing systems and networks are more usable. New and existing systems and software can be exploited, and new and existing industry and international standards and architecture can be introduced.

DCE isolates the application programmer from the communications code required for distributed applications, enabling the development of higher quality, more functional distributed applications. Directory and security functions are automatically invoked as part of RPC. Distributed application client and server routines, written for a target operating system are more easily ported to another operating system because OSF DCE API's are the same among operating systems that support the DCE standard.

CICS Translation Server for AS/400 (5769-DFH)

Previously referred to as CICS/400, CICS Translation Server for AS/400 comes packaged with two other products, CICS Universal Clients and CICS Transaction Gateway. The grouping of these products allows entry into e-business. Using application programs (pre-written or custom) to access and manipulate information in an AS/400 database, businesses can combine all of the methods of accessing information to provide an environment that is tailored to their particular needs. These application programs may, unknown to the users, employ one or more of the previously discussed database access methods, depending on the specific need. Using the CICS Translation Server for AS/400 extension to OS/400, programmers can run CICS application programs (COBOL) on an AS/400 and access data on the AS/400 or some other computer (e.g., an S/390 or OS2 computer) running CICS.

Application programs that use CICS are very common in the IBM S/390 user community. CICS Translation Server for AS/400 allows programmers to migrate S/390-based CICS application programs to the AS/400 or use their CICS experience to write new CICS application programs specifically for the AS/400. The communications functions provided by the CICS environment provide another way for AS/400 programmers to write/migrate application programs that give users access to information stored in the AS/400 and other computer systems. The CICS Translation Server for AS/400 functions have been extended to include client/server support, two-phase commit, and C application language support.

Many of these different methods and tools for creating, loading, and accessing AS/400 files and databases were carried over from the System/36 and System/38 product lines. Some of these different methods and tools provide functions that are highly redundant with others. This was done intentionally to provide application program compatibility with the System/36 and System/38. Providing all these different methods for managing AS/400 databases makes it easier to migrate System/3X application programs to AS/400. This helps preserve the significant investment made by businesses in application programs, user training, data accumulation, and so on. At the same time, improved database tools (e.g., SQL/400 and CICS/400) not available with System/3X computers are provided for the AS/400.

Communications Support

Communications facilities included in OS/400 allow a properly equipped AS/400 computer to communicate with different computing equipment in a variety of ways. First, OS/400 provides support for remote workstations, allowing terminals and printers to be located far away (e.g., across the country) from the AS/400 computer system itself. This allows remote offices to perform all the functions available to those users located in the same building as the AS/400. Further, OS/400 provides the programming support for communications with other computer systems (both IBM and non-IBM) such as System/390, personal computers, System/3X, Macintosh, and other AS/400s. In any case, there are different communications protocols that can be used, as discussed in "Wide Area Networks (WANs)" and in "The AS/400 and Local Area Networks" in Chapter 2. OS/400 includes support for the following protocols, the first five of which are used in wide area networks, the last four of which are used in local area networks:

- Async
- Bisync
- SDLC
- X.25
- IDLC (ISDN networks)
- IEEE 802.5 (IBM token-ring networks)
- IEEE 802.3 (Ethernet networks)
- ISO 9314 (FDDI networks)
- Wireless Local Area Networks

In addition, the ATM protocols and devices may be used to increase the information flow rate between networks and systems also using those protocols and devices.

Communications configurations provide some hardware and software configurations for various communications networks. For now, it is only necessary to understand that OS/400 comes with the programming required to support these different types of communications environments.

Additional information about additional subjects supported by OS/400 communications can be obtained by referring to the following sections:

- TCP/IP
- Systems Network Management
- Systems Network Architecture (SNA)
- Display Station/Printer Pass-Thru
- S/390 Communications Support

TCP/IP

Another extension to OS/400 called AS/400 TCP/IP Communications Utilities (#5738-TC1) allows AS/400 systems to participate in communications networks that use the **Transmission Control Protocol/Internet Protocol (TCP/IP)**. TCP/IP is commonly used over a Local Area Network (LAN) (e.g., Ethernet) in which computer systems (e.g., UNIX-based systems) of different brands communicate with one another. The IBM TCP/IP Server Support/400 product (#5798-RWY) gives clients access to AS/400 database files and folder files via Sun Microsystems' Network File System (NFS), which is commonly used in TCP/IP environments. The TCP/IP protocol has become increasingly significant as the client/server environment has moved into a networked environment including both intranets and the Internet.

Standards supported by AS/400 TCP/IP include **Dynamic Host Configuration Protocol (DHCP)** and **Domain Name Server (DNS)**. Dynamic Host Configuration Protocol support allows the AS/400 to dynamically assign Internet Protocol (IP) addresses when new hosts are added to the network, such as when a network station or PC is turned on in an intranet. Domain Name Server converts the text names as used in URLs to the 32-bit codes used for network routing. As an example it converts www.as400.ibm.com to 205.217.130.11. Other functions supported are TCP/IP dial-in via **PPP (Point to Point)** and ISDN as well as full TCP/IP routing. Operations Navigator provides a Windows-like graphical interface to the TCP/IP configuration function.

The network integration characteristics of TCP/IP have been enhanced through the addition of Graphical Users Interface (GUI) support of all TCP/IP configuration and administrative tasks. Filtering of the IP packets can be based on the remote system, IP address and applications, choosing to "allow" or "deny" for the remote access to filter. **Network Address Translation (NAT)** and filtering activities can be journaled. The entries will be added each time IP packets are examined, IP addresses are translated or rules are updated. The user can choose to start the journal or not. As discussed under firewall, users have the opportunity to change IP addresses of IP packets going out from the network, so the internal addresses are not known by the external hosts. This secures the internal network.

NAT provides a technology called IP masquerading, which allows multiple users to share a single public IP address. NAT translates the internal IP addresses to a single specific IP address using the unique port numbers assigned to the internal IP addresses. **Virtual IP Addressing (VIPA)** provides network load balancing and fault tolerance between multiple IP interfaces (adapters). Outgoing balancing and incoming balancing work differently. **Outgoing balancing** is done through the routing configuration. **Incoming balancing** needs an external router which is capable of distributing IP packets to multiple interfaces. The distribution information is provided to the routers by the RIP protocol. The load balancing using routers, enables multiple redundant paths from the server to the network, providing horizontal bandwidth growth, and high availability tolerance for link or router failures.

Figure 4.13 provides an example of TCP/IP enabled dial-on-demand networking. In Figure 4.13 a switched point to point (PPP) connection is established only when demanded by either the central site or one of the remote sites. The types of connections can be mixed and matched to the available connection capabilities, analog lines up to 33.6 Kb, switched digital up to 56 Kb, and ISDN at up to 128 Kb. Figure 4.14 shows an integrated TCP/IP load balancing connection for a high volume e-business server to either an intranet or the Internet. Appendix C summarizes the TCP/IP protocols, servers and services including related standards.

Figure 4.13. Example of AS/400 Dial-on Demand Networking.

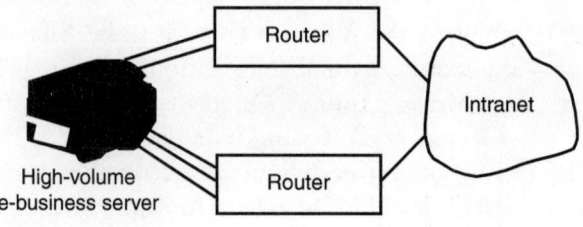

Figure 4.14. AS/400 Integrated TCP/IP load balancing for a high volume e-business server.

File Transport Protocol (FTP) graphical client support includes the UNIX list command. Directories other than database libraries can be used as the initial working directory, and files larger than 2 GB can be transferred. Options are added to create new database files. FTP supports the ability to transfer files larger than 2 GB in all file systems that support the large file sizes. Database files containing null field data can also be transferred.

SMTP scaleability has been improved by extending the number of inbound and outbound connections from 16 to unlimited and by changing the Domain Name Server (DNS) resolver to support large ISPs, as a result, the SMTP client processes all mail exchange records returned by a domain name server query. An option exists to track delivery status and mail statistics using journaling. There is an option which forces all mail received by the AS/400 SMTP to be processed by the AS/400 Mail Services Framework (MSF).

Telnet Server provides native support for Secure Sockets Layer (SSL), and the interactive capacity of TCP/IP attached workstations has been increased.

Virtual Private Networks

Virtual Private Networks (VPN) evolved from the need to insure secure communications between networked computers. At considerable expense companies established private networks. Firewall technology enabled these private networks to connect into the public networks including the Internet with some hope of protection against hackers.

As the trend of Network Computing and e-business continues to evolve, secure communications need to be extended within the enterprise while allowing the public networks to be utilized. Standards are evolving to allow a uniform VPN solution across vendors. The AS/400 VPN solution addresses four environments:

- Intranets - secure connections within an Intranet

- Extranets or ValuNets - secure connections between Intranets of different companies

- Remote office/Branch office - secure connections between Intranets of the same company

- Mobile Worker - secure connections from a mobile worker, using different ISPs to an Intranet.

TCP/IP Remote Access Extensions. The remote access dial-up solution for mobile users Virtual Private Network is used to support dial-in access to a corporate network whose users are all company employees. The standards group defined a tunneling protocol called Layer 2 Tunnel Protocol (L2TP) which extends the span of a point-to-point (PPP) connection. Instead of beginning at the remote host and ending at a local ISPs point of presence (PoP), the "virtual PPP" link now extends from the remote host all the way back to the corporate gateway. The remote host appears to be on the same subnet as the corporate gateway. When used in conjunction with IPSec, L2TP provides a cost effective and secure remote access for mobile users.

TCP/IP Protocol Stack. The TCP/IP protocol stack has improved capacity providing improved performance. Two Requests for Comments have been added to the protocol stack.

Systems Network Management

Having AS/400 systems participate in a communications network is one thing, but managing that communications network is something else. Systems network management tasks include such things as problem determination, problem tracking, making network configuration changes, and distributing necessary changes. In addition to this list of management tasks, the AS/400 can provide operations monitoring, automated operations, problem management, software distribution, change management, backup and recovery, media management, security, performance management, and capacity planning not only for the AS/400 systems in your network, but also for the attached clients. Rather than discuss each of these functions individually, we will discuss the benefits that arise for the business as a result of the management function.

Among the benefits is that the user is not involved in the following activities because the system performs them automatically: problem data collection and logging; hardware problem prediction and logging; automated configuration and resource data logging; performance data capture and logging; alert generation, logging, and reporting; and Electronic Customer Support (ECS), which provides automated problem reporting, electronic PTF selection/distribution, automated service dispatching, and an electronic interface to the IBM information/database. This automation allows a reduction in staff. The AS/400 will do the distribution automatically, take care of the security related to the software, detect the problems that occur on the clients whether those clients are from IBM or other vendors, and provide backup and recovery for those clients as required. The distribution of the functions that accomplish these tasks within the AS/400 is accomplished under a set of programs named Systems Manager/400 and Managed System Services/400 within OS/400. The next section shows how this might work between an AS/400 system and a System/390 computer.

Systems Network Management Example

The systems network management functions needed vary depending on the type of communications network involved. For example, in a simple token-ring network, OS/400 can automatically notify the network operator of any problems that develop in the token-ring adapter or cable and record the error to help in problem determination. In more complex communications environments, OS/400 has other functions that help manage the enterprise. Suppose an AS/400 in Pittsburgh, Pennsylvania, is part of a network managed from a central System/390 computer located in San Francisco. The network operator in San Francisco uses a System/390 program called NetView to manage the entire network. Now a problem develops in the communications link between the AS/400 in Pittsburgh and the System/390 in San Francisco. OS/400 automatically notifies the network operator in San Francisco that a network problem has been detected. This is done through an alert message that is automatically sent by OS/400 to the computer in San Francisco.

Once an alert notifies the network operator of the problem, several OS/400 functions help identify and correct the problem. First, the Network Remote Facilities (NRF) program allows the network operator to interact with the AS/400 as if the System/390 terminal in San Francisco were actually a remote AS/400 workstation in Pittsburgh. Using another OS/400 network management feature called the NetView/Remote Manager (NV/RM), the network operator can also issue network commands to test the health of network elements (e.g., modems). Once the cause of the problem is determined, the necessary fix can be put in place. If a change to some AS/400 programming is necessary, OS/400's SystemView Managed System Services (MSS) program provides a way to distribute and install new programs or changes directly from San Francisco. Alternately, to exchange files between the S/390 host (running MVS/ESA) in San Francisco and the AS/400 in Pittsburgh, the NetView File Transfer program (5730-082) can be used. Thus, the San Francisco-based network operator can use his or her expertise to analyze and fix the problem without having to travel to Pittsburgh. This kind of network management environment makes for speedy problem determination and correction, resulting in system downtime.

Systems Network Architecture (SNA)

OS/400 supports IBM's Systems Network Architecture (SNA). This is a published set of rules governing various aspects of computer communications from protocols (e.g., SDLC) to document formats (e.g., Document Content Architecture [DCA]) and electronic mail (e.g., SNA Distribution Services [SNADS]). It is SNA that provides the common ground on which different types of computer equipment can efficiently exchange information. OS/400's Advanced **Peer-to-Peer Network (APPN)** architecture, originally developed on the earlier IBM S/36 computers, has now been adopted as part of SNA. Further, APPN support has been expanded (APPN end-node support) to allow more direct interaction with traditional SNA networks.

Wireless Local Area Network

The IBM Wireless Connection for AS/400 (5798-TBW) is a networking software program for the OS/400 operating system based on the TCP/IP sockets program connecting real time, 5250 mobile devices with the AS/400. A separate feature allows multiple instances of the wireless connection program to run on the same AS/400 allowing large users to consolidate smaller AS/400 systems into one or more larger AS/400 data centers. The system administrator can name PTC device sessions, change the PTC configuration without first ending Wireless Connection for AS/400, re-map the PTC keyboard, and reformat the PTC screen to display existing applications. This networking software product uses Internet Protocol (IP) and TCP/IP sockets to support wireless networks through locally attached Ethernet and token-ring LANs and at remote locations through routers, allowing easy integration between wireless networks and installed LANs. An existing LAN wiring infrastructure can be used for this connection by dropping a #2480 Ethernet or token-ring access point from the existing wiring. This combination of remote access and support for multiple instances of the program allows the management of the 5250 devices anywhere in the world.

This networking software product is particularly applicable to the Model 150 and Model 170 because the #2668 Wireless LAN Adapter can only be attached to an SPD bus, and no equivalent is available for the only bus supported by these system models, a PCI bus. This software networking product does not work on the CISC-based Version 3 Release 2 systems, for which the #2668 Wireless LAN Adapter was designed.

Display Station/Printer Pass-Thru

Other communications functions provided with OS/400 include **Display Station Pass-Thru (DSPT)** and object distribution. DSPT allows a user of one system to sign on to some other computer in the communications network as if the two systems were directly attached. This allows one workstation to access any computer system in the network. The object distribution facility of OS/400 makes sending information or programs to remote locations much simpler. A common use for this facility is to distribute application programs developed at a central site to remote computers.

A recent addition to the pass-thru functions is printer pass-thru. This allows a print spool function to be performed on any computer in the systems network and later be printed either on the printer that is most local to the display station that originated the print spool function or at a printer located anywhere in the system network that the user selects. Figure 4.15 illustrates the connection for display or printer pass-thru.

S/390 Communications Support

The AS/400 Communications Utilities (5738-CM1) software product complements the communications function of OS/400 for interacting with System/390 computers. This set of programs augments OS/400 communications functions in the area of interchanging electronic mail and files with various System/390 computer environments over a SNA communications network. For example, AS/400 Communications Utilities allows AS/400 Office users to exchange information with users of the OfficeVision/VM and OfficeVision/MVS. These programs run on the System 390, providing those users with functions like those of OfficeVision/400 (e.g., electronic mail and calendaring). The other basic function provided by AS/400 Communications Utilities is called the Remote Job Entry Facility (RJE). RJE allows an AS/400 system to emulate an RJE workstation used to submit batch jobs to or receive output from System/390 computers. Figure 4.16 illustrates one methodology for connecting an AS/400 system to a System/390 computer.

Figure 4.15. All Application Systems use the cable-thru approach to attaching local workstations.

Figure 4.16. Example of a communications configuration used to attach an AS/400 to an S/390 computer.

Client Access

The Client Access family of products provides AS/400-to-Windows desktop connectivity and function. Client Access/400 has been divided into two separate components, AS/400 Client Access Family for Windows (5769-XW1) and AS/400 Client Access Family (5769-XY1). Client Access supports the full 32-bit version of Advanced Function Print (AFP) Workbench Viewer. Because this is the full-function version, there will be no need to update again. The Viewer can be used to display, on the PC, information stored in AS/400 spooled files (AFP and SCS). Full page documents are completely rendered on both Windows and OS/2. **Image files** (such as those stored in GIF, TIFF, or JPEG) can be viewed on a PC. AFP Viewer also provides end-user productivity aides such as the ability to zoom in or search for specific portions of a stored document.

This means business processes can extend beyond printed output, to: archival, indexing, retrieval, customer service viewing, reprint, and fax. AS/400 Client Access Express for Windows (5769-XE1) has been added to allow a client access environment which does not require SNA, and operates entirely in a TCP/IP environment, and is included with the AS/400 Client Access Family for Windows product along with the other client members. All functions of the Express client and the other clients can be used when the Client Access Family for Windows product is installed on the AS/400 system.

Client Access has been improved to provide better administrative control of Operations Navigator functions, including improved usability. Figure 4.17 demonstrates how the various Client Access functions support different operating systems.

AS/400 Client Access Family for Windows

AS/400 Client Access Family for Windows includes Client Access for Windows 95/NT and Client Access Enhanced for Windows, and it supports customer environments that concentrate on Windows as a client platform. Client Access Enhanced for Windows includes communications and management enhancements. Client Access Family for Windows supports Windows NT 4.0 workstation and server operating systems, Windows 95, and Windows 98 client, and includes Lotus Mail 4.5, providing desktop connectivity and function. Connectivity includes TCP/IP, IPX, and SNA for token-ring and Ethernet LAN's (IPX is only supplied with Client Access for Windows 95/NT). Support for Windows NT 5.0 will be added as it becomes available.

SNA supports SDLC, asynchronous, X.25, and twinax communications. AnyNet protocol independence provides the ability to run APPC over TCP/IP. Display and print emulators that can access AS/400 facilities are PC5250, Graphical Access, Systems Object Access, and Operations Navigator with Client Access for Windows 95/NT. The PC 5250 emulator can emulate printers over TCP/IP and can be configured to use a device ID over TCP/IP, and the user can bypass the Sign-on screen using TCP/IP auto-logon. Client Access for Windows extends the AS/400 resources to the desktop using end-user tools (e.g., graphical data transfer, network print, network drives, and file serving). API's (ODBC, Data Queues, Remote Commands, and Remote SQL) further extend the services and resources of the AS/400.

Client Access for Windows 95/NT provides e-mail support through Lotus Mail 4.5 on TCP/IP, IPX, and SNA/APPC networks to send and receive mail anywhere in the world. The support includes a single logon and directory function like the AS/400 System Directory. A connection type in the Netsoft Router called autosync1 allows users to connect

	Windows 95	Windows 3.1	Optimized OS/2	OS/2	DOS Ext	DOS
Function						
License Management						
Enhanced Security	x	x	x	x	x	x
Check Expired Password	x	x	x	x	x	x
Password Encrypted	x	x	x	x	x	x
Network Password Management	x					
5250 Display Emulation						
RUMBA/400 (SBCS/DBCS)		x	x	x	x	
PC5250 (SBCS/DBCS)	x(2*)	x(2*)	x(2*)			
WSF (SBCS)					x	x
AS/400 PC Console		x				
RUMBA/400		x	x			
PC5250			x	x		
5250 Print Emulation						
RUMBA/400		x	x	x	x	
PC5250	x(3*)	x	x			
WSF					x	x
GUI Interfaces						
Graphical Access	x	x	x			
System Object Access	x	x				
AFP Workbench Subset	x	x	x			
Graphical Operations		x	x	x		
Multimedia Enablers						
Ultimedia System Facility		x	x	x	x	

See Notes, page 307

Figure 4.17. Client Access detailed function chart vs. supported PC operating systems. *(continued on next page)*

Function	Windows 95	Windows 3.1	Optimized OS/2	OS/2	DOS Ext	DOS
File/Database Functions						
Integrated File System	x	x	x			
Transfer Function	x	x	x	x	x	
Database Access GUI		x	x			
ODBC Version 2 Level 2	x(8*)	x	x			
ODBC Version 1 Level 2	x	x	x		x	
ODBC Version 1 Level 1	x	x	x	x	x	
Remote SQL APIs	x(8*)	x	x	x		
Remote SQL Extensions	x		x			
Supports DRDA 1 Architecture	x	x	x	x	x	x
Supports DRDA 2 Architecture	x		x			
Checkin/Checkout			x	x	x	x
SNA Networks						
Twinax	x	x	x	x	x	x
Asynchronous	x	x	x (1*)	x (1*)	x (6*)	x
X.25	x	x	x	x (1*)	x	x
SDLC	x	x	x	x	x	x
Token-Ring	x	x	x	x	x	x
Ethernet	x	x	x	x (1*)	x	x
ISDN			x (1*)			
API's Supported						
EHNAPPC	x	x	x	x	x	x
CPI-C 2.0	x (7*)	x (7*)	x	x		
Sockets	x (9*)	x (9*)	x (9*)			

See Notes, page 307

Figure 4.17. Client Access detailed function chart vs. supported PC operating systems. *(continued on next page)*

Function	Windows 95	Windows 3.1	Optimized OS/2	OS/2	DOS Ext	DOS
Communications Programs Included						
Subset of CM/2			x	x		
NetSoft Router (32-bit)	x					
NS/Windows Router		x				
DOS Router (APPC)					x	x
Communications Programs Supported						
NetWare for SAA 2.0	x	x		x		
Microsoft SNA Server	x					
LAN Drivers						
MSDLC (32-bit)	x (9*)					
LAN Support Program (V1.38) included		x (5*)			x (5*)	
NTS/2 included			x (5*)	x (5*)		x (5*)
TCP/IP Networks (native)						
Token-Ring	x					
Ethernet	x					
Asynchronous (SLIP)	x(10*)		x			
TCP/IP Networks (AnyNet)						
Token-Ring	x	x	x			
Ethernet	x	x	x			
Asynchronous (SLIP)	x(10*)	x (10*)				
APIs Supported						
EHNAPPC (via AnyNet)	x	x	x			
CPI-C (via AnyNet) - Sockets	x	x	x			
Sockets	x (9)	x (9)	x (9)			
See Notes, page 307						

Figure 4.17. Client Access detailed function chart vs. supported PC operating systems. *(continued on next page)*

Function	Windows 95	Windows 3.1	Optimized OS/2	OS/2	DOS Ext	DOS
TCP/IP Stacks Supported						
IBM DOS (included)	x	x(4*)				
FTP OnNet 1.1 (Windows)	x					
Microsoft WFW (32-bit)		x				
Novell (V4.2)		x				
WRQ V4.01 (Windows)		x				
NetManage Chameleon (Windows V4.01)						
Microsoft Windows 95 (32-bit)	x					
IBM OS/2 (included)			x (5*)			
Client Management						
SNMP Client Management			x			
Desktop Management (DMI)			x			
PC Update	x	x	x	x	x	x
Central Administration Function	x	x	x	x	x	x
Migration Utility	x	x				
Node Operation Facility (NOF)						
Mail/Office Functions						
MAPI (to POP3 server)	x(11*)					
MAPI (to OV/400 only)		x				
PC Text Assistant (OV/400, SBCS)	x	x	x	x	x	x
Application Command Level APIs						
Data Queues	x (8*)	x	x	x	x	
See Notes, page 307						

Figure 4.17. Client Access detailed function chart vs. supported PC operating systems. *(continued on next page)*

Function	Windows 95	Windows 3.1	Optimized OS/2	OS/2	DOS Ext	DOS
Application Command Level (continued)						
Submit Remote Command	x (8*)	x	x	x	x	x
Distributed Program Call	x		x			
OLE Enablers (APIs)						
Custom Controls	x					
Automation	x					
Command Level APIs on AS/400						
Start PC Command (STRPCCMD)		x		x	x	x
Run Remote Command (RUNRMTCMD)	x		x	x	x	x
Copy to PC Document (CPYTOPCD)	x	x	x	x	x	x
Copy from PC Document (CPYFRMPCD)	x	x	x	x	x	x
Print Serving						
AS/400 Printers	x	x	x	x	x	
PC Network Printers	x	x	x	x	x	x
AFP Printer Driver	x	x	x	x	x	x
Integrated w/ FAX/400	x					
Programmer Tools						
PC Tools Folder (QIWSTOOL)		x		x	x	x
CA/400 Toolkit		x	x			
Shipped with client	x					
PC Code Installable						
From PC Diskettes	x	x		x	x	x
From PC CD-ROM	x	x		x	x	x
From PC Server/FSIOA	x	x				
Onto PC Server	x (12*)					

See Notes, page 307

Figure 4.17. Client Access detailed function chart vs. supported PC operating systems. *(continued on next page)*

Notes

(1) Stand-alone Communications Manager/2 (CM/2) can provide this connectivity. AS/400 Client Access can also be used in conjunction with this CM/2.
(2) DBCS is Japanese only.
(3) Not supported on native TCP/IP networks. Is supported on TCP/IP networks when using AnyNet.
(4) Applications (such as TELNET) are not provided with the stack. Supports English only SBCS (DBCS data transmission supported).
(5) Supports English SBCS/DBCS.
(6) Supports SBCS only.
(7) Windows 3.1 Client NS/Windows Router supports CPI-C Version 2.0 + optional classes for Data Conversion, Queue Level Non-Blocking, Full Duplex and Callback functions. Windows 95 Client NetSoft Router supports CPI-C Version 2.0 + optional classes for Data Conversion only.
(8) Windows 95 Client provides 32-bit APIs. The Windows 95 Client also supports the Windows 3.1 Client APIs, so applications written to those 16-bit APIs can also be run over SNA/APPC networks or TCP/IP networks (with AnyNet).
(9) Works with Client Access but is not included in Client Access package.
(10) OS/400 provides SLIP dial-in support for TCP/IP networks in V3R2 and V3R7. For PC users connecting to V3R1/V3R6 systems, PPP can be used to dial into a gateway, then connect to AS/400 via TRN or Ethernet. TCP/IP stack being used in PC must also support dial-up in order to use this capability.
(11) POP3 server provided in OS/400 V3R2 and V3R7 only.
(12) Limited support; client administration restrictions (for example, cannot customize functions available to individual users).

Figure 4.17. Client Access detailed function chart vs. supported PC operating systems. *(continued from previous page)* to a synchronous host using an asynchronous modem without the need for additional hardware on the host or PC. No longer required is the ASCII Workstation Controller on the AS/400 or the SDLC (multiprotocol adapter) on the PC.

The NS/Router configuration screens allow a user to specify a telephone number, location, and modem type. The NS/Router has a "dial from" asynchronous connection option, enabling users to configure multiple "dial from" locations. At connection time, the user is prompted for the location the number is being dialed from. Client Access supports connecting PCs to the AS/400 using TCP/IP with the IBM 5250 Express Twinax adapter cards as well as other selected IBM twinax and twisted-pair supporting adapters. When connecting to an AS/400 with a PC, error messages, online help, return codes, and a Verify function assist in determining what problems, if any, exist.

The AS/400 has access to the NT Client file system using the AS/400 Integrated File System (IFS) Application Program Interface components. This access methodology uses the TCP/IP transports to communicate with any NT Server in the domain, supports connection to both an NT Server on the Integrated PC Server, and to standalone NT Servers. As a result, the AS/400 becomes a management control point for distribution of applications, and any AS/400 application that can use data formatted on the NT Server can now have access to that data.

Support for Microsoft's Policies enhances the AS/400's ability to perform central administration for attached Windows 95/NT clients. With **policies** an administrator can configure software on a client for a specific user, a group of users, or specific personal computer. Policies are kept on a server and are downloaded to the PC when a user logs on. Client Access supports policies on the following components:

- Data transfer

- Directory update

- Install NLS support

- Passwords

- Incoming remote call

- Operations Navigator (and subcomponents)

- ODBC

- Service tab on Client Access properties

- Install and selective install

Network printing has been improved by adding parameters in the Device Settings panel to send output as text rather than graphics, reducing the size of the printed output file created with the AFP driver, thereby reducing the time required to send large documents across the network for printing on the locally-attached PC printers. Network print buffering has been changed to improve performance for applications making small write AS/400 print requests to redirected PC printers (i.e., DOS applications that send one character at a time are now buffered and sent as one request). This does not apply to the Microsoft Windows NT operating system.

The Client Access Software developer Toolkit, SDK for ActiveX and OLE DB, has been packaged on the family CD-ROM with the Windows 95/NT client. Using the SDK, developers can build applications to access AS/400 resources via record-level access, SQL, stored procedures, data queues, programs, and CL commands, supporting transferring AS/400 data over TCP/IP and SNA/APPC communications protocols. When using Visual Basic, wizards generate code to link to the AS/400 data and services. Documentation and end-users samples are provided for Delphi, PowerBuilder, Visual C++, Lotus 1-2-3, Internet Explorer, and Visual Basic environments. Client Server programs generated using the SDK can be run using the OLE DB for AS/400 provider (run-time driver) included with the Windows 95/NT client.

The Windows 95/NT client can access AS/400 database information over any supported connectivity by means of the Microsoft ODBC 3.0 Driver Manager enabling access to applications written to either ODBC 2.0 or ODBC 3.0. New client server applications can take advantage of the new functions provided by the Microsoft ODBC 3.0 specification, yet old applications do not require rewrite.

AS/400 Client Access Family

AS/400 Client Access Family includes Client Access for Windows 3.1, Client Access Optimized for OS/2, Client Access for OS/2, Client Access for DOS with Extended Memory, and Client Access for DOS, and is intended to be used in environments that are not predominantly using Windows as a client platform. The PC 5250 emulator can emulate printers over TCP/IP and can be configured to use a device ID over TCP/IP, and the user can bypass the Sign-on screen using TCP/IP auto-logon. Client Access Family continues to offer full, native TCP/IP support, both 16 bit and 32 bit SNA/APPC offerings, AS/400 administration through Operations Navigator, the latest Microsoft Windows platforms applications enablement, and national language enablement for worldwide users.

Both Client Access products provide fully graphical viewing of AS/400 output files, faxes, and image files. Full-page documents (such as AFP spooled files) are completely rendered on both Windows and OS/2 clients. The Client Access/400 Viewer means business processes can easily be extended beyond printed output, to archiving, indexing, retrieval, customer service viewing, reprinting, and faxing.

AS/400 Client Access Express for Windows (5769-XE1)

AS/400 Client Access Express for Windows is a new client program which does not require the presence of Systems Network Architecture (SNA) and uses only TCP/IP for its connectivity protocol. The TCP/IP program used is the standard TCP/IP program shipped with the Microsoft 32-bit operating systems. (Other Winsock-compatible stacks can also be used.) The new client does not support routers, and does not contain any screen scrapers. The AS/400 server must include OS/400 Version 4 Release 2 or later.

Client Access Express runs on PC's installed with Microsoft Windows 95, 98, NT 4.0, or server operating systems. Included with the Microsoft NT environment is support for Terminal Server Edition (TSE) which enables the NT server to be used as a gateway between end users and the AS/400. Also included is the Microsoft Internet Information Server (IIS) environment with a version called Peer Web Services which provides AS/400 database access from Web pages.

Secure Sockets Layer (SSL) is provided for client functions to improve TCP/IP security. The user-id and password sent between the desktop and the AS/400 is encrypted. The user has the choice to select what is encrypted. AS/400 server authentication is used to assure connection to the intended AS/400 diminishing the possibility of spoofing in an Internet environment.

AS/400 NetServer is used to provide file serving and network print support. NetServer unites the Integrated File System and AS/400 printers into Microsoft Network Neighborhood allowing user access to these resources using the same methods as accessing resources directly on the desktop. Previously when using Network drives or Network printers, the resources would be viewed as resources on the AS/400. The only directories or printers visible to the end user are those identified as shared by the system administrator or resource owner. Now NetServer hides these resources unless a specific share is created to enable viewing of that resource.

A full function AFP Workbench is included. The Viewer can display on the PC information stored in AS/400 spooled files (AFGP or SCS) as well as image files (files stored in GIF, TIFF, or JPEG formats).

Local and remote console access are included through Operations Console. Microsoft technologies are exploited through the inclusion of 32-bit client/server application enablers, OLE DB Data Provider and Active X, ODBC driver, Remote Command, and Data Queues.

Operations Navigator is used to work with AS/400 resources and for administering and operating AS/400 systems. New graphical interfaces are added to Operations Navigator for working with the following AS/400 functions:

- Folders in the Integrated File System can be created, deleted and renamed. Objects in the File System can be cut, copied, and pasted, or dragged and dropped between AS/400s and PCs.

- AS/400 NetServer file and printer shares are easier to create, locate and manage.

- Database improvements include SQL performance monitor, SQL scripts, SQL indexes, stored procedures, LOBs, DataLink data types, user defined functions, and user defined functions.

- Virtual Private Networks (VPN) and Application and Network Security have been added to TCP/IP for secure connections across a public network. Other TCP/IP functions include the ability to have multiple User-id's while using a single copy of Client Access. Each user-id can be using a different application.

- Management Central system group functions have been added to the hierarchy for object packaging and distribution, remote operations, PTF management, inventory, and job scheduler

- Application administration of third party plug-ins

Microsoft policies are also supported. A maximum of 150 different policies can be enforced. Policy restrictions can be enforced on a per-user or per-PC basis.

The Express client includes the PC5250 Operations console function, enabling PC workstations to locally or remotely perform AS/400 system operations and services from PC5250 emulation via an AS/400 System Console Session, including the Graphical Control Panel application.

Data Transfer provides an array of GUI's for both desktop users and programming enablers for application programmers to retrieve data from an AS/400 database or to store PC file data in the AS/400 database. Thirty-two AS/400 files can be selected and data transferred with a single request to either a desktop display, a PC printer, a PC file, an HTML file or directly into an Excel spreadsheet. Specified records or fields of records can be selected and transferred. Wizards can create, modify, and run transfer requests or save them for later use. Batch transfers are also supported. A transfer can be "auto-run" or part of a start up session. Wizards can be used to create a new AS/400 database file definition for PC file upload requests. Database information can be inserted directly into a section of an existing HTML file, enabling the update of part of a Web page while leaving the remainder intact. Datalink commands for linking to HTML tables are supported. All functions of the Express client, with the exception of the functions of PC5250 Display and the functions of Print Emulation and Data Transfer, can be used without acquiring a license for AS/400 Client Access for Windows product.

Lotus Notes 5.0 Client Support

The Lotus Notes 5.0 client can be used on all desktops running either the Express client or the Windows 95/NT client. Lotus Notes can be used with Lotus Domino for AS/400. Lotus Notes supports Internet SMPT/MIME mail standards and can be used as a client to the post office services (POP3) built in to OS/400. Lotus Notes client supports e-mail, calendaring, web browsing, and information management features.

Operations Navigator function is also packaged with AS/400 Client Access Express for Windows.

Client Access Express for Windows client uses Secure Socket Layer for Client Encryption. Client Encryption includes a SSL for Windows 95/NT and a SSL for Java. 5769-CE1 provides 40 bit encryption, 5769-CE2 provides 56 bit encryption, and 5769-CE3 provides 128 bit encryption for the US and Canada only.

SystemView

To bring more order to systems management tools, IBM defined a framework called SystemView to improve the efficiency and reduce the cost associated with systems management activities. The SystemView strategy is to publish a framework (blueprint) to guide the development of a family of integrated systems management tools. By publishing the SystemView framework, IBM has encouraged the many companies developing systems management software products to modify their systems management tools or to create new systems management tools that follow the SystemView framework. The user gets SystemView-compliant systems management tools. The SystemView framework is depicted in Figure 4.18. There are three elements in the SystemView framework: the *end-use dimension*, the *data dimension*, and the *application dimension*.

The end-use dimension addresses a consistent user interface for all systems management tools. All SystemView tools should present a common appearance and behavior to the user. Having a consistent user interface reduces the training requirements for the users because concepts and techniques learned on the first SystemView tool are transferable to other SystemView tools. The user interface specified by the SystemView end-use dimension complies with the **Common User Access (CUA)** interface.

The data dimension of SystemView defines the information types and formats shared by all SystemView-compliant tools and provides facilities for accessing data consistently. Re-entering the same data for independent data structures of systems management tools wastes time and provides opportunity for data inconsistency. By providing a set of shared data, SystemView allows for data to be entered one time and then be used by as many different systems management tools as necessary.

The application dimension of SystemView defines six types of systems management tools or disciplines:

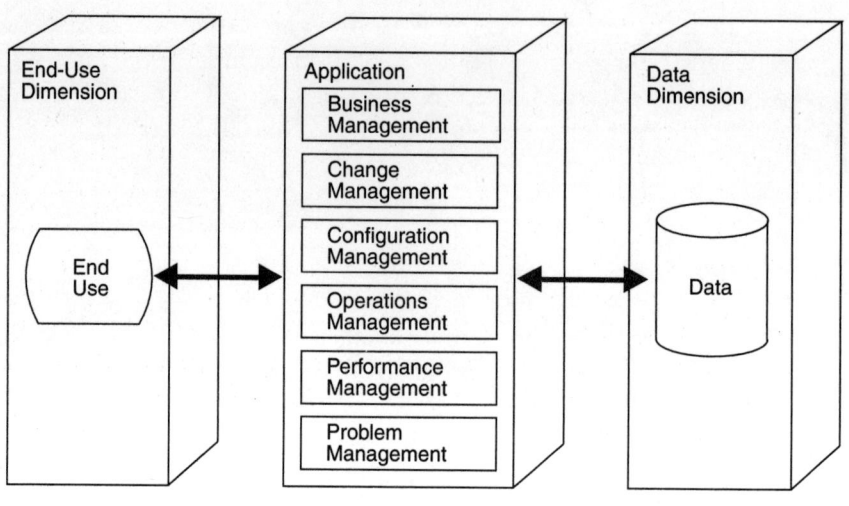

Figure 4.18. The System View framework.

- Business management allows users to track physical assets and manage the finance and accounting associated with a computer system(s).

- Change management allows systems management personnel to plan, implement, and track changes made to the computer system(s).

- Configuration management helps in documenting, planning, and modifying the configuration (physical and logical relationships between components) of the elements comprising the computer system(s).

- Operations management helps devise and maintain the policies and procedures used to efficiently process a business's workload with the computer system(s).

- Performance management helps define, monitor, and plan the level of performance users should expect from the computer system.

- Problem management helps plan how computer-related problems are prevented, detected, tracked, and resolved.

These functions have been combined under SystemView's Systems Manager/400 and Managed Systems Services/400 and have been extended to contain equivalent functions for remote AS/400 systems. The user can run remote programs and can remotely perform an **IPL (Initial Program Load)** on systems. All results are returned to the central site system for monitoring and tracking. Network-wide job schedules can be implemented by specifying when functions are to be run on the systems.

Figure 4.19 shows where OS/400 and some example extensions to OS/400 fit into the application dimension of the SystemView framework. As shown in the figure, many functions provided as standard in OS/400 can be mapped into the SystemView framework. For example, as users begin to use the AS/400 system, the disk storage begins to accu-

Business	Change	Configuration	Operations	Performance	Problem
APIs	COMMAND LANGUAGE INTERFACE			OUTPUT FILES FOR DATA	

• ECS
  - IBM Link Access
  - Hardware Upgrade
  - Order Processing
• Job Accounting
	• ECS
	  - Service Request
	  - PTF Ordering
	  - PTF Management
	• DSNX
	• Object Distribution
	• PC Support
		• Resource Manager
		• Auto Configuration
		• Vital Product Data
		• Inventory
		  - Hardware
		  - Software
		• Client Inventory
		  - Hardware
		  - Software
		• Retrieve Configuration Source
			• Remote Power Control
			• Remote IPL
			• Store Management
			• Backup/Recovery
			  - Save While Active
			• Security Management
			• Workstation Pass-Thru
			• SNMP
			• SNA/MS Transport
			• Remote PC Command Execution
			• DSNX Job Initiation
			• Network Routing Facility
			• Operations Navigator
				• Performance Monitor
				  - Performance Measurement
				  - Data Collection
				  - Scheduling
					• Problem Analysis
					• Alert Log and Manager
					  - Alert Filter/Router
					• Problem Log and Manager
					• Problem Log Filter/Router
					• ECS
					  - Service Request
					  - Question and Answer Facility
					• Remote Commands
					  - Copy Screen Image
					  - Pass Through
					• APPN Session PD

Figure 4.19. How OS/400 and other AS/400 system programs fit into the SystemView framework.

mulate business information that is often vital to the day-to-day operations of the business. This information becomes an asset to the business and should be protected as such. OS/400 provides several functions that protect against loss of information from user errors, hardware failures, intentional corruptions, and so forth. These include backup/recovery (BRMS/400), ADSM/400, commitment control and journaling, EDMSuite OnDemand for AS/400 Operations Navigator, disk failure recovery, utility failure recovery, and SMAPP.

Commitment Control and Journaling

Two other functions of OS/400 are commitment control and journaling. Commitment control allows an application program to be designed so that a user must complete all changes related to a database transaction before the transaction is permanently reflected in the database. This helps ensure the data integrity of the database in the event of a system failure in the middle of a transaction. It also allows a transaction to be canceled in process if the user feels the transaction is erroneous.

Journaling is a task performed by OS/400 in which every database transaction, in addition to changing the database, is stored in a separate file of transactions. This journaling works in conjunction with normal backup procedures to allow for recovery of database information in the event of information loss—for example, if the information in an AS/400 database becomes corrupted through a user error or hardware failure. The recovery process would involve loading a previously made backup tape and restoring the database through a simple restore command. However, none of the database transactions made since the backup tape was made would be reflected in the newly restored database. Thus, the database has been recovered only to the point at which the last backup copy was made. Thousands of transactions may have been made since the last backup, and these will have to be reapplied to the restored database.

This is where **journaling** comes in. Because all transactions performed since the last backup are stored in the separate journal area, these transactions can be automatically applied to the newly restored database to bring it to the point immediately before it was corrupted. Without journaling, every transaction performed since the last backup would have to be manually reentered, which can be a very time consuming process. **Remote journaling** allows database changes to be sent immediately to another system for high-availability applications to help off-load Central Processing Unit consumption from the source machine so that it can achieve more throughput by capturing and transmitting journal images between source and target systems. This can significantly reduce the time and effort required to reconcile source and target databases following a system failure, because database changes are transported immediately to the remote system assuring no loss of transactions.

Backup/Recovery

As users begin to use the AS/400 system, the disk storage will begin to accumulate business information that is often vital to the day-to-day operations of the business. This information becomes an asset to the business and should be protected as such. OS/400 provides several system management functions that allow the system's operator to protect against loss of information from user errors, hardware failures, intentional corruptions, environmental disasters, and so forth.

First, the system's operator can make backup copies of the information on disk storage to magnetic tape. With OS/400 these backup copies can be made while users are actively using the systems. This feature is called **save while active**. Before the save while active function was provided, the systems operator had to regularly reserve a block of time and dedicate the AS/400 system to backup operations, making it unavailable to the users. Now the backup operations occur while users are still performing useful work. If the information on the AS/400 disk storage is lost, the backup tapes can be used to restore the AS/400 disk storage to the state at which the last backup was made. With the additional journaling function and the BRMS/400 and ADSM/400 functions of OS/400, not only can all transactions subsequent to the backup but prior to the failure be posted to the restored information, the recovery of the lost data can be done without the user being aware of its occurrence. This typically completes the recovery procedure, and the information on the AS/400 system is restored to the point just before the failure occurred.

Support on save commands for generic library names and omit options provides flexibility in defining which libraries and objects to save and allow usage of multiple tape drives to reduce the time required for a save operation. Multiple concurrent restore operations using two or more tape units can be used to restore objects to a single library or to restore Document library objects to a single Auxiliary Storage Pool. Most Save and Restore commands support using multiple tape devices or multiple resources in a tape library in parallel. This reduces the amount of time required to save and restore very large objects. The previous save rate was limited to the throughput capabilities of a single tape, by using multiple tapes in parallel, the maximum throughput can be increased.

Save Menu option defaults have been added to simplify unattended save operations. The defaults include save entire system; , - save system data only; and save all user data. The operations console makes it possible to provide remote console support equivalent to a full function 5250 system console session. When the systems and operations staff are in separate locations, either can initiate remote backup/recovery operations.

Transferring programs between systems in a network has been simplified by means of the capability to use recovery program methodology to a different system than the backup was performed on. A restore menu option was added to all unattended restores and restores to a different system.

Operations Navigator

The AS/400 is designed for office environments in which technical skills are usually limited. Operations Navigator simplifies systems management tasks. This product allows an AS/400 system administrator to perform systems management tasks through a familiar Windows-based Graphical User Interface (GUI). This makes it easier for users unfamiliar with AS/400 systems to perform OS/400 tasks.

Operations Navigator supplies many AS/400 functions used by system administrators and users on a daily basis, including job manipulation, message handling, printer management, printer output handling, user and group administration, database administration, file systems, security functions, authorization lists, security and auditing policies, backup support, and hardware and software inventory. These functions may be accessed for a particular system from either a local or a remote system workstation. For example, a large company may have one AS/400 system at the headquarters location and multiple AS/400 systems distributed to other locations throughout the country or around the world. Rather than provide AS/400 and OS/400 personnel at each of the locations, it is often desirable to have a centralized staff of experts who can support all of the AS/400 systems throughout the company (a central **help desk**). That help desk can then coordinate all outside resources (e.g., IBM's customer support structure or an application software company's support system) as the single point of contact for the whole company.

Operations Navigator includes support for TCP/IP configuration, including DHCP and DNS. This support as well as all those following are simplified by the use of wizards and GUIs. Servers can be configured to start automatically when TCP/IP is started and the status of the servers can be monitored. Operations Navigator integrates the administration of Domino for AS/400, AS/400 NetServer software, and the administration of the AS/400 system's Internet capability by launching a Web browser interface to configure **HTTP Server for AS/400**, Firewall, and IBM Network Station. Plug-in Application Program Interfaces (API's) are provided for use by other applications to integrate into the AS/400 Operations Navigator program's interface.

From the Operations Navigator window it is possible to drag and drop printer output to various printers and to the desktop, to set the Operations Navigator Windows so that the Windows can refresh their content automatically, to open separate windows to monitor specific items of interest, to create desktop shortcuts to items within Operations Navigator, and to find text within Operations Navigator lists. PC users can view and end AS/400 messages.

Operations Navigator graphical interfaces provide capabilities for improving operation and administration of the AS/400 by means of the following:

- Security Configuration Wizard (See Appendix E)

- Real-time graphical performance monitor

- AS/400 DCE server setup and management

- TCP/IP security setup for Network Address Translation (NAT) and IP Packet filtering

- Network File System (NFS) server management

- Viewing AS/400 NetServer (SMB) server statistics

- Managing remote journals and aliases, updating AS/400 database table contents, and copying/moving capabilities between system database tables.

It is possible to selectively install only the needed Operations Navigator functions, and system administrators can select which Operations Navigator functions are available to specific users.

EDMSuite OnDemand for AS/400 (5769-RD1)

The EDMSuite OnDemand for AS/400, formerly referred to as Report/Data Archive and Retrieval System (R/DARS), consists of a set of four archive program features that allow the storage of large volumes of data and the retrieval of selected data. That data may be stored on disk, optical, or tape storage media. OnDemand helps maintain accessible and secure archives and can improve the cost and usability of long-term data storage. OnDemand archiving and print support functions include the OnDemand client and Internet document support. The OnDemand features can be ordered separately or in any combination of the following.

Spool File Archive can store large volumes of spooled print data from current applications on magnetic, tape, or optical storage media. Users can retrieve selected pages or documents on demand. The management features include automated capture, automatic indexing, immediate compression, and unattended storage migration.

Record Archive can use IBM's 3995 Optical Libraries to store and retrieve aged data records, such as historical sales or customer data. Users can continue to use existing applications with the added capability of retrieving historical data from optical files and current data from magnetic disk. For quicker access, only pointers to the data are stored on magnetic disk; the actual data is stored on optical disk.

Object Archive can compress and archive a variety of AS/400 objects such as program source files, database files, or entire application libraries on tape or optical media. Multiple generations of archived objects such as monthly or annual detail files can be managed.

AnyStore, which requires the Spool File Archive, allows the storage and retrieval of binary large objects (BLOBS) such as PC files (spreadsheets, X-rays, MRI's) and small scanned images (remittance slips, insurance cards). AnyStore is a toolkit of Application Program Interfaces (API's) intended for programmers to use to create archive/retrieval applications or to enhance existing applications with archive functions. The enhanced application passes the index data and BLOB to OnDemand Spool File Archive to manage the data. The application does the segmentation and extraction of the indices; OnDemand provides storage, migration, and retrieval capabilities to and from media, whether disk, optical or tape.

OnDemand is a client feature that delivers specialized client functions for report and document retrieval. The feature is available for Windows 3.1, Windows 95, Windows NT, and OS/2, and includes server code and the OnDemand client. The OnDemand client includes a GUI interface, and fill-in-the-blank queries help locate archived information, and supports Operations Navigator integration.

Note that the OnDemand Spool File Archive supports *AFP index fields*, a new capability for DDS.

Advantages of the system are many: From a workstation it is possible to electronically store, retrieve, distribute, print, and fax any customer document exactly as it was presented to the customer; large volumes of data can be stored or data can be retrieved selectively, whether on disk, optical or tape storage media; long-term storage becomes more affordable and usable because of the capability to maintain highly accessible, secure archives; and immediate servicing provides improved productivity and increased benefits.

Also note that the EDMSuite Content Connect enables multiple document repositories to be searched using a single search request.

EDMSuite OnDemand for AS/400 Product Preview. A Connection Server will be added to OnDemand for AS/400 and Visual Info for AS/400.

Backup Recovery and Media Services (BRMS/400)

Backup Recovery and Media Services/400 (BRMS/400) is a systems management tool for managing backup, archiving, and recovery environments for a single or multiple AS/400 systems at a single site or across a network where the principal data exchange is by tape. BRMS/400 is designed to perform complex backups easily. The definitions of a backup and changes to those definitions are easy. Full error checking is performed, and messages are provided to the operators to ensure that errors do not go unnoticed. BRMS includes "EXITs" to allow processing of user commands or programs during the backup procedures. BRMS performs full, incremental, or non-cumulative incremental saves, saves to save files, and save while active.

BRMS/400 offers a step-by-step recovery in the form of a report printed after the nightly backups are complete. Recovery includes full and detailed feedback during the recovery process by means of an auto-refresh screen, updated as each library is restored.

BRMS/400 archives data from DASD's to tape and tracks information about objects that have been archived. Locating data in the archives is easy, because the restore can be triggered from a work-with screen. Dynamic retrieval for database files is possible, archived files can be restored upon access with the user application. No changes to the user application are needed to initiate the restore. BRMS/400 provides a comprehensive inventory management system for all tapes, cataloging and managing an entire tape library, as well as outputting reports as instructions to operators about required actions.

BRMS/400 provides for policy-driven backup, recovery, tape media management, and archive services for tape devices. This means there is an automatic recall of archived database files from tape devices to direct access storage devices (DASDs) when required, which relieves the user from having to become involved. BRMS/400 is intended for the system environment with over 50 tapes and therefore may introduce excess complexity in the operation of a smaller system. Operations Navigator is intended to provide the backup/restore functions for this less complex environment.

In addition to these functions, BRMS can backup or archive low-volume AS/400 user data on any ADSM server including another AS/400, RS/6000, or S390, or on the 3466 Network Storage Manager. Using the policies and services provided by BRMS can automate the save and restore operations directed to ADSM servers. Objects saved from one system on an ADSM server storage can be restored to another system sharing the same ADSM server because BRMS can be used on multiple AS/400 systems with shared inventory support.

BRMS provides the ability to backup a single library, or single library object in parallel across any number of tape devices. Parallel backup enables a user to shorten the window of time required to perform backup by using more tape devices in the backup process. Using parallel backup with an automated tape library device allows the saving of a large library to all currently available resources. This reduces the administration involved in setting up a backup strategy by eliminating the need to design the strategy based on the current number of drives and the current objects.

BRMS interfaces can be controlled, allowing administrators to secure the setup and functionality of BRMS from users not skilled in the administration and usage of BRMS. The BRMS functional usage model can secure the following types of function from specific users, and each user can be allowed to use one function and not others (i.e., allow an operator backup functionality, but not the ability to recover objects):

- Backup
- Archive
- Recovery
- Retrieval
- Migration

The functional usage model allows the administrator to control specific setups such as a control group or policy. Users could use and view a policy but not be allowed to change the contents of the policy. Not supported by the base product are archive, dynamic retrieval, automated migration operations, or shared media.

BRMS Network Feature. The BRMS Network Feature enables a BRMS system to be connected to other BRMS network systems using a network. Networked BRMS systems can share the inventory and policies associated with media managed by a central BRMS system.

BRMS Advanced Functions Feature. The BRMS Advanced Functions Feature enables BRMS advanced functions like **Hierarchical Storage Management (HSM)** archive with HSM dynamic retrieval and automated **Application Storage Pool (ASP)** object migration. Parallel Backup also works with the Advanced functions, allowing for parallel archive and parallel dynamic retrieval of a single object. Parallelism used in the dynamic retrieval of a large database file reduces the required time window for the retrieval process. The Advanced Functions Feature can initiate archiving of database files, stream files, and documents based on frequency of usage. The frequency of use rule is based upon the number of days used and is calculated based on a month period. The user can specify the value into the archive control group driving the archive operation.

Adstar Distributed Storage Manager (ADSM)

The Adstar Distributed Storage Manager (ADSM) (5763-SV2) is a client/server product that provides administrator-controlled, highly automated, centrally scheduled, network-based back up and archive functions.

ADSM/400 protects data on workstations and LAN file servers by automatically backing up critical LAN and workstation data and archiving files that are used infrequently. A disaster recovery solution is provided for LANs and workstations. ADSM is administered from a client workstation attached to an AS/400, and with *BRMS/400* can be used to back up an entire AS/400 client/server environment.

ADSM also includes an AS/400 API to allow users to develop their own applications enabling the AS/400 system to function as an ADSM backup-archive client, an Oracle Backup Agent to allow ADSM to back up the Oracle database by providing an API into Oracles Enterprise backup Utility, and HSM for Solaris 2.5.

ADSM not only provides a backup agent for Lotus Notes database backup and recovery, ADSM backs up data from clients running on all of the following:

- AIX

- Apple Macintosh

- Auspex (supported by SunOS client)

- Bull DPX/2

- Bull DPX/20 (Bull AIX, supported by AIX client)

- Digital ULTRIX (formally referred to as DEC ULTRIX)

- Digital UNIX

- DOS

- Hewlett-Packard HP-UX

- Microsoft Windows and Windows 32-bit

- NCR UNIX SVR-4 (formerly AT&T GIS)
- NEC EWS-UX/V
- Novell NetWare
- OpenEdition MVS
- OS/2
- Pyramid Nile (supported by SINIX RISC client)
- SCO UNIX 386 and SCO Open Desktop
- Sequent PTX
- Siemens Nexdorf SINIX 386/486 and SINIX RISC
- Silicon Graphics IRIX
- Sun Microsystems SunOS and Solaris

ADSM participates in the Hierarchical Storage Management structure for the AS/400. ADSM can backup/archive AS/400 user data on any ADSM server including AS/400, RS/6000, S/390, and the 3466 Network Storage Manager. ADSM save/restore operations are automated with BRMS/400.

System Managed Access Path Protection (SMAPP)

A function called System Managed Access Path Protection (SMAPP), which automatically records the access path information according to a mathematical algorithm set by the user, has been added to the systems management function. Users tell the system manager how long they are willing to wait for recovery to take place after a long utility outage, and the system manager ensures that the access paths will be journaled frequently enough to achieve that recovery period. The recovery period may be identified to be either system-wide or by **Application Storage Pool (ASP)**. An application storage pool is a grouping of files related to a common set of applications. The file grouping is generally both logically and physically related. In the case of a utility outage on a system with internal battery backup or a UPS power system, when the main storage data has been dumped to disk and the system then powered down, the access paths to the data dumped to disk have been lost if SMAPP has not been enabled. Before the main storage contents can be reloaded and processing resumed, the access paths to the data resident in main storage must be rebuilt. This can take many hours of interaction with the systems administrator or SMAPP can journal the access path information and recovery time can be reduced to the identified time interval in SMAPP.

Hierarchical Storage Management

Hierarchical Storage Management (HSM) interface support provides data management within a storage hierarchy consisting of high performance disks, compressed disks, tape devices, and ADSM server storage. With HSM implementation, users can migrate data as it ages from fast disk devices to compressed disk devices, to optical, and then to tape devices. Data stored on tape devices is accessed just like data residing on disk.

BRMS/400 is the application program providing the foundation for the HSM customer interface. BRMS/400 defines a new set of policies under which the user can determine when the different object types can be moved or migrated to the different levels of storage. OS/400 enablers include a new API (FREESTG) to support archiving one object at a time (this also eliminates the temporary copy on disk.) The utility (WRKASP) handles the movement of data between the different levels of storage hierarchy. Using BRMS/400, the hierarchical storage management enables the migration of user libraries, folders and spooled files between Application Storage Pools (ASP's), **simplifying** the archiving of database files, database members, and documents. Stream files can be migrated from disk to tape or ADSM server storage, or from a high-performance disk to a compressed disk. Dynamic retrieval provides files on demand for application access. HSM operates automatically, and is policy based requiring no application changes to implement and minimal maintenance support. The fast access, high capacity, and high data transfer rate make the IBM Magstar MP3570 and 3575 Tape subsystems excellent HSM tape storage alternatives.

Utility Failure Recovery

So far, the backup and recovery methodologies discussed have related to data protection from hardware failure of a disk storage unit. A failure mechanism that occurs about thirty times more frequently is a utility failure. A utility failure will not as a rule cause any permanent damage to an AS/400 system, but it can severely damage the efficiency of your business operation. As discussed in "Packaging Technology" in Chapter 1, the AS/400 provides either an internal battery backup system or an interface for a Universal Power Supply (UPS). The primary purpose of these items is to protect the information resident in the main storage of the system that is related to the applications currently running on the system. In most situations, the internal battery backup system or the UPS can supply enough capability for the system to ride through the outage, even though the lights went out and your local screens went blank.

However, everyone has experienced the 15-minute or longer outage. Statistics on utility systems indicate that the frequency of the longer outage is increasing and that on the average seven outages of longer than 5 minutes per year will occur no matter where you are located in the United States. The AS/400 has been programmed to allow a certain period (changeable by the user) to pass after the first occurrence of an outage and then to dump the contents of main storage to disk storage. This process will prevent the loss of data from the current applications but will not achieve minimum recovery time for the user. The user will still experience significant recovery time because the access paths to the data have not been saved. To assist in the recovery of those access paths, the user has the option to turn on **System Managed Access Path Protection (SMAPP)**.

Disk Failure Recovery

Another recovery function in OS/400 used to guard against disk unit failures is known as **checksum (RAID-5 is a hardware checksum approach)**. With the checksum approach, a mathematical formula is used to store redundant information on disk storage in addition to the business information. If one of the disk units fails, the redundant information on the remaining disk units can be used to automatically regenerate the lost information on the replacement fixed disk. Checksum provides a way, at the cost of increased disk storage requirements and an additional load on the computer, to avoid having to do a restore from backups in the event of a disk unit failure. The RAID-5 controller hardware relieves the load on the central system computer for calculating the mathematical formula. (RAID-5 is a hardware methodology for performing the checksum function.)

The RAID-5 disk controllers on the AS/400 systems require a minimum of four drives of identical capacity to create a valid RAID-5 configuration. A maximum of three arrays are allowed per RAID-5 controller, and a maximum of ten drives per array. All drives in an array must be the same capacity. When an array consists of from four to seven drives, **parity** is spread across four drives. When an array contains from eight to ten drives, parity may be spread across either four drives or eight drives. If a system is started with from eight to ten drives in an array, parity will be spread across eight drives. If a system is started with less than eight drives and later upgraded to include from eight to ten drives in that array, the parity function must be stopped and then restarted before the parity function can be spread across eight drives. The AS/400 no longer uses the software checksum approach because of the impact on system performance.

Another data loss protection methodology available on the AS/400 is called **data mirroring**. In data mirroring, a second copy of the data is written to a second disk storage unit, which in the ultimate implementation is located on a separate disk unit controller located on a separate system bus. Data mirroring is the most expensive of the protection methodologies because it requires a total duplication of the data, which requires a doubling of the data storage space. When ranked in the order of highest reliability and minimum impact upon performance, data mirroring would be followed by RAID-5 and software checksum as **data protection methods**. Data mirroring also offers some performance improvements in a read-intensive database environment because the second copy of the data is available while the first copy may be busy being read by another application.

Systems Manager/400

SystemView System Manager/400 (#5769-SM1) provides facilities that allow a central AS/400 system/site/staff to perform systems management tasks for a network of remote AS/400 systems. It addresses the following systems management needs: problem management, change management, Client Access/400 clients inventory, problem tracking for those clients, and PC software management. System Manager/400 provides a Graphical User Interface (GUI), session management support, and support for a roving user, one who needs to use multiple workstations, but only one at a time. The user can move from one workstation to another and maintain the same capabilities and interface characteristics used on the prior workstation.

In the area of problem management, System Manager/400 provides a way to maintain an electronic **problem log**. That problem log is managed automatically and includes the clients attached via Client Access/400. As users or the AS/400 system itself report a problem, that problem is automatically noted in the electronic problem log. The problems are prioritized, and notes are kept on the activities associated with each problem. If IBM's customer service needs to get involved, the problem, with all of its notes, is sent electronically to IBM's support network. If the central support site has an S/390 computer system, System Manager/400 cooperates with the S/390, allowing all support activity to be performed from that system. In the area of hardware/software inventory and software management, System Manager/400 automatically detects what hardware is connected on the LAN networks and downloads the operating system required Windows, OS/2, etc.).

OS/400 V4R2 and Managed System Services working together can provide automated tracking and management of corequisite PTF's within corequisite PTF's as a group. The risks and complexity in managing corequisite relationships are reduced as a result of this cooperative effort. These PTF's can be downloaded across the Internet. With V4R3, customers with a network of AS/400 systems can use software intended for use on a remote system without having to install that software on the central site system. This saves DASD space and installation time. Previously, the remote system could only receive software that the central site could service, the list of which was the combination of a hard-coded list and a list of software installed on the central site system.

Management Central

Management Central provides immediate and up-to-the-minute information about the systems being managed, making it possible for systems administrators or operators with multiple systems and networks to gather, analyze and react to system information. Systems can be grouped to allow the control and monitoring of multiple AS/400 systems in a network from a central AS/400 server. It is possible to monitor:

- CPU utilization (average, interactive)
- Interactive response time
- Batch logical I/O
- Transaction rates
- Disk space utilization
- Communications IOPs
- Communications lines
- Local area networks
- Disk IOPs
- Disk arm utilization
- Machine pool faulting rates (maximum only)
- Base/user pool faulting rates
- CPU utilization (Lite) (average only)

With the capability of real-time graphical monitoring, it is possible to: monitor multiple systems or groups, establish thresholds for each monitor, automatically execute programs/actions on threshold events, and view threshold events.

TCP/IP security can be set up to include network address translation and IP packet filtering to accept or reject IP packets based on criteria. The latter capability providing one method for eliminating unwanted e-mail.

The system can also be set up to manage an AS/400 Network File System (NFS) server, including the exports and netgroups for that server.

If NetServer is operating on an Integrated PC Server, it is possible to view server statistics with optional automatic refreshing, shared objects being used by a session, and sessions using a shared object.

Within a database, Management Central enables table contents to be updated, remote journals to be managed, aliases to be managed, and tables to be copied and moved between systems.

In a Distributed Computing Environment, it is possible to set up and manage AS/400 DCE services.

For Lightweight Directory Access Protocols (LDAP), it is possible to set up and manage an AS/400 Directory Server and publish user information to an LDAP directory.

Management Central Methodology

Management Central provides a methodology for managing multiple systems, system groups, and system group functions. Management Central includes performance monitors, support for remote operations, inventory collection, packaged object distribution, management of software fixes, performance collection services, and job scheduling. The primary components of Management Central include the following:

Collection Services is a tool for data collection which replaces the performance monitor with an emphasis on capturing data with minimum system impact. The data is not processed until needed. Flexibility is provided in what data is collected and how that data is managed. Collected data is written into a Management Collection object. **Management Collection objects** may be created and destroyed automatically or retained indefinitely based on user defined parameters. A performance monitor database is created based on the data in the management collection object. The creation of the database can be deferred until a later time than the data collection or even on a different system. Also, only data of interest need be processed and only over time intervals of interest. Multiple database views may be created from the same management collection object.

Object Packaging and Distribution Graphical Interface provides a way to send objects from any file system to one or more AS/400s in a network. It also includes features for restoring objects, taking snapshots of objects, versioning packages of objects, and post execution of commands against objects. The functions can be performed on a group or network of AS/400s and be scheduled for a convenient time.

PTF Management Wizards for a distributed environment walks the user through comparing the PTF levels of multiple AS/400 systems to a model system on which a proven set of PTFs have been installed. The Wizard then performs the distribution and installation of any missing PTFs on the remote AS/400s by identifying the system or group of systems to be updated.

Inventory for Multiple Systems can be performed using a graphical interface which enables the scheduling of regular inventory collections of hardware, software and PTF information. The inventory collection can be for a group or network of AS/400 systems. Using the data collected, it is possible to search for a specific piece of information, and export that information to a PC application for analysis, or just compare information for multiple systems.

AS/400 Performance Tools (5716-PT1)

The IBM AS/400 Performance Tools (5716-PT1) feature accesses system load information automatically logged by the system. With these tools, the performance of the system can be "tuned" and future performance requirements projected. The tools provide performance reports that can be as high-level or as detailed as needed. System use, response time, and number of transactions are statistically treated. The expert systems–based "advisor" function assists the system manager in interpreting performance analysis and often recommends specific actions. AS/400 Performance Tools help the system manager determine where the system is and where it is going in terms of capacity and performance. For smaller systems or those not requiring the function of AS/400 Performance Tools, the Performance Tools/400 (5763-PT1) provides basic performance planning tools. Also, the Performance Investigator/400 (PRPQ #5799-PRG) runs on a PC under DOS/Windows and graphs in real time (15-second samples) items such as CPU use, response time, and so on. One PC can monitor up to 16 AS/400 systems.

Managed System Services for AS/400

SystemView Managed System Services for AS/400 (5769-MG1) makes it easier to distribute software and manage software changes for clients attached to AS/400 systems by adding a change control server function. The change control server enables unattended software distribution and installation for NetFinity clients. Software distributions to clients can be scheduled and tracked from the AS/400 system managing the network. Distribution and change requests can be sent to the clients over SNA and TCP/IP networks. Additional client management function is also provided for sending files, programs, and data to a client; retrieving files, programs, and data from a client; deleting files, programs, and data on a client; running a command or calling a program on a client; performing a remote IPL or reboot on a client; or applying or removing a software fix on a client. These changes might be **Program Temporary Fixes (PTFs)** that correct known problems or might involve installing a whole new version of OS/400. The updates can be sent electronically to the remote AS/400 systems over existing APPN or traditional SNA networks or over TCP/IP and the Internet.

NetFinity for AS/400

NetFinity for AS/400 (5716-SVA) enables the movement of systems management tasks from end users to more experienced system administrators. NetFinity contains an inventory server that collects hardware and software inventory information from the clients being managed and stores it in DB2/400 databases on the AS/400 server. This information is used to perform management tasks such as software distribution, distributed monitoring, and remote control. NetFinity enables the system administrator to perform remote control of the PC clients, allowing the identification and correction of potential problems before they impact business. NetFinity also provides a graphical interface to software distribution by defining custom reports for querying the hardware and software database, runs the reports and displays results, generates a node list for distributing software, and distributes the PC software. Other NetFinity capabilities include critical file monitoring, workstation discovery, performance monitoring, activity scheduling, enhanced security, user profile data collection, alert management and processing, and problem analysis and correction.

NetFinity for AS/400 has two components: NetFinity Server for AS/400 (5716-SVA) is the server component, installed on the AS/400 servers and the central site system. NetFinity AS/400 Manager (5716-SVD) is a manager component installed on a PC connected to an AS/400 server in its workgroup. NetFinity Services for AS/400 (5716-SVE) contains the PC client code supporting NetFinity for AS/400. All the PCs to be managed within the enterprise must include this code, which performs the responses directed by the NetFinity Manager and Netfinity for AS/400 software. NetFinity Server for AS/400 includes an easy-to-use GUI for setting up pro-active resource monitors and alert conditions on the clients. Client alerts notify the manager GUI when conditions are met, such as changes to critical files, the start or end of a critical process, and performance and capacity statistics. Administrators can view a snapshot of the screen, start a command-line session, transfer files, browse information in the desktop management interface, and view current hardware and software configurations on remote clients.

In order to support remote control of Windows NT Server on the Integrated PC Server, NetFinity requires a local managing workstation for the remote server, control of the remote console keyboard/mouse, the capability to inventory the software and hardware and to perform software distribution through the AS/400 using Managed System Services (MSS). PC systems supported as clients are Windows 3.1, Windows 95, Windows 98, Windows NT, and OS/2.

Application Development Facilities

Many businesses find that writing their own custom application programs is the best method of solving business problems through computers. To this end, the basic architecture of AS/400 has been optimized to make writing and maintaining custom application programs as easy as possible. The database built into all AS/400s is one example of this. The ability to create databases that do not reside in any one program (externally described data) and to create different logical views of the same or related physical data is a major benefit to programmer productivity. This is particularly true when it becomes necessary to modify or add programs that use the database information in a different way.

Single-level storage and the concept of objects help the programmer by automatically managing the complexities of main storage sizes, disk storage allocation and paging, and file sizes. Programmers can therefore spend their time making the application program more powerful or easier to use instead of managing internal computer logistics. Later in this chapter, we discuss the need to evolve (redevelop existing programs that executed in the host-centric environment so that they are usable in the client/server environment) and how object-oriented technology can be used to help solve that migration problem. The programmer has several programming languages from which to choose, including:

- AS/400 PL1
- IBM Pascal
- VRPG/400
- ILE RPG400
- AS/400 BASIC
- ILE COBOL400
- VisualAge C++ for OS/400
- ILE C for AS/400
- ILE C++ for AS/400
- RM/COBOL
- FORTRAN400

These commonly used programming languages can be thought of as the library of instructions from which a programmer constructs a program. The language selected depends on the requirements of the application program and the skills of the programmer(s). The "ILE" languages conform to the AS/400's Integrated Language Environment.

Designed into OS/400 are functions that allow the application programmer to participate in the **Document Interchange Architecture (DIA)**. The Document Interchange Architecture consists of a set of rules published by IBM that allow the smooth flow of electronic documents through different types of computers and programs, and allow the user to file and search for those electronic documents. Other OS/400 features make it easier for the programmer to provide online help text and use graphics (i.e., GDDM support), making the application program easier to understand and use. To further augment tools available to the programmer, the separately purchased IBM AS/400 Application Development Tools (ADTS/400) package is available. This programmer tool kit is based on programmer tools available with earlier System/3X computers and consists of the following tools, designed for use on a non-programmable terminal.

The IBM AS/400 Application Development Tools package has been divided into six sections.

1. The first section, Application Development Tool Set/400, contains the Data File Utility (DFU), Screen Design Aid (SDA), Source Entry Utility (SEU), and Program Development Manager.

2. The second section, Application Development Tools—Printing, contains the Advanced Printer Functions (APF) (5727-AP6), Advanced Function Printing (AFP), and AFP Font Collection.

3. The third section, Application Development Tools—Programs Group 1 includes Structured Query Language (SQL, 5763-WP1), Business Graphics Utility (BGU, 5716-DS1), and Query/400 (5769-QU1).

4. The fourth section, Application Development Tools—Programs Group 2, contains the Application Program Driver (5649-PD1), Application Dictionary Services/400 (5738-AD1), and WindowTool/400 (5798-RYF).

5. The fifth section, Application Development Tools—Debug and Maintenance, includes the Interactive Source Level Debugger (ISLD), the Cooperative Debugger, and the File Compare and Merge Utility (FCMU).

6. The last section contains other application development methodologies, CODE/400, VRPG Client, Computer-Aided Software Engineering (CASE), and Know-ledgeTool/400 (5798-RYE). The Neural Network Utility/400 (5798-RYB) has been absorbed by Intelligent Miner (5733-IM1).

Application Development Tools Set/400

This set of application development program tools eases the programmer's task of writing new applications and maintaining existing applications. The tools include capabilities for managing the development project, specifically designing a database management program, designing the appearance of the interface to the application, and editing and checking the program code itself as the design progresses. Any and all of the programming languages listed in Application Development Facilities are supported by each of these tools.

Data File Utility (DFU). This utility program is primarily intended to help a programmer write simple database management programs. Typical programs in this area include data entry (filling up a database with information), retrieving information (inquiry), and making necessary changes to a database (file maintenance). Although OS/400 itself provides a way to perform these tasks, DFU and user-written application programs make these tasks easier for the user.

Screen Design Aid (SDA). This program allows the application programmer to interactively design, create, and maintain the user interface of a program—that is, the screens seen by the user of an application program can be generated through the SDA. This tool saves the programmer considerable time that would otherwise have to be spent programming all screen images from scratch. Since SDA is interactive, the programmer can easily change the screen being designed (e.g., different color, text, and fields) and immediately see the results of the change. Once a screen image is completed, it can be printed for use in program documentation.

Source Entry Utility (SEU). This tool can be thought of as a specialized word processor for programmers that is used to write applications programs. It provides a full-screen editor, which means that you can work on an entire page of text at a time. It provides the basic capabilities of copying, deleting, and moving text (programming statements) as well as language-sensitive dynamic prompting and automatic syntax checking. A search function allows you to automatically locate particular statements in a program. The split-screen function allows you to simultaneously view two different areas of a program or two separate programs for purposes of comparison, change, and copying. Many of the commands used with SEU are similar to those used in development support utilities and source entry utility programs of System/3X computers.

Program Development Manager. This program provides all the elements of ADTS/400 assembled into one integrated programming environment. It allows the programmer to work with lists of items being developed. Rather than copying each item individually, the Program Development Manager allows you to perform the copy with one operation. It provides convenience that improves productivity and makes for a more pleasant programming environment. The Program Development Manager is similar to the Programmer and Operator Productivity (POP) environment on the System/36 with a few enhancements.

Application Development Tools—Printing

These tools address the needs of the programmer relative to setting up and managing the appearance of output documents, whether provided directly by a printer or indirectly by an electronic interchange methodology such as fax.

Print Services Facility/400. Print Services Facility/400 (**PSF/400**) is an integrated feature of OS/400 that provides full system-managed printing to IPDS printers. It is automatically invoked by OS/400 print management when its services are required. PSF/400 is the driver subsystem for Advanced Function Printing (AFP) on AS/400.

PSF/400 manages the printing of the following types of AS/400 spooled files to the IPDS printers:

- SCS files

- SCS with printer file options (i.e., front or back overlay)

- SCS with page or form definitions for print formatting

- AFP capabilities from the Client Access/400 AFP driver

- AFP capabilities from other systems or AFP Toolbox (a PrintSuite product)

- PostScript and image files converted by Host Print Transform (HPT)

- IPDS files

- AFP files created from DDS printer file specifications. DDS includes keywords to: switch between simplex and duplex printing within a spooled file. All of these spooled files (except IPDS) are transformed into IPDS and managed to the printer. As the system managed print driver, PSF/400 provides full document services, printer services, and print process management. In addition, PSF/400 provides full functionality when printing to TCP/IP-connected network printers.

AFP Font Collection. The AFP Font Collection provides a comprehensive set of Advanced Function Printing (AFP) fonts with over 1,000 fonts from the most popular type families, including Times New Roman, Helvetica, and Courier. A full range of sizes, resolutions (240 dpi, 300 dpi) and languages (over 48) are included. Outline formats are also supplied, enabling the creation of additional sizes or variations as well as support the full viewing of AFP output using the Client Access/400 Viewer.

Advanced Function Printing Utilities (5769-AF1). The Advanced Function Printing Utilities support expanded duplex, image, and application design support including color, bar codes (Australian Postal, Japan Postal, Royal Mail). AFP/U is a set of three utilities (Print Format Utility, Query for AFP utility, and AFP Toolbox) supporting the development of advanced print applications.

Print Format Utility and Query for AFP Utility support tumble duplex in addition to standard duplex. Element selection allows the specification of conditions under which any element within a record layout will be printed. Selection is determined by the values of one to five variable fields in the database file being printed. Color can be specified in overlay and print application design for lines and boxes. Image handling options support two image formats (IOCA and IMI), the specification of which uses the same manner and yields similar results.

Euro Currency Symbol. AS/400 support for the euro currency symbol includes changes to the following system functions:

- Code pages and CCSIDs

- Keyboard types

- Device configurations and device controllers

- Fonts and glyphs

- Specific currency processing

This phase of euro support is only for those countries that use the "Latin 1" based alphabet, including those countries initially participating in the European Monetary Union and other select countries. For the latest information and a road-map to euro currency sign support on the AS/400 visit the AS/400 Web site at:

http://www.as400.ibm.com/euro

For those who would like to see the symbol, it can be viewed by choosing coins at symbols at the following Web site address:

http://www.europa.eu.int/euro/html/home5.html?lang=5

Application Development Tools—Program Group 1

These application development tools are also application programs that fit the definition of cross-industry applications. As such, they are used by a wide variety of other applications as well as for developing new custom applications.

Structured Query Language (SQL). SQL provides the programmer with additional commands that can be embedded in application programs to efficiently manipulate database information.

Business Graphics Utility (BGU). BGU is a programmer's tool for creating computer-generated graphics. Although users with no programming experience can use BGU interactively to create their own graphs, the programming interface provided by BGU gives the application programmer convenient access to graphics functions.

Query/400. Query/400 can be used by the programmer to define database reports that can be executed by the user. Once the query has been defined, the AS/400 system need not have the Query/400 program to simply execute the query. Again, although the user can often use

Query/400 without the assistance of a programmer, a programmer can also take advantage of Query/400 when writing application programs.

Other Application Development Tools—Program Group 2

In addition to the Application Development Toolset/400, there are other separately purchased tools for the AS/400 programmer. Among these are the Application Program Driver (5730-095), Application Dictionary Services/400 (5733-080), WindowTool/400 (5798-RYF), and Lotus Notes.

Application Program Driver. The Application Program Driver (5769-PD1) is yet another tool for programmers that provides many of the services commonly needed by application programs (e.g., menu design, fast-path support around menus, and security). Further, the Application Program Driver can provide a single menu interface to all application programs. This makes for a consistent user interface for users who need access to more than one application program. The Applications Program Driver has received a GUI interface to make it easier to use for Windows 3.1 or Windows 95 users or customers with multiple applications in a single graphical environment. The GUI interface provides point and click capability, fast path commands, AS/400 connectivity, detailed help, and reduces the learning curve through increased consistency.

Application Dictionary Services/400. Application Dictionary Services/400 builds a directory of data and programs residing on the AS/400 system. It is used by the programmer to keep an inventory of the data and program items stored on the system and can be used to evaluate the impact of a proposed change to an application program and to re-create impacted objects if desired.

Window Tool/400. WindowTool/400 is a tool used to build a text-based windows user interface for existing AS/400 application programs on non-intelligent terminals. With WindowTool/400 systems, operators and programmers can subdivide the screen into boxes (called windows) and provide user interface items such as pull-down windows, pop-up menus, action bars, and so on. Although no graphics are supported with WindowTool/400, the user interface provided on non-intelligent text-only workstations with WindowTool/400 is a step toward the graphical user interface that has become so popular on intelligent workstations (e.g., Windows and OS/2 Presentation Manager on a PS/2).

Alternately, application programs can be written to some enhanced OS/400 application programming interfaces (**DDS Windows support**) to provide the best user interface available to the user. That is, a user with a personal computer or InfoWindow II workstation will automatically be presented an enhanced user interface with pop-up windows, scroll bars, and so on. A user of a workstation that doesn't support the enhanced user interface functions of OS/400 will be presented a standard user interface (e.g., a simple menu). The programmer writes the application programming using the DDS Windows application program interfaces. The OS/400 and associated hardware automatically tailor the user interface for each user's workstation based on its capabilities. RUMBA/400, mentioned earlier, recognizes and works with application programs that use the new DDS Windows application programming interfaces.

Application Development Tools—Debugging and Maintenance

Once the programs have been written using AS/400 programming tools, they must be tested for correctness and any problems must be diagnosed and fixed. OS/400 provides an interactive debugging facility for this purpose. This facility allows the programmer to closely control and monitor the new or modified application program as it is executing on the AS/400. Because one of the most frustrating tasks for the programmer is **debugging** the program (finding and fixing programming errors), this facility is very important. The only thing constant is change.

Even when an application program is completely tested and put into productive use, there will be a need to make changes as the business environment changes and to fix newly discovered program errors that were not caught during testing. This activity is called **supporting** or **maintaining** the application program. In addition to AS/400's externally described database design, there are some tools that help with this maintenance. OS/400's cross-reference facility and data dictionary support provide the programmer with the means to determine which application programs use what database information. With this information, the programmers can assess the impact of a proposed change to an application program or database. The data dictionary support also provides a single place to go for information concerning database field names, data types, and the like.

Interactive Source Level Debugger (ISLD). This tool provides the program developer with a debugging facility with which the developer can interact as the code is being designed.

Cooperative Debugger. This tool provides the developer with a debugging facility with which the developer can debug code on OS/400 from an OS/2 client. The tool applies to C++ and other ILE languages, including CODE/400.

File Compare and Merge Utility (FCMU). The functions of this tool are apparent from the name. It will compare a new file against an existing file, and it will merge two existing files together, making a single larger file.

Application Development Tools Programming

AS/400 Software Development Kit for ActiveX and **OLE DB** is a PC-based developers toolkit for building GUI client/server applications. The SDK works with AS/400 OLE DB data provider, and ships on Client Access for Windows Family CD-ROM.

IBM VisualAge for Java IDE and **Inprise's JBuilder/400 IDE** are PC-based development environments closely tied to the AS/400. These environments have been refreshed to include the Toolbox for Java.

Application Development Tools—Other Methodologies

A couple of IBM workstation-based products are emerging in application development: CODE/400 and VRPG Client. **CODE/400** is a tool for server- or host-based development, and **VRPG Client** is a visual programming tool to create RPG client/server applications. The built-in features of AS/400 and OS/400 along with additional tools (e.g., Application Development Tools, SQL, etc.) make for productive application program development and maintenance. However, there are other AS/400 programming tools for those wishing to implement the more structured **Computer-Aided Software Engineering (CASE)** methodology.

CASE is a structure and methodology for managing and executing application development projects from inception of the project through ongoing software maintenance activities. Finally, knowledge-based tools support the development of a class of custom application programs that employ expert system techniques for solving problems. **Expert systems** are application programs that attempt to capture the knowledge of a human expert and then draw conclusions on any presented information based on that expert knowledge. Although expert systems are not the answer to all application program needs, they can be very effective in addressing many business needs.

Two examples of *knowledge-based tools* are the **IBM Knowledge Tool/400 (5798-RYE)** and the **Intelligent Miner (5733-IM1)**. KnowledgeTool/400 is a tool used by programmers to write application programs that use rule-based expert system technology. These application programs are designed to capture the expertise of humans in a set of rules later used by the application program to make decisions and recommendations on any new data provided. For example, a rule-based expert system application program for the medical profession might try to diagnose an illness based on a set of symptoms entered into a computer system.

Neural networks take a different approach. Rather than having the expert and programmer develop a set of rules, the **neural network** analyzes a set of existing information in order to identify and classify patterns in the information. For example, if a bank has a database containing information about loan applicants and their subsequent payment records, neural networks can be employed to look for patterns in the information and identify characteristics that tend to indicate that the party will pay off a loan on schedule. During this analysis phase, the neural network is said to be training on the data. Once the neural network is trained, it can then look at the information collected from new loan applicants and help management determine the risk associated with each applicant based on history. Neural networks for the AS/400 have been repackaged under the Intelligent Miner/400 (5733-IM1) product.

In the next phase of the application program development project, production and maintenance, the test, maintenance, and redevelopment tools are introduced. Building tools are used to "assemble" all the pieces of the application program(s) (e.g., object code modules, subroutine libraries, etc.) into a working system. **Testing tools** help the programmers simulate inputs to the application program and monitor outputs. Tests can be defined and then run during initial testing and rerun later to validate any changes made to the application program after it is in use. **Maintenance tools** include things to increase the productivity of the programmers when they correct errors or implement changes in the application program while it is in use. An example of a maintenance tool is an impact analysis tool, which allows programmers to assess the amount of effort needed to implement a requested change before the change is started. This allows the level of effort required for the change to be measured against the value of the change in order to help prioritize work.

AS/400 Kernel Threads

A **thread** is an independent unit of execution within a program. The amount of system resources used for a thread is far less than the resources used for a job. Threads share a common address space and have access to all job resources. They are used to run different parts of an application concurrently. Multithreading provides simplified algorithms and more responsive programs in that the functions of I/O, calculations, and user interface are each dealt with through separate threads, and threads use less resources than a multiprocess solution. Initial implementations of threads will be in Java, C, and C++.

When **POSIX** Application Program Interfaces (API's) are used, there are multithreading considerations including the added complexity of managing shared resources and data, concerns with data synchronization and race conditions, a potential for deadlocks, and a non-threadsafe environment. The Java language eliminates many of the POSIX multithreading considerations. The AS/400 positioning relative to threads support is to provide kernel threads at a level sufficient to support porting of multithreaded applications and servers from other platforms, such as Domino, to provide a competitive platform for multiuser/multithreaded servers, to provide thread performance equal to or better than the best of AIX and Windows NT, to support integration of existing code with threads, and to stage threadsafe OS/400 functions over several releases, based on application requirements.

A threadsafe function can be invoked simultaneously in multiple threads. A function is **threadsafe** if and only if all functions it calls are threadsafe. OS/400 is not threadsafe. OS/400 will allow access to non-threadsafe functions with the following exceptions:

- Thread-unsafe file systems

- Thread creation in non-multithread-capable jobs

- File types other than database files or print files with SPOOL

- File overrides

- Reclaim resources
- Save/restore

The following list identifies the threadsafe support at V4R3:

- Basic System services (job management, security, librarian, performance and service tools)
- UNIX style APIs (signals, process management)
- Root, Qopensys, user-defined file systems
- Sockets support (TCP/IP)
- Data base record I/O
- SQL
- SQL server (shipped as PTF)
- Multithreaded support for batch immediate and pre-start jobs
- Command analyzer
- Threadsafe CL commands (user indexes, user queues, user spaces, data queues, and data areas)
- Shared file opens
- Thread scoped transactions through SQL server
- Change user attributes
- QnetClient File system
- Multithread job capability for SBMJOB, autostart jobs, and reading jobs from a database file.

Thread safe functions/facilities supported at V4R4 are: (1) C++ access class libraries, (2) ILE RPG and ILE Cobol, (3) IFS and DB file management, and (4) allowing native method access from Java to legacy functions.

The following listing identifies the limitations of AS/400 thread support:

- It performs batch jobs only (no interactive support).

- Startup costs are higher.

- Special considerations must be taken (I/O, data sharing, function results) in order to share information with interactive jobs.

- The shell product provides equivalent support to UNIX platforms.

- If the Activation Group encounter conditions that would result in destruction of the activation group, the job will be terminated. (This is expected behavior on UNIX and Windows platforms.)

- Non-threadsafe AS/400 functions must be accessed in separate jobs.

- Integration of existing code into multithreaded applications requires separation of the job or synchronization to access the function.

Integrated Language Environment (ILE)

The Integrated Language Environment (ILE) provides a new set of tools and system support designed to enhance program development on the AS/400 System. Benefits that ILE offers over previous program models include binding, modularity, reusable components, common run-time services, and coexistence. ILE also offers better control over resources, better control over language interactions, better code optimization, and a better environment for the supported languages. ILE produces a **mod-**

ule object (**MODULE**) that can be combined (*bound*) with other modules to form a single executable unit, that is, a program object (PGM).

The module objects may be written in several languages, and the binding is performed by calls from each individual module. The development of the modules results in faster compiling time, simplified maintenance, simplified testing, better use of programming resources, and easier porting to other platforms. The presence of reusable components in ILE means that a segment of code that has been developed previously does not have to be rewritten to be used in a new application, but can be picked up as a module and integrated with the new application. The ILE's common runtime services include a selection of off-the-shelf components (bindable APIs) that are supplied as part of the ILE, ready to be incorporated into your applications. These APIs provide services such as these:

- Date and time manipulation

- Message handling

- Math routines

- Greater control over screen handling

- Dynamic memory allocation

ILE programs can coexist with existing programs, each being able to call the other. ILE program modules may be written in C, C++, RPG, COBOL, and CL. In addition to the traditional programming languages (C, RPG, and COBOL), OS/400 provides another language, called **Command Language** (CL), that can be used as a scripting language to control flow within an application and to perform operating system tasks. Command Language can be used to issue a single operating system request or to create complex programs that present the user with menus and initiate other application programs.

ILE RPG for AS/400 supports variable-length fields, allows you to use your own data structure for indicators to communicate values to data, and enables the use of built-in functions instead of result indicators. Built-in functions have been added to query the results of input/output operations and for error handling. Control-specific keywords can be used to specify compile options, and the specified compile options will be used on every compile of the program. In addition, support is provided for import and export of mixed-case procedures and variables, built-in functions have been added to make string manipulation easier, and application profiling support is provided.

ILE COBOL for AS/400 now supports user defined data types; supports date, time, and timestamp data types within the FORMAT clause of the Data Description entry; allows profiling a program for optimization; and permits manipulation of null values in database records and locale-sensitive categories. ILE COBOL for AS/400 also supports locale sensitive categories, includes native thread enablement of ILE COBOL run time and more XPG4/ANSI functions for the POSIX locale, and provides argument optimization support. ILE COBOL for AS/400 supports a 64-bit integer as a data type, and can read the Integrated File System directly.

ILE C++ has a native compiler that runs on the AS/400 under theVisualAge C++ for AS/400. The language is 64-bit enabled, can compile C++ programs natively on the AS/400 and can read the Integrated File System directly.

Emerging Application Development Environments

Although the preceding paragraphs provide a valid insight into the world of third- and fourth-generation language application development, they fall somewhat short of describing the emerging programming environment. The following paragraphs provide the reader with an overview of application development in the time frame of emerging programming languages and evolved computing paradigms that provide a new environment for the old host-centric programs. And we discuss the need to somehow migrate these old programs to a new computing paradigm that includes client/server and distributed computing as a base.

Like the evolution of hardware from the ability to mix and match parts from different vendors within the same system (personal computer systems, the IBM-compatible phenomenon) to the ability to mix and match computing systems from many different vendors (the Distributed Computing Environment [DCE] as defined by the Open Systems Foundation [OSF], X-Open, and other standards groups), emerging programming languages are defining interfaces that enable programs to be picked up in pieces that are developed by different groups and will be guaranteed to work together without the need for additional programming glue. What this means is that it is possible to take existing third-generation language applications (**procedural languages** such as RPG, COBOL, and Pascal), add an input interface and an output interface around them, add them to other programs that provide a distributed computing environment, and, after compiling, execute them in a distributed computing environment. The programming languages that provide this capability are the **object-oriented programming languages**, foremost among which are SmallTalk, C++, and Java.

Five possible steps may be taken along the path to full client/server distributed computing as applications are moved from a host-centric environment. A business may elect to stop at any one of those steps, depending upon the investment needed to move along the path. Figure 4.20 illustrates the steps, and the text in "Client/Server Computing Model" describes how the client and server relate to the function of executing programs using the environment provided at each step. Over the last few years the definition of client/server computing has been clarified, and most vendors accept the set of models defined by the Gartner Group—the base for Figure 4.20, which focuses on three facets of computing:

- The distribution of the presentation part of the application, whether or not it is graphic, and whether the software that manages the screen is on the server or on the workstation (called "Presentation" in Figure 4.20).

- The distribution between client and server of function or "logic"—the processing or procedural part of the application (called "Logic" in Figure 4.20).

- The distribution of data—where it resides, how it is accessed, and who accesses it (called "Data Management" in Figure 4.20).

Client/Server Computing Model

What Figure 4.20 shows is that there are many ways to view the client/server application approach. They cover a wide range of ways to distribute data, logic, and presentation, but they appear to the end user to all be client/server. The AS/400 supports all of the models just as it supports the original host-centric non-programmable terminal model.

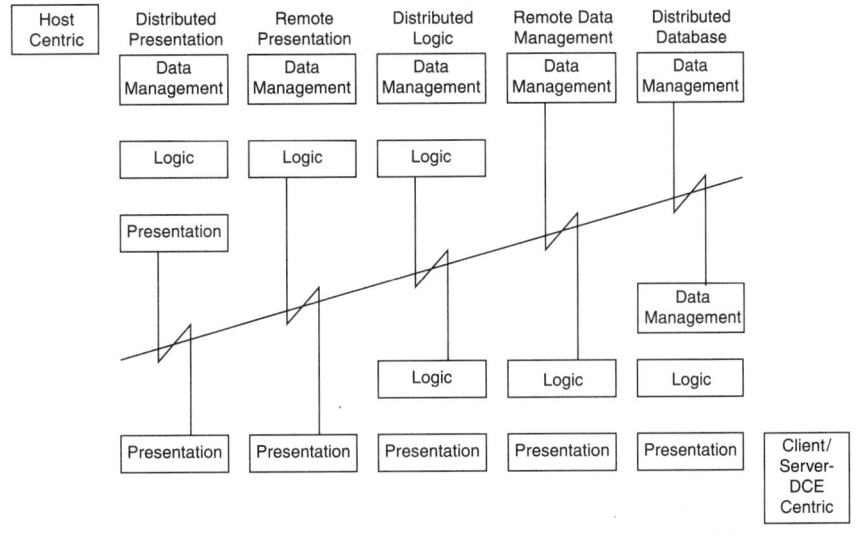

Figure 4.20. Client/server computing models.

The next few paragraphs describe each of the models, describing the level of function that is executed on both the client and the server.

Host-Centric Model. All processing functions are performed in the central processing system for presentation, logic, and data management—no intelligence is required to exist in the terminal. The terminal may have intelligence, but the intelligence is not being used to support the programming function. Only the display and keyboard of the terminal are effectively functional. The greatest proportion of existing applications have been written for this model, and there is no additional cost to maintain that software.

Distributed Presentation Model. Presentation services in this model are provided by both the client and the server. The server completely formats the presentation, then a client-based application intercepts and interprets the display data stream generated by the server. For the AS/400, the communication between client and server could be either the 5250 data stream or TCP/IP. The original applications remain unchanged. This technique is relatively simple to implement, and software costs can be minimal. The user benefits of this type of applications conversion should not be downgraded: the ease of use and integration advantages for the user's workspace can be significant.

Remote Presentation Model. In this model, the remote client provides the presentation services via some form of dialogue manager. The application drives the remote display as in an application programming interface, typically a conversational interface such as Advanced Program-to-Program Communications (APPC). System services (at the server) provide the protocol and data streams to transport the application commands to the client. A dialogue manager in the client then provides the screen formatting and user interface, and sends the results to the server application, which is performing the data management and application logic functions. Using the AS/400 fourth-generation languages and application generators, it can be quite easy for a user to achieve client/server applications employing remote presentations. The code generator will optionally create a set of application interfaces, communications code, PC programs, and local PC data to accomplish screen display.

Distributed Logic Model. In this model the application logic is split between the client and the server, with pieces residing on both. Application components interact with each other using some form of remote access. The communications style can vary from conversational (APPC), to Remote Procedure Call (RPC), to queued messages (MQI or DAE), to the emerging distributed object-oriented messages (CORBA). The logic could be split, with the server executing a transaction processing subsystem to handle the business rules and procedures, interfacing to a rules-driven database, also on the server, while the client carries the application flow as directed through user-driven events.

Remote Data Model. Presentation services and application logic reside on the client while the server provides data services, usually through an SQL interface. Remote data management typically involves a PC-oriented application generator that accesses data on the server through SQL. These SQL-based tools are generally highly open to the server of choice. This type of development provides an inexpensive start because it only requires a PC development license, but additional costs come when data integrity and security become important. The AS/400's integrated relational database and systems management provide advantages both in data integrity and security not generally available with other server platforms.

Distributed Computing Model. Data is distributed across the clients and the servers by means of the networks and requires sophisticated data management. The data security, locking, and file structure may be on the client or distributed between client and multiple servers. When data is distributed, the interface is normally one of the database-to-database standards, such as IBM DRDA, Oracle Transparent Gateway for SQL/400, and Sybase Open Client-Open Server. The AS/400 provides support for all of these standards.

Object Technology

The following paragraphs answer these questions: Why object technology? What is object technology? How is object technology different from the other programming languages and development paradigms described here? A set of definitions are provided to identify the fundamental concepts of object technology, and three benefits of object technology are described. The AS/400's support for object technology and strategic direction are outlined, and application development tools currently on the AS/400 supporting object technology (such as frameworks and Java) are described.

Why Object Technology? As discussed earlier, when speaking of application development, there is a need to reduce the cost of software in every phase of application development. That need is being driven by the fact that the business environment is changing at a faster and faster pace, and no two businesses operate in exactly the same way. Businesses need application packages tailored to their specific operation, or at the least application packages modifiable to their operations—and the testing and maintenance of those packages has to be made simpler. Software developers need new tools and methodologies to provide application packages faster and with less expense. Object technology offers significant promise of being able to deliver those capabilities.

What Is Object Technology? Object technology is not a product, it is an enabling technology that provides an approach to software development supported by several products and system and network enablers. The approach models the business world and has properties that support the reuse of software components. The AS/400 currently supports C++ and SmallTalk (supported on client, not native) object-oriented application development and Java execution and services for the Internet. Modeling the business world and reusing software components leads to reducing development expense and providing software applications faster. These application packages can be built with existing methodologies (procedural, structured programming) or object technology. The transition to object technology is expected to take several years for software developers; as a result, coexistence with existing procedural applications is a critical requirement of object technology.

What Makes Object Technology Different from Procedural Programming Approaches? Object technology holds out the promise of being able to build applications from parts of other applications. Procedural programming technologies had no capabilities for achieving this. It was difficult to separate the beginning of one procedure from another, and it was difficult to identify what a particular procedure was actually doing, which is what made maintenance so expensive. Data was easy to access and change, many times by accident. In object technology data is hidden from the rest of the program and action must be taken overtly to change data. Object technology allows the inheritance of properties from other objects and the ability for objects of a subclass of a particular class to respond to the same message with different results. These differences are clarified in the definitions of the fundamental concepts in object technology. Two subjects that result from the move to object-oriented technology are frameworks and Java. These two subjects have achieved sufficient importance in the AS/400 strategic direction that they deserve separate sections devoted uniquely to that specific subject.

Fundamental Concepts of Object Technology. In this section, we will present some fundamental concepts of object technology and explain their functions.

An **object** is a software entity that combines data elements and the operations that can be performed on the data. This combination of data and operators into a single entity differentiates object-oriented programming from procedural programming, in which data and operators are separate. An object is a specific individual entity. For example, a car with a particular serial number is an object. Its data elements might include the serial number, the make of the vehicle, the owner's name, the date purchased, the date sold, the purchase price, the interest rate, and the down payment. Its operators might include addition, subtraction, remainder, logical, assignment, and greater than. **Instance** is the same as object.

Class is the abstraction that describes all objects that share the same data elements and operations. For example, all vehicles constitute a class. Your particular car is an instance of the class.

Inheritance is the derivation of a new subclass from an existing base class by using the "kind of" hierarchy. For example, a truck and a car are kinds of vehicles, so they can be derived from the vehicle class. In addition to operation descriptions and data elements unique to the subclass, the derived subclass contains information from the original base class. That information enables the subclass to reuse the code and data in the base class without having to repeat them. Reuse is the main reason why object technology leads to increased programmer productivity. Inheritance allows programmers to derive subclasses to meet specific needs by customizing applications and extending designs.

Encapsulation is the hiding of internal data structure and operations of an object from client programs. Client programs cannot see the implementation details inside the object. All they can see is the interface to the object.

Polymorphism (many forms) is the ability of subclasses of the same class to respond to the same message and produce different results. Polymorphism combines inheritance and dynamic binding.

Dynamic binding is the ability of some languages (including C++, Java, and SmallTalk) to bind the names of variables and expressions to their types at run time instead of at compile time. Sometimes referred to as *late binding*.

Framework is a set of classes that provide infrastructure and the flow of control in an application. Frameworks call your code; you do not call the frameworks. Well-designed frameworks provide the general design and implementation for a specific problem, allowing the developer to customize it to a particular situation.

Message is the mechanism by which one object requests services of another. The message identifies the method that the object will use to perform the request. This term is used only in SmallTalk, not in C++ or Java.

Method is another name for an operation that an object performs. An object may have many methods.

An **Object Request Broker (ORB)** is the mechanism that enables objects to communicate with each other across a network. The ORB handles services for security, registration, and object management. The Object Management Group (OMG) is an industry consortium that has defined the **Common Object Request Broker Architecture (CORBA)** to specify standards so that different ORB implementations in the industry can work together.

And, finally, a **part** is a preexisting software component that can be combined into an application by visual programming and construction.

Benefits of Object Technology. Software developers benefit from solving complex business problems by assembling or extending reusable software components. Since object applications model business problems more closely than procedural applications do, object applications are easier to develop, particularly once many frameworks exist. Object applications are easier to maintain, because if objects model real-life business processes, as processes change, corresponding object changes are both obvious and containable, with modularity and encapsulation data hiding. Maintenance is the greatest part of development expense. Programming effort can be used again and again. This reuse results in shorter development cycles, customizable delivery, and lower development expense.

To be useful across systems, objects must reside in open, distributed environments. To allow movement of objects within the network, these objects must be portable. This portability enables dynamic re-engineering of the application to match the evolving flow in the business. Distributed objects that are CORBA compliant provide software developers with a simple method to develop open, distributed applications for the client/server market. The end user benefits because object technology can result in solutions that address many end-user requirements:

- More consistent accessibility to information and to the computer system resources with better integrity.

- Better integration of applications.

- Greater flexibility of applications. The end user can create or customize visual applications instantly.

- Investment protection. Object-oriented applications can be phased in gradually and can coexist with procedural applications.

The information technology industry benefits because adoption of object technology facilitates two significant changes in the marketplace: distributed computing and component software.

Distributed computing means that remote objects and information can be created and used across platforms in a network. Software reuse from component software will operate the way component hardware is reused today, facilitating both quality and productivity. Every major vendor in the computer industry has declared object technology key to its strategic business goals. Industry standards are emerging, led by the OMG and the open cross-platform CORBA specification for distributed objects. Object-oriented languages are moving to ANSI standards.

How Can the AS/400 Participate in Object Technology? The AS/400 perceives the existence of object technology in an environment that is multiuser, business oriented, adaptable, customizable, reliable, integrated, simplified, and distributed. Not only is data to be distributed, so is the function. The distribution is across many vendor platforms connected by local networks (LANs, intranets) and remote networks (the Internet). Applications are perceived as distributed networking computer models that support task-centered client applications as well as server- and host-centered collaborative applications running the business.

This business environment has certain requirements for tools, base operating system support, and parts/frameworks. The tools need to support team development of projects that scale from small to large, that support legacy and object-oriented code development and run time, and that span low-level (system) to high-level (visual) development. The operating system must support multiuser, commercial business applications in a manageable way that hides complexity and provides low cost of ownership. The frameworks must span the industry segments and be shareable and portable across platforms and businesses.

AS/400 Object Technology Development Tools. Before object-oriented applications can become a success, programming languages and tools integrated into the development environment must be available. The integrated environment must encompass the development, run-time, and administration of distributed client/server applications. The three dominant **object-oriented languages**—C++, Java, and SmallTalk—are included in the AS/400 application development environment. VisualAge is an integrated application development environment designed for commercial client/server applications through visual programming and construction from components.

The **C++** application development environment is provided by the VisualAge C++ family of products. Cross platform development using C++ is enabled as a central technology by the VisualAge C++ family of products. VisualAge C++ for AS/400 (5716-CX4) and VisualAge for C++ for AS/400 (5716-CX5) combine the development environment of C++ for OS/2 with the capability to develop C++ code that is targeted for the AS/400. By enabling the development of powerful client/server applications to be written in C++, this combination takes advantage of the advanced data and security features of OS/400. Object interfaces to OS/400 functions and data are provided by the AS/400 Access Class Library (ACL).

VisualAge/SmallTalk is the repackaging of ENVY/400 with its access class libraries. It is not just a Graphical User Interface (GUI) builder or prototyping tool, it is a power tool designed to build online transaction processing and decision support applications. In visual programming, the user selects interface components and reviews the results as the interface is built. Applications can be built by selecting from a palette of categories of parts that are laid out and connected. The connected code is then automatically generated. A part may represent a database, a communications link, or an external source such as another program.

Team programming, including version control, change management, and library functions, enables multiple developers to work on the same application simultaneously. More experienced programmers have the benefit of the underlying SmallTalk language, including an integrated suite of productivity tools (editors, browsers, debuggers, and inspectors). The AS/400 Access Class Library (ACL) provides object interfaces to OS/400 functions and data, and similar Access Class Libraries are in VisualAge/SmallTalk for AS/400.

Emerging Applications Environments

Three application environments are on the verge of being available, Frameworks, OpenDoc, and Java. Those environments are being developed by many vendors. OS/400 is putting in place the support structures to embed these environments as quickly as they are available. Frameworks is the nearest to reality, so it is described in some detail.

Frameworks

The **frameworks environment** is one in which a company such as IBM develops the skeleton of an application, leaving to the final user the tuning of the application to the businesses needs. Object-oriented technology provides for programming—the reuse of parts and components that have been a part of the hardware environment for the last 5 to 10 years. Frameworks groups those components into compatible software sets, capturing the collective experience of a design team and providing a model for a common solution to particular problems, thereby automating much of the development effort. Examples of what frameworks can do include the following:

- Automating tasks associated with distributed applications

- Allowing applications to move easily between different operating systems by disguising the differences in those operating systems

- Automating graphical user interface development

- Masking/dealing with the complexities within and between transactions and communications.

Two different types of frameworks are being developed. One type deals with applications, the other with systems. The application frameworks provide a basic set of cross-industry and vertical functions/objects, which include basic financial management objects, distribution objects, and customer/supplier objects. Over time, application frameworks are expected to provide a rich base of application frameworks to enable the software parts business. IBM is developing a set of frameworks using the code name San Francisco. San Francisco focuses on business management software.

Within the second type of framework, the system framework, the system developer will provide the frameworks to support the traditional operating system functions in an object-oriented environment. These functions include graphical operations, data access, and network management. In addition, security, data integrity across multiple cooperating systems, save/restore, activation, and national language support need to be included as business objects. The concept of frameworks has been introduced here to set the stage for what to expect in the long run in system development.

The San Francisco Framework. San Francisco is a framework that focuses on business management software. San Francisco is written in Java. The user can elect to build an application starting from any of the three layers of San Francisco:

1. Base Layer. This provides the technical infrastructure needed before object technology can be used above it.

2. Common Business Objects Layer. These are the building blocks application developers can use to create business applications.

3. Core Business Processes Layer. This is built for one specific application containing the basic functions all applications of this type require.

The final layer of San Francisco is the Commercial Applications layer created by the software developers who buy and extend the San Francisco frameworks. In most cases this final layer will be created using Java. The layers of San Francisco are illustrated in Figure 4.21, together with its positioning relative to the Java virtual machine and the technology-independent interface.

SanFrancisco supplies a set of cross-platform, business process components including:

- Common Business Objects

- General Ledger

- Accounts Receivable/Accounts Payable Ledger

- Order Management

- Warehouse Management

San Francisco is designed to support the distributed object environment, and reduces the complexity, expense, and time-to-market factors related to the building of customized, multi-platform business applications. Performance has been enhanced to 3 times the initial release performance.

OpenDoc

OpenDoc is a cross-platform compound-document architecture designed to simplify creation of documents, including the multimedia elements of text, spreadsheets, charts, tables, graphics, images, video, and sound. End users can combine the parts as desired.

Figure 4.21. San Francisco block diagram.

ORB Support

AS/400 supports Iona's Orbix product which is a full implementation of OMG's Common Object Request Broker Architecture (CORBA). Orbix 2.3 is a C/C++ ORB implementation. OrbixWeb 3.0 is a Java ORB designed for use in the Java environment. Significant companies which have adopted this ORB are SAP, Intentia, and Baan.

AS/400 also supports Inprise's VisiBroker product which provides similar CORBA distributed object services. VisiBroker provides high-level services (naming, transaction, security, etc.), and DCOM connector. Significant companies which have adopted VisiBroker are Netscape and SUN.

Java

Java is a standardized cross-platform (running on many different types of computers) object-oriented programming language. The standards are being established by Sun Microsystems. The AS/400 representatives who have studied Java state that it is a pure object-oriented language similar in syntax to C++ and similar in behavior to SmallTalk. Java is an interpreted language and is machine independent, meaning programs written in Java will execute on any system. The Java Developer's Kit (JDK) from Sun includes a standardized set of Class Libraries (packages), a Java compiler, and the Java virtual machine.

The Class Libraries support creating Graphical User Interfaces (GUI's), controlling multimedia data, communicating over networks, accessing data in stream files and relational databases, and more. The Java compiler (also known as the **"javac"** compiler) compiles the Java source code to machine-neutral instructions. The instructions are then interpreted and run on the Java Virtual Machine (JVM).

The JVM is a fictional processor that is emulated in software. The instructions, called Java **bytecodes,** for that fictional processor are identical no matter what hardware or OS platform the virtual machine is running on. As each bytecode arrives, the virtual machine reads it, interprets it, and executes the native instructions appropriate for that particular local environment. Each operating system that supports Java has its own platform-dependent JVM to interpret the Java bytecodes. Many common Web browsers, such as Netscape or Internet Explorer, also contain their own Java virtual machines so that Java applets from the Internet can be run inside the browsers.

In addition to the Java compiler included in the JDK, many operating systems support just-in-time compilers for Java. A just-in-time compiler can be plugged into the Java virtual machine, and when the virtual machine is ready to execute a method in a class or object, it passes the bytecodes for that method to the just-in-time compiler, which then compiles the bytecodes on the fly to native code. Without a just-in-time compiler, the Java virtual machine must interpret and execute each bytecode in succession, a much slower process. Java applets will be downloadable to any system from the Internet.

AS/400 has a Java virtual machine residing below the Technology Independent Machine Interface for fast interpretation and execution. In addition to supporting Sun's javac compiler, there is also a direct-execution static compiler, called the Java Transformer, to generate AS/400-dependent machine code. The Java Transformer is IBM's solution to improve Java runtime performance which replaces the use of a just-in-time compiler. The AS/400 Toolbox for Java includes a set of enablers that support an Internet programming model. Provided is a set of client/server programming interfaces for use by Java applets and applications plus a set of applets that can be integrated into HTML documents. Client support required is Java virtual machine and AS/400

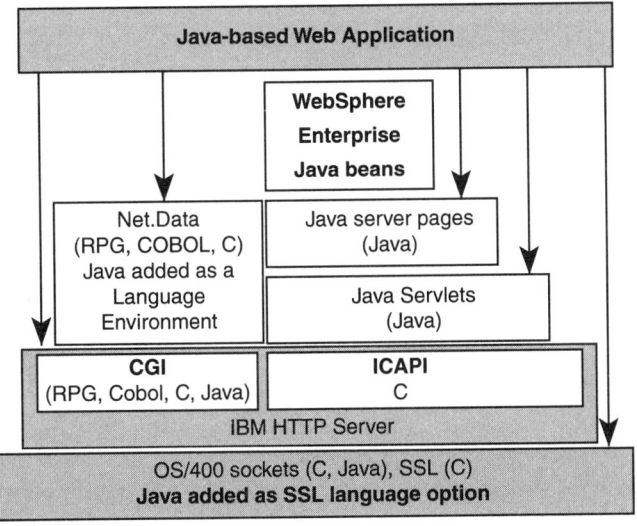

Figure 4.22. Java with OS/400.

Developer Kit for Java. Because graphical user interfaces cannot be displayed by an AS/400 green-screen, AS/400 implements something called Remote AWT. Java on AS/400 intercepts GUI requests coming from a Java program and reroutes the requests to an attached workstation running its own JVM, which will interpret and display the JAVA.AWT graphical components. Other Java packages are being integrated with OS/400 to improve ease-of-use and performance. Java objects on AS/400 are full-fledged AS/400 objects that can be persistent, shared, secure, backed up, and restored, something not available in two-level-store operating systems. Figure 4.22 positions Java in relation to OS/400.

Java security extensions leverage the integrated Secure Sockets Layer (SSL) functionality built into the AS/400. All data exchanged between the client and server can be encrypted using the SSL protocol. Customers and business partners can build secure client/server applications using Java.

Structured Query Language Java (SQLJ). SQLJ is Structured Query Language embedded in Java. SQL statements include queries (SELECT), data manipulation statements (INSERT, UPDATE, DELETE) and others that operate on data stored in tables in relational databases. SQLJ is a conventional method for embedding those SQL statements in Java. It allows programming tools to perform translation-time (compile-time) analysis of SQL in Java, for syntax checking of SQL statements, for type checking to determine that the data exchanged between Java and SQL have compatible types and proper type conversions, and for schema checking to assure the SQL constructs are well-formed and valid (in the database schema where they will be executed). Embedded SQL statements are referred to as "static" because they are textually evident in the Java program, and can be compiled when the containing Java program is compiled. SQLJ provides a standard for tightly integrated Java/SQL programs.

SQLJ finds compatibility with multiple translation approaches. SQLJ can be processed by a stand-alone SQLJ-to-Java translator in a client environment or by a Java integrated development environment, to emit standard Java code with calls to any appropriate database API. When Java is supported as a stored procedure language (in a RDBMS server), SQLJ translation can be integrated with Java and SQL compilation for ease-of-use and performance.

Dynamic SQL is a call interface for passing strings to a database as SQL commands. No analysis or checking of those strings is done until the database receives them at execution time. JavaSoft has specified a dynamic SQL API called JDBC. Because a calling program can compose SQL strings at run-time, dynamic SQL is more flexible than static SQL. Because the SQL commands many applications use are fixed, those applications do not have to compose SQL dynamically. Embedded SQL is a better solution for those applications because error checking is allowed at development time, and because it permits pre-compilation of SQL for faster execution at run-time. Other static SQL advantages over dynamic SQL include that the source programs are smaller than equivalent JDBC programs and provide greater opportunity for optimization.

Also included is a standardized set of Class Libraries (packages) that support creating Graphical User Interfaces (GUI's), controlling multimedia data, communicating over networks, and accessing data in stream files and relational databases.

The AS/400 Developer Kit for Java, available with OS/400 V4R2, is a no-cost tool designed to produce Java applets and full-scale applications. Included are a collection of development tools, help files, and documentation for Java programmers. The Developer Kit is compliant with Sun's Java 1.1.6 specifications and provides improved performance either through improved transaction rates or through lower CPU utilization on applications that use the database. A single AS/400 can support a wide range of installed Java developer Kits concurrently.

Toolbox for Java. The AS/400 Toolbox for Java, available on AS/400 and other Java-compliant platforms, enables Java applets and applications to access AS/400 data and resources, by providing a collection of classes that represent AS/400 data and providing AS/400 client/server program interfaces for Java programs. The AS/400 Toolbox for Java provides access to the following AS/400 system resources:

- Connections to the AS/400 Security

- Database access via JDBC 2.0

- Database access via record-level file input/output

- AS/400 program call

- AS/400 command call

- AS/400 Integrated File System

- AS/400 Print Resources includes a spooled file viewer class, a GUI for showing print output

- AS/400 data queues

- Data description and conversion

- AS/400 user space classes, allowing Java to create, read from, write to, and delete AS/400 user spaces

- Digital certificates stored on AS/400 allowing Java to manage AS/400 digital certificates

- Job listing, allowing Java to list active jobs and retrieve information about those jobs including listing messages in the job log of a job

- AS/400 message queues allowing Java to list, delete, and answer messages in a message queue.

- User and group classes allowing Java to list users on the AS/400 and retrieve information about the users

- Visual access classes that provide a set of classes using Java's Swing 1.0 framework to retrieve data and then present the data to the user

- An Integrated File System class extends Java's java.io.File class to applications so the applications can act on files in the Integrated File System.

- Access to AS/400 message files

- Access to AS/400 data areas

- Access to AS/400 system values (both low level and GUI classes)

- Access to AS/400 authority on an object (both low level and GUI classes)

- Access to AS/400 system status
- Access to information about jobs running on the AS/400
- Access to information about users on the AS/400

With the AS/400 Toolbox for Java, Graphical API's are available to access the following AS/400 resources:

- Database data via JDBC
- Database data via record-level database access classes
- AS/400 program call
- AS/400 command call
- AS/400 data queues
- Files in the AS/400 Integrated File System
- AS/400 Print Resources
- Active jobs on the AS/400
- AS/400 messages and message queues
- AS/400 users and groups

With the AS/400 Toolbox for Java, AS/400 data can be presented in the following formats:

- List pane presents a list of AS/400 resources and allows a selection of one or more resources.
- Details pane presents a list of AS/400 resources in a table where each row displays various details about a single resource. The table allows the selection of one or more resources.

- Tree pane presents a tree hierarchy of AS/400 resources and allows selection of one or more resources.

- Explorer pane combines an AS/400 Tree Pane and AS/400 Details Pane so that the resource selected in the tree is presented in the details.

The AS/400 Toolbox for Java also includes a set of enablers that support an Internet programming model. Provided is a set of client/server programming interfaces for use by Java applets and applications.

The AS/400 Toolbox for Java supports the secure Sockets Layer specification. Data flowing between a workstation and an AS/400 running OS/400 can have data encryption and server authentication through the used of an SSL connection.

A user interface framework is included in the Toolbox to provide a development environment for building graphical panels. The framework handles the exchange of data automatically. The developer creates one or more data beans and binds them to the panel component using tags from the **Panel Definition Markup Language (PDML)**. The user interface framework can also create a platform and technology independent representation of graphical panels based on the **Extensible Markup Language (XML)**. Also provided is a pure Java framework for interpreting XML and constructing user interface panels based on the Java Foundation Classes. Windows dialogs can be converted to equivalent Java panels using a resource script converter. A WYSIWYG GUI editor can be used to develop Java GUIs. A **Program Call Markup Language (PCML)**, a tag language, is used to provide a program call framework to support the program call function of the Toolbox. The language fully describes all parameters, structures and field relationships necessary to call an AS/400 program.

The AS/400 Toolbox for Java requires that both the TC1 Licensed Program (TCP/IP Connectivity Utilities for AS/400) and the Host Server option of OS/400 to be installed and configured on the AS/400. Client machines and Web browsers must contain a Java virtual machine that fully supports Java Version 1.1.2. The AS/400 Toolbox for Java Classes can access data and resources on V3R2, V3R7, V4R1 and above.

Other Java packages are being integrated with OS/400 to improve ease-of-use and performance. Java objects on AS/400 are full-fledged AS/400 objects allowing them to be persistent, shared, secure, backed up and restored, something not available in two-level-store operating systems.

Product Preview—Enterprise Java Beans

Enterprise Java Beans (EJB) is an emerging industry standard initiated by Sun for a program model for developing portable, cross platform, server side, distributed business components using Java. The EJB programming model supports scalable, distributed, transaction-oriented three tier business applications. EJBs are easy to develop. The IBM AS/400 ESJ provides a fully compliant EJB server and container for hosting EJBs. The EJB server and container provides transaction, security, and persistence support which makes development of server-side business logic considerably easier. EJBs are reusable, portable, server-side business logic components. The EJB server hides complexities of transaction management, security, and persistence. EJB support is available now via BEA/Weblogic's Java Application Server, and EJB support will be delivered as an e-pack to the WebSphere Application Server LP in 3Q99.

Using Java at the Client

The AS/400 will also include a copy of Borland's J-Builder on a "try and buy" basis for those who do not like VisualAge for Java and who still need to develop Java applications.

Open Standards (UNIX)

In the early 1980s a movement started toward open standards computing, which eventually evolved to become known as **UNIX**. The objectives of open standards computing were to achieve interoperability and portability. UNIX is an operating system created by AT&T and adapted by everyone else. Today no two UNIX operating systems are identical, so the objectives of interoperability and portability touted for open standard computing have not been 100% achieved, but they are quite close (some say 90 percent, others say better). The **Open Standards Foundation** has its own UNIX version called AIX. OS/400 is compatible with most of the various UNIX operating systems in the world and addresses the two questions of interoperability and portability by compliance to the standards upon which the UNIX operating systems are based.

Open Standards-Based Interoperability

Support for the open standards environment (client/server) has been enhanced by incorporating the popular database standards and transmission protocols. There is significant overlap between the characteristics of this support and the needs of the UNIX environment, which will be addressed in the next section. The DB2/400 capability provides support for:

- ANSI X3.135.1992, ISO 9075-1992, and FIPS 127-2 Structured Query Language (SQL)

- IBM's Distributed Relational Database Architecture (DRDA)

- Distributed Unit of Work—Application Directed

- Remote Unit of Work

- Microsoft's Open Database Connection (ODBC)

- Apple's Data Access Language

The AS/400 supports the TCP/IP, APPC, and APPN transmission protocols. The combination of the database and transmission protocols supported allows the user to exploit the maturity and stability of the AS/400 database server with a wide range of client applications running on OS/2, DOS, Windows, AIX, and Apple Workstations. Over 25,000 commercially available AS/400 application solutions take advantage of the power, flexibility, and ease of use of the DB2/400 database manager. These applications are written for a wide range of industries and users, ranging from the small business with basic accounting needs to the large corporation with complex computing environments. The Data Propagator Relational (5716-DP1) product enables easy management of DB2-family distributed databases containing local copies of master databases by providing automatic update support for the shadow copies.

UNIX C Portability

The AS/400 supports over 80 percent of the POSIX 1003.1 APIs, and together with the BSD sockets, TCPIP, and X-Open (often referred to as UNIX Spec 1170) support, the portability of UNIX Commercial APIs has nearly doubled. With the addition of the Integrated File System (IFS), the support of DCE Base Services/400 (5798-TBF), the improvements for sockets and Anynet400 over TCP/IP, and the addition of Security

Level 50, most UNIX/AIX applications are now portable to the AS/400 and execute with performance competitive with the industry.

System/3X Compatibility

To preserve most of the System/3X user's current investment in application programs, OS/400 provides a way to use most existing System/3X application programs on an AS/400. OS/400 and related products allow most programs written for a System/36 or System/38 to be migrated with little or no change to an AS/400. OS/400 supports this capability by providing multiple programming interfaces, as shown in Figure 4.23.

First is the AS/400 native programming interface. This provides support for functions such as the Structured Query Language. The System/38 programming interface provides a high level of compatibility with System/38 application programs. Because AS/400 was based on the same basic architecture as the System/38, the two are naturally very

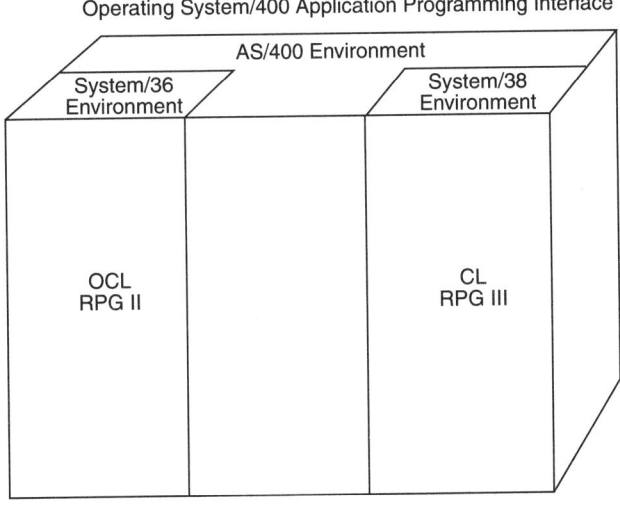

Figure 4.23. The three basic elements of the OS/400 application programming interface provide a high level of compatibility with application programs written for System/3X computers.

compatible and there is little system performance impact to operating in OS/400's System38 environment. OS/400 is automatically switched into the System/38 environment when a System/38 program is executed. OS/400's System/38 environment can also be activated through CL.

The System/36 programming interface of OS/400 with the changes instituted in Version 2 is nearly as clean a fit as that for the System/38 and provides a migration path for most System/36 application programs. OS/400's System/36 environment interprets the OCL used with the System/36 and can execute RPG II and COBOL application programs after they are adapted to the AS/400 environment. Since applications originally written for the System/36 don't take advantage of the AS/400 architecture, the performance of the AS/400 is reduced when executing in the System/36 environment. With the System/36 and System/38 environments of the AS/400, programs for the S/36 and S/38 can be developed on an AS/400.

However, they must be compiled on the S/36 or S/38 before they can be used on those systems. As discussed in ("SSP—An Executive Overview"), it is now possible to run up to three copies of the SSP operating system concurrently with a single copy of OS/400 on the same system. This guarantees S/36 code compatibility at both the object code and source-code levels. When S/36 programs are executed in an SSP environment on the AS/400 the performance improvements to be realized by that environment are achieved.

Two tools are available to help migrate System/3X application programs to AS/400: the AS/400 System/38 Migration Aid and the OS/400 System/36 Migration Aid. These tools run on their respective System/3X systems and provide the programmer with a way to analyze data, libraries, files, and programs that are to be migrated to AS/400. Migration (S/36 and S/38) are further discussed in Chapter 6.

Software Solution Packages

IBM is offering two software solution packages at a reduced price. One of those software solution packages is tailored for the *entry client/server environment* (AS/400e Server 150 BasePak [5649-EP5]) and offers support for improved performance, Internet functions, and new versions of Client Access Family for Windows clients, including capability for wireless connection on the entry model and support for Windows 95 and NT. The second software package is for the business that has an overloaded **ISIT (Information Systems/Information Technology)** staff and is finding it difficult to manage the scheduling of the necessary backup functions required to control the state of recovery in the case of a system emergency (device or system crash, or environmental disaster).

AS/400e server 150 BasePak (5649-EP5)

The newest versions of e-server 150 system packages are preloaded with selected functions of Version 4 Release 4 of BasePak (5649-EP5), including OS/400 Version 4 Release 4 (5769-SS1) and Extended Base Support.

Extended Base Support includes these listed features (note that the items with an asterisk are not preloaded):

- Online Information
- Extended Base Directory Support
- Host Servers
- Common Programming APIs Toolkit
- PSF/400 Base and Fax Support
- Extended NLS Support
- Object Connect
- Advanced 36 (Enablement only)
- Qshell Interpreter
- Domain Name System
- Directory Services
- Digital Certificate Manager
- PSF/400 1-20 IPM Printer Support
- Performance Management/400

- TCP/IP Connectivity Utilities for AS/400
- NetQuestion for AS/400
- IBM HTTP Server for AS/400
- S/36 and S/38 Migration*
- S/36 Environment*
- S/38 Environment*
- Example Tools Library*
- AFP Compatibility Fonts*
- PRV CL Compiler Support*
- S/36 Migration Assistant*
- System Openness Includes*
- GDDM*
- Ultimedia System Facilities*
- Lotus/Notes Enhanced Integration*
- AS/400 Integration for Windows NT Server*
- CCA Crypto Service Provider*
- Integration Services for FSIOP*
- OS/400 Integration for Novell NetWare*
- AS/400 Toolbox for Java*
- AS/400 Developer Kit for Java*

In addition to the features described above, the software solution package AS/400e Server 150 Software, includes the following:

- AS/400 Client Access for Windows (5769-XW1)

- Query for AS/400 (5769-QU1)

- DB2 Query Manager and SQL Development Kit for AS/400 (5769-ST1)

- Facsimile Support for AS/400 (5798-TBW)

- Advanced Function Printing (AFP) DBCS Fonts for AS/400 (5769-FN1)

The following items are either new or enhanced for V4R4 and included in e-server 150 BasePak:

- Virtual Private Networking (VPN) improves Internet security

- Network Address Translation

- Certificate Management Services to manage access to secure applications

- Crypto Framework enables writing secure applications

- IBM HTTP Server for AS/400

- Domino for AS/400

- TCP/IP Communications

- NetQuestion

- Net.Commerce V3

- Net.Data

- DCE for AS/400
- Java for AS/400
- AS/400 Toolbox for Java
- IONA Orbix implements OMG's CORBA architecture
- Source in stream files
- Threads Safe POSIX and UNIX98 APIs
- Large Address Space
- Integrated File System
- Expanded SQL Join Support
- Intelligent query Optimization
- Universal Database Compatibility supports user-defined functions and data types
- Datalink Support allows storing a pointer to an object in a database field
- Large Objects support images, video, audio, etc.
- Welcome Center for AS/400
- Information Center
- Technical Studio
- DB2 Query Manager and SQL Development Kit for AS/400
- Facsimile Support for AS/400
- AS/400 Client Access Express for Windows

The following product is a new one for V4R4 e-server 150 BasePak as an option: Client Encryption for AS/400 (5769-CE1, 5769-CE2, and 5769-CE3, 40 bit, 56 bit, and 128 bit respectively). These are client *encryption* products which complement the previously available server encryption products available as Cryptographic Access Providers forAS/400 (5769-AC1, 5769-AC2, and 5769-AC3).

The following Products have been enhanced as optional V4R4 software for e-server 150 BasePak:

- Advanced Function Printing Utilities for AS/400 (5769-AF1)

- Application Development ToolSet for AS/400 (5769-PW1)

- Application Development ToolSet Client Server for AS/400 (5769-CL3)

- FireWall for AS/400 (5649-FW4)

- ILE C for AS/400 (5769-CX2)

- ILE Cobol for AS/400 (5769-CB1)

- ILE RPG for AS/400 (5769-RG1)

- OnDemand for AS/400 (5769-RD1)

- Wireless Connection for AS/400 (5769-TBW)

AS/400 Operations Productivity Pak (5716-OPK)

- IBM Job Scheduler for AS/400 (5716JS1)

- Backup Recovery and Media Services (BRMS) for AS/400 (5716-BR1)

- ADSTAR Distributed Storage Manager (ADSM) for AS/400 Version 2.1 (5716-SV2).

5

AS/400 and Communications—
An Introduction

AS/400's standard functions plus the many communications options and supporting software provide users with flexibility when configuring AS/400 for various environments. However, this flexibility can also cause confusion when trying to determine which options and programs are needed for a particular setting. This section provides a guide through the jungle of business communications available. "Communications Options" in Chapter 2 looked at some communications hardware for Application Systems, and "Communications Support" in Chapter 4 looked at communications software support in OS/400. In this section, some of the most popular communications environments are examined, and, where appropriate, example configurations are provided.

Computer Communications in the Office—An Introduction

If one activity is most crucial to a business of any size, it is the act of communicating accurate, timely, and manageable information to the proper decision maker. Based on the information available important choices are made that can have far-reaching effects on the success of the business. Improve communications in a business and productivity and profitability are likely to improve. As a business grows, it becomes both more important and more difficult to maintain efficient, accurate communications—the very thing that facilitates business growth in the first place. Communications difficulties grow geometrically with the size of the business.

Today's businesses are quickly finding that computers are a communications tool unequaled in significance since Bell invented the telephone. Computers are already commonplace in the business environment, and now there is an increasing emphasis on computer communication. This communication can occur between two computers or among a group of computers in a communications network and allows business information to move at electronic speeds. Furthermore, communication allows users at remote locations access to vital business information on a distant computer. AS/400 computers represent a powerful communication tool. All provide a choice of standard communications features to facilitate getting computer support through IBM **Electronic Customer Support (ECS)**. As was seen in "Communications Options," there is a full complement of communications options and peripherals, which, with the associated software, allows AS/400 to participate in many different communications environments.

This chapter discusses System Networks Architecture (SNA), Electronic Customer Support (ECS), remote workstation communications, distributed computer communications, AS/400 distributed networks, AS/400 system clustering, IBM's overall network blueprint, and network computing, including environments created by intranets, retail systems, electronic business (e-biz), and the Internet.

What Is SNA?

In the not too remote past, computers were like islands, each performing very specific tasks independent of any other computer. As computer systems became more popular, they grew in number and spread over wide geographic distances. Then, almost as an afterthought, it became desirable to attach remote users to computers as well as to link distant computer systems. This led to specialized communications hardware and programming that limited the flexibility of both the communications configurations and the communications functions available. Businesses were constantly faced with massive programming changes and incompatible hardware elements when trying to grow or adapt to new requirements. For this reason, in 1974 IBM introduced a set of communications conventions called the **Systems Network Architecture (SNA)**. This set of published communications standards provided a direction for the evolution of flexible, cost-effective communications.

SNA is the set of standards that IBM committed to support as a strategic direction for future products. It defined communications protocols, hardware specifications, and programming conventions that made for coherent growth of communications facilities. Since 1974, IBM and many other companies have provided computer hardware and programming products that conform to SNA, and SNA is now a widely accepted direction for computer communications in the business environment. Furthermore, SNA itself has been expanded and updated in an evolutionary way to meet the changing and growing needs of business environments. All Application Systems support SNA communications. Since SNA is still IBM's strategic direction for communications, investments in SNA hardware and software will be protected over time.

IBM Electronic Customer Support Communications

AS/400 systems come standard with the communications equipment necessary to participate in IBM Electronic Customer Support (ECS). This is a link to IBM or other support providers that allows you to obtain answers to technical questions, report problems, receive **Program Temporary Fixes (PTFs)**, and the like. Although its not necessary to be a communications expert to use IBM Electronic Customer Support, understanding the basic communications link can remove the mystery.

Figure 5.1 shows the AS/400 communications link to IBM Electronic Customer Support. Every AS/400 system comes standard with a EIA 232/V.24 adapter used to communicate over a switched telephone line. The EIA 232/V.24 adapter provides the electrical interface and handles the communications protocol used with IBM Electronic Customer Support. A **modem** adapts the computer information into electrical signals suitable for telephone line transmission. OS/400 comes standard with the necessary functions to manage the telephone communications link. When IBM Electronic Customer Support is desired, the

Figure 5.1. Communications configuration used for Electronic Customer Support.

user instructs OS/400 to place a toll-free call to the IBM Information Network.

The IBM Information Network is a nationwide communications network that provides many services, including connections to the appropriate Electronic Customer Support computer system. The user is then linked to IBM Electronic Customer Support and can perform the desired tasks. For simplicity, the rest of the communications configurations provided in this chapter do not show the IBM Electronic Customer Support communications link. You should understand that all communications configurations shown are in addition to the IBM Electronic Customer Support link that is provided with most AS/400 systems.

No matter what computer system a business chooses, the system and its users will require ongoing support. They will have questions that need answering, hardware problems that must be addressed, software updates that must be installed, and so forth. This support can be delivered in many different ways. Personnel from the computer manufacturer, the software company, or the business's own staff are generally involved in supporting the computer system and its users.

With AS/400 systems (as well as with other IBM systems) much of this support can be provided electronically over communications networks. This is called IBM Electronic Customer Support (ECS). Just as electronic mail and online business information streamline a business's operation, the delivery of the various types of support needed can also be improved through IBM Electronic Customer Support. IBM provides five basic areas of IBM Electronic Customer Support:

- IBMLink

- RETAIN

- Question-and-answer database

- File transfer

- Copy screen

The communications hardware and software necessary to participate in IBM Electronic Customer Support are provided with every AS/400 system. Access to IBM Electronic Customer Support is provided through the **IBM Information Network (IIN)**. The kinds of things provided through **IBMLink** include electronic announcement letters, product catalogs, education catalogs, publication catalogs, pricing information, product configuration aids, and lists of local dealers. Users can exchange electronic notes with IBM marketing and support personnel. With proper authorization, you can also place orders, access a database of technical questions and answers, author new questions, report service hardware or software problems, and so on, all electronically over IBMLink.

IBM Electronic Customer Support also provides direct access to IBM's **RETAIN** network. Over RETAIN, you can electronically report a hardware problem and send accompanying information helpful in diagnosing the problem. IBM service personnel can then automatically be dispatched—all over the RETAIN network. Similarly, software problems can be reported, and any missing **programming fixes (PTFs)** that are indicated by the symptoms can often be automatically sent over RETAIN. With the addition of the SystemView System Management

Utilities for the OS/400, the user's central AS/400 system can become a repository for PTFs and service any other AS/400 systems over a communications link, thus becoming centralized support for their own organization. Another element of IBM Electronic Customer Support is the technical **question-and-answer database**. Each AS/400 system is shipped with its own electronic copy of the most commonly asked questions and their answers. If the question is not contained in this local database, IBM Electronic Customer Support provides access to an IBM database with additional questions and answers. With proper authorization, the user can also author new questions that will be answered (electronically) by IBM support personnel.

The **file transfer capability** of IBM Electronic Customer Support allows you to exchange information (e.g., a file containing your system's configuration) with IBM marketing and support personnel as necessary. The **copy screen** facility of IBM Electronic Customer Support allows remote support personnel to see the same image you see on your display for the purpose of education or problem troubleshooting. With IBM Electronic Customer Support, help is delivered electronically, improving access to technical and product information and streamlining communications between IBM and the users. AS/400 online education and IBMLink tutorials are provided along with the online user's guide and help text to make the interaction with IBM Electronic Customer Support easier to use.

Remote Workstations

Often those who need access to Application Systems are not conveniently located at the same location as the computer system. In these cases, Application Systems' communications can be employed to provide access to distant or remote users. The way to provide computer access to remote users is to provide them with workstations (terminals and printers) attached to Application Systems over telephone lines. Figure 5.2 shows an example of how remote workstations can be attached to an AS/400 (9406). As with local users, the remote users are provided with workstations including terminals and printers. The remote workstations are attached to the 5494 Remote Workstation Controller. This device helps manage the traffic between the remote workstations and

384 EXPLORING IBM AS/400 COMPUTERS

Figure 5.2. Remote workstations can be attached to an Application System through remote workstation controllers.

the AS/400. It provides the same services to remote workstations as the Twinaxial Workstation Controller provides for locally attached workstations.

The telephone line in our example is a **leased line,** meaning that it provides a continuous connection between the remote site and the AS/400. The modems at each end handle the electronic details associated with sending and receiving information over the telephone line. The 7861 Modems were chosen because they allow for communications at up to 19,200 bps on leased telephone lines. Any of the workstations can be remotely attached in this fashion. In our example, we have 3486 and 3487 Terminals, a personal computer, and 4234 and 4230 Printers. Except for the 4230 Printer, all these workstations are attached directly to the 5494 Remote Workstation Controller with twinaxial cable. To illustrate how the printer port provided on the 3487 (and 3486) Display can be used, the 4230 Printer is cabled directly to the printer port on the 3487 Display. With this type of arrangement, the 4230 is still under direct control of the remote AS/400. It is simply another way of cabling the printer, one that may be more convenient, depending on the user's environment.

The personal computer (PC) workstation is equipped with the System 36/38 workstation emulation adapter. This provides the electrical interface necessary to attach the PC to the twinaxial cable used with Application Systems. AS/400's Client Access Family for Windows program provides the programming for both the PC (running DOS, Windows, or OS/2) and the AS/400 allowing the PC to act like an Application Systems workstation. In this configuration, the PC has access to the information, disk storage, printers, and so on, of the AS/400 (i.e., the AS/400 is a server for the PC client). Alternately, specially written application programs residing on the PC and AS/400 can directly interact (cooperative processing), allowing for a highly flexible computing environment.

On the AS/400 side, OS/400 provides the necessary communications functions to support the remote workstations as if they were locally attached—that is, the application program need not be specially written to support the remote workstations. In fact, the application program cannot tell the difference between local and remote users. In our example, we have provided 5 separate communications lines that can be used to attach remote workstations from 5 different locations. Larger AS/400 systems can support up to 300 lines. This allows a single AS/400 to serve the needs of users at many different remote locations.

In the preceding example, we achieved the first line by installing a 2699 Two-Line WAN I/O Adapter and a 0330 EIA 232/V.24 Cable, which is supported by the Multi-Function I/O Processor provided as standard with all AS/400 systems (on the Models 150, 170, and 720 systems, the MFIOP functions are performed by a base system controller but are still there). The remaining four lines were provided by installing a 2623 Six-Line Communications Controller and two 2699 Two-Line I/O Adapters and two 0330 Cables.

Distributed Computer Communications

In some cases, the computing needs of a business can be met with a single computer system. This is particularly true for smaller businesses or businesses in which most computer needs are at a single location. In many cases, however, the needs of a business may be best satisfied by using multiple computer systems. Instead of providing remote users with remote workstations, as discussed earlier, remote users may be provided with their own small computer system. For example, a retail chain may want a computer system at each retail location as well as a computer system at headquarters as illustrated in Figure 5.3. As shown, all computer systems are joined through a communications network that allows them to easily move information (for example, daily cash register receipts) from place to place as necessary. This is called a **distributed computing network**.

When computer systems are placed or distributed at the site where they are needed, several nice things happen. First, because all users are locally attached to their respective computer system, they often enjoy

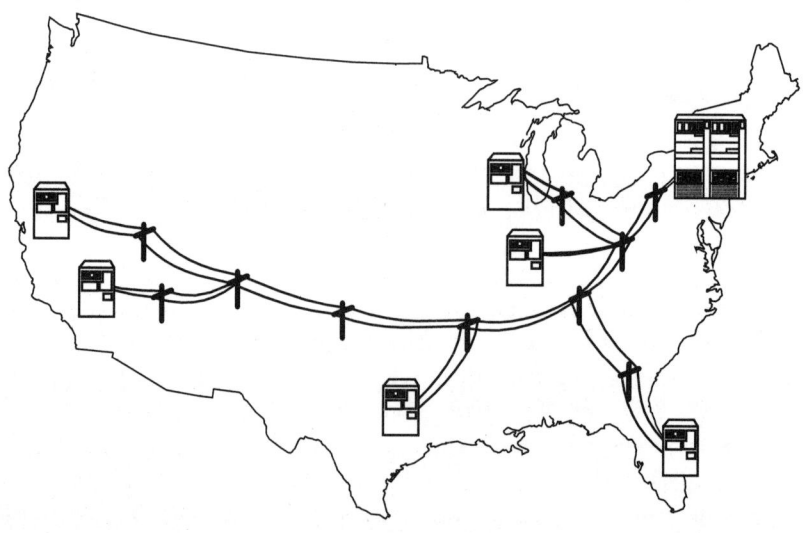

Figure 5.3. Example of a distributed network for a retail chain headquartered in New York City.

improved system performance (reduced response time) as compared with remotely attached workstations, which are slowed down by communications line limitations. Further, the distributed computer system can consolidate communications. This is particularly true at larger remote locations, which may need a large number of communications lines to support all the remote workstations. With a distributed computing approach, remote users would be locally attached to their distributed system, which could then communicate summary information to other computers through a single communications line.

In some cases, it may be an advantage to provide the remote location with some control over the distributed system. It may have unique requirements that can be met by an available pre-written application program. It could then acquire the program and get the support of the software firm in meeting its unique needs, all without becoming computer experts or blindly relying on the headquarters' computer staff. This makes the remote location more productive while reducing the workload at headquarters. The disadvantage is that a large distributed computer network is often more difficult to manage than a single computer system. However, because Application Systems were designed for a distributed environment, there are system management and network management tools that ease this task. As discussed in OS/400, SystemView System Manager/400 provides some of these tools. An example communications environment in which Application Systems participate in a distributed computing environment is shown next, in "AS/400 Distributed Networks."

AS/400 Distributed Networks

Multiple AS/400 systems can be attached together through communications lines to create a distributed computer network. An example distributed network of this type might consist of five small AS/400s (e.g., Model 150s), each distributed to a remote location, and a larger AS/400 (e.g., a 9406 Model 640) at the business's headquarters. Figure 5.4 is an example of AS/400 hardware and software configurations for one of the remote locations and the headquarters location. The remote location configuration (Model 150) would be duplicated for every remote location. Furthermore, the AS/400 at each end would be equipped with the appropriate local workstations to support the users at the respective locations. These are not shown to avoid confusion with options needed

Figure 5.4. Configuration used for attaching distant AS/400 systems together.

to support the communications link. The hardware configurations needed to meet the communications requirements for this distributed network are listed in the following paragraph.

Distributed AS/400 Network Example

The 9401 Model 150 used at the remote location is equipped with a 2721 PCI Two-Line WAN Adapter and 0330 EIA 232/V.24 Cable that provide one communications line (in addition to the standard communications line used for IBM Electronic Customer Support). This adapter is supported by the equivalent Multi-Function I/O Processor function provided as standard equipment with all 940X systems. Since the remote AS/400 system needs to communicate only with the central AS/400 system, this is the only adapter needed. The 7861 Modem allows for communications at 19,200 bps over leased telephone lines. OS/400 has the communications functions necessary to manage the communications link. At the central location, the larger AS/400 is in constant communication with all remote locations. It collects the summary information needed by headquarters to consolidate all remote location activity.

In our example, one communications line is used for each remote location. This means the central AS/400 must have at least five communications lines (in addition to that used for IBM Electronic Customer Support). To meet this need, a 2699 Two-Line WAN I/O Adapter and an EIA 232/V.24 cable is first added. This adapter works with the Multi-Function I/O Processor provided as standard with all AS/400 systems. Next, a 2623 Six-Line Communications Controller and two additional 2699 Two-Line WAN I/O Adapters and EIA 232/V.24 Cables are added. Thus, the AS/400 system now has five communications lines (in addition to the one used for IBM Electronic Customer Support). One 7861 Modem is required at the central site for each communications line, making a total of five (one is shown).

With our example communications configuration and appropriate application programs, there are several different ways in which the distributed AS/400 systems can work together. In the simplest form, the distributed computing environment could use OS/400's **Distributed Data Management (DDM)** support, which allows a user of a remote AS/400 to query a database on the central AS/400 or any other AS/400 in the network. The user need not even know that the database needed is located on another computer system. The DDM function of OS/400 will automatically locate, retrieve, and present the information to the user, reducing the complexity of the system from the user's viewpoint. Alternately, a user of one system may actually want to sign on and directly interact with one of the other systems in the network. Another OS/400 function, called **Display Station Pass-Thru (DSPT)**, supports this type of interaction by allowing a user to sign on and interact with any other AS/400 in the distributed network as if the user were directly attached to that system.

The preceding example is a network connected by Wide Area Network (WAN) communications, using non-intelligent workstations; an alternative would be to use the Internet to connect and communicate between the AS/400 systems. A configuration of this type will be discussed in the section of this chapter on the Internet.

Often, the central location provides technical support to all remote locations. This support includes troubleshooting network communications problems and distributing new software and software updates. Through IBM Electronic Customer Support, the central site can also provide its own technical question/answer database. This database can contain any type of company-related information from operating procedures to technical information about a custom application program. Thus, any user anywhere in the distributed network can look up questions and the corresponding answers without playing telephone tag or waiting for the headquarters staff to respond. If a question is not covered in the database, it can be submitted to the headquarters staff. Once the staff responds with an answer, it is added to the database so that it will be available the next time that question is asked. SystemView System Manager/400 provides functions that allow the central support site to manage changes to the AS/400 systems in the network and any problems that are reported.

APPC/APPN

Sophisticated cooperative processing between the central and remote AS/400 systems is becoming more prevalent. OS/400 functions such as **Advanced Program-to-Program Communications (APPC)** and **Advanced Peer-to-Peer Networking (APPN)**, along with OS/400 extensions such as Client Access and Structured Query Language/400, let programmers write application programs that can efficiently delegate processing tasks and share information among the various AS/400 and personal computer systems in a network. APPC is a communications convention that allows a program on one AS/400 system to initiate actions on a remote computer system (e.g., start a program or perform a database query) without any assistance from the user. APPN is a networking scheme that manages the logistics necessary for one AS/400 in the network to know details (location, communications links, available application programs and data, etc.) about all of the other AS/400 and personal computer systems in that network. APPN also dynamically selects the most appropriate communications link (if more than one is available) based on variables such as cost, line speed, and security level.

IBM's Systems Network Architecture (SNA) has adopted APPN as a strategic networking scheme, making it important in other environments (e.g., personal computer and S/390 communications networks). Since OS/400 supports SNA, documents can be freely exchanged between nodes using **SNA's Distribution Services (SNADS)** conventions. This provides a coherent electronic mail environment in which users need not concern themselves about who is where in the network. Furthermore, any AS/400 file can be sent from any node to any other node on the network. This can be useful for distributing program or data updates from a single point in the network. Further discussion of these OS/400 communications functions can be found in "Communications Support" in Chapter 4.

APPN support includes two different types of filter lists, the session endpoint filter list and the directory endpoint filter list, that provide a firewall security operation for local networks as well as for the Internet.

Filter Lists

Filter Lists enable the invocation of security functions for either local network protection or Internet network isolation. Two filter lists are provided under Advanced Peer-to-Peer Networking (APPN). The **session endpoint filter list** controls access to and from local locations, and the **directory endpoint filter list** controls access to and from peripheral nodes.

The session endpoint filter list defines the remote locations that are allowed or rejected from communicating with local locations. As a rule, the session endpoint filter list should be used in conjunction with the APPN remote location list and password security. There is no need to duplicate location in the remote location list. The session endpoint filter list controls user and control-point sessions, and supports generic and wildcard naming.

The directory search filter list is used to restrict the locations with which peripheral nodes can establish sessions by using the network identifier and control-point name of the peripheral node. Locations on the peripheral node are called **filtered locations**. Locations that peripheral nodes want to access are called **partner locations**. The directory search firewall is only as strong as its weakest link. When both session endpoint filter and directory search filter lists have been identified for a single location, the session endpoint filter list will manage the security access function for that location.

AS/400 System Clustering

As described earlier, the networking function supports both local and wide area network capabilities on the AS/400. The local area networks provide one method for horizontal growth of the system. Horizontal growth implies the ability to increase the networked system from both a capacity and performance perspective by adding components to the existing system without having to exchange existing system components. The capacity increase occurs because the addition of a system implies the capability to add all functions of the system independent of the path by which the interconnection is achieved. The performance of a system cluster connected in a local area network is limited by the performance of the local area network itself.

The types of local area networks supported on the AS/400 are the token-ring and Ethernet networks. The **instantaneous bandwidth** of each of these local area networks is 16 and 100 Mbps, respectively (FDDI is a special case of a token-ring network with 100-Mbps instantaneous bandwidth). The instantaneous bandwidth identifies how fast data can be passed from one system in a cluster to a different system in that cluster once a connection has been established. More important than instantaneous bandwidth is the utilization rate of the network. The utilization rate is the proportion of the instantaneous bandwidth that is available for information exchange between systems after contention for network resources, the overhead of the network, and recovery from errors has been accounted for. The following ratios for utilization rate are approximate, but they illustrate that local area networks, although a vast improvement upon wide area networks, still leave significant room for performance improvement.

Utilization starts to saturate for token-ring networks at 70 percent, for Ethernet at 40 percent, and for FDDI at 70 percent. A second methodology for adding system performance and growth via system clustering is offered by the AS/400 Optical Interconnect with Object Connect/400. The hardware necessary to perform the interconnect is described in "Opticonnect/400 Systems" and "Packaging Technology," both contained in Chapter 1. The hardware has the capability of interchanging data between any two systems at an instantaneous data rate of 1063 Mbps, with a theoretical utilization rate of 70 percent.

Furthermore, if more than three systems are in the cluster, as many as $n/2$ simultaneous conversations (where n is the total number of systems in the cluster) may be going on at the same time, as long as the data needed exists on at least one set of each pair of systems. Data Propagator Relational/400 also works over this connection and may be used to ensure that the needed data replication exists. Opticonnect/400 with Distributed Data Management (DDM) is the application support needed to exploit this capability.

In this environment, if an application needs greater performance than is available in the existing systems, an additional system is added to the clustered system network. Using the capability of parallel threads, that system will decrease the load on the other existing systems in the network, thereby providing the performance boost that previously required the replacement of the existing processing system (vertical growth).

An additional capability, besides the system and performance growth (occurring as a result of the ability to cluster systems levels) is the capability to build redundancy into the processing, data files, and networking functions. The redundancy methodology may include a mixture of approaches—including N+1, mirroring, RAID-5, and checksums—at system and subsystem levels as needed to achieve the protection desired. All of the pass-thru functions for displays and printers continue to function in the clustered system environment. In fact the user of the application has no perception of which system in the cluster of systems is actually executing the application. LANs and WANs may coexist on each system in a system cluster. Opticonnect/400 is the loosely coupled connection referred to in Chapter 3, in "Data Warehousing" and "Data Mining."

ObjectConnect/400

ObjectConnect/400 is a **PRPQ (Program Request Per Quote)** that simply and efficiently moves individual objects, entire libraries, or entire **Integrated File System (IFS)** directories from one AS/400 system to another over a standard communications connection or over a high-speed fiber optic bus.

IBM's Overall Networking Blueprint

The IBM Networking Blueprint (Figure 5.5), is a guide to IBM's networking commitments. The Blueprint lays out the framework for integrating into a single network multiple separate networks and their

Figure 5.5. IBM's Networking Blueprint structure.

applications that use different communications protocols, different hardware components, different bandwidths, and different network management techniques. The Blueprint incorporates existing and anticipated industry standards and open systems standards. It complements the Systems Network Architecture (SNA) communications standards as well as **Open Software Foundation's Distributed Computing Environment (DCE)** and ISO communications specifications, but it does not replace them.

The IBM Networking Blueprint framework provides the freedom to choose network elements to meet application and business needs, rather than force-fitting those requirements to inappropriate networking solutions. The Blueprint allows a mixture of international standards, industry standards, and architectures. As standards evolve, the Blueprint will change to keep pace. The Blueprint is divided into four layers, representing the elements necessary to make up a network: the Applications layer, the Applications Support layer, the Transport Network layer, and the Subnetworking layer.

Applications Layer

The IBM Networking Blueprint provides all major interfaces for distributed computing. The first layer, starting from the top of the Blueprint, is the Applications Layer (see Figure 5.6), which represents the full range of applications and application enablers (e.g., high-level languages and program generators) that support an organization's business. The applications and enablers make use of the underlying capabilities of the network.

Figure 5.6. AS/400 Multi-Protocol Networking Blueprint Interface-applications layer.

Application Support Layer

The second layer, the Application Support layer, represents multi-vendor application interfaces and services. There are three primary interfaces (see Figure 5.7): Common Programming Interface for Communications (CPI-C), Remote Procedure Call (RPC), and the Messaging and Queuing Interface (MQI). Each of these interfaces is described in greater detail in "Multi-vendor Application Program Interfaces."

Figure 5.7. AS/400 Multi-Protocol Networking Blueprint Interface-applications support layer.

The Application Support layer also contains a set of distributed networking services for handling messages, security, directory, and transaction processing. Standard networking applications, such as file transfer programs, also fall within the Application Support layer. Although not shown on the IBM Networking Blueprint, CICS/ESA and CallPath could be considered to span both the Applications layer and the Application Support layer. Both products contain APIs and provide application support services, so they fit within the Application Support layer, but the APIs are application-enabling APIs, also making them part of the Applications layer. The CICS API may be thought of as an extension to many of the application development languages, allowing application development without the concern for the underlying network. CallPath provides an API that allows applications to combine voice functions of the telephone with the data processing capability of a computer.

Multivendor Application Program Interfaces

The following paragraphs discuss the CPI-C interface, the Remote Procedure Call, and the messaging and queuing interface.

The CPI-C Interface

The CPI-C interface supports communication between application programs over private logical connections called **conversations**. Conversational communication is a sophisticated method of program-to-program communication requiring simultaneous execution of partner programs. It is designed primarily for a structured exchange of information between programs and requires that a network session be reserved exclusively for the communicating programs. CPI-C applications are generally client/server or peer-to-peer implementations.

The operating systems implemented **Advanced Program-to-Program Communication (APPC)** services to assist in the implementation of conversational applications through CPI-C. In spite of the sophistication of conversational applications, they are surprisingly easy to implement. **APPC/MVS** in MVS/ESA, for example, offers built-in server functions that can be used in client/server conversations. APPC/MVS services are *callable* services, so they can be accessed from a high-level language application without the necessity of writing assembler language routines.

The Remote Procedure Call

The **Remote Procedure Call (RPC)** function provides communications between applications using a call/return mechanism, much like doing FORTRAN library subroutine calls. RPC applications are client/server implementations. The client program (the caller) is responsible for determining the server location (the called procedure) in the network, establishing the necessary communication, and passing the required parameters for the procedure execution. This is a synchronous operation. The caller waits until the procedure finishes execution, and the results are passed back. Again using MVS/ESA as the example, different vendor implementations of Remote Procedure Call are supported. Today, workstations with applications implementing RPC can operate as clients with MVS/ESA using the TCP/IP product. TCP/IP also supports Apollo Computers' Network Computing System RPC. The OSF/DCE RPC is supported using the POSIX-compliant application programming interface.

The Messaging and Queuing Interface

The Messaging and Queuing Interface (MQI) MQSeries (5716-MQ1) is an asynchronous program-to-program interface that supports message-driven, deferred processing. Communication is through **queues**, not through private connections. Programs that use MQI fill and empty message queues. The calling program places the request in a queue but does not wait for a response; instead, it continues with its processing, and when the response arrives, it is placed in a queue to await processing. MQI services route the messages to the appropriate destinations in the network for access by the programs servicing the queue. MQI applications can be client/server, peer-to-peer, or more complex implementations. MQI provides guaranteed message delivery, recover ability, and, where applicable, sync-point participation.

When messages are broken into multiple packets that are sent over separate routes, the packets do not necessarily arrive in the correct order, and the sync points allow the message to be reconstructed regardless of the order of the packet reception at the final destination.

MQSeries allows use of distribution lists to put a single message in multiple queues with a single call. Channel definitions can be automatically created for receiver and server channel connections. Large transactions can use message segmentation ordering and grouping to improve checking of transactional data. The ability to reference messages with chained exits allows large amounts of data to be transferred between nodes. The ability to use C++ for MQI applications and the ability to perform static bindings in ILE RPG programs make programming easier. Channel heartbeats provide faster recovery when the system stops or resets, and when data needs fast delivery, more programs can take advantage of fast nonpersistent messages.

Transport Network Layer: SNA-TCP/IP-MPTN-APPN

The third layer, the transport network layer (see Figure 5.8), is the layer for integrating multi-vendor network protocols into one efficient network. Networking protocols are used for sending and receiving information throughout the network. Typically, applications and application services are bound to a specific networking protocol. CPI-C applications use SNA networking; RPC applications use TCP/IP; X.400 applications use Open System Interconnection (OSI); other applications use NetBIOS, Internet Packet Exchange (IPX), DECnet, or other protocols, but within this layer, the Common Transport Semantics framework (see Figure 5.8) provides a structure for supporting multi-protocol networking capability.

Multiprotocol Transport Networking (MPTN)

The Multi-Protocol Transport Networking (MPTN) architecture defines much of the Common Transport Semantics. MPTN architecture is open and general, eliminating the forced networking protocol bindings between the application support layer and the transport layer. In other words, the application support APIs and their services can communicate over a protocol other than the one for which they were originally implemented. The applications must be matched pairs, however—both designed to communicate using the same communication protocol. For example, two APPC programs originally designed to communicate over SNA could now communicate over TCP/IP, two socket programs originally designed to communicate over TCP/IP could now communicate over SNA, but an APPC program cannot communicate with a socket program over either SNA or TCP/IP.

Client Access offers a multi-protocol transport feature (called AnyNet/400), which allows the application to be separated from the

Figure 5.8. AS/400 Multi-Protocol Networking Blueprint Interface-Transport Network layer.

network transport. This feature provides OS/2 functions. The OS/2 function is installed at the host and downloaded to the workstation. CICS/400, IMS400, TM, DB2/400, DRDA, or any APPC application is able to communicate with an OS/2 workstation in a TCP/IP network that has the APPC API (e.g., OS/2). APPC over TCP/IP can be host to workstation, workstation to workstation, or host to host. AnyNet/400 also supports an interface for **Berkeley Software Distribution (BSD)** sockets over SNA for OS/2. The sockets interface uses APPC as the underlying network service. AnyNet/400 also supports Client Access for users who use Windows 3.1. Even before the introduction of the MPTN architecture, NetBIOS, IPX, and some other protocols' traffic could be transported over TCP/IP. NetBIOS and X.25 traffic could also be transported over SNA. Novell's Internetwork Packet Exchange (IPX) protocol is now available on AnyNet/400.

Advanced Peer-to-Peer Networking (APPN)

Advanced Peer-to-Peer Networking (APPN) provides value to existing SNA networks by reducing the complexity of maintaining network definitions. APPN minimizes the need for coordinated systems definition. Network resources are defined only at the node at which they are located, and APPN will distribute information about these resources through the network as it is needed. Switching to an APPN network can save considerable system programmer time because a high percentage of network definitions are eliminated by the dynamic nature of APPN routing. Device definitions, link definitions, and path definitions are all significantly reduced. The APPN end-node and network-node specifications are published as Common Communications Support protocols, facilitating implementation by others. Because APPN is based on LU 6.2 and T2.1 protocols, existing Original-Equipment Manufacturers' (OEMs') T2.1 LEN nodes and LU 6.2 applications can take advantage of APPN networking.

The APPN program has been enhanced to improve network reliability by automatically rerouting around failures, by automatically adjusting to network congestion to get data through without a timeout, and by automatically using high-speed links through increasing throughput on underutilized links.

Subnetworking Layer

The fourth layer, the subnetworking layer (see Figure 5.9), represents a piece of a larger network, a connection to Local Area Networks (LANs), Wide Area Networks (WANs), host channels, or other high-speed transmission services. The IBM Networking Blueprint provides a framework for integrating LAN and WAN networks, providing management services, efficient link utilization, and high availability, all with predictable response time. A key component of the Blueprint, systems and network management, applies to all four Blueprint layers. It encompasses all management disciplines and supports multi-protocol and multi-vendor

Figure 5.9. AS/400 Multi-Protocol Networking Blueprint Interface-Subnetworking layer.

environments through industry standards such as SNA management services, the TCP/IP Simple Network Management Protocol (SNMP), and the OSI Common Management Information Protocol (CMIP).

SystemView is the framework for providing enterprise-wide systems and network management, planning, coordination, and operations. It enables both centralized management and distributed management. The proposed OSF Distributed Management Environment (OSFDME) fits with the SystemView structure. Two SystemView-conforming products, NetView and NetView/400, help manage applications in an MPTN environment, where the applications use transport protocols different from the ones for which they were originally designed.

Intranet

An intranet is a local area network, or network of local area networks, which uses Internet tools such as a WWW browser, File Transfer Protocol (FTP), or TCP/IP to move data and programs between the server and the clients. As a rule, the security functions on an intranet are more relaxed than they are on the Internet because the users are trusted users. Some security policy still needs to be used, and this should include user authentication, resource protection, system integrity, data integrity, and a security audit. Being trusted users means that the users do not fit the definition of hackers, or crackers, at least as far as the enterprise using the intranet is concerned. The transport protocols for the local area network may still be token-ring or Ethernet, but the messaging protocols embedded within the token-ring or Ethernet delimiters is web compliant. A **hacker** is any unauthorized person who tries to break into the system. A **cracker** is a hacker with malicious intent.

AS/400 and Retail Terminals

Figure 5.10 shows a typical retail system configuration. In many of those configurations, the AS/400 has been the in-store processor. The 4680/4690 Point of Sale Controller controlled the StoreLoop, which interfaced to the AS/400, and if the store was a member of a chain, the AS/400 received information from and sent information to a host processor at the chain's home site. Initially the 4680/4690 Point of Sale Controller talked directly to the host controller, which in many cases was an AS/400. The point of sale terminal is described in "Retail Workstations" in Chapter 2, but basically it is a personal computer with some specialized I/O functions and a cash drawer. As a result, it already has the capability of participating in a token-ring local area network, either connected with wire in one form or another or with the new wireless technology.

With wireless technology, several desirable capabilities become available: additional security and password control, elimination of the 4680/4690 segment of the link, which increases the reliability of the network, portable terminal replacement of a potentially failing terminal, and redundancy in the network provided by the token-ring connection. To incorporate this connection a suite of applications has been developed by IBM and the AS/400 business partners and integrated with

Figure 5.10. The AS/400 in a retail environment.

the AS/400. That suite of applications includes the following retail-based functions: price lookup, electronic funds transfer, credit authorization, time and attendance, labor scheduling/forecasting, shelf price audit, store accounting, store reports, sales analysis, merchandise replenishment, pharmacy, direct store delivery, e-mail, word processing, clienteling, and so on. Figure 5.11 contains a business functions chart for retail applications and Figure 5.12 contains a listing of IBM business partners and the area(s) of the retail industry in which they offer products.

Intranet/Internet Security

You might say that an intranet/Internet system is only as good as its security mechanism. The following sections discuss the Internet Connection Secure Server and the Cryptographic Access Provider.

Business Functions	Retail Application Set				
Business Management	General Ledger	Accounts Payables	Billing and Accounts Receivables	Cost Accounts	Fixed Assets
(B/M)	Payroll	Human Resources	Lease Management		
Supply Chain	Stock Control	Stock Movement	Forecasting & Replenishment	Inventory Management	Stock Ordering
(S/C)	Distribution Operations	Warehouse Management	EDI Management	Category	
Store Operations	Customer Management	Store Management	Staff Management	Space Management	Inventory
(S/O)	Cash Management	Time and Attendance			
Business Intelligence (B/I)	Data Mining	Data Warehouse	Executive Info System	Geographic Info System	
Market Space (M/S)	Electronic Commerce	Kiosks	Catalog/ Mail Order		

Figure 5.11. Relational mapping of the retail application set against business functions.

Internet Connection Secure Server

Internet Connection Secure Server for AS/400 (5769-NCI/NCE) replaces HTTP Server. Among the differences from HTTP Server are the ability

Business Partner (Business Function) (Business Function)	All Retail	Apparel	Auto	Books & Music	Mail Order	Home Improvement	Consumer Electronics	Pharm. Drugs	General & Mass	Super Market	Video	Wholesale
JDA (B/M, S/C, S/O, B/I)	X					X	X		X	X		X
InfoSystems of N.C. (B/M, S/C, S/O, B/I)								X	X	X		
Island Pacific (B/M, S/C, B/I)	X	X				X			X			
Open Retail Systems (B/M, S/C, S/O, B/I)	X											
Intrepid Systems (B/M, S/C)	X		X	X		X	X		X			
Nordic Information Systems (B/M, S/C, B/I)					X							
Gateway Data Science (S/C, S/O, B/I)	X							X	X		X	
BCMS (B/M, S/C, S/O, B/I)	X	X										
CSI (B/M, S/C, B/I)		X										
Computer General Solutions (B/M, S/C, B/I)			X									
JBA International (B/M, S/C, B/I)		X										

Figure 5.12. AS/400 retail industry solution matrix. (*Continued on next page.*)

Business Partner (Business Function)	All Retail	Apparel	Auto	Books & Music	Mail Order	Home Improvement	Consumer Electronics	Pharm. Drugs	General & Mass	Super Market	Video	Wholesale
Grocery Support Systems (B/M, S/C, S/O, B/I)										X		
Park City (B/M., S/C, B/I)	X											
ADS (S/C, S/O, B/I)	X							X		X		
Worldwide Chain Store Systems (B/M, S/C; DC/warehouse mngt.)	X	X										
American Software (B/M, S/C; DC/warehouse mngt)	X							X		X	X	X
Exeter (S/C; DC/warehouse mngt.)	X											
Computer Associates (S/C; DC/warehouse mngt.)	X											
Manhattan Associates (S/C; DC/warehouse mngt.)	X											

Figure 5.12. AS/400 retail industry solution matrix. *(Continued on next page.)*

Business Partner (Business Function)	All Retail	Apparel	Auto	Books & Music	Mail Order	Home Improvement	Consumer Electronics	Pharm. Drugs	General & Mass	Super Market	Video	Wholesale
E3 (S/C; Forecast/ Replenishment)	X											
IBM INFOREM/400 (S/C; Forecast/ Replenishment)	X											
Computer Solutions Inc. (M/S; Mail order/ catalogue)	X											
ASA/Commercialware (M/S; Mail order/ catalogue)					X							
Lawson (B/M; Financial/HR mngt.)	X											
Software 2000 (B/M; Financial/HR mngt.)	X											
Silvon Software (B/I; Data Warehouse)	X											
SAMAC (B/I; Data Warehouse)	X											
Hoskyns (B/I; Data Warehouse)	X											
I/NET (M/S; Internet)	X											

Figure 5.12. AS/400 retail industry solution matrix. (*Continued on next page.*)

to name a user profile from which HTML is served and a different profile from which CGI-bin (Common Gateway Interface-binary) programs are run. This allows the authorization of different profiles to different Web applications and data, providing assurance that the correct data is served to applications. The capability for basic authentication (a user must provide at least some type of identification and password) before allowing access to certain data has been added.

With basic authentication come the concept of an "Internet user," who may be allowed to see certain data but is not a real AS/400 user, complete with an AS/400 user profile and password (allowing access to all publicly authorized objects). The Internet users are managed using a validation list: When an application requires user authentication, the information is requested on the browser, returned to the Internet Connection Secure Server and verified using the data in the validation list defined for the Web application. The validation list is one-way encrypted, making it secure. CGI applications can use AS/400 Activation Groups in their AS/400 Web Server solutions.

The AS/400 Secure Web Server is enabled by the IBM Internet Connection Secure Server (ICSS) for AS/400. ICSS provides the security to send proprietary or confidential information over the Internet and corporate intranets, enabling online transactions including electronic commerce to be performed. The security level comes from the Secure Sockets Layer (SSL) protocol, which provides end-to-end security. Data transferred between a server and a client is encrypted to ensure privacy. Before the data transmission starts, the identity of the server is authenticated by the client through the use of a **certificate** (digital ID). In a data transfer operation, the Web browser authenticates the identity of the AS/400 server and then the encrypted data is transferred.

Two different encryption algorithms are supported by ICSS: 5769-NC1 supports 128-bit data encryption capability, and ICSS_5769-NE1 supports 40-bit encryption capability. Although 128-bit encryption cannot be exported outside the United States and Canada; 40-bit encryption can be exported to other countries.

ICSS includes a Digital Certificate Manager (described next) to enable the creation of your own corporate certificate authority for your intranet or Internet sites. The certificate authority can sign certificates for clients and servers and download the needed certificates into users' browsers.

Cryptographic Access Provider

The below listed cryptographic products enable encryption in the AS/400 for use by such products as HTTP Server for AS/400. One of these products must be installed to enable the secure sockets layer (SSL) function. The 56 bit encryption product is now available for most countries. SSL protects data exchanged between a Web server and a browser.

The following products provide software encryption on the AS/400 servers:

- 40-bit encryption for AS/400 (5769-AC1)*
- 56-bit encryption for AS/400 (5769-AC2)*
- 128-bit encryption for AS/400 (5769-AC3)**

Whereas the following products provide software encryption on the AS/400 clients.

- 40-bit encryption for AS/400 (5769-CE1)*
- 56-bit encryption for AS/400 (5769-CE2)*
- 128-bit encryption for AS/400 (5769-CE3)**

Approved for export by the U.S. Government
** Available only in U. S. and Canada

Hardware Cryptography

The 4758 PCI card is a common hardware solution across IBM server platforms. The 4758 supports IBM's **Common Cryptographic Architecture (CCA)** APIs offering a unique support for finance applications. As a hardware-based cryptographic solution the 4758 provides the performance and secure key storage capabilities required by the advanced commercial applications operating over the Internet and Intranets. The 4758 was designed to meet FIPS 140-1 key protection standards. Banking and payment gateways require that the cryptographic keys a customer uses to run a business be stored in hardware. It is anticipated that requirement will apply to merchants running applications like eTill and net.commerce.

HTTP Server for AS/400

HTTP Server for AS/400 known previously as **Internet Connection Server** provides secure Internet connections. Security is improved through the use of digital certificates. Authentication includes both client and server authentication through the use of **Secure Sockets Layer** (SSL) V3. **Client certificates** can be associated with AS/400 **user profiles** or **validation lists**, allowing users seamless access to Web server resources without having to sign on.

If the environment has Socks-based **firewall** for access to the Internet, the HTTP server for AS/400 can be used as a *proxy server* to access destinations outside the firewall. Client connections using SSL are tunneled through the proxy server, eliminating the need to decrypt and encrypt the data at the proxy. CGI support includes Java, REXX, and C++. The server can be bypassed on output using the no parsed header CGIs. Any code page conversions the server performs on a Web application's input or output can be full configured. The HTTP Server for AS/400 is transformed into a Java-enabled Web server using the WebSphere Application Server as a portable, Java Servlet-based execution environment. Support is provided for the latest session-tracking APIs, personalization support, and Java Server pages. Java servlets can be used to provide additional server cache functions and dynamic Web applications.

Users can write applications that extend or customize how the Web server handles client requests with Server API Support a follow on to ICAPI. The unique capabilities of customer browsers can be exploited using **Automatic Browser Detection**, e.g., different documents can be provided to different clients based on the browser those clients are using.

Improved management is provided by the addition of: SNMP Subagent, Web Activity Monitor, Web usage mining, logging and archiving of reports, the extended Log format is supported, and NLS enabled logging. PICS support allows a security rating of information on a Web site. LDAP support enables storage of ACLs and configuration files.

SET Internet Security Manager

The SET level of Internet security involves the use of **digital certificates**. A digital certificate is a file of information that when used with **Public Key Cryptography Standard** (**PKCS**) cryptography can serve to authenticate that respondents to a certificate request are exactly who they claim to be. It is the "fingerprint" of the digital world, used to ensure that sensitive information is going to exactly the trusted receiver expected. The X.509 certificates are supported on AS/400. A user wishing to exchange secure data with a server applies to an authorized certificate issuer (certificate authority) for a digital certificate to be issued to the user's ID and password. The Certificate Authority (CA) "signs" a digital certificate to verify its authenticity. It is the CA's public key that lets a certificate requestor unwrap it to verify its veracity. Certificate authorities are the "Notary Public's" of the digital signature world.

After receipt of a certificate, the user exchanges that certificate with the secure server with which secure information exchange is desired. Upon receipt of the certificate and the user ID and password, the secure server sends the user the encryption algorithm to be used and the key to be used. The PKCS system uses an *asymmetrical encryption algorithm* such that one key (the private key) encrypts the data and a second key (the public key) decrypts it. This solves the problem of *symmetrical encryption* (the same key is used to encrypt and decrypt a file of how to provide the key to the remote user across the unencrypted line) related to making the key itself available to both end users.

Digital Certificate Manager

The AS/400 is able to serve as a Digital Certificate Manager. This means that the AS/400 can set up an intranet certificate authority, sign client and server certificates, distribute client certificates via a Web browser, and provide support for MD5 and SHA-1 hash algorithms.

The AS/400 accepts Digital Certificates for authentication. Both the HTTP and LDAP servers support Digital Certificates. The Certificates are used for identification only. A Digital Certificate is associated with a user profile and with a user in a validation list. Digital Certificates are also accepted as a Web server sign-on. The support for X.509 certificates is generalized to allow it to be used by Web Server, secure Sockets Layer, IPSec, AS/400 Client Access, and other applications.

Global Server Certificate support has been added to the certificate services available on the AS/400. This support can be used by the Web Server and other applications which use Certificates for network and web-based security.

The Digital Certificate Manager can provide certificates for multiple applications in a single system certificate store. Applications can also register to use system certificates, and clients can renew certificates. The AS/400 Digital Certificate Manager is intended to provide a limited certificate authority, i.e., manage a few certificates, not supply the function of a Net Registry or a Vault Registry.

IBM Payment Server V1.2 for AS/400

IBM Payment Server for AS/400 (electronic cash register) provides electronic payment processing for merchant systems such as Net.Commerce by coordinating the communications between a consumer (eWallet) and an acquiring bank (payment gateway). IBM Payment Server for AS/400 supports the **Secure Electronics Transaction (SET)** standard. SET is the Secure Electronics Transaction standard developed by Visa and Mastercard

The process (Figure 5.13) works by having the client (eWallet) send its credit card payment information to the Merchant System which cannot see the encrypted credit payment information. The Merchant System forwards the credit payment information to the Payment Gateway, which does the credit payment processing during a dialogue with the eWallet client. Then the Merchant System is updated on the transaction completion results.

Among the functions provided are:

- Funds authorization

- Funds capture

Figure 5.13. IBM Payment Server V1.2 Registry for SET.

- Refund

- Deposit

Security Wizard

The AS/400 continues the theme of making the system easier to interface to by providing a security wizard to assist in the setting up of the security function with a Windows like methodology. The security wizard asks questions about the AS/400 system and recommends how base system security should be configured. It is possible to apply some or all of the recommendations or to save the recommendations for later application. If the decision is to save the recommendations, the next time the security wizard is executed, the recommendations can be applied from the first screen. If changes are applied, the next time the wizard is started, a "reset changes" option appears on the first page to change the security configuration back to what it was before the changes were applied.

The security wizard generates an administrator report showing the recommended settings and how those settings affect the behavior of the system. The security wizard also generates a user report containing the information that users need to know about the system, including password composition rules and job time-out intervals. Appendix E contains sample screen capture images from the Security Wizard function. The selected images illustrate the process used by the wizard and the extent of the resulting security management.

Both reports are NLS enabled and are saved as text files that can be loaded into an editor or word processor.

Firewalls

A **firewall** controls the access and flow of information between a secure (trusted) network and an unsecure (un-trusted) network. Usually a combination of hardware and software provides firewall function. IBM suggests the use of firewalls where any connection to the Internet may possibly occur. The firewall may be formed using a separate system. Firewalls can provide the following benefits when your network is connected to the Internet:

- Controlled access to internal systems

- Concentrated security administration

- Enhanced privacy and secrecy of your network configuration

- Enforcement of your security policy

- Protection of vulnerable services, such as network file systems

- Improved system availability by blocking denial-of-service attacks

- Statistics of network use and misuse

- Protection of your organization's reputation as secure and reliable

Some *common firewall functions* are Traffic Blocking, Network Gateway, and Domain Name Serving. **Traffic Blocking** blocks unwanted traffic between the secure and the unsecure networks. The **Network Gateway** function hides both the Internet Protocol (IP) addresses and domain names of your internal network (intranet) from the Internet. The **Domain Name Serving** function makes it appear to the Internet that the firewall name is the source of all outbound traffic and also manages the routing of inbound traffic to the appropriate Intranet addresses. It is critical that other domain servers be unable to use your firewall to resolve your intranet domain names.

Most firewalls involve a separate system with separate programming. The AS/400 firewall is implemented using the **Integrated PC Server (IPCS)** internal to the AS/400 server system. This allows processor separation without requiring an additional system. Security functions running on the IPCS are separate from applications running on the AS/400 processor. The software used by the firewall is on a read-only disk, eliminating the possibility of a virus being introduced and preventing modification of programs that carry out the communications security functions. Communication between the main processor and the firewall is over an internal system bus immune from *sniffing programs* on local area networks. The firewall can be disabled by the main processor when it detects tampering, independent of the state of the firewall. Installation of firewall software is the same as for any other AS/400 software. The administrator is guided through the initial installation and configuration. The firewall is administered by a Web browser on the internal (secure) network. The Secure Sockets Layer (SSL) protocol can be used to protect the administration session. Authentication of the administrator is done with OS/400 security support.

IBM Firewall for AS/400 (#5769-FW1) is an application gateway firewall using Internet Protocol (IP) packet filtering to prevent undesirable traffic from reaching the internal network. Figure 5.14 shows how the AS/400 Integrated PC Server is positioned in the AS/400 system between the Internet and an intranet. The packets may be filtered by source IP address, protocol, port number, direction, and network interface. RealAudio is supported through dynamic packet filtering technology. A proxy server provides Web access to servers on the Internet without revealing the name or address on the browser, and can cache Web pages for better response time. All internal users have a single mail domain with hidden internal e-mail addresses. Various levels of logging are supported, ranging from logging all traffic to logging only exceptions. Figure 5.15 illustrates the generalized firewall environment where the firewall isolates the internal secure environment from the external public network environment.

Figure 5.14. Integrated PC server firewall inside the AS/400 system (available on all models except Model 436).

Using the AS/400 Socks Client program, AS/400 TCP/IP client programs such as FTP client can communicate with server programs running on systems outside the IBM Firewall for AS/400 program. Socks proxy support on the IBM Firewall for AS/400 program is used by the client programs to safely transmit data packets to external servers. Funneling these requests through the firewall proxy protects the customer's secure internal network from data packets coming from an unsecured network. The AS/400 Socks Client program is transparent to TCP/IP client programs and works for all client programs written to the sockets interface. The IBM TCP/IP clients programs, including Telnet and FTP, can be enabled to use a Socks proxy. The sockets API also supports TCP/IP multicast.

The IPCS uses Network Address Translation (NAT) to conceal internal network addresses while allowing direct access from secure clients to the external network without proxies. This simplifies exposing secure hosts, protected by the firewall to the Internet community without exposing internal network addresses. A virtual private network is enabled by the establishment of encrypted connections between firewalls to safeguard data transported through the network. Database tables are created from firewall log files, allowing SQL queries to tailor reports on usage or identify potential attacks. Log files can be deleted when they are no longer needed. The list of Firewall services includes a Web Traffic Express Proxy Server.

SafeMail Mail Relay provides protection against spamming while bridging multiple mail domains, hiding internal mail addresses, and ensuring that mail is not stored on the firewall.

Figure 5.15. The firewall environment.

WebSphere Application Server (5769-AS1)

The IBM WebSphere Application Server provides a run-time environment for Java servlets. WebSphere is intended to leverage Java to dynamically extend server function, to run in the context of the server process, and to enable the "write-once use everywhere" concept. WebSphere is built on the JavaServer toolkit from JavaSoft, uses connectors to common database formats with the industry standard object request broker, and on the server side is included with the HTTP Server. The WebSphere uses the *Java virtual machine* as a servlet engine, provides an application server manager as an applet interface for servlets and operates within a session-tracking framework that allows personalization of the applets. The database connection management function is through the Web and has persistence, which means that it remembers what activity occurred previously across the connection.

WebSphere **Studio** is an AS/400 development tool for programmers, and includes wizards and a Web workbench to help those programmers get started. Also included are site management and analysis tools. This is a separately ordered PC Tool package used to create WebSphere applications for WebSphere servers.

Product Preview: WebSphere provides Enterprise Java Bean support, uses LDAP directories, includes an XML parser, and the WebSphere performance pack provides caching, load balancing and Web site replication.

AS/400 and the Internet

This section considers the system connection shown in Figure 5.14. In this connection there are several AS/400 systems and PCs linked via a local area network. One of the AS/400 systems is a server to the local network and acts as a firewall to the modem connection to the Internet systems. The Internet, which grew out of the ARPA net defined as a result of the Cold War and today consists of over 44,000 total networks, is composed of a worldwide network of networks connected to each other and a suite of cooperating applications that allow computers connected to this network of networks to communicate with each other.

The Internet provides browsable information, file transfer, remote logon, electronic mail, news, and other services. Often referred to as the Web or the Net, the Internet is based on TCP/IP communications and basically uses the addressing and protocols defined in TCP/IP to provide access to its users. Internet terminology is defined at the Application Protocol level (because that is the level at which most users interact with the Internet), and in the process AS/400-supported functions are identified. Information exchanges on the Internet proceeds as follows

1. A client requests connection to a URL through an Internet browser.

2. The Internet server containing that URL provides the ability to browse that location through a home page and links, transfers files from the server to the client, or allows electronic commerce such as the requesting of information or ordering of products. In any case, the Internet server writes the information to the client's main storage or disk storage and disconnects from the client while the user takes time to investigate the information received.

With the AS/400 support for the Internet and the appropriate set of identifiers and passwords, it is possible to access the Web through the AS/400 to obtain information, but as an Internet user, the AS/400 can also be used to develop a program, download that program to your system from a remote site, download the information to execute against that program, and execute the program at a local system. A user has the option of accessing information in any of the files on the AS/400 and having that information HTML formatted on its way to the user's system. The user can have the AS/400 execute the program and only present the output in HTML format to the Web browser, and can develop an application on the AS/400 using CGI/WGS or the Net.Data and have that application downloaded to the browser.

Finally, to make this all work, the Internet connection server requires that the system administrator grant object access to the user profiles under which the server runs and then grant permission to the server to serve specific objects. If the server is on a system with multiple network addresses, it can be configured to serve different files based on the IP address that comes in on a request. Multiple server instances can also be configured by using either a different IP address or a single IP address and different ports for each server instance. As an example, an Internet service provider can configure a single server for multiple Web site customers with different welcome pages, mapping rules, and access control. Both Java and Java applets fit within this scenario.

To complete the discussion of the Internet, let's reconsider the Distributed AS/400 Network Example. Instead of connecting the AS/400

Servers with Wide Area Network communications, let's connect them through the Internet. Each system requires a single communications line with a modem. The system user requires a connection to a service provider like America On-Line, Compuserve, or Prodigy, or to an independent service provider. Assuming maximum security measures have been implemented, data, e-mail, and files as well as programs can be exchanged between the systems at lower costs because there is no charge for leased lines or long-distance telephone services other than the charge for the Internet service provider. Starting with Version 4 Release 2, IBM will allow you to download PTFs via the Internet.

Electronic Business (e-business)

Electronic commerce encompasses four Internet application enablers, IBM HTTP Server for AS/400, IBM Payment Server V1.2 for AS/400, Net.Data, NetQuestion, OS/400 Directory Services, Firewall for AS/400, Net.Data, Net.Commerce, and Domino.Merchant. Electronic business is a rapidly emerging environment in which the Internet is used to provide opportunities for building strong customer relations in addition to performing sales transactions. Both Net.Data and NetQuestion can be used by Net.Commerce.

Net.Commerce is a member of the CommercePoint offering from IBM. CommercePoint is a family of products designed to provide an extensive set of e-commerce solutions. The CommercePoint offerings look beyond local sales transactions to embody the core processes to doing electronic business on a global scale. CommercePoint enables the differentiation of the electronic sales channel for maintenance of a competitive edge.

Domino.Merchant is a product offering by Lotus that provides similar storefront establishment capability to Net.Commerce.

Net.Data

Net.Data is a compatible follow-on version of DB2 WWW Connection that builds on that tool's database access and reporting capabilities and provides a comprehensive Web development environment for the creation of simple dynamic to complex Web-based applications (i.e., it builds Web pages). Net.Data is a CGI program that creates a dialog with the user of a Web browser. The macro processor provides searches to the DB2-based database via SQL queries without the use of programming languages. Responses are provided to the Web browser in HyperText Markup Language

(HTML). Net.Data is contained in HTTP Server for AS/400. TCP/IP Connectivity and Utilities for AS/400 is required to use Net.Data.

Net.Data includes Web registry and flat file support as built-in functions. These functions increase the ease of creating Web pages. Web registry functions allow macro variables to be stored and retrieved, giving these variables persistence across **macro** boundaries. (The term "macro" as used here identifies a set of short programs that perform specific functions.) A macro variable and its value can be saved into a Web registry by one macro and later retrieved for use in another macro. Flat file functions allow the storage and retrieval of user data into files containing single field records. This single field record can contain multiple pieces of data separated by user-defined delimiters, enabling the performance of such tasks as saving a Net.Data table built in one macro and retrieving the table with a second macro used to create a report. Documentation on Net.Data can be found in Net.Data/Documentation.

Net.Data supports the LOB and DATALINK data types of DB2/400. SQL stored procedures can be called and multiple result sets returned by those procedures can be handled. It is possible to make direct program calls to AS/400 ILE programs that use input and output parameters. Java support allows access to Java applications or generation of Java applets from Net.Data. Macros are only parsed once and the results are saved for subsequent requests for that macro. Trace/logging support makes it easier to find errors in new programming macros. Net.Data includes built-in functions to send e-mail, generate browser cookies, and manipulate Net.Data tables.

NetQuestion

NetQuestion is the text search engine for Domino Go Webserver (also called IBM HTTP Server for AS/400) to find HTML information that will search any Single-Byte Character Set (SBCS) language. NetQuestion builds a global Internet or centralized intranet search service. It is capable of handling the large amounts of information that are typically stored on Web sites. Documents to be indexed by NetQuestion should be in either plain text or text with HTML markup. Net.Question enables the creation of searchable indexes over AS/400's Web server information.

Web surfers can search using a mixture of **Boolean logic,** proximity searching and free text searching via any standard browser. NetQuestion's user interface translation is for single-byte character languages and features the ability to build and maintain indexes, perform Boolean searches

(AND, OR, NOT), perform proximity and wildcard searches, and perform a free text search with ranked results. Precise term searches are optimized for Web applications in both Internet and intranet environments. High speed is provided in indexing and retrieval where one precise index is built. Net.Question also provides a Spell Wizard. NetQuestion can be used with Net.Data, Net.Commerce, or Domino.Merchant Common Gateway Interface (CGI) scripts and HTML forms are provided for search and administration. Command line functions can also be used for administration.

AS/400 NetQuestion search and index capability supports Double-byte Character Sets.

Net.Commerce

Net.Commerce for AS/400 enables the building of an **electronic storefront** on the Web. The storefront can range from a static Web site to a high-volume megasite providing secure links to thousands of consumers. Net.Commerce comes with sample storefronts that can be customized to provide product catalogs and search engines. Net.commerce allows a user to browse a store's categories and products. All data presented to the user is dynamically generated from the Net.Commerce specific back-end database. Net.Commerce also seamlessly manages the shoppers basket as well as letting the user register as a preferred shopper. When the shopper decides to check out, Net.Commerce will present the proper screens to determine quantities, shipping information, and payment method.

Features include virtual shopping carts and credit card validation (third party software allows real time credit card, and SET has been supported for this function since V4R3). There is a capability to check on order status, and frequent buyer discount programs can be established for multiple groups. Net.Commerce uses Net.Data to generate dynamic Internet pages using its own DB2/400 **database tables**. Management components are Site Manager, Store Manager, and Template Designer. Security functions include Internet Connection Secure Server(ICSS), and Secure Electronic Transaction (SET). Net.commerce currently uses Secure Socket Layer (SSL) for encryption.

Net.Commerce includes: Net.Commerce Server manages the customer interface enabling the customer to browse, save, query, and order items in the interactive catalog, and Net.Commerce Administrator enables the store and site personnel to create online catalog layouts, product templates and an interactive product catalog. Net.Commerce Administrator includes designers for site managers, store managers, and templates. Euro currency support is included. Net.Commerce includes Enterprise Commerce Connection for integration with backend ERP systems.

Net.Commerce Version 3 includes the following functions:

- Access Group

- Command Security

- Store level tax rates

- Payment module (IBM Payment Server and SET support)

- Product Advisor

- Tutorials

- Sample mall and stores

- Store Creator Wizard

- Staging Server

- Extended data log

- Documentation

- Euro currency support

- (Product preview) Enterprise Commerce Connection for integration with backend ERP systems

- Password Reset and Change

Domino 5.0 for AS/400

Domino 5.0 for AS/400 combines the AS/400 systems' features of strength of integration, ease of use, and scalability with Lotus's leading groupware offering Domino. Domino for AS/400 is a full-function Domino server incorporating the Domino architecture. The AS/400 system implementation of Domino includes full integration with the OS/400 operating system. Domino software runs as an application on the AS/400 system using PowerPC technology, provides the Notes client and Notes applications with direct access to the DB2/400 database, and can coexist with the Integrated PC Server, running the Domino software. Figure 5.16 illustrates the Domino development environment and the close relationship of that environment with Java for developing Domino applications.

The key features of Domino for AS/400 include:

- The latest release (a full fledged Lotus Domino Server) is Lotus Domino 5.0.

- AS/400 is enabled to be a server in a Notes network. Multiple (partitioned) Domino servers can run on a single AS/400. Up to 16 Domino servers are supported on one AS/400. Remote dial-in and dial-out are enabled.

- Universal mail exchange among multiple e-mail offerings including Lotus Notes, OfficeVision, JustMail, POP3, and Internet e-mail are provided.

- Data is integrated between Domino and DB2/400 in both directions.

- Simple-to-use mobile computing through the use of Notes replication is provided.

- Enables the building of e-commerce solutions by supporting the serving of Domino.Merchant databases and other web content databases.

- Coexists with Lotus Domino servers on the AS/400 Integrated PC Server and supports replication with all other Lotus Domino servers.

- The maximum file size for a Domino file has been increased to 4 GB.

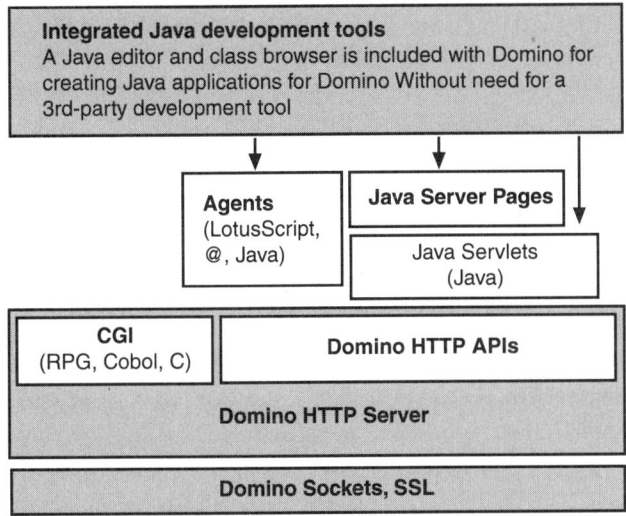

Figure 5.16. Java with Domino.

- Domino servlets support can be enabled.

- Delivers a highly reliable and available Domino server through AS/400 availability features, such as Raid-5 and mirrored protection, integrates Domino for AS/400 backup with standard AS/400 backup, runs as an OS/400 application, which isolates the server from other applications and provides server recovery without restarting the entire system.

- LDAP V3 support and a lightweight directory.

- Lotus Enterprise Integrator (formerly NotesPump) is extended with connectors to the Enterprise Resource Planning (ERP) applications.

- Lotus Domino.Doc 2.0 support.

- OfficeVision/400 has been migrated to Domino for AS/400 allowing migration of users, groups, mail, calendars, and folders to Domino from OV/400. Lotus Calendar Connector for

OfficeVision enables freetime search and sending meeting notices between Domino and OfficeVision/400.

- Supports Integrated File System stream files up to 250 GB in size in the root, QOpenSys, and user-defined file systems. OS/400 supports 64-bit integers and 64-bit APIs to work with the file system.

The AS/400 Kernel Threads model is leveraged by Domino software to save time by avoiding job initiation and to allow the software to scale to thousands of mail users on the AS/400 system.

Lotus Notes clients, both with and without an ODBC driver, can access the DB2/400 program database to import DB2/400 data directly into Notes databases. Notes C and C++ interfaces are provided, enabling AS/400 versions of standalone applications, server add-ins, database hook drivers, extension manager hook libraries, and external database drivers.

Two-way directory synchronization between the AS/400 System Distribution Directory and the Domino Name and Address Book is provided in real time, and any change in either location is automatically reflected in the other location to minimize administration activity related to both locations.

The AnyMail framework incorporates the **Lotus Simple Mail Transport Protocol/Mail Transfer Agent (SMTP/MTA)**, enabling the Domino for AS/400 to interact with other mail systems on the AS/400 system including OfficeVision/400. OfficeVision/400 is migrating to Domino for AS/400. The migration is being automated to minimize the impact on OfficeVision/400 users. Elements already migrated include:

- Nicknames, distribution lists, and groups moved to Domino/Notes registered users.

- Allows for private nicknames and distribution lists.

- Folders, notebooks, note logs move to Notes mail database folders.

- Mail items (with, without attachments) move to Notes mail database documents.

- Calendar data moves to Notes mail database documents.

Domino for AS/400 has been benchmarked at over 10,000 mail users. The high availability and reliability of the AS/400 result from the combination of the overall reliability of the AS/400 system and the incorporation of data mirroring and RAID-5 capabilities. The capability to support multiple instances via partition server support for up to 16 partitioned Domino servers, provides additional scalability. This partitioning of the Domino servers on a single system enables the workload to be split up for various applications. In addition to the Domino program's real-time Web serving capability with its HTTP server, the support and synchronization of the Domino.Merchant and DB2/400 databases enable the establishment of e-commerce storefronts.

Domino for AS/400 supports Lotus Domino.Doc, a robust "object" filing system providing a secure (easy to use and administer) document management solution. Lotus Domino.Doc also supports a distributed environment and leverages the AS/400 reliability and scalability while taking advantage of Domino's replication, security, and object storage capabilities. Lotus Domino.Doc features include document checkin/checkout, use of common terms (file rooms, file cabinets, binder, documents, etc.), and can be accessed from Web browsers, Notes Client, or ODMA-compliant applications.

Lotus Learning Space provides collaborative learning and management tools enabling media-rich online training and education. Lotus Learning Space can be accessed from the web or Notes clients to enable cost effective training where the students can access the product anytime from anywhere. Lotus Learning Space can be used to include the benefits of traditional classroom teaching—team oriented and instructor facilitated. Features of Lotus Learning Space include scheduling assignments, testing and grading tools, private or team discussions, and student based "home pages."

Lotus Script is receiving extensions to support SAP R/3, and MQSeries interfaces.

Domino.Merchant

Domino.Merchant is supported by the AS/400 at Version 4 Release 1. Domino.Merchant is a Lotus product that provides a set of functions similar to those of Net.Commerce. Domino.Merchant separates site design from creation and management. Templates are used to enable development and publication of site pages, using text, graphics, and multimedia.

Any Web browser can be used to design the store. Reviewers receive finished pages via automatic routing using the workflow capability of Domino.Merchant. Content authoring and updating are controlled, and distribution is managed using roles-based access management. User access is controlled through the Domino server's name and address book. Domino.Merchant supports a shopping basket equivalence in which customers accumulate selections, review choices, and place orders and provides links to data sheets and product reviews as additional product information if available. Multiple payment options are supported.

Net.Commerce vs. Domino.Merchant

How should the AS/400 user position Net.Commerce relative to Domino.Merchant? Net.Commerce is a packaged set of integrated software components used to develop flexible and scalable solutions to use electronic sales channels to address the growing e-business market. It is possible to integrate your e-business with existing enterprise applications using API functions. Net.Commerce addresses the needs of larger businesses, providing sophisticated catalog and Web site design for businesses expecting a high volume of traffic.

Domino.Merchant is intended for the smaller business interested in establishing an Internet presence and seeking a low-cost, easy-to-use solution and for Notes/Domino customers with a preference for a Notes-based solution for e-commerce. Domino.Merchant is complemented by Domino collaboration and tools for workflow and pre- and post-sales tasks. Catalog creation requires collaborative transactions and workflow for approvals. Ultimately, both products provide an equivalent function—establishment of an Internet storefront.

OS/400 Directory Services (LDAP)

The OS/400 Directory Server is based on LDAP v2 with some extensions. The OS/400 Directory Server utilizes DB2/400 to store LDAP information by means of a new Application Control Language (ACL) design to protect LDAP entries, and uses Operations Navigator's graphical user interface for presentation of the LDAP information. The directory server also includes LDAP Data Interchange Format (LDIF) interchange utilities to exchange data between the DB2/400 back-end and other servers.

Lightweight Directory Access Protocol (LDAP) Directory Services is the emerging Internet standard protocol for looking up information, such as e-mail addresses, phone numbers, and certificate information.

Distributed directories providing distributed name space and interoperability for operating systems and applications have been available for years (some of these are X.500, Novell's Netware Directory Service (NDS), and DCE's Cell Directory Services [CDS]), and each promised to be the network provider of a directory. However, none was completely accepted by the industry. LDAP functionality has been increased to be the equivalent of IBM eDirectory 2.1.

In addition to the LDAP server, AS/400 Directory Services includes an AS/400 based LDAP client and a Windows 95/NT LDAP client. The AS/400 based LDAP client includes a set of API's that can be used in OS/400 C programs. The Windows 95/NT LDAP client also includes a set of APIs. Other services which exploit LDAP include NetFinity, Management Central, IBM HTTP Server, WebSphere Application Server, Telnet Server, DDM and DRDA, Client Access Services and eNetwork On-Demand Server. In addition, with SSL support, these services are able to establish secure communications sessions with their corresponding clients. Data exchanged between the clients and servers is encrypted, and not subject to eavesdropping.

LDAP-enabled applications, such as Internet mail clients, can access, update, and manage the AS/400 directory. OS/400 applications can be developed to use LDAP for managing distributed information across the Internet and intranets using LDAP directories for both IBM and Non-IBM platforms. LDAP applications like mail clients can access AS/400 user information, such as e-mail addresses. System directory entries in the AS/400 can be converted to the entries of LDAP.

Internet Terminology

Internet terminology will be discussed in the context of AS/400 functions provided to perform useful work with the Internet.

HyperText Transfer Protocol (HTTP) is the protocol between a client and a server that gives World Wide Web browser clients access to AS/400 multimedia objects such as HyperText Markup Language (HTML) documents.

HyperText Markup Language (HTML) is a markup text language that allows hypertext links to be defined. A hypertext link can point to a different position in the same document or to a different document.

File Transfer Protocol (FTP) allows data to be transferred between local and remote host systems. Files may be transferred using either ASCII or binary mode. ASCII mode is used to transfer data sets that contain only text characters. FTP provides functions such as listing the remote directories, changing the current remote directory, creating and removing the remote directories, and transferring one or more files in a single request.

AS/400 TCP/IP TELNET provides client and server support for the TELNET protocol that allows remote logon to hosts within an Internet, and the *AS/400 TCP/IP Simple Network Management Protocol (SNMP)* provides a means for managing an Internet environment. SNMP allows network management by elements, including gateways, routers, and hosts. Network elements act as servers and contain management agents that perform the management functions requested. Network management stations act as clients: They run the management applications that monitor and control the network. SNMP provides a method of communicating between these elements and stations to send and receive information about network resources. The AS/400 can be an agent, but not the SNMP manager in a TCP/IP network.

Serial Line Internet Protocol (SLIP) allows the connection of systems over a pair of modems that are connected through a telephone line. The communication runs over a point-to-point link. X.25 and Frame Relay are other examples of point-to-point TCP/IP communications that AS/400 supports.

Multipurpose Internet Mail Extensions (MIME) is the Internet standard for sending mail with headers containing information describing the contents of the messages to the receiving client. The messages can be video, image, audio, or binary files or text.

Simple Mail Transfer Protocol (SMTP) allows the sending or receiving of electronic mail over a TCP/IP network. SMTP supports the distribution of notes, messages, and final-form text documents. SMTP can be sent with the OfficeVision for OS/400 licensed program. SMTP can be used for sending MIME formatted mail, but it cannot be used to distribute objects or to transfer revisable-form text (RFT) documents.

The *Post Office Protocol, Version 3 (POP3)* mail server allows AS/400 systems to act as POP servers for any clients that support the POP mail interface. This includes clients running on Windows, OS/2, AIX, and Macintosh. The POP3 server allows for the exchange of mail using the AnyMail/400 framework.

Uniform Resource Locators (URLs) are used by browser clients to make requests of the HTTP server. URLs are identifiers and instructions (e.g., programs) that tell the HTTP server what object to process and how to process it. The following AS/400 objects can be accessed using URLs:

- Source physical files and physical files containing EBCDIC, HTML, or plain text. **EBCDIC** is the IBM format for defining the contents of a byte, as opposed to ASCII which is the American Standard Committee format.

- Binary objects from file systems other than the AS/400 native file system. The binary objects can be multimedia objects, program applets, graphical objects, audio objects, etc.

- Common Gateway Interface program requests.

- DB2 database requests.

- Image map requests.

Common Gateway Interface (CGI) is the standard that specifies the interface between information servers and gateways, and defines the requirements for programs that the HTTP administrator allows browsers to request. The HTTP server recognizes a URL containing a request for a CGI program and calls that program on behalf of the client browser. The CGI specification dictates how the CGI program gets its input and how it will produce any output.

Workstation Gateway Server (WGS) is a TCP/IP application that transforms AS/400 5250 data streams to HTML for dynamic display on Web browsers, allowing AS/400 applications to be run from any workstation that has a Web browser.

Anonymous FTP enables a general access to certain information on a remote host. The remote site determines what information is made available for general access. Such information is considered to be publicly accessible and can be read by anyone. A user may logon to these hosts using the user ID *ANONYMOUS*. Typically the only operations allowed with this ID are logging on using FTP, listing the contents of a limited set of directories, and retrieving files from these directories and libraries. As a rule, the anonymous user is not allowed to transfer files to the FTP server system, although some systems do provide an incoming directory for anonymous users to send data. Some sites primarily used for archives ask for the user's e-mail address as the password. In Figure 5.14, the anonymous user is never allowed beyond the server system.

6

Application Systems and Your Business

An important first step in bringing Advanced Systems, or any computers, into your business environment is planning. Largely depending on how well you plan, introducing new computer resource(s) can be like pouring either water or gasoline on a fire. Many readers will already have a significant number of computers in their business and will add Application Systems to their computer arsenal, whereas others will be bringing Application Systems in as their first business computer.

In either case, the information in this chapter should help you understand how to introduce Advanced Business Systems computers into your particular environment. The chapter starts by discussing what you should consider when looking at Application Systems versus personal computers versus local area networks. Then it covers software selection, followed by some specific Application Systems hardware configurations appropriate for small, medium, and large businesses. In addition, the following topics will be discussed:

- Business decisions

- Implementation management

- Physical planning
- Training
- Ergonomics
- Security
- Technical support
- Service
- Migrating from System/3X to AS/400 systems
- Migrating from AS/400 CISC to AS/400 RISC

This chapter is not a complete guide to introducing Advanced Business Systems into any business, but it does provide a starting point for developing your plan and discussing some important issues.

What Are My Business Computing Needs?

Many businesses today use some type of computer system(s) to help run their business. These businesses must constantly evaluate whether their current system is good enough. Those businesses still using manual methods must determine whether automating their business might help. This book certainly cannot answer the question for you, but it can provide a starting point.

Whether your business has millions of dollars worth of computer systems or none at all, the way to begin answering these questions is to forget about computer hardware and software, and look very closely at your business. Too often, businesses buy computer systems and then look for problems to solve. A properly managed computer project should start by careful consideration of the collective business needs of all functional areas within the business. Independently attacking specific business problems can often result in a "dead-end" computer solution that provides no coherent growth strategy for the future.

From the very start, key people from all business areas should be collected into a project team. Since all business areas will be involved, the top management of the business must consistently demonstrate a commitment to the project. Without top management involvement, disagreements among the peer business areas are slow to be resolved and the sense of priority is diminished. Lack of consistent top management commitment at either the investigation or implementation phases of a computer project is a common cause of unsuccessful projects, which can be quite expensive.

The project team should start by reviewing the overall goals of the business (or segment of a larger business) over the next few years. In some cases, these goals will be well known, but in others a great deal of soul-searching will be necessary. These goals should be as specific as possible and should include any business strategies in place to achieve these goals. After the business goals are clearly defined, the project team should look closely at the current day-to-day operations of the business as it is and document the movement of information through the entire organization. Only after the information flow is understood can the team candidly discuss what is good and what is bad about the current way of doing business. Work to identify the sources of problems rather than focusing on symptoms. Understand the interaction between the various areas of the business. Consider the flow of information from one group to another as you trace the business cycle.

Chances are, not every problem that you will uncover can be solved through a computer. For example, a computerized inventory tracking system will not solve inventory problems if just anyone can casually walk into the inventory storeroom and walk out with what he or she needs with no controls. Computers are only a tool for effectively managing a business. They will not manage your business for you. Only after you have examined your current operation with a critical eye can you begin to see if a computer solution makes sense for your business. In the case of small businesses, this type of analysis can be done in a matter of weeks or even days. In larger businesses, it can span months or even years and is typically done on an ongoing basis. Some businesses choose to do the analysis on their own. If you want assistance with solving business problems with computers, there are plenty of places to turn, including consultants and computer manufacturers.

What About Personal Computers?

Although this book is about IBM's midsize computer systems, to make good buying decisions it is important to understand how these differ from personal computers (PCs). The first difference between Application Systems and PCs is that PCs were primarily designed to be used by one person at a time (single user) and Application Systems were initially designed to be simultaneously shared by many users (multiuser) running several applications at the same time. (Single User and Multiuser are contrasted in Chapter 4.) More recently, Application Systems design has been changed to incorporate the server function, which includes downloading operating systems, programs, and data to PCs.

Although there are some environments in which PCs can be used as small multiuser computers, their hardware and software architectures are primarily geared for single-user computing. Because Application Systems are multiuser computers, multiple PC systems must be purchased to serve an equivalent number of users. Furthermore, because all users of an Application System share a single computer, they can share equipment (printers) and information (inventory data). To obtain this sharing of equipment and information, the multiple PCs must be networked together through a Local Area Network (LAN). With the LAN, PCs can also freely share equipment and information as long as the PC programs were written for the LAN environment. So which is best? The PC LAN versus multiuser system debate still rages, and it is clear that both approaches have merit. Here are some things to consider to help make the decision.

Multiuser systems are more mature than LANs simply by virtue of having been around longer. Because PCs were originally used as independent computers, many of the application programs for PCs do not support LAN environments. The definition of the distributed computing environment helped to solve the problem for UNIX and the more recently written personal computer applications, but the second component, the distributed management environment, is really just beginning to achieve some definition. In general, it is much easier to extend the management principles of the multiuser Applications System to a LAN environment for shared data, applications, and security functions than it is to extend a single-user system environment to that same set of shared data, applications, and security functions.

The AS/400 development group with its new system management functions for the AS/400 servers and their clients under Client Access Family for AS/400 and Client Access Family for Windows for AS/400 are working with the Open System Foundation (OSF) to get the SystemView interfaces and constructs identified as the basis for the Distributed Management Environment (DME). Application programs for Application Systems are typically more comprehensive and support the multiuser environment. This means that there are more tried-and-true business applications for Application Systems than there are for PC LANs.

Furthermore, multiuser systems were designed to be just that, whereas PC LANs were more of an afterthought. This often means that a fair amount of technical skill is required to support a PC LAN. Such variables as the number of workstations, the technical support level, and systems management activity determine which approach yields the lowest cost. Do not forget to consider the PC LAN with Application Systems as the server. This can often provide the best of both worlds. Finally, the most important thing to consider is the application program(s) under consideration for each approach, because PCs and Application Systems are not software compatible and application programs written for one will not always run on the other. This distinction is becoming blurred with the recent announced support for the **Integrated Language Environment (ILE)**. For example, application programs written in C may be capable of execution on both the PC and the AS/400, assuming that you have the source code and recompile (because the code is not object compatible). It is possible that there will also be differences in screens and other I/O interfaces. The approach with the best-fitting application program will normally provide the best results.

What About RISC System/6000 Computers?

The RISC System/6000 family of computers is IBM's entry into the "open systems" area, where international standards take precedence over the proprietary innovations of individual companies. RISC System/6000 computers have a split personality in that they can be used as high-function workstations for a single user or as general-purpose multiuser computer systems in typical business environments. Since the AS/400 is not designed for use as a high-function workstation, the RS/6000 is a better choice if the computer is to be used primarily for activities such as computer-aided design and technical publishing.

In the general-purpose multiuser computer system arena, however, there is certainly room for confusion when deciding between the RISC System/6000 and the AS/400 families of computers. To resolve this confusion, let's look at some of the design points of each family. The AS/400 system's architecture includes a built-in relational database. In other words, the AS/400 hardware and operating system have been designed specifically to provide the database function commonly needed in business environments. Most other computer systems (including the RISC System/6000) require separately purchased database programs that sit on top of the operating system to provide users with a relational database. Since the AS/400 system's database is implemented in the hardware and operating system, the performance and elegance of the database implementation are improved. Further, the programmer productivity afforded by the built-in AS/400 database makes it a good system for those writing and maintaining their own business application programs. Finally, AS/400 systems led the way in the implementation of IBM's Systems Application Architecture (SAA).

As was stated in Chapter 3, IBM no longer enforces the SAA architecture across its systems but leaves it to its systems houses to reach agreement on the level of compatibility they will provide. All things being equal, if you need to coexist with a network of other IBM systems, an AS/400 may be indicated both because of the vast AS/400 application portfolio and because the AS/400 with AnyNet/400 and other integrated communications protocols will interface to those systems, whereas those systems may not always talk to each other. It should be noted, however, that AS/400 computers can also participate in the UNIX "open systems" environments (the primary target of RISC System/6000 systems) through OS/400's support of the OSI and TCP/IP communications protocols including SNMP and the X-OPEN standards. Although the RISC System/6000 has no built-in database, relational database programs that add this capability to the system are available. This added database will add an additional workload on the RISC System/6000, but this is only problematic if not considered when selecting which model is needed.

Those migrating programs and data from a UNIX multiuser computer system will find the *migration* to a RISC System/6000 much more natural than migrating to an AS/400. Those migrating programs and data from System/36 or System/38 computers will find the migration to the AS/400 much more natural than migrating to a RISC System/6000. If you need to coexist with computer systems of many different brands, the open systems foundation on which the RISC System/6000 is built will be a plus, but with the recent announcements, the AS/400 is approaching equivalent capabilities in this environment. Additionally, if you need to coexist in this environment but would like the computer to manage the complex resources provided by the mixed-brand environment, then the AS/400 should be the choice because the RS/6000 does not offer that management capability and requires the business to integrate the various communications and other programs needed to support that management need.

What About System/390 Computers?

The IBM System/390 (and System/370) computer family is also widely used to fill business needs. Like Application Systems, System/390 computers are multiuser computer systems that allow many users to share the system. Some System/390 computers offer the same level of computing power as that provided by all but the smallest Application Systems, but other System/390 computers provide computational power well beyond even the largest Application Systems. Although System/390 and Application Systems can share information, one cannot run object-code application programs written for the other. In some cases you can recompile source-code applications programs that use common languages such as Cobol and ANSI C.

What should you consider when choosing between System/390 computers and Application Systems? Again, the system that can run the application program that best fits your needs has a strong advantage when it comes to making a selection. There are more *prewritten* business applications for Application Systems than there are for System/390 computers. In the event you intend to write your own *custom* application programs from scratch, the programmer productivity features of Application Systems are a strong point, and it has been established that the System/390 typically requires a somewhat larger staff to support the system and its applications. However, your business may have already developed the System/390 application programs you would like to use, in which case the System/390 is desirable. Another reason to select a System/390 approach may be that you need more computing power than is available in the Application Systems family. This may often be the case in a highly technical environment, in which the System/390 architecture is a better fit than that of the Application Systems. One final and important consideration is that System/390 computer *operators* (not necessarily users) require more data processing experience than is needed by the operator of Application Systems.

When Should I Consider Application Systems?

When looking for ways to meet business computing needs, there seems to be an endless series of questions to be answered. Before getting into how to select an Advanced System to meet your needs, let us pause and glance at some other alternatives. Among the alternatives considered were Networked PCs, RS/6000s, and System/390s. Among the reasons identified for choosing AS/400 over the solution offered by the alternatives were multiuser capabilities; range of applications; number of applications; cost of support staffing; and integrated solutions resulting from the integration of database, file system, communications, security, and service.

Ease of use results from integrated system management of not only the system (but including workstations and intranets as well). Here are other benefits: ease of program development (for those involved with writing custom applications); and range of system growth. System growth could range from an entry system supporting as few as 7 users to a Model 740 supporting greater than 10,000 users, with the option of horizontal growth using optically connected local systems to support 32 times the capacity of a single system, all running the same applications without needing to recompile or change data structures across the entire range.

Parallel capability exists in the server environment, where an equivalent server model exists for each general-purpose computing model in the product line. All models support connectivity and development on the Internet from simple home pages to storefront management, which is scalable from a single-department-size store to a multi-department store.

Logical Partitioning of Symmetrical Multi-Processor systems provides the capability of consolidating multiple diverse servers into a single system with multiple partitions functioning independently or cooperatively with resilient data and programs may be another reason to select an AS/400 over a competitive product.

Choosing the Software

Application Systems computers become a useful business tool only when they are executing the appropriate software. Although there are many ways of generating a strategy for introducing computers, considering software needs before selecting detailed hardware configurations usually makes sense. The hardware requirements, such as memory size and disk storage space, will in part be based on the needs of the software selected. With the emerging applications providing a scalable Lotus Notes/Domino server (which may be required to grow to several times larger than available today anywhere), a system that can grow to support data warehousing and, through RISC power, analysis of data through data mining introduces scalability as a new consideration in the decision process. The application programs you select must perform the tasks needed by your end users both today and in the foreseeable future. Chapter 3 has already discussed some application programs commonly used with Application Systems.

Selecting the basic type of application program is often fairly simple: An accounting department needs an accounting application program, a secretary needs a word processing application program, and so on. What is more difficult is identifying the specific application program that best fits your particular needs. Is a custom application program preferred, or will a prewritten application program be acceptable? If a prewritten application program is desired, exactly which one is the best for your needs? If a custom application program is desired, who should write it and what should it include? The answers to these questions depend largely on the specifics of a given business environment and thus are beyond the scope of this book. However, a few basics remain the same whether you are selecting a program for a multinational corporation or one for a corner fish market.

First, you must precisely understand the tasks you are trying to put on a computer before pursuing any application program alternatives. A thorough knowledge of these helps you to identify specific requirements your application program must meet. After a detailed understanding of the tasks is obtained, a search can begin through the many prewritten or off-the-shelf application programs. If you can find an appropriate prewritten application program that fits your needs, you can avoid the expense, delay, and ongoing effort associated with custom software development and maintenance. Good prewritten application programs can be quite flexible. However, because everyone typically has slightly different needs and methods even within a given business function, you can bet that any prewritten application will have some features you do not need and will not have other features you will wish it did.

Do not forget to consider the more specialized type of prewritten application program—vertical market applications. **Vertical market application** programs address a highly specific segment of users such as lawyers, doctors, distributors, and manufacturers. There are several sources of information about the many prewritten application programs on the market. Of course, computer companies and consultants can help you select particular application programs to fit your needs. There are also many popular computer and trade magazines that periodically conduct extensive reviews of prewritten application programs. These can be excellent and timely sources of information. For specific or highly specialized needs, prewritten application programs may not be adequate. In this case, custom-developed software may be desirable. Although the development and maintenance of custom software is a long-term commitment that is typically expensive, it may be less costly in the long run to pay for the development of custom software than to settle for a prewritten application program that does not do the job. If you do select the custom software route, an important step is to select the proper developer.

Businesses that have their own programming staff can do their own custom program development. If you do not have your own programmers, it will be necessary to seek outside help—that is, an outside software developer. In either case, the developer will have the largest effect on the ultimate success or failure of the custom development activity. The developer's job is not an easy one. In addition to programming expertise, the developer must become an expert in all aspects of your business, must be a good communicator to understand and discuss software requirements, must understand human psychology when defining the user interface for the program, must be a proficient teacher to train the end users on the new program, and, finally, must be dependable and reliable, and therefore available to provide technical support, software maintenance, and any needed modifications.

Choosing the Hardware

Selecting the proper Application Systems hardware components that will together fit your needs can be confusing. You must select among the Application Systems and their disk configurations, feature cards, peripherals, and so on. Although we cannot possibly cover all needs for all environments in the limited scope of this book, we can examine some business environments—for example, a small retail franchise establishment, a small manufacturing establishment, a medium business, and a large business—and outfit them with the appropriate Application Systems configurations. With the insight provided by outfitting these hypothetical business environments, you will be better prepared to properly select the Application Systems components useful in your environment. Assistance in selecting specific Application Systems configurations is available from IBM or authorized remarketers.

Small Business Environment, Retail—Anatole's Sub Factory

The first hypothetical small business is a submarine sandwich fast food franchise outlet. Jerry is the owner of the franchise located on the south side of Milwaukee in a predominantly Mexican-American neighborhood. As a result, Jerry has found that the demographics of his location require that he market a taco and a chile relleno sub, which are not in high demand at the other Anatole's Sub Factory locations either in Milwaukee or outside of Texas. Also, the demographics make the normal supply methodology for other Anatole Sub Factories invalid, so Jerry has installed a personal computer connected to an AS/400 Advanced Entry Model 150 configuration in addition to the two cash drawer personal computer retail terminals used at his customer checkout locations. The cash drawer terminals, the personal computer, and the Entry Model 150 are connected by a token-ring local area network operating at 16 Mbps. The Entry Model 150 is connected to an AS/400e system 740 located at the Anatole Sub Factory headquarters in Detroit through the Internet by an EIA 232/V.24 line operating at 19.2 Kbps. This configuration is illustrated in Figure 6.1.

Before Jerry installed his own personal computer notebook and began doing his own demographics studies, the franchise manager had been shipping Jerry supplies for his customers on the same basis as had

Application Systems and Your Business   **443**

Figure 6.1. Jerry's Anatole Sub Factory—small business retail franchise.

been done for the other franchisees in the Milwaukee area. After installing the personal computer and the Relational Database Facility on the AS/400, Jerry was able to modify the order process with the franchise manager to control the inventory received to more closely match his sales projections. Jerry also became the test marketing site for two new sub sandwiches resulting from his suggestions to Anatole's Sub Factory—an enchilada sub and a tamale sub. Jerry also uses the PC notebook system and the Entry Model 150 to handle his payroll, attendance, cost/revenue projections, and so on. The PC notebook system allows Jerry to take some of the business work home at night, using the Internet interface to download and upload the results to the Model 150 while also being able to make inquiries into Anatole's Sub headquarters for information on how they are processing his inventory and managing the supplying of his franchise.

Small Business Environment, Manufacturing—Bob's Gearbox Co.

The second hypothetical small business is a gearbox manufacturer named Bob's Gearbox Co. Bob's has a standard line of gearboxes and also accepts orders for custom gearboxes. It is a private corporation (owned by Bob, of course) and has 32 employees. Bob has been in business 5 years and has experienced moderate growth. He currently conducts business by noncomputer methods but finds himself needing to streamline his operation as the business grows. Bob is particularly concerned that his profits seem to be shrinking as his sales increase. A study of Bob's business shows that there are two basic causes for this. First, his sales staff often commits to discounted pricing on a gearbox order to capture the business. The trouble is that Bob never really knows what it actually costs him to produce a given gearbox. He uses standard cost estimates to price a customer's order and hopes that the actual cost of building the gearbox is close to this. The second basic problem uncovered in the study is that Bob's inventory is not well managed. The production department is often hampered by not having the right parts and raw materials in inventory. This often causes slips in the delivery of customer orders that hurt customer satisfaction and fuel heated arguments among the marketing manager, the production manager, and the materials manager. Finger pointing is commonplace. The study also showed that 25 percent of the inventory items in stock are obsolete and will never be used.

In this scenario, it is clear that Bob has outgrown his manual methods of doing business. Bob needs a better way to track the actual costs associated with manufacturing his products. This may uncover the fact that his sales staff often sell gearboxes at or below cost. Bob also needs help tracking his inventory. He needs to know when critical parts are getting low and what parts are moving slowly. The deficiencies in Bob's business can be addressed with the proper computer solution.

Let us examine the Application Systems configuration suitable for Bob's Gearbox. Bob will use the Manufacturing Accounting Production Information Control System (MAPICS/DB) to help gain better control over his business. By selecting the appropriate modules (programs) within the MAPICS/DB family of software, Bob can track manufacturing costs more closely (Production Control and Costing, and Product Data Management modules) and better manage his inventory (Inventory Control module). Bob also chooses to take advantage of the computer system to automate the general accounting functions of his business such as payroll, accounts receivable, accounts payable, and general ledger, and he will use the Order Entry and Invoicing module to track and bill customer orders. The Cross-Application Support module is required on all systems. Through a questionnaire, this module allows Bob to customize MAPICS/DB for his particular business environment. Furthermore, the Cross-Application Support module automatically passes information among the various MAPICS/DB modules, making them function as a single system.

Based on the requirements of the software and Bob's business transaction volumes, Bob will get the AS/400e server 170 shown in Figure 6.2. The Model 170 system was selected for its low cost and the Model 170's ability to be first upgraded to higher-performance processors and then replaced by a larger AS/400 system. The standard 4196 MB of disk storage will be expanded to 16,000 MB to provide enough storage for

Figure 6.2. Bob's AS/400 Advanced System 400.

the system software, the MAPICS/DB modules, and associated data. The Model 170 system's ability to expand to 175,400 MB of disk storage will allow for expansion as Bob's business grows. Bob will also expand the standard 64 MB of main storage to 128 MB by adding a 64-MB main storage option. The optional Uninterruptible Power Supply unit will help prevent disruption of the system by power failures—Bob can do without the extra headache. The 7861 Modem will be used to access IBM's Electronic Customer Support (ECS) network.

The System Console function is performed by a 3489 Modular Display Unit. For the users, four 3488 Displays are provided initially. One display is for the inventory clerk, one is for the purchasing agent, one is for the production department, and one is for Bob so that he can get the management information he needs to make intelligent decisions. The 4234 Printer will be used to produce the various reports provided by MAPICS/DB. The 7-GB cartridge tape unit will allow data stored on disk to be backed up on tape. This will help prevent important business information from getting accidentally lost. Since OS/400 V4R4 is now bundled with the Model 170 hardware, Bob has no need to concern himself with AS/400's operating system. Bob will also get the Query/400 and OfficeVision/400 programs so that he and his staff can generate customized reports and manage schedules as needed.

Bob expects to participate in electronic commerce through the Internet, so he insists on having a 7852 Modem attached. He also figures this will provide him with closer contact with his sales force (whom he plans on providing with notebook computers) through e-mail while they are interacting with customers for his gearboxes. Because he has no programming skills on his staff, Bob anticipates consulting with IBM about setting up his Internet site and storefront.

Medium Business Environment—Johnson & Thornbush

The hypothetical medium-sized business is an advertising agency named Johnson & Thornbush. This company has been in business for 12 years. Their business started with one major account, and today they have 17 active clients. Steve Johnson and Perry Thornbush are both still active in managing the business. The main office has 74 people and is located in Chicago, Illinois. A second office, with 7 people, is located in Fort Lauderdale, Florida, to handle several large accounts in the Southeast.

Almost every person at each location has a personal computer (PC) providing personal productivity tools for such tasks as market analysis, trend analysis, word processing, and financial modeling.

Steve Johnson recently sponsored a company-wide study to find a way to address the business goals of increasing marketing effectiveness and reducing operating costs. The results of the study revealed that the market analysis being done by one PC user seldom correlated with the market analysis done by another PC user. The cause of the disagreement in information was that there were different versions of the area demographic information residing on the various PC disk units used in the market analysis. Even though one person had responsibility for periodically updating the demographic information and distributing the updates, eventually different versions of the information emerged, making the market analysis inaccurate. Further, as the company's market coverage grows, the demographic information is growing in size and becoming impractical to distribute via diskettes. It is apparent that more sophisticated data management and analysis techniques will become necessary as the firm continues to grow.

Another area needing improvement uncovered in the study was that basic office operations could be streamlined, increasing productivity and thereby reducing operating expense. Mail delays between the two offices were slowing down many day-to-day business operations. Because of busy schedules, it was often difficult to schedule meetings, as the last attendee contacted would often have a conflict. Although the secretarial staff also had PCs and WordPerfect for word processing, turnaround time for even a simple memo was getting longer as the workload increased.

The project team recommended a computer solution that streamlined office functions and centralized the area demographic information. All PCs were to be connected in such a way that they could share information and facilitate business communications. Figure 6.3 shows the system configuration suitable for Johnson & Thornbush. In this solution, the PC users retain their PCs, protecting that investment in hardware, programs, and training, only now all PCs (in Chicago and Fort Lauderdale) are attached to an AS/400 located in Chicago, allowing them to double as PCs and AS/400 workstations. As PCs, they can do everything they could before. As workstations on the AS/400, the PCs allow users to interact with the AS/400, providing some additional capabilities provided by AS/400 programs.

448 EXPLORING IBM AS/400 COMPUTERS

Figure 6.3. AS/400e system 730 for Johnson & Thornbrush.

Hardware Configuration

Based on the number of users and the growth being experienced by the business, an AS/400 9406 Model 730 with processor option 2062 with interactive feature 1503 is selected. For now, 1024 MB of main storage should meet the need. Two additional 6713 integrated 8.58-GB disk units will expand the standard 4.19 GB to over 20 GB of disk storage—more than enough for now. The 6390 7.0-GB 8-mm cartridge tape unit provides for efficient backup of the information stored in the AS/400 disk storage. The 16/4-Mbps Token-Ring Network Adapter/HP will allow the AS/400 to participate in a 16-Mbps token-ring network. A 16/4-Mbps Token-Ring Network Adapter/A must also be installed in each of the local PCs, allowing them to participate in the network. The 6262 Printer will provide high-speed printing to all local users.

In Fort Lauderdale a 5494 Remote Workstation Controller is attached to a communications line to Chicago, where the PCs are equipped with the System 36/38 Workstation Adapter/A and attached to the 5494 so they can be used as AS/400 workstations. The smaller 4230 Printer, along with the PC printers they already have, will meet printing needs for the Fort Lauderdale users. Although the PCs will be attached to the 5494 via twinaxial cable for now, a token-ring network could be installed later at the Fort Lauderdale location. The PCs can then be attached to the 5494 via the token-ring network to provide for more efficiency and flexibility as the Fort Lauderdale location grows.

Johnson & Thornbush Software Scenario

The OfficeVision/400 application program provides the basic office functions needed to streamline operations. The electronic mail feature of OfficeVision allows any user to electronically send documents or quick notes to any other user. This eliminates mail delays and reduces the word processing workload, because simple notes and messages can be typed and sent by the users themselves. The calendar management function of the OfficeVision application can automatically schedule a desired meeting by electronically checking the calendars of all attendees and finding a time suitable for all.

Although OfficeVision has a word processing function, those with primarily word processing activities to perform will continue to use the

WordPerfect word processing program on the PCs. Since both offices have a heavy word processing workload, using the intelligence in the PCs for this function will provide the highest productivity (lowest response time). This is particularly true in Fort Lauderdale, because AS/400 response time will be reduced by the relatively slow telephone line communications speeds. Furthermore, removing the word processing tasks from the AS/400 provides improved response time for the electronic mail, calendaring, and demographic activities performed on the AS/400 system.

The Client Access Family for Windows program allows AS/400 disk storage to act as the central repository (file server) for the demographic information. In effect, a portion of the AS/400 disk storage appears to be a giant PC disk unit shared by all PCs. With Client Access Family for Windows, all PC users can simultaneously share this single copy of the information, ensuring that all are using the same current data for their marketing analysis. This will result in a more accurate market analysis and thus more effective marketing efforts for the firm's clients.

With the AS/400 Application Development Tools Structure Query Language Development Kit for OS/400, ILE RPG/400, DB2 Query Manager for OS/400(5769-ST1), and AS/400 Query (5769-QU1) — Johnson & Thornbush will develop custom application software over time that will allow the AS/400 to act as a database repository and interact with the PCs in a cooperative processing environment. Through the token-ring network, all of the PCs located in Chicago are attached to the AS/400.

The token-ring network was selected for its high-speed information transfer rate and because it could use the twisted-pair wiring already installed throughout much of their building. All of the PCs in Fort Lauderdale will be attached to the AS/400 system as remote workstations through a 5494 Remote Workstation Controller, appropriate modems, and a leased, voice-grade telephone line. This allows every PC, no matter where it is located, to double as an intelligent AS/400 workstation. Whether PC users are in Chicago or Fort Lauderdale, they will have access to the same functions. However, because the Fort Lauderdale PC users are attached via a telephone line, their response time will not be as good (fast) as that of those in Chicago, who are attached over the high-speed token-ring network.

To improve the exchange of ideas and responsiveness of the people to people interactions, Domino 5.0 was installed on the AS/400 Model

730, and Lotus Notes was installed on the PC's both in Chicago and in Fort Lauderdale.

Large Business Environment—Atole Enterprises

The hypothetical large business that will be outfitted with Application Systems is Atole Enterprises. This multinational corporation is a distributor of canned foods and enjoys financial prowess worthy of its Fortune 500 membership. The many benefits afforded by computers are well known at Atole Enterprises. They have been using computers in their day-to-day operations for many years. The U.S. headquarters is in New York City and currently has a large System/390 computer complex. There are 17 distribution centers located from coast to coast. Each distribution center has its own small System/36 and Atole-written application programs to track orders and local inventory, and to transmit information to the System/390 in New York. System/36s were originally selected for their ease of operation, which minimizes the need for technical skills at each distribution center.

A companywide study sponsored by headquarters came to the following conclusions: Most of the System/36s are fully depreciated and in many cases are not providing enough computing power to meet growing demands. The custom-written application programs written for the System/36s have been around a long time and need major updates to keep the company's competitive edge in customer service. The study therefore recommended that Atole convert the distribution centers from System/36s to entry level AS/400e server 170s using processor 2289 with improved application programs.

Also, the System/390 located in New York will be right-sized to an AS/400e server 740 with processor feature 2069 and interactive feature 1510, which will save significant operating cost over the next 5-year period. In addition, future applications will be developed on the 740 and verified before being shipped to the distribution centers, thus avoiding the need to install a separate Model 170 at the main office. A difficult decision existed between the Advanced 36 Model 436 and the Model 170 systems because of the capability of the Advanced 36 to directly apply the existing System/36 applications, but since the decision had already been made to rewrite the applications, the greatest gain in performance and growth could be attained with the Model 170s. It was decided to get a SSP license for the Model 170 systems during the transition interval related to the application rewrite.

Atole Solution Scenario

The first step in implementing the solution is to install Model 170 systems at the distribution centers. The distribution-center staff will use the migration tools to quickly move the current distribution-center application programs from the System/36 to that AS/400 system, since the Model 170 can execute SSP and OS/400 concurrently. After the initial migration is complete, the headquarters staff on the Model 740 will exploit the programmer productivity features in the AS/400 system to enhance the distribution centers' application programs. It is critical to get the improved application programs ready as soon as possible. Once this is done, each distribution center will download the updated application programs. The headquarters staff will assist each distribution center in performing systems management on the new systems.

Figure 6.4 shows the AS/400 distribution-center configuration that will be used by Atole. The AS/400e system model 170 with processor option 2289 was selected because its performance and capacity best matched the need and because of its continuing upgrade path. The standard Model 170 configuration will be expanded to 8380 MB of disk storage and 256 MB of main storage to provide enough capacity to meet the needs of the distribution centers for an estimated 5 years. In the event of a power failure, the UPS power unit will provide power to sustain critical components while they ride through short power outages and will allow the system to perform an orderly shutdown in case of longer power outages. This will reduce the disruption associated with power failures at the distribution centers.

The 7852 Modem will be used for IBM Electronic Customer Support (ECS), which will derive from the base 9720 PCI WAN/Twinaxial IOA which will support up to 28 twinaxial attached workstations in addition to the ECS communications line. In this case, however, Atole chooses to provide the ECS for each distribution center from the headquarters location; that is, headquarters will maintain a help desk and a technical question-and-answer database pertaining to their custom software in addition to the IBM question-and-answer database. They will be the first line of support for the distribution centers. A second communications line is provided by the 2721 PCI Two-Line Wan IOA

Application Systems and Your Business **453**

Figure 6.4. AS/400 distribution center configuration that will be used by Atole.

and 0331 EIA 232/V.24 50-foot cable and the 7852 Modem. This leased line will be used to communicate with the Model 740 at headquarters to consolidate information needed from each distribution center much as before. This will allow for communications at 33,600 bps.

The NetView program running on the AS/400e system 740 will work with the 7852 Modems to manage the communications network. Further, the SystemView System Manager for OS/400 program will be loaded on the central site's AS/400 to allow the retrained S/390 personnel to perform change and problem management for the remote AS/400 systems. Atole will use 3487 Display Stations as color terminals to allow their custom application programs to exploit color to associate and highlight information on the screen. This will result in improved ease of use. Each distribution center will have a 4234 Printer to produce reports and correspondence-quality documents. The standard streaming tape drive provided with every 9406 Model 740 will be used to back up disk storage. Backup will only be performed to the Model 740 at the central headquarters site.

The AS/400 software needed, in addition to OS/400, includes IBM's Communications Utilities, Query, and ILE RPG/400. IBM's Communications Utilities provides some additional communications functions between the AS/400s. Query/400 will allow local distribution center management to develop their own custom reports, giving them more flexibility. Finally, OfficeVision/400 will facilitate communications between headquarters staff and each distribution center.

Server Selection

The medium business environment of Johnson & Thornbush could equally well have used an AS/400e server 730. Performance within the locally connected personal computers would have been improved with no degradation at the remote site. In fact, performance would appear to improve if the process of maintaining the database concurrent between the two server systems were managed properly. Figure 6.5 illustrates the preferred configuration for Johnson & Thornbush in a server-based implementation. Note that the 5494 Remote Workstation Controller has been replaced with a LAN-configured AS/400 Advanced Entry Model 150. This transformation is possible because the servers are specifically set up to manage LAN-connected personal computers.

The only non-LAN-connected terminals on either of the systems are the system console and the printers. If the 9720 Base PCI WAN/Twinaxial IOA feature had been chosen using an additional com-

Figure 6.5. Johnson & Thornbush configuration as a set of servers.

munications line, both the console and printers could have been LAN connected. It is worthwhile for the business that has almost all its terminals as personal computers to consider the server configurations because specially priced packages to meet those configurations are available. Figure 6.6 illustrates the Johnson & Thornbush system configuration as it would appear if implemented as a network configuration. In a network computing configuration, the leased line connecting the two modems in Figure 6.6 would be replaced by an Internet cloud, which would give each group of users (those on the Model 730 and those on the Model 150) access not only to each other's groupings, but to all the information on the Internet. Of course, it would cost more to provide security—including a firewall, an encryption card to send corporate information encrypted, and the Internet Connection Secure Server software on each system.

Figure 6.6. Johnson & Thornbush system configuration in a network computing environment.

The Competitive View of 64-Bit Processing

One other aspect needs to be considered before deciding which computer system does the best job in the long term for your business. That consideration is the turmoil associated with getting your applications to execute as the industry migrates from **16-bit** and **32-bit processing** to **64-bit processing**. As described in "RISC PowerPC AS Microprocessors" in Chapter 1, the AS/400 is based on a 64-bit RISC processor. So are DEC's Alpha and HP's Precision architecture-based systems and Microsoft's NT architecture. In the case of DEC and HP, the processor is 64 bit, but the applications that exist are 16 bit and 32 bit; and because they were *processor-centric* (written with a direct relation to the processor that they were intended to execute on), they must be rewritten to perform in a 64-bit manner on the 64-bit processors. This is not to say that those applications will not run on the 64-bit processors from those vendors, but that they will run as 16-bit or 32-bit applications, dissipating the value of the 64-bit processors they are using.

The NT Architecture defined by Microsoft has the same problem except that rather than being processor-centric, it is *API-centric* and the 16-bit and 32-bit applications must be rewritten to match to the interfaces of a 64-bit world before they can leverage the hardware when it becomes available from Intel, Motorola, Sun, or whoever provides it. The IBM AS/400, because of the **Technology-Independent Machine Interface (TIMI)**, can take applications written for 16-bit or 32-bit environments and translate them (i.e., the applications execute as 64 bit applications) to a 64-bit environment. This translation is intrinsic in the AS/400 system and has happened with each release of new processing hardware, which did not affect the applications that executed from previous releases. Figure 6.7 illustrates the impact of the architectural decision upon the applications for these companies as it relates to the movement to 64-bit processing.

Figure 6.7. Positioning 64-bit processing, a competitive view.

The Business Decisions

In addition to selecting the hardware and software to solve identified business problems, you must also consider financial questions before you install your computer solution. Two important areas that must be addressed are cost justification and the lease or buy decision.

Cost Justification

All businesses are the same in one respect: They exist to make a profit. In the final analysis, the only reason for a business to buy a computer is to increase profits. In other words, the computer system must be **cost justified**. There are two parts to the cost justification analysis: costs and benefits. The price you pay to the computer company is easily identified early in the project. What many people fail to consider are the costs of owning a computer system beyond the original price paid. The costs of operating the computer installation after you buy it should also be considered over several years. Some costs that should be considered beyond the price tag are identified next.

Costs

Hardware Maintenance

This is usually a monthly or annual fee you pay that basically is an extended warranty for the computer hardware. There are various alternatives, but the basic deal is that if your computer system breaks down, the service company will come out and effect repairs at no charge. You do not have to put your system on a maintenance contract, but if you do not you will have to pay an hourly fee and parts costs when your system breaks down. Since this parts/labor billing approach can be extremely expensive, most businesses choose to put their system on a maintenance contract.

Software Maintenance

In some cases, you will have to pay the software supplier a fee to get fixes and updates to your programs. Users who have been purchasing applications that use two-digit year designations in date codes should consult "Year 2000 Challenge," because they may be approaching an expensive software maintenance job unless they are using or have updated to OS/400 Version 3 Release 2 or Version 3 Release 7 or later. IBM is making Version 3 Release 1 and Version 3 Release 6 suitable for development of year-2000-ready applications through the PTF process. Those with this concern should contact their IBM Technical Support Center.

Technical Support

Technical support provides answers to your questions and resolves any technical problems in either the hardware or software. This kind of support ranges from providing a telephone number to having permanently assigned personnel from the computer company on your premises. Sometimes this support is provided free of charge; other times it is on a fee basis. In Chapter 4 and earlier in this chapter ("What about Personal Computers?"), we discussed the relative positioning of the AS/400 and personal computers relative to systems management. Whether you are operating a large, medium, or small business, if you have more than one computer functioning within that business, you have a system management concern. That system management concern has a very real cost associated with it. It is difficult to associate a dollar value because each system configuration is different, but estimates of the cost do exist. Whether you hire someone directly to deal with the concern, do it yourself, or get technical support from an external company, you must pay that cost. *Cost estimates* indicate that for 3 to 40 computers or terminals the cost is one full-time person and increases with the addition of one full-time person for each added 40 computers or terminals.

Facilities

It is often necessary for you to modify your building to accommodate a computer system. These modifications might include adding additional air conditioning, running cables between workstations and the computer, or modifying the electrical power services available. Fortunately, the costs of such building modifications are relatively low with Application Systems as compared with large computers, which often require water cooling and raised floors. The new packaging reduces these costs for new installations, because only the largest systems require two-phase service to operate.

Education/Training

The people who will be using the new computer system will need education. The computer operator(s) will need to understand how to manage the day-to-day operations of the computer. The users of the computer system will have to understand the application programs. It may also be necessary to train your own programmer(s) to write custom application programs for your business. Fortunately, Application Systems are easier to operate and use than larger computer systems. However, some education is still necessary. Many different types of education are available, some of which are discussed later in this chapter.

Communications Line Costs

If your computer system is attached to remote workstations or other remote computers, you will incur communications line costs. There are many different communications services available today, and these costs should be considered in your justification.

Environmental Costs

Environmental costs are the costs to operate the system over a period of time. It has been calculated that the difference in operational costs for an existing System/36 Model D24 and an Advanced 36 over a period of 60 months is $20,220. This difference results from the reduced heat load on air conditioning systems, reduced cost in electrical requirements, and reduced cost of a maintenance agreement. That *cost reduction* will pretty much pay for the new system, and you will reap the benefit of improved performance that increases the efficiency of your workers.

Enhancing Applications

Anytime you either downsize or modify your computer installation to modernize it, it is expected that you will have to pay the cost of updating your applications or purchasing new applications to operate within that new environment. This was dealt with in greater detail in the discussion of application development in Chapter 4, but the one thing you can trust is that your host-centric applications will *not* operate in a distributed client/server-centric environment.

Benefits

On the brighter side, the computer is being purchased to solve identified business problems and/or address new business opportunities. You will receive benefits after the computer system is installed (or else why install it?). Although it is fairly easy to identify and quantify the costs associated with a computer system, it is often difficult to do the same for the benefits. This does not mean that benefits are any less real than costs; it simply means that they require more work to uncover. Benefits are also more specific to your business, so it would be impossible to list all of them here, but we can consider some common benefits associated with the application of computer systems to basic business functions.

Improved Business Cycle

The basic cycle of most businesses has the same components: The business buys goods/equipment, takes customer orders for goods or services, makes deliveries, and bills the customer. The classic application of computer systems to these areas produces improvements in the basic business cycle that result in real dollar savings. These savings can result from such basic things as collecting accounts receivable more quickly and taking better advantage of accounts payable discount terms.

Inventory Reduction

Many carrying costs are associated with a business inventory. These include items such as warehouse space, insurance, taxes, and interest expense. The proper application of computers can reduce the level of inventory that must be kept on hand, thus reducing carrying costs.

Improved Productivity

Given the proper tools, anyone in any part of a business can do his or her job more efficiently. This allows a business to get the same amount of work done more quickly or with less people. Excess time can then be redirected to performing other tasks that help meet the business objectives. Further, as natural attrition reduces the work force, it may not be necessary to hire replacements, allowing for a reduction of the work force over time.

Improved Quality

By providing more timely or better organized information to personnel, businesses can often improve the quality of the services and/or products they provide. This is particularly true in manufacturing environments, in which computers can be applied to everything from design simulations to statistical quality control. It has also been found that providing the needed information in a more timely fashion (reduced wait time) results in fewer errors being made by the users, increasing productivity.

Improved Customer Service

By allowing a business to respond to customer orders, questions, and special requests, computer systems can improve customer service. These improvements can involve quickly responding to requests for price quotations and accurately quoting/meeting delivery dates.

Competitive Advantage

The items that have been discussed contribute to reducing costs, improving quality, and improving customer service, so they all work to improve the competitive posture of the business. The flexibility provided by a computer system can also help improve your competitiveness by allowing you to more quickly respond to changing market demands. The business additionally has the opportunity to use advanced software technology products such as multimedia, telephony, and so on to increase revenues.

This list of general benefits is in no way comprehensive. Every business can add to the list based on its current position and business objectives. Once benefits have been identified, however, you have still not finished. You should try to quantify the benefits in dollars and cents where possible, to help focus on the areas with the largest payoff first. *Quantified benefits* also help when comparing computer investments with any other capital projects under consideration. However, quantifying benefits can be difficult and subject to judgment. Unlike the price of a computer, which can be looked up in a catalog, benefits must be calculated according to expected results.

For example, if you feel that inventory can be reduced by 10 percent by installing an inventory management application program, you would multiply 10 percent of your inventory value times the carrying costs to determine the annual benefit. This is not very difficult, but other areas are more difficult to quantify accurately. For example, if an engineer's productivity is increased by 15 percent, then you might multiply the annual salary and benefit costs by 15 percent, yielding the annual savings. In this case, some would argue that because the engineer is still paid full salary, nothing is saved. However, if the time is devoted to developing a product to enter a new market, for example, the actual benefit may be much higher than 15 percent of the engineer's salary. You will have to decide what a benefit is worth to your business.

Other benefits that are typically difficult to quantify and thus are often overlooked when tallying savings include increased sales (resulting from improved customer service) and lower employee turnover (resulting from improved working conditions and pride). The fact that these benefits (and others like them) are difficult to quantify does not make them any less valuable, but it does mean that they are often overlooked. After the costs and benefits have been quantified, you can begin to evaluate the proposed computer project against other capital projects.

Two often-used guidelines with which to measure a proposed computer system are:

1. The *payback period*, in which the time to recover the investment from accrued benefits is calculated.

2. The *net present value*, in which the cash flows are calculated and then discounted based on the cost of money and risk associated with the project.

Although this type of analysis can be valuable, do not overlook other aspects of the capital project such as its strategic value and its effect on customer perceived quality and professionalism. Classic accounting techniques are easy to defend but do not always reveal the entire picture.

Lease or Buy?

Just when you think you are through analyzing all the software and hardware alternatives, you are faced with a whole new set of questions concerning the acquisition method you will use. Several methods are commonly used to acquire a computer system. The most obvious alternative is to simply pay cash for the computer system—**outright purchase**. This is the least expensive way to acquire a computer system. However, it has a direct and usually substantial impact on the business's cash flow and capital position.

The next acquisition alternative is to finance the purchase price over a period of time, just as you would finance a new house. In this case, you simply make a down payment, typically 10 percent, and take out a loan for the balance. The loan and interest are repaid through monthly payments (over a period of from 2 to 5 years typically). Since you must pay back the interest on the loan, this is a more expensive alternative than a cash purchase, but it can reduce cash flow requirements. In either case the title of the computer system passes to the business, as do any tax benefits such as depreciation.

The purchaser of a computer also has the ability to sell the computer when it is replaced or no longer required, thus recovering the **residual value** of the computer system.

Another acquisition alternative is the **term lease**. In this alternative, the lessor (computer owner) grants use of a computer system to the lessee (the using company), which in turn agrees to make lease payments for some specified period of time or **term**. The term of a lease can be any length, but typically runs from 2 to 5 years. If the lessee decides to terminate the lease before the end of the term, there is usually a termination fee, which can be substantial. Some of the advantages offered by the term lease alternative include the conservation of business capital and lines of credit, which can then be used to finance other investments.

Two commonly found lease types are a **capital lease** and an **operating lease**. Capital leases are rent-to-own, in which, at the end of the term, you can purchase the computer system for a relatively small fee (e.g., 5 or 10 percent of the original cost). With a capital lease, the lessee is considered the owner and gets the tax benefits of ownership. Capital leases are much like a financed purchase, the major difference being that a capital lease does not require the user to make a down payment as does a financed purchase. Operating leases are real leases in which there is no discounted purchase option at the end of the lease term. The lessor is considered to be the owner and thus retains the tax benefits of ownership. Because of this, the lessee typically makes a lower payment than with the capital lease alternative.

A final acquisition alternative is to rent the computer system month by month. This provides the most flexibility, because this kind of arrangement typically requires only 1 to 3 months' notice to discontinue. Of course, you usually must pay higher rental payments to get this flexibility; and because the payment is usually not fixed, you are subject to increases.

The acquisition of computer software is a whole different story. Typically, you will not have the option to buy software. Most companies **license** software. A software license grants the licensee the right to use the software under the conditions specified in the document supplied by the software company, called the **license agreement**. Typically, these licenses allow the licensee to use the software on a specified computer system for a specified fee. Three common ways to pay for this license agreement are *one-time charge, lease,* or *monthly charge*. With the one-time charge, the licensee pays a set price and retains the right to use the software indefinitely. The price can be paid in cash or financed. The leasing alternative is really just another way to finance the one-time charge with no down payment. Finally, the monthly charge is like renting the software month to month indefinitely.

Although some basic lease/purchase alternatives have been introduced in this section, the rules governing these various alternatives are complex and subject to change. The effects on a company's cash flow, income statements, balance sheets, taxes, and so on can also be strongly affected by the various acquisition methods. You should consult the proper professionals to determine the best alternative for your situation.

Education

The discussions in the chapter so far should assist you in selecting the appropriate software and hardware to fit your needs. However, no matter what computer hardware and software you select, they will require people to interact with them. To maximize efficiency, these people or users must be educated in the use of the computer system itself as well as its software. Proper education is critical to the success of any computer automation project. Inadequate education prevents reaping the productivity benefits of moving a task to the computer.

The first goal of education is to make users (and system operators) proficient at using the computer hardware and software they need to do their jobs. Another important goal of education is to make the users' interaction with the computer system enjoyable. If using the computer is enjoyable, users will be more motivated. However, if using the computer is a frustrating struggle (because the users have inadequate education), they will be less productive or perhaps avoid the computer altogether. AS/400-specific education is available from IBM Education and Training, IBM's training subsidiary, as well as from other non-IBM companies.

The IBM Education and Training educational offerings come in the following forms:

- *Classroom courses* are traditional lectures/discussions led by an IBM instructor. These forums provide for direct interaction between students and instructors. Hands-on, in-class exercises are often part of a classroom course. Public courses are held regularly at IBM facilities. Alternately, private courses can be arranged and held either at IBM locations or customer locations.

- *Personalized learning series* courses are basically duplicates of classroom courses except in self-study format. Student are provided with transcriptions of the classroom course lectures in electronic form. Transcribed lectures are loaded on an AS/400 system using a CD-ROM and read on the user's display screen. Also provided is a booklet containing the foils (illustrations) normally presented in the classroom lectures. An additional offering in the self-study format is a set of diskettes containing the self-study courses for the AS/400 that may be loaded on to a personal computer and studied from there.

- *Discover/education series* courses cover additional AS/400-related topics in a format identical to the online education provided as standard with AS/400 systems.

- *Learning centers* are educational facilities where students come in and use the materials just discussed (for a fee) without having to buy them. They also sell these educational offerings.

There is also a set of self-study courses shipped with every AS/400 system. Those courses are listed in Figure 6.8.

Ergonomics

No plan would be complete without addressing the human needs that directly affect the day-to-day productivity of computer users—**ergonomics**. Ergonomics is a science dedicated to investigating the designs for effective interaction between devices and human beings. Human beings have many physiological and psychological characteristics that should

PS586	Self-study	AS/400 Getting to Know Your System
PS587	Self-study	AS/400 Administrator-Work Management and Basic Tuning
PS588	Self-study	AS/400 Administrator-Security Planning and Implementation
PS589	Self-study	AS/400 Administrator-Availability and Recovery Management
PS590	Self-study	AS/400 Administrator Library
PS682	Self-study	Lotus Notes R4 System Administration I: Extending A Notes
PS684	Self-study	Lotus Notes System Admin II: Cross Certificates and Multiple???
PS685	Self-study	Lotus Notes R4 System Admin II: Server Activity and Performance
DE204	Self-study	AS/400 Basic Education Series
DE205	Self-study	AS/400 Implementation Series
DE206	Self-study	Office Vision/400 Support Series
DE208	Self-study	AS/400 Implementation for Entry Systems
DE209	Software	AS/400 Overview and Introductory Topics
PS153	Software	AS/400 Implementation and Operation Series
PS154	Software	COBOL/400 and SQL/400 Programming Series
PS155	Software	RPG/400 and SQL/400 Programming Series
PS156	Software	AS/400 Library
PS163	Software	AS/400 System Using the S/36 Environment
PS164	Self-study	AS/400 System for the Experienced S/38 Implementer
PS274	Self-study	SQL/400 Programming Workshop

Additional information on each of these courses can be obtained by accesing the Internet at *httpf://www.training.ibm.com/ibmedul/news/400f96.htm.*

Figure 6.8. List of self-study courses available for the AS/400 on CD-ROM.

be considered when designing computers, software, desks, lighting, chairs, and so on. Attention to ergonomics increases effectiveness, work quality, health and safety, and job satisfaction.

Application Systems workstations have been designed with careful attention to ergonomics. Everything from the power switch location to the length of the keyboard cable has been scrutinized. Much effort is also expended fine-tuning the ergonomics of most application programs. To get the most out of your Application Systems, you must also provide an ergonomic environment for the users. Organizations such as the **American Optometric Association (AOA)** and the **New York Committee for Occupational Safety and Health (NYCOSH)** as well as IBM have probed deeply into the relationship between the computer and the user. Items such as desks, chairs, lighting, noise, and the like are important to productivity. Some of these steps are inexpensive and easily accomplished. Others may be expensive and accomplished gradually over time. Let us explore some specific steps that will help improve the ergonomics in your environment.

Comfort for the Eyes

The eyes, like any other part of the human body, can get tired as a result of intensive use. This fatigue, called eyestrain, is not new to people who work long hours reading material. With the increase in computer use over recent years, however, we have seen an increase in eyestrain. Although eyestrain is only a temporary condition, it can cause users to feel tired and irritated, particularly if they continue to work under the pressures of deadlines. The eyes function most naturally at distances greater than or equal to arm's length. After all, throughout the majority of history, the eyes were used to pick fruit, not read contracts. When the eyes focus on anything closer than arm's reach, be it a computer terminal or newspaper, they are forced to look inward toward the nose. This is extra work for the muscles that move your eye within its socket, resulting in fatigue. To reduce this effect of fatigue, the computer user should take breaks and go to an area in which the tendency is to focus on more distant objects.

Another factor contributing to eye fatigue results from the work done by a muscle in the eye that reforms the eye's lens to maintain sharp focus. Frequent changes in the distance at which objects are viewed (such as a computer display and a paper on your desk) make the focusing muscles effectively do "push-ups." This also leads to tired eyes. To help prevent these eye "push-ups," it is desirable to put any paper that is frequently referenced during a computer session at the same distance and orientation as the computer screen. A clip-type holder used by secretaries to hold documents as they are typing works well for this. Poor image quality can cause the eyes to constantly change focus in a futile attempt to correct the image. Application Systems terminals provide a high-quality image that helps to minimize eyestrain. As if all this were not enough, there is still another contributor to eye fatigue commonly found in offices, namely, improper lighting. The eye adjusts to all of the light in the field of vision. Unwanted light reflections called glare can appear in the user's field of vision, causing nonuniform light intensities. If the light intensity varies widely, the iris in the eye will continuously expand and contract to adjust for the light-level variance. To reduce the glare in the user's environment, Application Systems displays have an antiglare screen.

Similarly, the workstation (desk, table, etc.) surface should have antiglare or nonreflective surfaces. Windows are big culprits in causing glare, but almost everyone likes windows. You can reduce the amount of glare caused by windows by positioning your computer display screen at right angles to any window. You can also use curtains or (preferably) horizontal blinds to direct the light away from the screen. Diffused office lighting will provide fewer "hot spots" and tend to provide the most uniform light and soften harsh shadows. For using computer displays, 30 to 50 foot-candles of ambient light is optimum. The goal is to have the screen brightness three or four times the ambient light. Since typical offices were originally designed to work with paper, not video displays, there is usually more light than this in an office. This may be difficult to change, depending on the type of lighting used. You can try using fewer or lower-intensity bulbs or fluorescent tubes. Another possibility is to install dimmer switches.

Workstation Comfort

The workstation furniture shared by the computer and the user can also affect productivity. For this reason, attention should be given to the details of the user's workstation; that is, the chair and desk/table to be used. A properly designed chair can help reduce back problems and make the user more comfortable and more productive. An improperly designed chair can lead to reduced alertness and shorter concentration spans. A user may not even be aware of being uncomfortable, yet may unconsciously but constantly seek a more comfortable position.

What makes a chair a good chair? First, because a chair is typically used by many different people during its life with a company, it should be adjustable. The height of the seat pan should adjust from around 16 to 22 inches and should allow the feet to rest flat on the floor. Weight should be distributed through the buttocks, not the thighs. The front of the seat pan should roll off smoothly as in the **waterfall** design to provide for proper blood flow in the legs. A 20-mm compression is about firm enough. Backrests should adjust up or down over a 2-inch range and backward or forward between 80 and 120 degrees for good support. Both the seat pans and the backrests should be upholstered and covered in a material that absorbs perspiration.

If mobility is required, wheels or casters are recommended unless the floor is slippery, making the chair unstable. Hard casters should be used for soft floors and vice versa. A five-legged chair will provide stability and prevent tipping. Seats should swivel if lateral movement is required. Once the users are seated, their relationship with the computer display and keyboard directly affects comfort and thus productivity. The computer display should be positioned properly, with the top of the computer display 10 degrees below eye level and the center of the display at about 20 degrees below eye level and between 14 and 20 inches away. A tilt/swivel stand under the display allows the user to adjust the display angle as desired. Users should avoid bifocal lenses because they force the head to be tipped back while reading the screen.

This can lead to discomfort in the back and shoulders. The keyboard should also be in a comfortable position. Application Systems' separate keyboard, attached by a flexible cable, allows the user to position the keyboard as desired. The keyboard height should be such that the elbow is bent at about 90 degrees when typing. Finally, provide sufficient desk space for documents used during the computer session.

What About Noise?

Noise is not conducive to efficiency. Irregular noise is more distracting than constant noise. Unfortunately, irregular noise is common in the office environment, resulting from nearby conversations, telephones, printers, copy machines, and many other things. If possible, isolate noise sources such as impact printers and copy machines by placing them in isolated areas or separate rooms. Noise can also be reduced by installing doors, carpets, and other sound-insulating materials.

Security

In many business environments, computer systems are the very backbone of business operations. This makes the information stored on the computers a corporate asset at least as valuable as cash. Because of the new methods of accessing the data on your business computer (Internet, intranet), it is necessary to rethink the security aspects of your system. One of the items that distinguishes the AS/400 family from most other computer systems families is the flexibility of its security features. System security has three important objectives:

- **Confidentiality:**

  - Protecting against disclosing information to unauthorized people

  - Restricting access to confidential information

  - Protecting against curious system users and outsiders

- **Integrity:**

  - Protecting against unauthorized changes to data

  - Restricting manipulation of data to authorized programs

  - Providing assurance that data is trustworthy

- **Availability:**

  - Preventing accidental changes or destruction of data

  - Protecting against attempts by outsiders to abuse or destroy system resources

System security is often associated with external threats, such as hackers or business rivals. The intent of these paragraphs is not to minimize the external exposure but to present a more balanced approach to system security. More damage can be caused by the accidental depression of the wrong key at the wrong time. A well-designed security system will provide protection against system accidents by authorized system users.

As with an application, good results from the system security functions cannot be obtained without good planning. Setting up security in small pieces without planning can be confusing and difficult to maintain and to audit. Planning does not imply designing the security for every file, program, and device in advance. Planning *does* imply establishing an overall approach to security on the system and communicating that approach to application designers, programmers, and system users. The following questions need to be considered when planning the security on your system and deciding how much security is needed:

- Is there a company policy or standard that requires a certain level of security?

- Do the company auditors require some level of security?

- How important is your system and the data on it to your business?

- How important is the error protection provided by the security features?

- What are your company security requirements for the future?

Like a business's cash, computer information must be protected from loss or theft. Let us look at how this vital information can be protected.

Loss Prevention

An ever-present hazard when dealing with information (with or without computers) is the possibility that the information will be lost. This loss can occur in many different ways. A computer system's breakdown, such as a disk unit failure, can result in lost information; operator error can cause data to be accidentally corrupted, resulting in lost information; or a disaster (such as a fire or flood) can result in a loss of vital business information. For this reason, **recovery** from the loss of vital business information must be addressed.

One way to deal with the risk of losing vital information is to make backup copies of computer information at regular intervals (e.g., daily). Multiple backup copies should be made on a revolving basis and kept in a place safe from damage or loss. Three copies will allow at least one copy to be kept in safe storage at all times and provide for different levels of backup. In the event of an information loss, the computer system can be restored to the point at which the most recent backup copy was made. Application Systems' operating systems and the various tape devices discussed in Chapter 2 are designed for these kinds of **save/restore** operations. Any changes to information after the point of the last backup will have to be recreated after the backup copy is used to restore the system. This may involve manually reentering the transactions since the last backup or exploiting OS/400 features such as journaling and checksum, discussed earlier in this book.

Any good disaster recovery plan will also consider how the business will operate in the event the current computer system is destroyed. Many companies, including IBM, offer disaster recovery services that essentially provide you with emergency access to a similarly configured computer system located elsewhere. Usually, a test allowance is part of the deal so that you can run disaster recovery drills to ensure readiness. The "AS/400 Backup and Recovery Guide" (SC41-8079), available from IBM, is a good reference when planning your backup strategy.

Theft Prevention

Theft prevention deals with protecting sensitive information from unauthorized disclosure. These security requirements vary widely from environment to environment. Consider your particular needs early in your planning. Application Systems provide various levels of security that help deter unauthorized access. All Applications Systems are now designed to meet the C2 level of security, although the current rating is specifically for Version 2 Release 3, Version 3 Release 0.5, Version 3 Release 1, and Version 4 Release 1 of OS/400, Source Entry Utility, Query/400, SAA Structured Query Language/400, and Common Cryptographic Architecture Services/400.

The AS/400 is the first system to achieve a C2 security rating for a system (hardware and operating system) with an integrated full-function database. The requirements for the C2 level of security are defined by the **United States Department of Defense (DoD)** in the **Trusted Computing Systems Evaluation Criteria (TCSEC)**. Additional detail related to the C2 operating environment can be found in IBM publication "AS/400 Security - Enabling for C2."

AS/400 security is integrated into the computer system hardware along with the associated operating system. Depending on the needs of the user environment, one of *five levels of security* can be activated. The *first* level is basically no security at all. People can access the system and can do anything they wish. The *second* level of security requires the user to enter a password before access is granted to the system. After the proper password is entered, the user can perform any task. The *third* level of security is user access control, which is just like the second level except that the user can be restricted to various functions as well. A security officer is usually assigned to manage the security of the system. The *fourth* level of security adds operating system integrity by restricting the use of certain operating system functions and unsupported interfaces. The *fifth* level enhances the integrity protection provided at the fourth level and is designed to meet the requirements of C2-level security.

For sensitive environments, you may wish to consider restricting access to the area in which the Application Systems itself is located. It may also be necessary to restrict access to the area(s) in which workstations are located. These needs should be considered early in a computer automation project. For additional discussion of security subjects and AS/400 security capabilities obtain "Tips and Tools for Securing Your AS/400" (SC41-3300-00) from your local IBM branch or IBM representative.

Additional Security issues relating specifically to Internet/Intranet security and Operating system security are discussed in Chapters 4 and 5. The complete picture of the security capabilities of the AS/400 systems should include all the discussed offerings and the additional capability of the hardware *keylock function* included with every system.

Service

Although every effort has been made to make Application Systems as reliable as possible, some computers will fail. If yours does, you must have a way of getting it fixed. All Application Systems come with a 1-year warranty that provides free on-site repairs from IBM's service division 7 days a week, 24 hours a day. Each of the various terminals and printers associated with Application Systems has its own warranty terms and periods ranging from 3 months to 3 years. After the warranty period, you become responsible for maintenance of the system.

IBM and other companies offer service agreements that, for a fee, provide postwarranty on-site service just like that provided during the warranty. Various maintenance discounts are available, depending on the level of system management procedures you are willing to implement in your business. Appendix A contains a listing of some of the many IBM Service offerings. If your system fails and you do not have any type of service contract, you will have to pay for parts and labor, which can become extremely expensive. For this reason, most people choose to keep their systems on maintenance after warranty.

Year 2000 Challenge

The AS/400 Division is the first organization in the computer industry to receive the **Information Technology Association of America's (ITAA) ITAA*2000 certification,** the industry's first year-2000-readiness certification program. The certification recognizes AS/400 Advanced Series systems, Advanced 36 included, using OS/400 Version 3 Release 2, Version 3 Release 7, and Version 4 Releases 1 and 2 **and later** as being year-2000-ready now. In addition, these systems have some powerful tools for getting the rest of your applications ready. More information is available on the IBM AS/400 Partners in Development Year 2000 home page at:
http://www.ibm.com/as400/developer/year2000.html

Migrating from System/3X to AS/400

Some businesses may be replacing System/34, System/36, or System/38 computer(s) with an AS/400. AS/400 has been designed to ease the migration of most programs and data from these earlier System/3X computer systems to AS/400. OS/400 functions plus available tools provide a guided and highly automated procedure for these types of migrations. Although programming skills are still required to guide the migration activities, the tools reduce the manual work of analyzing, documenting, saving, and restoring application programs. Programs are migrated to either the AS/400 System/36 Environment or the AS/400 System/38 Environment discussed in Chapter 4. If desired, the programs can be further adapted to take advantage of new AS/400 functions at your own pace after the migration is complete. Now let us look at some topics related to migrating from S/3X to AS/400:

- Sizing a replacement AS/400

- Migrating System/3X I/O devices to the AS/400

- Migrating programs and data from the System/36

- Migrating programs and data from the System/38

- Migrating programs and data from the System/34

Sizing a Replacement AS/400

Whether AS/400 will be your first computer system or you will be replacing a System/36 or System/38, you will have to choose the appropriate size AS/400. "Size" refers to the processor speed and capacity, which by model depends on memory size and amount of disk storage. There are many things to consider when choosing the size AS/400 needed in a given situation. If you are migrating from a System/3X, you can use that system as a starting point for your sizing activity. Here, you know your current memory size, disk storage size, and so on. If you are migrating programs and data from a System/36 to an AS/400, you will need more disk storage and main storage capacity on the AS/400 system than you needed on the System/36 for several reasons: First, the AS/400's operating system (OS/400) takes up significantly more disk space than that of the System/36 (SSP). Further, the AS/400 automatically generates extra program debugging and external data definition information during the migration process that are not present in the System/36. Finally, the "blanks" in programs are not compressed as they were on the System/36.

The net effect of these factors is that load members (object code) will need about 7 times more *disk storage* (this can be reduced to a factor of 2.5 by removing the extra debugging information after migration), source members will require about 3.6 times more disk storage, and data files will require about 1.2 times the space. Mail logs and data dictionaries are approximately the same size on the AS/400 as they are on a System/36. You will also need more main storage when migrating to the AS/400 from a System/36 because the more powerful (and more complex) OS/400 requires more main storage to operate, keeps more information about the current jobs resident in main storage, and uses larger control blocks. The bright side of these facts is that the number of disk storage operations (each of which takes a long time in the context of a computer system) is reduced because more information is in main storage and ready for immediate use.

Those migrating from the System/38 to the AS/400 will also need more disk storage and main storage capacity than they did with the System/38 for similar reasons. In this case, more disk storage space is necessary mostly because of the increased requirements of OS/400. More main storage is needed because more information about each task remains resident in memory. More information in main storage has been a traditional advantage of the System/38 because it makes for better system performance. The AS/400 takes further advantage of the same concept. Whether you are migrating from a System/36 or a System/38, you must also select the correct AS/400 processor model. The performance section of Chapter 1 will give you a rough idea of the relative performance of the various computer systems of interest.

To refine your model selection, you must start by examining your current computer system very closely. Tools like the **Systems Management Facility (SMF)** and the **System/38 Performance Measurement Tools** can be used to determine the workload on your current system. The capacity planner portion of the AS/400 Performance Tools (discussed in Chapter 4) can help analyze your current system to determine which AS/400 model is appropriate. An IBM document that will help in using these sizing tools and determining AS/400 disk storage requirements is the "AS/400 Performance and Capacity Planning Newsletter" (GC21-8175). If you are adding additional functions (programs and data) or more users to the new AS/400 system, you must also consider the effect of these new requirements on performance, memory, and disk storage requirements. IBM personnel have tools and resources available to them to help you size the appropriate AS/400 system.

Migrating System/3X I/O Devices to the AS/400

Most of the twinaxially attached input/output devices, such as terminals and printers, are supported on AS/400 systems. One of the design points of AS/400 was to protect current investments in I/O devices. Not all System/3X I/O devices, however, can be supported by AS/400. These include some old terminals and disk storage devices. These older devices should therefore stay with the System/3X system being replaced, whether it is sold, redistributed, or otherwise disposed of. Information stored on System/3X tape or diskettes can be read by a properly configured AS/400 system. However, because AS/400s do not come standard with a diskette drive, it is possible that System/3X users who use *diskettes as the backup media* (no tape drive) may not be able to exchange information with a particular AS/400. Furthermore, because AS/400 does not support a diskette magazine (a System/3X device that holds a group of diskettes), diskettes must be fed to an AS/400 one at a time.

Transferring large amounts of information one diskette at a time is time-consuming at best and often impractical. For situations like this, the **0059 Transition Data Link** provides an alternative method to move information between a System/3X and an AS/400. The 0059 allows for the direct attachment of an AS/400 system with a System/3X as shown in Figure 6.9. A twinaxial cable, like that used to attach workstations, attaches the 0059 to the workstation controller of each computer system. With this configuration, information can be transferred at twinaxial cable speeds, resulting in efficient information transfer. Dedicating multiple workstation addresses to the 0059 data transfer function (up to seven) can further improve information transfer performance. The 0059 can also be used to attach workstations to both computer systems during migration activities. This allows the user of a single terminal to switch from one system to another by simply striking a key. Although printers can also be attached via the 0059, they can be accessed only by one system or the other, not by both.

Figure 6.9. The 0059 migration data link can be used to transfer information between AS/400 and System/3X computers. It can also be used to provide workstations with access to both systems.

Migrating Programs and Data from the System/36

With the announcement of compatible operation for SSP programs on all models of the AS/400 Advanced Series RISC-based systems (Models 7XX), the migration of System/36 programs and data just got easier. Those who are considering that upgrade must first create a **logical SSP machine** (Advanced 36 models already contain that logical SSP machine, but other AS/400 models must be licensed to use the SSP as an operating system) and then load the application programs and data as described in the previous paragraph. The following can be migrated from a System/36 to an AS/400:

- Source members for programs, screen formats, messages, and menus

- Procedures

- Data files and alternative indexes

- Libraries

- Folders

- Data dictionaries

- Security and master configuration information

You can also migrate the following items (e.g., files, folders, directories) used by System/36 SSP and licensed programs:

- Advanced Printer Function (APF)

- Business Graphics Utilities/36 (BGU/36)

- Data File Utility (DFU) programs

- Distributed Data Management (DDM)

- Multiple Session Remote Job Entry (MSRJE)

- PC Support/36

- Personal Services/36

- Query/36

Migrating Programs and Data from the System/38

The migrating of System/38 programs and data is accomplished using the same basic steps as migrating from the System/36. You first load the System/38 Migration Aid on the System/38. You can then analyze and select the objects (data, libraries, files, and programs) to be migrated. The purpose of this step is to look for things that must be changed to work properly on an AS/400 system. You can select objects to be migrated by libraries, categories, and other groupings, or you can choose to migrate the entire system. The System/38 objects to be migrated are then transferred to the AS/400 through diskette, tape, or a communications link. Once on the AS/400 system, facilities are available to make the necessary changes to System/38 objects.

Personal Services/38 documents and virtual disks are automatically converted to be usable by AS/400. Unlike System/36 programs, System/38 programs can be transported to AS/400 as object code that is automatically adapted (reencapsulated) to run on AS/400 without recompiling. This is true for programs written in RPG III, COBOL '74, PL/1, BASIC, or Command Language (CL). Because a few things are supported on System/38 but not on AS/400 (96-column cards and diskette magazines), consideration must be given to programs using those items. As with System/36 migration, menus provide guidance throughout the migration process and reports show the status of migration activities. Since AS/400's architecture is based on that of the System/38, the migration of programs and data is more direct than when migrating from the System/36, this is true whether the processor architecture is IMPI or RISC. For the same reason, you do not pay a significant performance penalty when running System/38 programs as you do when you run System/36 programs (except when the System/36 programs are run on a licensed SSP operating system). The following can be migrated from the System/38:

- User profiles

- Most system configuration descriptions.

- User libraries, including library QGPL (General Purpose Library)

- Objects in user libraries, except for

  - Printer Images

  - Documents

  - Document lists

  - Edit descriptions

  - User-defined message queues

  - Card files

- Many of the system values

Another migration aid, called the **System/38 Utilities**, runs on the AS/400 and provides support for programs written using the System/38 Data File Utility and Query/38. The Text Management/38 functions of this tool also provide word processing capabilities to AS/400 users not using OfficeVision/400. The AS/400 document that discusses the details of this migration is "Migrating from System/38 Planning Guide" (GC21-9624).

Migrating Programs and Data from the System/34

Users of the IBM System/34, a predecessor to the System/36, can also migrate many of their programs to AS/400 systems. As with the System/36, System/34 programs and data are first saved to diskettes and then restored on an AS/400. Optionally, the **System/34 to System/36 Migration Aid (5727-MA1)** can be used to identify missing source members and provide an audit trail during this process. System/34 programs can be modified if necessary, recompiled, and run in OS/400's System/36 Environment. As with the System/36, BASIC subroutines must be converted to source code. The migration of System/34 Data File Utility routines, security, and configuration members is a manual process. A technical newsletter, "System/34 to AS/400 Migration Tips" (GC21-8161), is helpful in such migrations.

Migrating C, D, E, and F 9402, 9404, and 9406 Models to the Advanced Series

Most of the I/O processing adapters used on the old models will be usable on the new system unit package. In some cases, disk units and tape units in particular, I/O devices will require repackaging to properly adapt to the new system unit package. The 9402 and 9404 base and expansion towers must be replaced. The 9406 system unit racks are convertible to expansion/extension racks with the removal of the system unit. The 9406 rack-mounted devices and expansion/extension units may be attached to the new system units. In the new system units, processors, expansion memory cards, MultiFunction I/O Processor cards, and battery backup units are unique to the Version 4 Release 1 and 2 hardware. In general, B-level hardware cannot be migrated.

Migrating Advanced Series 20X/30X System Units to AS/400e server System Units: CISC to RISC

Because the RISC processor and memory interface has changed relative to the CISC processor/memory interface, it is necessary to change the backplane to migrate the system units. The processors and memory from the CISC models must be replaced, and no net-priced exchange of memory cards is supported. All of the I/O and IOPs are preserved and can be used with the new models, except in the case of the Model 150 or Model 170 or a non-expanded version of the Model 720 which use only PCI based I/O adapters. Also over time, some of the lower capacity internal disk and tape units are migrated because the performance impact on the new system is too large as a result of the low performance interfaces supported by those devices. See Chapter 2 for a listing of the devices which are supported, or contact your IBM representative. All of the expansion units can be migrated. The new method for preserving the contents of main storage does not make it necessary to change the batteries. For migrating programs and data from the CISC-based system to the RISC-based system, it is recommended that the user obtain a copy of the "AS/400 Road Map for Changing to PowerPC Technology" (SA41-4150-01) and follow its suggestions religiously.

System Performance Tables for AS/400 Systems

System Performance of AS/400 systems prior to V3R6 are presented to allow comparison to the V4R4 performance capabilities for those older systems. Figures 6.10 through Figure 6.15 illustrate the performance capabilities of all previous AS/400 system and processor models.

484 EXPLORING IBM AS/400 COMPUTERS

Model/Feat. Code	V3R6 CPW Value	V3R7 CPW Value	% Increase Over V3R6	V4R1 CPW Value	% Increase Over V3R7
400/2130	12.3	13.8	12	13.8	0
400/2131	18.3	20.6	13	20.6	0
400/2132	24.5	27.0	10	27.0	0
400/2133	30.6	33.3	9	35.0	5
500/2140	18.7	21.4	14	21.4	0
500/2141	26.9	30.7	14	21.4	0
500/2142	38.3	43.9	15	43.9	0
510/2143	66.7	77.7	16	81.6	5
510/2144	85.0	104.2	23	111.5	7
530/2150	107.1	131.1	22	148	13
530/2151	132.5	162.7	23	188.2	16
530/2152	198.7	278.8	40	319.0	14
530/2153	299.0	459.3	54	598.0650	30
530/2162	349.8	509.9	46	650.0	27

Figure 6.10. AS/400 Advanced System—V4R2 Performance for V3R6 general-purpose-based processors as a result of V4R2 actions.

Model/Feature Code	V3R6 CPW Value	V3R7 CPW Value	% Increase Over V3R6	V4R1 CPW Value	% Increase Over V3R7
40S/2109	24.5/8.4	27.0/9.4	10/12	27.0/9.4	0/0
40S/2110	30.6/12.3	33.3/13.8	9/12	35.0/14.5	5/5
40S/2111	52.9/18.3	59.8/20.6	13/13	63.0/21.6	5/5
40S/2112	77.3/26.9	87.3/30.7	13/14	91.0/32.2	5/5
50S/2120	66.7/18.7	77.7/21.4	16/14	81.6/22.5	5/5
50S/2121	85.0/26.9	104.2/30.7	23/14	111.5/32.8	7/7
50S/2122	106.8/26.9	130.7/30.7	23/14	138.0/32.8	5/7
53S/2154	132.5/26.9	162.7/30.7	23/14	188.2/32.8	16/7
53S/2155	198.7/26.9	278.8/30.7	40/14	319.0/32.8	16/7
53S/2156	299.0/26.9	459.3/30.7	54/14	598.0/32.8	30/7
53S/2157	349.8/26.9	509.9/30.7	46/14	650.0/32.8	27/7

Figure 6.11. AS/400 Advanced Server CV4R1 Performance for V3R6 server-based processors as a result of V4R1 actions.

Model Group	Feature Code	Memory Capacity (MB, min-max)	Disk Capacity (GB, min-max)	Relative Performance Ratings		Relative System Performance Metric (CPW Value)
				Internal Processor	System (RAMP-C)	
200	2030	8-24	1.03-23.6	2.5	2.5	7.3
	2031	8-56	1.03-23.6	4.0	4.0	11.6
	2032	16-128	1.03-23.6	5.8	6.2	16.8
300	2040	8-72	1.03-117.4	4.0	4.2	11.6
	2041	16-80	1.03-117.4	5.8	6.0	16.8
	2042	32-160	1.03-117.4	7.2	7.5	21.1
310	2043	64-832	1.03-159.3	10.9	12.0	33.8
	2044	64-832	1.03-159.3	19.0 (2)*	20.2	56.5 (2)*
320	2050	128-1536	1.03-259.6	23.2	25.7	67.5
	2051	128-1536	1.03-259.6	41.3 (2)*	45.8	120.3 (2)*
	2052	128-1536	1.03-259.6	61.2 (4)*	71.5	177.4 (4)*

Power PC Models						
400	2130	32-160	1.96-23.6	3.8	4.1	12.3
	2131	32-224	1.96-23.6	5.7	6.1	18.3
	2132	32-224	1.96-23.6	8.3	8.7	24.5
	2133	32-224	1.96-23.6	10.6	10.9	30.6
436	2102	32-224	1.96-23.6	1.0 (SSP mode)	4.8 (OS/400 mode)	14.4 (OS/400 mode)
	2104	32-224	1.96-23.6	1.3 (SSP mode)	6.1 (OS/400 mode)	18.3 (OS/400 mode)
	2106	64-256	1.96-23.6	2.4 (SSP mode)	8.7 (OS/400 mode)	24.5 (OS/400 mode)
500	2140	64-768	1.96-151	5.7	6.4	18.7
	2141	64-768	1.96-151	8.3	9.3	26.9
	2142	64-1024	1.96-151	11.4	12.6	38.3
510	2143	256-1024	1.96-318.7	19.7	21.6	66.7
	2144	256-1024	1.96-318.7	26.6	28.5	85.0
530	2150	512-4096	1.96-520	32.9	37.4	107.1
	2151	512-4096	1.96-520	43.4	48.9	132.5
	2152	512-4096	1.96-520	66.6 (2)*	74.0	198.7 (2)*
	2153	512-4096	1.96-520	101.4 (4)*	119.2	299.0 (4)*

Figure 6.12. Relative performance of AS/400 Advanced System (CICS and PowerPC RISC models).

Model Group	Feature Code	Memory Capacity (MB, min-max)	Disk Capacity (GB, min-max)	Relative Performance Ratings (RPR, B10=1.0)		Relative System Performance Metric (CPW Value)
				Internal Processor	System (RAMP-C)	
9401	P02	8-16	1.0-2.1	2.5	2.1	7.3
	P03-2114	8-24	1.03-2.99	2.5	2.5	7.3
	P03-2115	8-40	1.96-3.93	3.3	3.3	9.6
	150-2169/70	32-96	4-16			10.9
	PO3-2117	8-56	1.96-3.93	5.8	3.9	16.8
9402	C04	8-12	0.6-1.3	1.0	1.1	3.1
	C06	8-16	0.6-1.3	1.3	1.3	3.6
	D02	8-16	0.8-1.2	1.3	1.3	3.8
	D04	8-16	0.8-1.6	1.5	1.5	4.4
	E02	8-24	1.0-2.0	1.5	1.5	4.5
	D06	8-20	0.8-1.6	1.9	1.9	5.5
	E04	8-24	1.0-4.0	1.9	1.9	5.5
	F02	8-24	1.0-2.1	1.9	1.9	5.5
	F04	8-24	1.0-4.1	2.5	2.5	7.3
	E06	8-40	1.0-7.9	2.5	2.6	7.3
	F06	8-40	1.0-8.2	3.3	3.3	9.6
9404	B10	4-16	0.6-1.9	1.0	1.0	2.9
	C10	8-20	0.6-1.9	1.3	1.3	3.9
	B20	4-28	0.6-3.8	1.7	1.7	5.1
	C20	8-32	0.6-3.8	1.8	1.8	5.3
	D10	8-32	0.8-4.8	1.8	1.9	5.3
	C25	8-40	0.6-3.8	2.1	2.2	6.1
	D20	8-40	0.8-4.8	2.3	2.4	6.8
	E10	8-40	1.0-19.7	2.6	2.6	7.6
	D25	16-64	0.8-6.4	3.3	3.4	9.7
	F10	8-72	1.0-20.6	3.3	3.4	9.6
	E20	8-72	1.0-19.7	3.3	3.5	9.7
	F20	16-80	1.0-20.6	4.0	4.2	11.6
	E25	16-80	1.0-19.7	4.0	4.2	11.8
	F25	16-80	1.0-20.6	4.7	4.8	13.7

Figure 6.13. Relative performance of AS/400 Systems (9401, 9402, and 9404 models).

Application Systems and Your Business **487**

Feature Code	MemoryCapacity (MB, min-max)	Disk Capacity (GB, min-max)	Relative Performance Ratings (RPR, B10=1.0)		Relative System Performance Metric (CPW Value)
			Internal Processor	System (RAMP-C)	
B30	4-36	0.6-13.7	1.3	1.4	3.8
B35	8-40	0.6-13.7	1.5	1.6	4.6
B40	8-40	0.6-13.7	1.8	2.0	5.2
B45	8-40	0.6-13.7	2.3	2.3	6.5
D35	8-72	1.3-67.0	2.5	2.6	7.4
B50	16-48	0.6-27.4	3.3	3.2	9.3
E35	8-72	1.3-67.0	3.3	3.4	9.7
D45	16-80	1.3-67.0	3.7	3.7	10.8
D50	32-128	1.3-98.0	4.5	4.8	13.3
E45	16-80	1.3-67.0	4.7	4.8	13.8
F35	16-80	2.0-67.0	4.7	4.8	13.7
B60	32-96	0.654.8	5.1	5.2	15.1
F45	16-80	2.0-67.0	5.9	6.0	17.1
E50	32-128	1.3-98.0	6.2	6.4	18.1
B70	32-192	0.6-54.8	6.8	7.0	20.0
D60	64-192	1.3-146	8.1	8.3	23.9
F50	64-192	2.0-114	9.5	10.2	27.8
E60	64-192	1.3-146	9.7	10.2	28.1
D70	64-256	1.3-146	10.9	11.2	32.3
E70	64-256	1.3-146	13.5	14.2	39.2
F60	128-384	2.0-146	13.7	14.7	40.0
D80	64-384	2.0-146	19.0 (2)*	19.8	56.6 (2)*
F70	128-512	2.0-256	18.9	21.0	57.0
E80	64-512	1.3-256	23.8 (2)*	25.2	69.4 (2)*
E90	64-1024	1.3-256	32.6 (3)*	34.4	96.7 (3)*
F80	128-768	2.0-256	33.5 (2)*	36.5	97.1 (2)*
E95	64-1152	1.3-256	40.2 (4)*	42.1	116.6 (4)*
F90	128-1024	2.0-256	43.8 (3)*	50.5	127.7 (3)*
F95	128-1280	2.0-256	51.0 (4)*	59.0	148.8 (4)*
F97	128-1536	2.0-256	61.2 (4)*	71.5	177.4 (4)*

Note: *The number in parentheses shows the number of CPUs contained in that model.

Figure 6.14. Relative performance of AS/400 System 9405 models.

Model Group	Feature Code	Memory Capacity (MB, min-max)	Disk Capacity (GB, min-max)	Relative Performance Ratings (RPR, B10=1.0) Internal Processor C/S Interactive	Relative System Performance Metric (CPW Value) C/S Interactive
9402	S01	8-56	1.96-3.9	5.9-1.9	17.1-5.5
	100	16-56	1.0-7.9	5.9-1.9	17.1-5.5
9404	135	32-384	1.0-27.5	10.9-3.3	32.3-9.6
	140	64-512	1.0-47.2	22.5-4.0 (2)*	65.6-11.6 (2)*
20S	2010	16-128	1-23.6	5.9-1.9	17.1-5.5
2FS	2010	16-128	1-7.8	5.9-1.9	17.1-5.5
2SS	2010	16-128	1-7.8	5.9-1.9	17.1-5.5
2SG	2010	16-128	1-7.8	5.9-1.9	17.1-5.5
30S	2411	32-384	1-86.5	10.9-3.3	32.3-9.6
	2412	64-832	1-86.5	23.5-4.0 (2)*	68.5-11.6 (2)*
40S	2109	32-224	1.96-23.6	8.3-2.6	24.5-8.4
	2110	32-224	1.96-23.6	10.6-3.8	30.6-12.3
50S	2120	64-1024	1.96-318.7	19.7-5.7	66.7-18.7
	2121	64-1024	1.96-318.7	26.6-8.3	85.0-26.9
53S	2154	512-4096	1.96-520	43.4-8.3	132.5-26.9
	2155	512-4096	1.96-520	66.6-8.3 (2)*	198.7-26.9 (2)*
	2156	512-4096	1.96-520	101.4-8.3 (4)*	299.0-26.9 (4)*

The number in parentheses shows the number of CPUs contained in that model.

Figure 6.15. Relative performance of AS/400 Advanced Servers CISC and RISC models.

Appendix A
AS/400 System Support Services

The following list identifies and briefly describes the system support services available for the AS/400 family of systems as well as the older S36 and S38. It is adapted with IBM's permission from IBM document G325-0740-03.

- **AS/400 PerformanceEdge** provides standard maintenance agreement services with 24-hour telephone access to technical hardware support, on-site access to IBM customer engineers, plus AS400 Service Director, PM/400-subset, and AS/400 Forum.

- **AS/400 and AS/400 Advanced 36 Support Line** provides prime shift 2-hour response, access via IBMLink, management activity reports detailing usage, additional contacts option, and software defect and usage questions answered by Rochester specialists.

- **AS/400 and AS/400 Advanced 36 Associate** will assign a specific support representative who possesses in-depth knowledge of your account and system, is your advocate to pursue technical concerns and questions beyond the limits of the Support Line service, and will call you back within an hour during prime shift.

- **AS/400 and AS/400 Advanced 36 Consult Line** provides you access to experts in such areas as availability and recovery; systems management; communications, including multiple platforms, personal computers, and LANs; cooperative processing; client/server applications; system migration; rightsizing; database design; application design; and other areas to meet your needs.

- **PM/400** performs many of the resource-intensive manual operations required to record and track system throughput and response. It helps you maintain optimal system performance and plan future capacity requirements with minimal resources, and it provides reports by schedule or on demand.

- **AS/400 Forum** provides access to the cumulative experiences of the AS400 community from which you can share technical ideas, tips, and techniques of other midrange professionals. In addition, you have access to a software tools repository for downloading both source and object code.

- **AS/400 Alert** will make you aware of critical software and hardware fixes, which could cause system interruptions and expensive system downtime. System availability can be improved by anticipating and preventing problems before they occur.

- **AS/400 VitalSign** is a systems administration assessment that evaluates your existing system administration practices and provides comments and recommendations specific to your business and IS operations. This is done by collecting information from your system and using an interactive questionnaire to gather customer input.

- **AS/400 Recovery Express** provides an entry-level recovery service from IBM Business Recovery Services. This service is provided to assist customers in responding to an unplanned interruption of critical information processing (disaster) at a specified location due to causes beyond the customer's control.

- **AS/400 SiteManager** alerts you to small problems before they become disasters. It monitors your hardware, business applications, and systems environment, and alerts you to problem conditions 365 days a year, day and night.

- **AS/400 RemoteInstall** provides a remote installation service to keep you current on the latest releases and software fixes (PTFs).

- **IBM HouseCall** provides scheduled assistance at your location for basic, task-oriented services. Specialists trained on each hardware platform are available to work at your place of business.

- **AS/400 Support Solutions** supplements your technical staff with AS/400 experts to provide, either on site or remotely, services such as performance and capacity planning, cooperative processing, client/server, client series, application design reviews/application development, recovery readiness exams, installation services, availability and recovery audits, security audits, or voice integration programs.

- **AS/400 SysMigration** provides an IBM specialist to assist in moving data and applications from existing systems to new systems using tape to restore.

- **AS/400 SoftInstall** provides customers with expert planning, verification, installation, and education for all new OS/400 releases. This service offering is used for all new OS/400 releases. This service offering is used for all release-to-release upgrades.

- **AS/400 Advanced 36 Installation** provides IBM specialists who will assist customers with the installation of their new Advanced 36 system.

- **AS/400 SmoothStart** provides an IBM specialist on site with customers to assist with the installation of their new AS400 system.

- **AS/400 GigMigration** provides an IBM specialist to assist with the DASD data migration from an existing system to a new configuration.

- **AS/400 Gopher Client Internet Installation** provides an IBM specialist to assist customers in connecting their AS/400 to the Internet.

- **AS/400 Novell Client Works** provides an IBM specialist to enable customers to successfully install and configure ClientAccess/400 (or PC Support) on PCs that must access Novell servers at the same time.

- **AS400 OMEGAMON/400 Installation** provides an IBM specialist to assist in getting this software in production and running quickly.

- **AS/400 Version 3, Release 6 System Transition Services (SysTransition)** provides an IBM specialist to plan, transition, and verify the transition of your current IMPI-based system to the new AS/400 RISC-based PowerPC processor. This service is comprised of three offerings: (1) Upgrade Assistant, (2) System Transition, and (3) Total Project Management.

- **SmoothStart Service for Lotus Notes** provides planning, installation, and configuration of Lotus Notes for the AS/400 FSIOP Server, and also provides on-site installation training.

- **Integration Services for OS/400 for Novell Netware** provides installation of OS/400 software features and PTFs, integration of Novell Netware into your OS/400 Operating System, and integration of the new AS/400 server into your new or existing Novel Network.

- **AS/400 Security Review** provides an IBM specialist to assist the customer in running the OS/400 provided security tool to analyze their system security procedures.

- **SmoothStart Service for Web Server/400 from I-Net, Inc.** provides the install, configure, and tailor the INet Web Server/400 to allow your business to be connected to the World Wide Web.

- **Planning for Internet Connection for AS/400** is a planning service to provide information and guidance to determine which are the best functions of your AS/400 to offer Internet users.

- **SmoothStart Service for Internet Connection for AS/400** provides for the AS/400 HTTP Web Server to be installed and configured. Gain visibility on the Internet with your own home page, and reach your clients around the world through Web servers.

- **AS/400 BRMS Installation Services** provides an IBM specialist to assist with the planning and implementation of the plan to install and operate Backup Recovery Media Services.

Appendix B

User Groups

In addition to the AS/400 technical conferences, which are conducted every year by IBM and other companies, yet another educational forum is provided by user groups. **Guide, Share,** and **Common** are the user groups most easily recognizable to users of IBM equipment. Guide and Share are user groups associated with the enterprise- or mainframe-sized systems and are of interest to those readers who will network their AS/400 with a mainframe system. Common is a large association of IBM users of small and midrange systems. Like Guide and Share, it is a member-run organization, although IBM provides considerable support. Common has two national conferences each year in the United States (April and October), as well as one in Europe each May, run by European Common. There is a large MAPICS user group within Common, and each conference has many sessions on using the various functions in MAPICS, and others on upcoming enhancements. You can contact Common at:

> Common
> 401 North Michigan Avenue
> Chicago, IL 60611-4267
> Phone: (312) 644-6610
> Fax: (312) 565-4658

Common also has user groups in other countries that meet at various times each year: Common Peru, Common Australasia, and Common Europe. Information on the times for meetings of these groups located outside of the United States may be obtained from the Common location identified earlier.

Share and Guide are primarily related to mainframe systems functions. However, because the relationship between mainframe systems and the midrange systems covered by the AS/400 is no longer obvious, contacts for those user groups are provided to enable the potentially needed information exchange.

Share can be contacted by either mail or phone at:
Share U.S.
401 N. Michigan Ave.
Chicago, IL 60611-4267
Phone: (312) 822-0932
Fax: (312) 321-6869

Guide or G.U.I.D.E. user groups can be reached at:
Guide International Corporation
401 N. Michigan Ave.
Chicago, IL 60611-4267
Phone: (312) 644-6610

G.U.I.D.E. Headquarters
c/o Schindler Information, Ltd.
CH-6030
Ebikon, Switzerland
Phone: +44-41-33-28-27

Appendix C
TCP/IP Protocols, Servers, and Services

TCP/IP Servers and Services:

- GUI Configuration support

- File Transfer Protocol (FTP) client and server

- Simple Mail Transfer Protocol (SMPT)

- Post Office Protocol (POP) version 3

- IBM HTTP server (HTTP)

- Web-based Administration server

- Network File System (NFS) client and server

- Domain Name Service (DNS) server

- IP Printing to HP-compatible network printers

- Line printer daemon (LPD) server
- Line printer requester (LPR)
- 5250/HTML workstation gateway
- TELNET client and server
- REXEC client and server
- BOOTP server
- Remote IPL TFTP server
- REXEC client (Run Remote Command - RUNRMTCMD)
- Dynamic Host Configuration Protocol (DHCP) server
- Internet Key Exchange (IKE) server
- Layer 2 Tunneling Protocol (L2TP) server (LNS)

TCP/IP Protocols Supported:

- Transmission Control Protocol (TCP)
- User Datagram protocol (UDP)
- Internet Protocol (IP)
- Simple network management protocol (SNMP)
- APPC over TCP/IP
- Internet protocol over SNA
- Network status (NETSTAT)
- Packet Internet grouper (PING)

- Internet control message protocol (ICMP)
- Address resolution protocol (ARP)
- Proxy address resolution protocol (Proxy ARP)
- Routing information protocol (RIP) ver 1 and 2
- Sockets application program interface (API)
- IP multilink load balancing
- Serial line internet protocol (SLIP)
- Point-to-Point protocol (PPP)
- SOCKS proxy enablement
- UDP multicast support
- CORBA ORB
- IP Security (IPSec)
- Internet Security Association Key Management Protocol (ISAKMP)
- Layer 2 Tunneling Protocol (L2TP)

Physical Interfaces to TCP/IP:

- IBM token-ring LAN
- Ethernet LAN
- Ethernet 100 Mb LAN
- Distributed data interface (DDI - fiber or STP)
- Frame relay

- Wireless (LAN)
- X.25 (PVC and SVC)
- X.25 over ISDN
- Integrated PC Server LAN
- Asynchronous Support
- ATM
- Twinax

Appendix D
EZ-Setup Wizard

The following screen captures illustrate the operation of the EZ-Setup Wizard. As the user provides responses to the questions asked by the EZ-Setup Wizard about the desired computer environment, the AS/400 system becomes adapted to fit that environment.

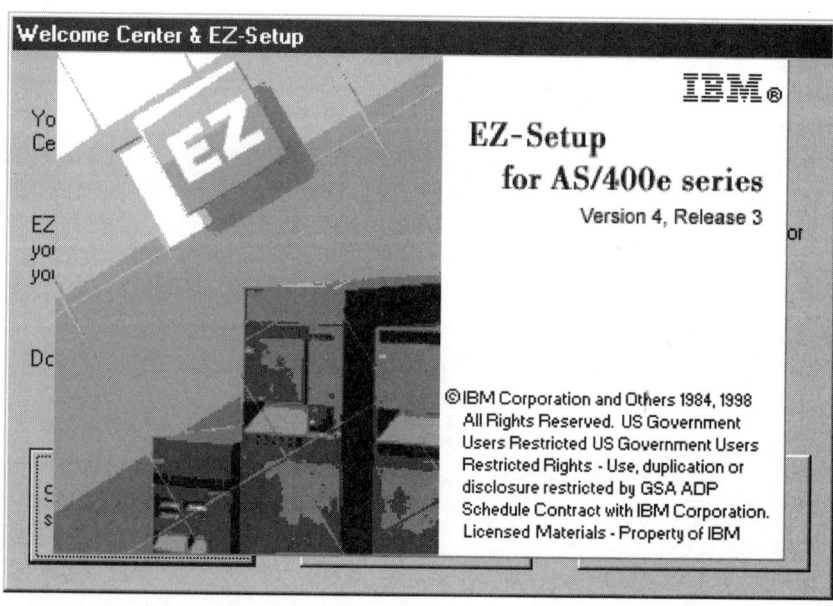

AS/400 EZ-Setup Wizard 501

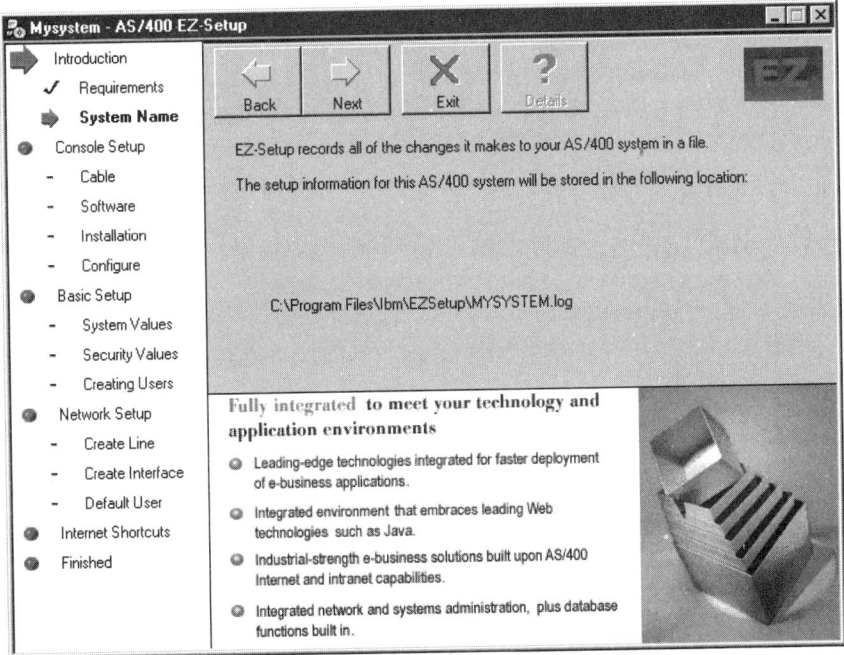

502 EXPLORING IBM AS/400 COMPUTERS

AS/400 EZ-Setup Wizard

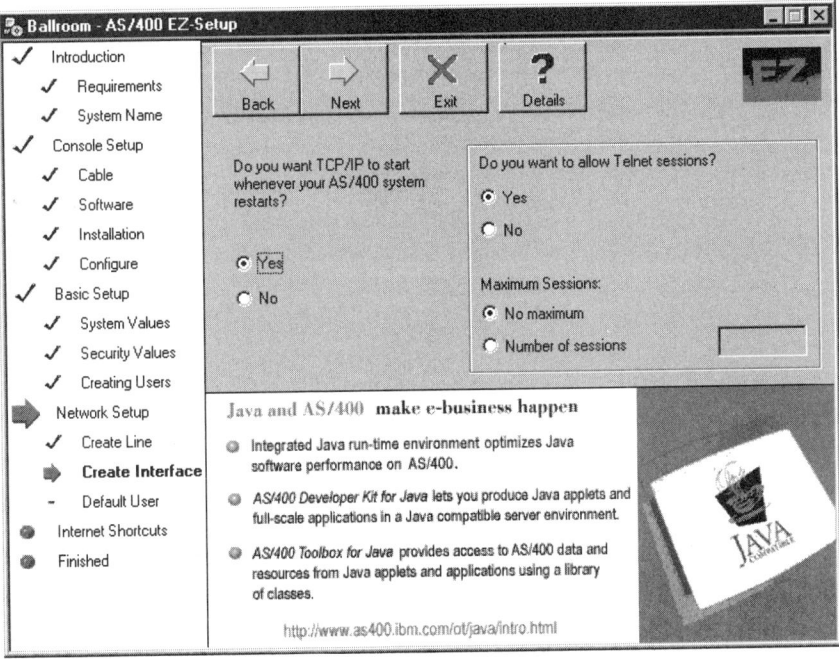

504 EXPLORING IBM AS/400 COMPUTERS

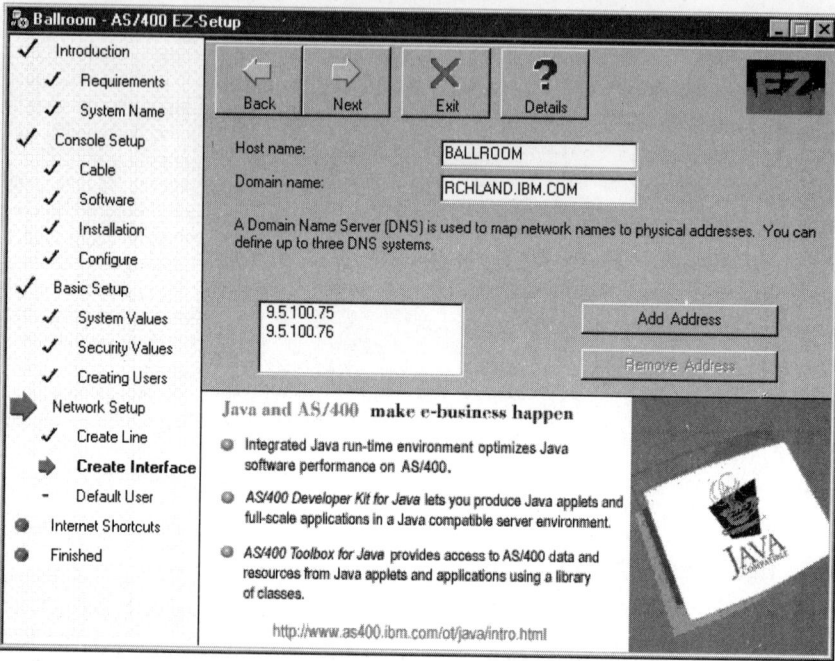

Appendix E

Security Wizard

The AS/400 continues the theme of making the system easier to interface to by providing a security wizard to assist in the setting up of the security function with a Windows-like methodology. The security wizard asks questions about the AS/400 system and recommends how base system security should be configured. It is possible to apply some or all of the recommendations or to save the recommendations for later application. If the decision is to save the recommendations, the next time the security wizard is executed, the recommendations can be applied from the first screen. If changes are applied, the next time the wizard is started, a "reset changes" option appears on the first page to change the security configuration back to what it was before the changes were applied.

The security wizard generates an administrator report showing the recommended settings and how those settings affect the behavior of the system. The security wizard also generates a user report containing the information that users need to know about the system, including password composition rules and job time-out intervals.

Both reports are NLS enabled and are saved as test files that can be loaded into an editor or work processor.

To provide a flavor for what the security wizard contains, 8 of the screens are reproduced below. The first two screens introduce the appearance of the wizard, and the final six screens present the appearance of the results after execution of the wizard.

Security Wizard **507**

508 EXPLORING IBM AS/400 COMPUTERS

Security Wizard

Appendix F

Multiple Upgrade Paths

The following figures illustrate the upgrade paths from previous models of the AS/400 to the V4R4 models and the recommended upgrade paths within the V4R4 models. These figures were moved to this appendix because they interrupted to flow of the text, and also made it difficult for the reader to maintain continuity with what was being read.

From: Processor	To: 2159	2160	2164	2176	2183	2289	2290	2291	2292	2385	2386	2388
2159		X	X	X	X					X	X	X
2160			X	X	X					X	X	X
2164				X	X					X	X	X
2176					X					X	X	X
2183											X	X
2289						X	X	X	X	X		
2290							X	X	X	X	X	
2291								X	X	X	X	X
2292										X	X	X
2385											X	X
2386												X

Figure F.1. Migration from AS/400e server 170 to AS/400e server 170.

From: Model/Processor	To: Model ISV 2340	Model ISV 2341
S20-ISV/2170		X
S20-ISV/2177	X	X
S20-ISV/2178	X	X
S30-ISV/2320	X	X
S30-ISV/2321	X	X
S30-ISV/2322	X	X

Figure F.2. Custom mixed-mode servers upgrade.

From: Model/Processor	To: Model SB1 2312	Model SB1 2313
SB1/2310	X	X
SSB1/2311	X	X
SB1/2312		X

Figure F.3. Upgrades to new custom application servers.

From: Model/Processor	Interactive Capacity	740/2069 1514	740/2069 1510	740/2069 1511	740/2069 1512	740/2070 1514	740/2070 1510	740/2070 1511	740/2070 1512	740/2070 1513
S20/2170	1490	X				X				
S20/2177	1491	X				X				
S20/2178	1492		X	X			X	X		
S30/2320	1492		X	X			X	X		
S30/2321	1493		X	X	X		X	X	X	
S30/2322	1494		X	X	X		X	X	X	X
S40/2340	1495			X	X			X	X	X
S40/2341	1496								X	X

Figure F.4. Model and processor upgrades custom mixed-mode servers to 740.

512 EXPLORING IBM AS/400 COMPUTERS

From: Model/Processor	Interactive Capacity	To: 720/2061				720/2062					720/2063				720/2064					
		150	150	101	102	150	150	101	102	103	150	150	102	103	150	150	101	102	103	104	105
236/2100																					
400/2130		X	X																		
400/2131		X	X	X																	
400/2132		X	X	X	X	X	X														
400/2133		X	X	X	X	X	X	X	X	X											
436/2102		X	X	X	X	X	X	X	X	X											
436/2104		X		X	X	X		X	X	X											
436/2106				X	X			X	X	X											
500/2140		X	X	X	X																
500/2141		X	X	X	X	X		X	X	X											
500/2142			X	X	X				X	X											
510/2143				X	X						X	X	X	X		X	X				
510/2144					X							X	X	X			X	X			
600/2129		X	X	X	X	X	X	X	X	X											
600/2134		X	X	X	X		X	X	X	X											
600/2135			X	X	X			X	X	X									X			
600/2136				X	X		X	X	X	X	X	X	X	X							
620/2175			X	X	X			X	X	X	X	X	X	X							
620/2179				X	X			X	X	X	X	X	X	X			X	X	X	X	
620/2180					X				X	X		X	X	X		X	X	X	X	X	X
620/2181					X				X	X				X			X	X	X	X	X
620/2182					X					X				X						X	X

Figure F.5. RISC to 720 models and processor upgrades.

From: Model/Processor	Interactive Capacity	To: 740/2069				To: 730/2070				
		154	150	151	152	154	150	151	152	1510 3
530/2153			X	X	X		X	X	X	X
530/2162			X	X	X		X	X	X	X
620/2182			X	X	X		X	X	X	X
640/2238			X	X	X		X	X	X	X
640/2239			X	X	X		X	X	X	X
650/2240				X	X			X	X	X
650/2243					X				X	X
650/2188									X	X
650/2189										

Figure F.6. Model and processor upgrades 9406 systems to 740.

From: Model/Processor	Interactive Capacity	To: 740/2069				To: 740/2070				
		154	150	151	152	154	150	151	152	153
53S/2156		X				X				
53S/2157		X				X				
S20/2165		X				X				
S20/2166		X				X				
S30/2258		X				X				
S30/2259		X				X				
S30/2260		X				X				
S40/2256		X				X				
S40/2261		X				X				
S40/2207						X	X			
S40/2208						X				

Figure F.7. Model and processor upgrades 9406 servers to 740.

From: Model/ Processor	720/2061			720/2062				720/2063				720/2064			
To: Interactive Capacity	1500	1501	1502	1500	1501	1502	1503	1500	1502	1503	1504	1500	1503	1504	1505
40S/2109	X														
40S/2110	X	X													
40S/2111	X	X	X												
40S/2112	X	X	X	X	X	X	X								
50S/2120	X	X	X	X	X	X	X	X	X	X	X				
50S/2121	X	X	X	X	X	X	X	X	X	X	X				
50S/2122	X	X	X	X	X	X	X	X	X	X	X				
53S															
S10/2118	X	X		X	X										
S10/2119	X	X	X	X	X	X		X	X	X					
S20/2161	X	X	X	X	X	X	X	X	X	X	X				
S20/2163				X	X	X	X	X	X	X	X	X	X	X	X
S20/2165												X	X	X	X
S20/2166												X	X	X	X

Figure F.8. RISC servers to 720 models and processor upgrades.

	720/2061			720/2062				720/2063				720/2064			
To: Model/Processor	1	1	1	1	1	1	1	1	1	1	1	1	1	1	1
Interactive	5	5	5	5	5	5	5	5	5	5	5	5	5	5	5
Capacity	0	0	0	0	0	0	0	0	0	0	0	0	0	0	0
From:	0	1	2	0	1	2	3	0	2	3	4	0	2	3	4	5
S20-ISV/2170 1490								X	X			X	X		
S20-ISV/2177 1491												X	X	X	
S20-ISV/2178 1492													X	X	X

Figure F.9. Custom mixed-mode servers to 720 models and processor upgrades.

From: Model/Processor	Interactive Capacity	To: 720/2061			720/2062				720/2063				720/2064				
		1500	1501	1502	1500	1501	1502	1503	1500	1502	1503	1504	1500	1502	1503	1504	1505
720/2061	1500		X	X		X	X	X		X	X	X		X	X	X	X
720/2061	1501			X			X	X		X	X	X		X	X	X	X
720/2061	1502							X			X	X			X	X	X
720/2062	1500					X	X	X		X	X	X		X	X	X	X
720/2062	1501						X	X		X	X	X		X	X	X	X
720/2062	1502							X			X	X			X	X	X
720/2062	1503											X				X	X
720/2063	1500									X	X	X	X	X	X	X	X
720/2063	1502										X	X			X	X	X
720/2063	1503											X				X	X
720/2063	1504																X
720/2064	1500													X	X	X	X
720/2064	1502														X	X	X
720/2064	1503															X	X
720/2064	1504																X
720/2064	1505																

Figure F.10. 720 to 720 models and processor upgrades.

Figure F.11. RISC to 730 models and processor upgrades.

518 EXPLORING IBM AS/400 COMPUTERS

From: Model/Processor	Interactive Capacity	To: 730/2065 1506	1507	1508	1509	730/2066 1506	1507	1508	1509	1510	1511	730/2067 1506	1508	1509	1510	1511	730/2068 1506	1508	1509	1510	1511
720/2063	1500					X	X					X					X				
720/2063	1502						X	X	X				X	X	X			X	X	X	
720/2063	1503							X	X	X				X	X	X			X	X	X
720/2063	1504								X	X	X				X	X				X	X
720/2064	1500											X					X				
720/2064	1502												X	X	X			X	X	X	
720/2064	1503													X	X	X			X	X	X
720/2064	1504														X	X				X	X
720/2064	1505															X					X
730/2065	1506		X	X	X		X	X	X	X	X	X	X	X	X	X	X	X	X	X	X
730/2065	1507			X	X			X	X	X	X		X	X	X	X		X	X	X	X
730/2065	1508				X				X	X	X			X	X	X			X	X	X
730/2065	1509									X	X				X	X				X	X

Figure F.12. Model and processor upgrades from 720/730 to 730. *(continued on next page)*

		To:																		
		730/2065				730/2066					730/2067					730/2068				
From: Model/ Processor	Interactive Capacity	1506	1507	1508	1509	1506	1507	1508	1509	1510	1506	1508	1509	1510	1511	1506	1508	1509	1510	1511
730/2066	1506						X				X	X				X				
730/2066	1507							X	X		X	X	X				X	X		
730/2066	1508								X	X		X	X	X				X	X	
730/2066	1509									X			X	X	X				X	X
730/2066	1510													X	X				X	X
730/2067	1506											X	X			X	X			
730/2067	1508												X	X			X	X		
730/2067	1509													X	X			X	X	
730/2067	1510														X				X	X
730/2067	1511																			X
730/2068	1506																X	X	X	X
730/2068	1508																	X	X	X
730/2068	1509																		X	X
730/2068	1510																			X
730/2068	1511																			

Figure F.12. Model and processor upgrades from 720/730 to 730. *(continued from previous page)*

		To:								
		740/2069					740/2070			
From: Model/ Processor	Interactive Capacity	1 5 1 4	1 5 1 0	1 5 1 1	1 5 1 2	1 5 1 4	1 5 1 0	1 5 1 1	1 5 1 2	1 5 1 3
720/2064	1500	X				X				
720/2064	1502	X	X			X	X			
720/2064	1503		X	X			X	X		
720/2064	1504		X	X	X		X	X	X	
720/2064	1505		X	X	X		X	X	X	X
730/2066	1506	X				X				
730/2066	1507	X	X			X	X			
730/2066	1508		X	X			X	X		
730/2066	1509		X	X	X		X	X	X	X
730/2066	1510			X	X			X	X	X
730/2067	1506	X				X				
730/2067	1508		X	X			X	X		
730/2067	1509		X	X	X		X	X	X	X
730/2067	1510			X	X			X	X	X
730/2067	1511				X				X	X
730/2068	1506	X				X				
730/2068	1508		X	X			X	X		
730/2068	1509		X	X	X			X	X	X
730/2068	1510			X	X			X	X	X
730/2068	1511				X				X	X
740/2069	1514		X					X		
740/2069	1510			X	X			X	X	X
740/2069	1511				X				X	X
740/2069	1512									X
740/2070	1514						X			
740/2070	1510							X	X	X
740/2070	1511								X	X
740/2070	1512									X
X740/2070	1513									

Figure F.13. Model and processor upgrades 720/730/740 to 740.

	To: 730/2065				730/2066						730/2067						730/2068					
From: Model/Processor	Interactive Capacity																					
	1506	1507	1508	1509	1506	1507	1508	1509	1509	1510	1506	1508	1509	1509	1510	1511	1506	1508	1509	1510	1511	1511
53S/2154	X	X			X	X																
53S/2155	X	X			X	X																
53S/2156					X	X	X	X			X	X					X	X				
53S/2157					X	X	X	X			X	X	X				X	X	X			
S20/2165					X	X	X				X	X	X	X			X	X	X	X		
S20/2166					X	X					X	X	X	X			X	X	X	X		
S30/2257			X	X	X	X					X	X	X									
620/2258					X	X	X	X	X		X	X	X	X	X		X	X	X	X	X	
620/2259								X	X		X	X	X	X	X		X	X	X	X	X	
620/2260									X	X	X	X	X	X	X		X	X	X	X	X	

Figure F.14. RISC servers to 730 models and processor upgrades.

Appendix F 521

		To:																					
		730/2065				730/2066					730/2067							730/2068					
From: Model/ Processor	Interactive Capacity	1506	1507	1508	1509	1506	1507	1508	1509	1510	1505	1506	1508	1509	1510	1511	1511	1505	1506	1508	1509	1510	1511
S20/2170	1490	X				X	X				X							X					
S20/2177	1491						X					X	X	X					X	X	X		
S20/2178	1492							X	X				X	X	X					X	X	X	
S30/2320	1492							X	X					X	X	X					X	X	X
S30/2321	1493														X	X	X					X	X
S30/2322	1494															X	X						X

Figure F.15. Custom mixed-mode servers to 730 models and processor upgrades.

Index

1 1/4-Inch Tape Unit Cage (#7130), 178
2.5-GB 1/4-Inch Cartridge Tape Unit, 137
3 1/2-Inch Disk Unit Cage (#7128), 177
4-GB 1/4-Inch Cartridge Tape Unit, 138
7-GB 8-mm Cartridge Tape Unit, 138
13-GB 1/4-Inch Cartridge Tape Unit, 138
16-bit to 64-bit processing, 456-457
0059 Transition Data Link, 181-182, 478
64-bit processing, 456-457
1063 Mbps PCI Expansion Tower #5065, 176, 177
3270 protocol, 116
#3995 Optical Library, 142-143
5250 protocol, 116
5394 Remote Workstation Controller, 172
5494 Remote Workstation Controller, 172-174
#6618 Integrated NetFinity Server, 155
9331 Model 11 and 12 Diskette units, 123
9402, 9404, 9406 Models, 482-483

A

A10 Microprocessor, 14-15
A35 Microprocessor, 15-16, 17
A50 Microprocessor, 16, 18
Acacia Technologies-Acacia Suite for AS/400, 42-43
access points, 159
ActiveX, AS/400 Software Development Kit for, 343
actuator of disk units, 83
actuators, 124
adapter (other) options, 180-183
    0059 Transition Data Link, 181-182, 478
    Cryptographic Processors (#2620/2628), 180-181
    PCI Cryptographic IOA (#4800), 181
    Terminal Multiconnector and Telephone Twisted-Pair Adapter, 182-183
ADSM (Adstar Distributed Storage Manager), 324-325
advanced application architecture, 8-18
    A10 Microprocessor, 14-15
    A35 Microprocessor, 15-16, 17
    A50 Microprocessor, 16, 18
    branch prediction, 12
    Bus Control Adapter Logic (BCAL), 16, 18
    client application layer, 5, 8-9
    commercial versus scientific/engineering workloads, 13
    Complementary Metal-Oxide Semiconductor (CMOS), 14, 15, 16
    Complex Instruction Set Computer (CISC), 11
    hardware layer, 5, 10
    Integrated File System (IFS), 5, 9
    integrated midware layer, 5, 9-10
    machine interface, technology-independent, 5, 10
    object-oriented server applications, 5, 9
    op code, 12
    optimal decoding, 12
    overview, 5
    pipelining, 12
    Reduced Instruction Set Computer (RISC), 11-12
    RISC PowerPC AS microprocessors, 11-18
    separate storage control chip (STGCTL), 16, 18
    Serial Control Interface Logic (SCIL), 16, 18
    server layer, 5, 9
    superscalar, 12
    System Licensed Internal Code (SLIC), 5, 10
Advanced Function Presentation. *See* AFP
Advanced Function Printing
    Font Collection, 339
    overview, 102-103, 110
    Utilities (5769-AF1), 339
    Workbench Viewer support, 300, 311
Advanced Peer to Peer Communications (APPC), 72
Advanced Peer-to-Peer Networking (APPN), 297, 390, 391, 401
Advanced Print Utility (APU), 210
Advanced Program-to-Program Communications (APPC), 390, 397
Advanced Series 20X/30X System Units, 483
Advanced Series #2686 Optical Link Processor (266 Mbps), 179-180
Advanced Series Base Optical Bus Adapter (#2696), 178-179
Advanced Series Optical Link Processor (#2688), 180
AFP (Advanced Function Presentation), 265-280
    built-in database, 272-279
    concurrency (synchronization), 277-279
    DB2 for AS/400, 266-270
    Distributed Data Management (DDM), 279-280
    Distributed Relational Database Architecture (DRDA), 280
    index fields, 321
    Intelligent Printer Data Stream (IPDS), 266
    lock management, 264, 279
    logical files, 276-277
    Mixed Object Document Content Architecture-Presentation (MODCA-P), 265
    physical files, 275-276
    telephone book, 274-275
AFP PrintSuite, 209-211
AFP Toolbox, 211
American Optometric Association (AOA), 468

523

analog communications, 167
Anonymous FTP, 431
AnyMail/400, 211-212, 426
AnyStore, 320
AOA (American Optometric Association), 468
APIs (Application Program Interfaces), 76, 211, 247, 252-253
APPC (Advanced Peer to Peer Communications), 72
APPC (Advanced Program-to-Program Communications), 390, 397
application architecture, 195-198
application-centric computing, 3-7
application development facilities, 334-377. *See also* application programs; business and Application Systems; migrating from System/3X; software; *specific programming languages*
    Advanced Function Printing Font Collection, 339
    Advanced Function Printing Utilities (5769-AF1), 339
    Application Development Tools Set/400, 336-341
    Application Dictionary Services/400, 341
    Application Program Driver, 341
    AS/400e server 150 BasePak (5649-EP5), 373-377
    AS/400 Kernel Threads, 345-347, 426
    AS/400 Object Technology Development Tools, 357-358
    AS/400 Operations Productivity Pak (5716-OPK), 377
    AS/400 Software Development Kit for ActiveX and OLE DB, 343
    Business Graphics Utility (BGU), 340
    for client/server computing model, 350-353
    CODE/400, 343
    Command Language (CL), 348
    Computer-Aided Software Engineering (CASE) methodology, 343-344
    Cooperative Debugger, 343
    for cross-industry applications, 199, 200-201, 340-341
    Data File Utility (DFU), 337
    DDS Window support, 342
    for debugging and maintenance, 342-343
    distributed computing model, 4, 7, 353
    distributed logic model, 352
    distributed presentation model, 351-352
    Document Interchange Architecture (DIA), 335
    Euro Currency Symbol, 339-340
    File Compare and Merge Utility (FCMU), 343
    frameworks, 359-361
    host-centric computing, 2, 3-4, 351
    IBM Knowledge Tool/400, 344
    IBM VisualAge for Java IDE, 343
    ILE C++, 349
    ILE COBOL for AS/400, 349
    ILE RPG for AS/400, 348-349
    for Integrated Language Environment (ILE), 347-349
    Intelligent Miner, 233-236, 344
    Interactive Source Level Debugger (ISLD), 343
    for Java, 343, 357, 362-369
    JBuilder/400 IDE, 343
    for kernel threads, 345-347, 426
    knowledge-based tools, 344
    maintenance tools, 342-343, 344-345
    module object (MODULE), 347-348
    neural networks, 344
    for object-oriented languages, 350, 357-358
    Object Request Broker (ORB) support, 355, 362
    for object technology, 353-358
    OpenDoc, 361
    Open Standards (UNIX), 369-371
    overview, 334-336
    POSIX Application Program Interfaces, 345
    for printing, 338-340
    Print Services Facility/400, 338-339
    Program Development Manager, 337-338
    for programming, 343
    programming languages, 334-335
    Query/400, 340-341
    remote data model, 352
    remote presentation model, 352
    San Francisco Framework, 360-361
    Screen Design Aid (SDA), 337
    single-level storage, 334
    Source Entry Utility (SEU), 337
    Structured Query Language (SQL), 340
    System/3X compatibility, 193-198, 371-372
    testing tools, 344
    for threadsafe functions, 345-347
    UNIX, 369-371
    UNIX C portability, 370-371
    VisualAge/SmallTalk, 358
    VRPG Client, 343
    Window Tool/400, 341-342
Application Development Tools Set/400, 336-341
Application Dictionary Services/400, 341
application dimension of SystemView, 313-316
Application Program Driver, 341
Application Program Interfaces (APIs), 76, 211, 247, 252-253
application program layer, 185, 186
application programs, 198-245. *See also* application development facilities; business and Application Systems; migrating from System/3X; software; *specific programming languages*
    Advanced Function Presentation (AFP) PrintSuite, 209-211
    Advanced Function Presentation (AFP) Toolbox, 211
    Advanced Print Utility (APU), 210
    AnyMail/400, 211-212
    Application Program Interfaces (APIs), 211
    AS/400 Client Series, 241-242
    automation, 229
    batch job stream management, 228
    business data, 233
    Business Graphics Utility (BGU), 216-217
    calendar management, 203, 204

Index

CallPath/400, 222-223
capacity of data mining, 235
cleansing data, 231
Client Access Ultimedia Tools, 224-225
collaborative computing, 236-241
Command Language (CL), 222
contextual help, 207
costs of enhancement, 460-461
cross-industry, 199, 200-201, 340-341
  custom, 244-245, 440, 441
data mining, 233-236, 284
data structures, multiple, 235
data warehousing, 230-233, 234, 235, 269
Decision Support Systems (DSS), 233
directory management, 207
Distributed Data Management (DDM), 229
distribution, Client Access for, 308
document management, 203, 205
Domino 5.0/Notes, 237
electronic mail, 203, 204, 211-212
enabler, 223
Encoded Vector Index (EVI), 214-216
Executive Information Systems (EIS), 233
Facsimile Support/400, 220-222
forward planning, 229
Graphics Data Format (GDF), 217
groupware, 236
IBM Job Scheduler/400, 227-230
ImagePlus/400, 217-220
industry-specific, 199, 242-244
informational data, 231
Intelligent Miner, 233-236, 344
Internet addressing, 207-208
Internet mail protocol (MIME), 212
Local Data Areas (LDAs), 229
Lotus Enterprise Integrator (NotesPump), 239-241
Lotus Notes 5.0, 236, 237-239
Manufacturing Accounting and Production Information Control System/Database (MAPICS/DB), 243
metadata, 233
migrating from System/3X, 479-482
migrating to AS/400, 245, 358-371
Multimedia, 223-227
OfficeVision, 201-209, 426
OfficeVision JustMail (5798-TBT), 209
On-Line Analytical Processing (OLAP), 232-233
On-Line Transaction Processing (OLTP), 230
open interfaces of data mining, 235
operational data, 230-231
Page Printer Formatting Aid (PPFA), 210
paging support, 229
performance of data mining, 234-235
Post Office Protocol, Version 3 (POP3), 212
prewritten, 199-200, 440, 441
and printing technology, 100, 102-103
production forecasting, 229
Query/400, 212-214
Rapid Application Development (RAD), 238
relational database system, 232
SAP R/3 AFP Print, 211
scalability of data mining, 235
technical data, 233
Ultimedia Business Conferencing/400, 225-227
word processing, 205-206
Workfolder Application Facility, 219, 220
Applications Layer, 395
Applications Support layer, 396-397
Application Storage Pools (ASPs), 259, 323, 325, 326
Application Systems. *See* AS/400 systems
APPN (Advanced Peer-to-Peer Networking), 297, 390, 391, 401
APU (Advanced Print Utility), 210
AS/400 Advanced Entry Model 150
  auxiliary storage options, 128
  main storage expansion, 117
  overview, 19, 20-24
AS/400 and the Internet, 419-431
  Anonymous FTP, 431
  AnyMail/400, 426
  AS/400 Kernel Threads model, 345-347, 426
  AS/400 TCP/IP TELNET, 430
  Boolean logic for searching, 421-422
  CommercePoint, 420
  Common Gateway Interface (CGI), 409, 431
  Domino 5.0 for AS/400, 423-427
  Domino Go Webserver (IBM HTTP Server for AS/400), 421
  Domino.Merchant, 427-428
  Electronic Business (e-business), 420
  electronic storefront for the Web, 422
  File Transfer Protocol (FTP), 429-430
  HyperText Markup Language (HTML), 429
  HyperText Transfer Protocol (HTTP), 429
  Internet terminology, 429-431
  Java with Domino, 424, 425
  Lightweight Directory Access Protocol (LDAP), 428-429
  Lotus Domino.Doc support, 427
  Lotus Learning Space, 427
  Lotus Script, 427
  Lotus Simple Mail Transport Protocol/Mail Transfer Agent (SMTP/MTA), 426
  Multipurpose Internet Mail Extensions (MIME), 430
  Net.Commerce, 420, 422-423
  Net.Commerce versus Domino.Merchant, 428
  Net.Data, 420-421
  NetQuestion, 421-422
  OfficeVision, 201-209, 426
  OS/400 Directory Services, 428-429
  overview, 418-420
  Post Office Protocol, Version 3 (POP3), 430
  Serial Line Internet Protocol (SLIP), 430
  Simple Mail Transfer Protocol (SMTP), 294, 430
  Simple Network Management Protocol (SNMP), 430

TCP/IP Simple Network Management
  Protocol (SNMP), 430
TCP/IP TELNET, 430
Uniform Resource Locator (URL), 430-431
Workstation Gateway Server (WGS), 431
AS/400 Client Access Express for Windows
  (5769-XE1), 310-313
AS/400 Client Access Family, 301, 308-310
AS/400 Client Series, 241-242
AS/400 Developer Kit for Java, 363-364, 365
AS/400 distributed networks, 387-390
AS/400e server 150 BasePak (5649-EP5),
  373-377
AS/400e server 170
  main storage expansion, 117-119
  overview, 3, 19, 25-27, 28
AS/400e server 720
  auxiliary storage options, 128-129
  main storage expansion, 119-120
  overview, 19, 27, 29-31
AS/400e server 730
  auxiliary storage options, 129-130
  main storage expansion, 120-121
  overview, 19, 31-34, 35, 36, 37
AS/400e server 740
  auxiliary storage options, 131
  main storage expansion, 121, 122
  overview, 19, 34-40
AS/400 Kernel Threads model, 345-347, 426
AS/400 Object Technology Development Tools,
  357-358
AS/400 Operations Productivity Pak
  (5716-OPK), 377
AS/400 Performance Tools (5716-PT1), 332
AS/400 Secure Web Server, 409
AS/400 Software Development Kit for ActiveX
  and OLE DB, 343
AS/400 System Clustering, 392-393
AS/400 systems, 1-87. *See also* advanced
  application architecture; application
  programs; auxiliary storage; business and
  Application Systems; communications;
  custom application servers; custom
  mixed-mode servers; memory or main
  storage; operating systems; performance;
  software; system availability; system unit
  members
    Advanced Peer to Peer Communications
      (APPC), 72
    application-centric computing, 3-7
    Application Program Interfaces (APIs), 76
    C2 security rating, 473-474
    cable-thru, 86
    cache memory, 68, 69-70
    client/server computing, 4, 5, 6-7
    clustering technology, 47, 50-52, 71-76,
      392-393
    Complementary Metal-Oxide Semiconduc-
      tor (CMOS), 85
    components of, 2
    DB2 Multi-system, 74
    distributed computing systems, 4, 7, 353
    Distributed Data Management (DDM),
      72-73, 74

Distributed Relational Database Architecture (DRDA), 74
family overview, 19-20, 21
fiber optic bus, 87
flexibility and change management over
  time, 6
freedom of choice, 6
hardware architecture overview, 68-71, 73
high availability, 76
horizontal growth, 76
host-centric computing, 2, 3-4, 351
Integrated PC Server (IPCS), 7
Internet Packet Exchange (IPX), 7
interoperability, 5
investment protection, 6
I/O bus, 70-71
I/O processors, 68, 70, 73
lasting value, 6
multiuser computer systems, 1, 249-250,
  435-436
Novell NetWare 4.10, 7
N-way multiprocessor architecture, 71, 72
open systems computing, 4, 5-6
OptiConnect/400, 49, 71-76
packaging technology, 3, 85-86
portability, 5
printers, 2
Programming Request Per Quote (PRPQ),
  76
software layers comparison to traditional,
  189-191
Structured Query Language (SQL), 74
Symmetrical Multi-Processors (SMPs), 71,
  72
System 3/X comparison to, xxvii-xxx
system console, 2
System Licensed Internal Code (SLIC), 70
System Network Architecture Distribution
  Services (SNADS), 74
system performance tables, 483-487
system processor, 68-69
terminals, 2
Very Large Scale Integration (VLSI), 85
AS/400 TCP/IP TELNET, 430
AS/400 Toolbox for Java, 363, 365-368
ASCII workstation controllers, 114-115
ASPs (Application Storage Pools), 259, 323, 325,
  326
ASW, International Business Systems-IBS, 41
asymmetrical encryption algorithm, 412
Async protocol, 166
ATM (Asynchronous Transfer Mode), 157-159
authentication, 288
Automatic Browser Detection, 411
automation, 229
auxiliary storage, 81-85. *See also* auxiliary
  storage options
    actuator of disk units, 83
    Compact Disk-Read Only Memory
      (CD-ROM), 84
    Direct Access Storage Devices (DASDs), 82
    diskette storage, 81, 82
    disk storage, 82-84
    latency of platters, 82

optical libraries, 84-85
performance of disk units, 82-83
seek time of disk units, 82
tape storage, 85
Write Many, Read Many (WMRM), 85, 141
Write Once, Read Many (WORM), 84-85, 141
auxiliary storage options, 121-143
    2.5-GB 1/4-Inch Cartridge Tape Unit, 137
    4-GB 1/4-Inch Cartridge Tape Unit, 138
    7-GB 8-mm Cartridge Tape Unit, 138
    13-GB 1/4-Inch Cartridge Tape Unit, 138
    #3995 Optical Library, 142-143
    9331 Model 11 and 12 Diskette units, 123
    actuators, 124
    for AS/400 Advanced Entry Model 150, 128
    for AS/400e server 720, 128-129
    for AS/400e server 730, 129-130
    for AS/400e server 740, 131
    Compact Disk-Read Only Memory (CD-ROM), 141-142
    compression, 124-125, 127
    controllers, 143, 144
    Direct Access Storage Devices (DASDs), 124
    disk adapters, 132-136
    disk compression, 125, 127
    diskette storage, 122-123
    disk storage, 123-136
    external tape units, 139, 140
    F-mode configuration for tape drives, 139
    IBM Magstar MP 3575 Tape Library Dataserver, 139
    Initial Program Load (IPL), 142
    Input/Output Processors (IOPs), 132-136, 143
    integrated hardware disk compression, 125, 127
    internal tape units, 137-138
    Model 2100 Versatile Storage DataServer, 131-132
    Model SB1 disk options, 130-131
    Multi-Function I/O Processor (MFIOP), 124, 133-134, 143
    optical storage, 141-143
    PCI Integrated PC Server, 134
    for QIC tape formats, 138
    tape libraries, 139
    tape storage, 136-140
    Write Many, Read Many, (WMRM), 85, 141
    Write Once, Read Many (WORM), 84-85, 141
availability of system security, 471

B
Baan-BaanERP, 42, 46
backup/recovery, 317-328
    Adstar Distributed Storage Manager (ADSM), 324-325
    Advanced Function Presentation (AFP) index fields, 321
    AnyStore, 320
    Application Storage Pools (ASPs), 323, 325, 326
    Backup Recovery and Media Services (BRMS/400), 321-323
    BRMS Advanced Functions Feature, 323
    BRMS Network Feature, 323
    checksum, 327-328
    data mirroring, 328
    data protection methods, 328
    disk failure recovery, 327-328
    EDMSuite OnDemand for AS/400 (5769-RD1), 320-321
    Hierarchical Storage Management (HSM), 323, 325, 326
    HTTP Server for AS/400, 319
    journaling, 316-317
    Object Archive, 320
    Operations Navigator, 318-320
    RAID-5 disk controllers, 327-328
    Record Archive, 320
    remote journaling, 316-317
    save while active feature, 317
    Security Wizard, 319, 505-509
    Spool File Archive, 320, 321
    System Managed Access Path Protection (SMAPP), 325-326, 327
    SystemView, 317-318
    utility failure recovery, 327
Backup Recovery and Media Services (BRMS/400), 321-323
band printers, 104, 105-107, 108
BasePak, 24
batch job stream management, 228
batch versus interactive processing, 248-249
BCAL (Bus Control Adapter Logic), 16, 18
benchmark testing, 57-66
Berkeley Software Distribution (BSD), 400
BGU (Business Graphics Utility), 216-217, 340
Bisync protocol, 166-167
Boolean logic for searching, 421-422
Borland J-Builder, 369
branch prediction, 12
BRMS/400 (Backup Recovery and Media Services), 321-323
BRMS Advanced Functions Feature, 323
BRMS Network Feature, 323
BSD (Berkeley Software Distribution), 400
BSF (Byte Stream File), 52
built-in database, 272-279
Bus Control Adapter Logic (BCAL), 16, 18
business and Application Systems, 432-488. *See also* application development facilities; application programs; hardware selection; migrating from System/3X; software
    applications enhancement costs, 460-461
    availability, 471
    benefits, 461-463
    business conferencing, 225-227
    business cycle improvement, 461
    business data, 233
    C2 security rating, 473-474
    capital lease, 464
    communications lines costs, 460

competitive advantage, 462-463
computing needs, determining, 433-434
confidentiality, 471
cost justification, 458-461
custom application programs, 244-245, 440, 441
customer service improvement, 462
ease of use, 439
education/training, 460, 465-466, 467
environmental costs, 460
ergonomics, 467-471
eye comfort, 468-469
facilities costs, 459-460
hardware maintenance costs, 458
IBM Education and Training, 466
integrity, 471
inventory reduction, 461
lease or buy decision, 464-465
logical partitioning of Symmetrical Multi-Processors (SMPs), 48-49, 439-440
loss prevention, 472-473
multiuser computer systems, 1, 249-250, 435-436
net present value, 463
noise comfort, 470-471
and open systems computing, 6
operating lease, 464-465
parallel capability, 439
payback period, 463
and personal computers (PCs), 435-436
prewritten application programs, 199-200, 440, 441
productivity improvement, 461-462
quality improvement, 462
residual value of computer system, 464
and RISC System/6000 computers, 436-438
security, 471-474
service, 474-475
software license agreement, 465
software maintenance costs, 458-459
software selection, 440-441, 449-451
and System/390 computers, 438-439
system performance tables, 483-487
technical support costs, 459
theft prevention, 473-474
vertical market application programs, 441
workstation comfort, 469-470
Year 2000 challenge, 459, 475
Business Graphics Utility (BGU), 216-217, 340
bytecodes, 362
bytes, 69
Byte Stream File (BSF), 52

C
C++, 349, 358
C, D, E, F 9402, 9404, 9406 Models, 482-483
C2 security rating, 473-474
cable-thru, 86, 113
cache memory, 68, 69-70
calendar management, 203, 204
CallPath/400, 222-223
capability-based addressing, 80
capacity of data mining, 235
capital lease, 464
CASE (Computer-Aided Software Engineering) methodology, 343-344
CCA (Common Cryptographic Architecture), 410
CD-ROM (Compact Disk-Read Only Memory), 84, 141-142
certificates (digital IDs), 409, 411, 412-413
CGI (Common Gateway Interface), 409, 431
check bits, 77
checksum, 327-328
CICS Translation Server for AS/400 (5769-DFH), 289-290
CISC (Complex Instruction Set Computer), 11
CISC to RISC, 483
class, 355
Class Libraries, 362
CL (Command Language), 222, 348
cleansing data, 231
Client Access, 94, 300-313
    Advanced Function Printing Workbench Viewer support, 300, 311
    for applications distribution, 308
    AS/400 Client Access Express for Windows (5769-XE1), 310-313
    AS/400 Client Access Family, 309-310
    AS/400 Client Access Family for Windows, 301, 308-309
    communications support, 301
    e-mail support, 301, 308
    functions and operating systems support, 301, 302-307
    Lotus Notes 5.0 support, 312-313
    Microsoft's Policies support, 308-309
    NetServer, 310-311
    Netsoft Router, 301, 308
    network printing support, 309
    Open DataBase Connection (ODBC), 309
    Operations Navigator, 311-312
    Peer Web Services, 310
    Secure Sockets Layer (SSL) support, 310, 313
    Software Developer Toolkit (SDK), 309
    Terminal Server Edition (TSE) support, 310
Client Access Ultimedia Tools, 224-225
client application layer, 5, 8-9
client certificates, 411
Client Series, 241-242
client/server computing
    application development facilities for, 350-353
    OS/400 for, 250-251
    overview, 4, 5, 6-7
Client Server Labs, 66
clustering technology, 47, 50-52, 71-76, 392-393
Cluster Resource Groups and Services, 50-52
CMOS (Complementary Metal-Oxide Semiconductor), 14, 15, 16, 85
COBOL, 349
CODE/400, 343
cold fusion printing, 109, 111
collaborative computing, 236-241
Collection Services (Management Central), 331
Command Language (CL), 222, 348

Index **529**

CommercePoint, 420
Commercial Processing Workload (CPW) benchmark test, 61-62, 63
commercial versus scientific/engineering workloads, 13
commitment control, 316
Common Cryptographic Architecture (CCA), 410
Common Gateway Interface (CGI), 409, 431
Common Object Request Broker Architecture (CORBA), 355
Common Programming Interface for Communications (CPI-C), 397
Common User Access (CUA), 198, 313
communications. *See also* communications support; distributed computer communications; IBM's networking blueprint; intranet/Internet security; LANs; WANs
    copy screen facility, 383
    costs of lines, 460
    file transfer capability, 383
    IBM Electronic Customer Support (ECS) for, 379, 380-383
    IBM Information Network (IIN), 381, 382
    IBMLink, 382
    Program Temporary Fixes (PTFs), 380, 382
    question-and-answer database for, 383
    for remote workstations, 383-385
    RETAIN network, 382
    Systems Network Architecture (SNA), 379-380
    SystemView System Management Utilities, 382-383
communications support, 290-300. *See also* LANs; WANs
    Advanced Peer-to-Peer Networking (APPN), 297
    and Client Access, 301
    dial-on-demand networking, 293
    Display Station Pass-Thru (DSPT), 298-299
    Domain Name Server (DNS), 292
    Dynamic Host Configuration Protocol (DHCP), 292
    extranets, 295
    File Transfer Protocol (FTP), 294
    incoming balancing, 293
    Integrated Services Digital Network (ISDN) protocol, 292
    intranets, 295
    Layer 2 Tunnel Protocol (L2TP), 295
    Mobile Worker, 295
    NetView/Remote Manager (NV/RM), 297
    Network Address Translation (NAT), 292-293
    Network Remote Facilities (NRF), 297
    outgoing balancing, 293
    overview, 290-292
    Point to Point (PPP), 292
    printer pass-thru, 298-299
    remote office connections, 295
    S/390 communications support, 299-300
    Secure Sockets Layer (SSL), 294
    SMTP scaleability, 294, 430
    Systems Network Architecture (SNA), 297
    Systems Network Management, 295-297
    SystemView Managed System Services (MSS), 297, 332-333
    Transmission Control Protocol/Internet Protocol (TCP/IP), 292-295, 496-499
    ValuNets, 295
    Virtual IP Addressing (VIPA), 293
    Virtual Private Networks (VPN), 294-295
    wireless local area networks, 159-161, 162, 163, 297-298
Compact Disk-Read Only Memory (CD-ROM), 84, 141-142
compatibility, software, 193-198, 371-372
competitive advantage, 462-463
compiler, Java, 362-363
compiling a program, 195
Complementary Metal-Oxide Semiconductor (CMOS), 14, 15, 16, 85
Complex Instruction Set Computer (CISC), 11
Complex Object Support, 270
compression, 124-125, 127
Computer-Aided Software Engineering (CASE) methodology, 343-344
computer terminals (display station), 89
computing needs, determining, 433-434
concurrency, 277-279
confidentiality of security system, 471
constrained performance, 23
contextual help, 207
continuous availability clustering, 47, 50-52, 71-76
Continuously Powered Main Storage (CPM), 27, 30, 33, 39, 44, 46, 53-54
controllers, 143, 144
Cooperative Debugger, 343
copy screen facility, 383
CORBA (Common Object Request Broker Architecture), 355
cost justification, 458-461
costs
    of application programs enhancement, 460-461
    of communications lines, 460
    of education/training costs, 460
    environmental costs, 460
    of facilities, 459-460
    of hardware maintenance, 458
    of printing, 101
    of software maintenance, 458-459
    of technical support, 459
CPI-C (Common Programming Interface for Communications), 397
CPM (Continuously Powered Main Storage), 27, 30, 33, 39, 44, 46, 53-54
CPW (Commercial Processing Workload) benchmark test, 61-62, 63
crackers, 403
cross-industry application programs, 199, 200-201, 340-341
cryptographic access provider, 410-414
Cryptographic Processors (#2620/2628), 180-181
CSMA/CD (Carrier Sense Multiple Access/Collision Detect), 146-147

CUA (Common User Access), 198, 313
custom application programs, 244-245, 440, 441
custom application servers, 20, 43-46
    Baan-BaanERP, 46
    Continuously Powered Main Storage (CPM), 44, 46
    Model 740-SB1, 44
    Model S40-SB1, 44
    Model SB1, 43-44
    Multi-Function I/O Processor (MFIOP), 44
    SAP-Base R/3 Package, 46
    Symmetrical Multi-Processors (SMPs), 44
customer service improvement, 462
custom mixed-mode servers, 20, 40-43
    Acacia Technologies-Acacia Suite for As/400, 42-43
    Baan-BaanERP, 42
    Infinium-Infinium Suite for IBM AS/400, 42
    Intentia-The Movex System, 41
    International Business Systems-IBS - ASW, 41
    JBA International-JBA System 21, 41
    Lilly Software Associates-Visual Manufacturing, 43
    MAPICS-MAPOCS XA, 41
    SAP-Base R/3 Package, 43
    SAP-Ready to Run R/3, 43
    SSA-BPCS Client/Server or Mixed Mode, 40

D
DASDs (Direct Access Storage Devices), 82, 124
data
    dimension, 313, 314
    integrity, 286, 288
    loader utility, 268
    migrating from System 3/X, 479-482
    mining, 233-236, 284
    mirroring, 328
    protection methods, 328
    resiliency, 47, 50
    striping, 267, 283
    structures, multiple, 235
    warehousing, 230-233, 234, 235, 269, 284
databases. *See also* DB2 for AS/400
    application programs for, 212-216, 340-341
    data mining, 233-236, 284
    data warehousing, 230-233, 234, 235, 269, 284
Data Encryption Standard (DES), 288
Data File Utility (DFU), 337
DataLink data types, 271
DataMirror, 50
DataPropagator Relational Capture and Apply, 269, 282
DB2 for AS/400, 266-270, 280-290. *See also* DB2-Universal Database support
    authentication, 288
    CICS Translation Server for AS/400 (5769-DFH), 289-290
    database definition, independent, 267
    database management, 285-286
    database monitor, 284-285
    database transactions, 285
    Data Encryption Standard (DES), 288
    data integrity, 286, 288
    data loader utility, 268
    data mining support, 284
    Data Propagator Relational Capture and Apply, 269
    DataPropagator Relational Capture and Apply, 282
    data striping, 267, 283
    data warehousing support, 230-233, 234, 235, 269, 284
    Distributed Computing Environment (DCE) Base Services/400, 286-289, 394
    Distributed Time Services, 289
    Encoded Vector Index (EVI), 269
    hash joint algorithm, 270
    integrated with OS/400, 267
    interface definition language (IDL), 286
    for Internet application serving, 268-269
    Java Database Connection (JDBC), 283
    logical files support, 267
    massively parallel database, 284
    Open DataBase Connection (ODBC), 267, 281, 282
    Operations Navigator, 269
    Optimizer, 269-270
    overview, 280-282
    parallel access path maintenance, 268
    as partitioned database, 281, 283-284
    performance of, 270
    record level locking, 286
    Remote Procedure Calls (RPCs), 286-287
    Structured Query Language (SQL), 267, 269, 281
    Symmetric Multi-Processors (SMPs) support, 268
DB2 Multi-System, 74
DB2 Query Manager, 262-263
DB2-Universal Database Support, 270-272
    Complex Object Support, 270
    DataLink data types, 271
    Uniform Resource Locator (URL), 271
    User Defined Functions, 272
    User Defined Types, 272
DCE (Distributed Computing Environment), 286-289, 394
D Channel, 164
DDM (Distributed Data Management), 72-73, 74, 229, 279-280, 389
DDS Window support, 342
debugging and maintenance, 342-343
Decision Support Systems (DSS), 233
DFU (Data File Utility), 337
DHCP (Dynamic Host Configuration Protocol), 292
DIA (Document Interchange Architecture), 335
dial-on-demand networking, 293
digital communications, 167
Direct Access Storage Devices (DASDs), 82, 124
directory endpoint filter lists, 391
directory management, 207
disaster tolerance, 47, 52-54
disk
    adapters, 132-136
    compression, 125, 127

failure recovery, 327-328
    storage, 78, 82-84, 123-136, 477
    units, performance of, 82-83
diskette storage, 81, 82, 122-123
Display Station Pass-Thru (DSPT), 298-299, 389
distributed
    computing, 4, 7, 353
    logic model, 352
    networks, 387-390
    presentation model, 351-352
distributed computer communications, 386-393
    Advanced Peer-to-Peer Networking (APPN), 390, 391
    Advanced Program-to-Program Communications (APPC), 390
    AS/400 distributed networks, 387-390
    AS/400 System Clustering, 392-393
    clustering, 47, 50-52, 71-76, 392-393
    directory endpoint filter lists, 391
    Display Station Pass-Thru (DSPT), 389
    Distributed Data Management (DDM), 389
    Ethernet, 146-147, 392
    filtered locations, 391
    Filter Lists, 391
    IBM Electronic Customer Support (ECS) for, 390
    instantaneous bandwidth, 392
    Integrated File System (IFS), 393
    ObjectConnect/400, 393
    partner locations, 391
    performance of, 392-393
    Programming Request Per Quote (PRPQ), 393
    security functions, 391
    session endpoint filter lists, 391
    System Network Architecture Distribution Services (SNADS), 391
    Systems Network Architecture (SNA), 391
    SystemView System Manager, 387, 390
    token-ring networks, 148-150, 392
Distributed Computing Environment (DCE), 286-289, 394
Distributed Data Management (DDM), 72-73, 74, 229, 279-280, 389
Distributed Relational Database Architecture (DRDA), 74, 280
Distributed Time Services, 289
DNS (Domain Name Server), 292
document characteristics and printing technology, 100, 101-103
Document Interchange Architecture (DIA), 335
document management, 203, 205
Domain Name Server (DNS), 292
Domain Name Serving function, 415
Domino 5.0, 237, 423-427
Domino Go Webserver (IBM HTTP Server for AS/400), 421
Domino.Merchant, 427-428
double words, 69
DRDA (Distributed Relational Database Architecture), 74, 280
DSPT (Display Station Pass-Thru), 298-299, 389
DSS (Decision Support Systems), 233
dynamic binding, 355

Dynamic Host Configuration Protocol (DHCP), 292

E
ease of use, 439
e-business, 420
ECC (Error Correction Code), 23
ECS (Electronic Customer Support), 379, 380-383, 390
EDMSuite, 220
EDMSuite OnDemand for AS/400 (5769-RD1), 320-321
education/training, 460, 465-466, 467
EIS (Executive Information Systems), 233
EJB (Enterprise Java Beans), 369
electronic
    documents, 101-102
    mail, 203, 204, 211-212, 301, 308
    storefront for the Web, 422
Electronic Business, 420
Electronic Customer Support (ECS), 379, 380-383, 390
enabler, 223
encapsulation, 355
Encoded Vector Index (EVI), 214-216, 269
encryption algorithms, 409
end-use dimension, 313, 314
Enterprise Java Beans (EJB), 369
environmental considerations and printing technology, 101
environmental costs, 460
ergonomics, 467-471
Error Correction Code (ECC), 23
Ethernet, 146-147, 392
Euro Currency Symbol, 339-340
event logs, 151
EVI (Encoded Vector Index), 214-216, 269
Executive Information Systems (EIS), 233
Exploring IBM Personal Computers, 9th Edition, 96
Extensible Markup Language (XML), 368
external tape units, 139, 140
extranets, 295
eye comfort, 468-469
EZ Setup Wizard, 196-197, 500-504

F
facilities costs, 459-460
Facsimile Support/400, 220-222
fax, 220-222
FCC (Federal Communications Commission), 160
FCMU (File Compare and Merge Utility), 343
FDDI (Fiber Distributed Data Interface), 150
Federal Communications Commission (FCC), 160
Fiber Distributed Data Interface (FDDI), 150
fiber optic bus, 87
File Compare and Merge Utility (FCMU), 343
File Server Input/Output Processor (FSIOP). *See* Integrated PC Server (#6616)
file systems supported, 258, 260-262
file transfer capability, 383
File Transfer Protocol (FTP), 294, 429-430

filtered locations, 391
Filter Lists, 391
firewalls, 152, 414-417
F-mode configuration for tape drives, 139
forward planning for application programs, 229
frame relay, 168
frameworks, 355, 359-361
FSIOP. See Integrated PC Servers
FTP (File Transfer Protocol), 294, 429-430
full words, 69

G
Gartner Group, 53, 350, 351
GDF (Graphics Data Format), 217
Global Server Certificate, 412
graphics, 216-217
Graphics Data Format (GDF), 217
groupware application programs, 236
growth version of system unit members, 21, 23-24

H
hackers, 403
half words, 69
hardware
    architecture overview, 68-71, 73
    cryptography, 410
    layer of advanced application architecture, 5, 10
    maintenance costs, 458
    solutions for system availability, 46-47
hardware selection, 442-457
    16-bit to 64-bit processing, 456-457
    64-bit processing, 456-457
    for large business environment, 451-454
    for manufacturing environment, 444-446
    for medium business environment, 446-451, 454-456
    for retail environment, 442-443
    server selection, 454-456
    for small business environment, manufacturing, 444-446
    for small business environment, retail, 442-443
    Technology-Independent Machine Interface (TIMI), 457
hash joint algorithm, 270
heartbeat monitoring, 52
Hierarchical Storage Management (HSM), 323, 325, 326
high availability, 76
horizontal growth, 54, 76
host-based development tool, 343
host-centric computing, 2, 3-4, 351
HSM (Hierarchical Storage Management), 323, 325, 326
HTML (HyperText Markup Language), 429
HTTP (HyperText Transfer Protocol), 429
HTTP Server for AS/400, 319, 411

I
IBM Application Systems. See AS/400 systems
IBM Education and Training, 466

IBM Electronic Customer Support (ECS), 379, 380-383, 390
IBM Information Network (IIN), 381, 382
IBM Job Scheduler/400, 227-230
IBM Knowledge Tool/400, 344
IBMLink, 382
IBM Magstar MP 3575 Tape Library Dataserver, 139
IBM Network Station #8361, 97-100
IBM Payment Server V1.2 for AS/400, 413-414
IBM's networking blueprint, 393-404
    Advanced Peer-to-Peer Networking (APPN), 401
    Advanced Program-to-Program Communications (APPC), 397
    Applications Layer, 395
    Applications Support layer, 396-397
    Common Programming Interface for Communications (CPI-C), 397
    crackers, 403
    for Distributed Computing Environment (DCE), 286-289, 394
    hackers, 403
    intranets, 403
    for ISO communications specifications, 394
    Messaging and Queuing Interface (MQI), 398-399
    Multiprotocol Transport Networking (MPTN), 399-401
    multivendor application program interfaces, 397-399
    Remote Procedure Calls (RPCs), 398
    retail terminals, 403-404, 405, 406-408
    Subnetworking layer, 401-402
    for Systems Network Architecture (SNA), 394
    Transport Network layer, 399-401
IBM Solutions Packaging Web site, 40
IBM VisualAge for Java IDE, 343
ICSS (Internet Connection Secure Server), 405, 409
IDLC (ISDN Data Link Control) protocol, 164
IDL (interface definition language), 286
IFS (Integrated File System), 257-265
    advanced application architecture and, 5, 9
    Application Storage Pools (ASPs), 259
    benefits of, 158-259
    DB2 Query Manager, 262-263
    file systems supported, 258, 260-262
    Large Objects (LOBs), 262
    lock management, 264, 279
    Network File System (NFS), 263-264
    and ObjectConnect/400, 393
    Physical File System (PFS), 263
    QDLS, 261
    QLANSrv, 261, 262
    and QNTC for Windows NT, 259
    QOPENSYS, 261
    QOPT, 262
    QSYS.LIB, 260, 262
    Remote File System, 264-265
    Remote Procedure Calls (RPCs), 263-264
    root file system, 261

SQL Development Kit, 262-263
stateless design, 264
stream files, 259-260, 261
system monitor, 264
Windows NT File System, client for, 265
IIN (IBM Information Network), 381, 382
ILE C++, 349
ILE COBOL for AS/400, 349
ILE (Integrated Language Environment), 347-349
ILE RPG for AS/400, 348-349
ImagePlus/400, 217-220
impact printers, 103-108
incoming balancing, 293
industry-specific application programs, 199, 242-244
Infinium-Infinium Suite for IBM AS/400, 42
informational data, 231
InfoWindowII 3486/3487 Display Stations, 90-92
InfoWindowII 3488/3489 Modular Display Station, 93-94
inheritance, 355
Initial Program Load (IPL), 53-54, 142, 315
inkjet printers, 109, 110
Inprise JBuilder/400 IDE, 343
Inprise VisiBroker, 362
Input/Output Processors (IOPs), 132-136, 143
instance, 354
instantaneous bandwidth, 392
Integrated Analog Modem #2761, 169-170
Integrated FAX Adapters, 168-169
Integrated File System. *See* IFS
integrated hardware disk compression, 125, 127
Integrated Language Environment (ILE), 347-349
integrated midware layer, 5, 9-10
Integrated PC Server (#6616), 154
Integrated PC Server (#6617), 154-155
Integrated PC Server (IPCS), 7, 150-157, 415, 416, 417
Integrated Services Digital Network (ISDN) protocol, 167-168, 292
integrity of security system, 471
Intelligent Miner, 233-236, 344
Intelligent Printer Data Stream (IPDS), 103, 110-112, 266
intelligent workstations, 96
Intentia-The Movex System, 41
interactive
    batch processing versus, 248-249
    jobs, 61
    performance, 66, 67
Interactive Source Level Debugger (ISLD), 343
interface definition language (IDL), 286
internal tape units, 137-138
International Business Systems-IBS - ASW, 41
Internet. *See also* AS/400 and the Internet; intranet/Internet security
    addressing, 207-208
    application serving, DB2 for, 268-269
    terminology, 429-431
Internet Connection Secure Server. *See* ICSS

Internet mail protocol (MIME), 212
Internet Packet Exchange (IPX), 7
interoperability, 5
intranet/Internet security, 404-431. *See also* AS/400 and the Internet
    AS/400 Secure Web Server, 409
    asymmetrical encryption algorithm, 412
    Automatic Browser Detection, 411
    certificates (digital IDs), 409, 411, 412-413
    client certificates, 411
    Common Cryptographic Architecture (CCA), 410
    Common Gateway Interface (CGI), 409, 431
    cryptographic access provider, 410-414
    defined, 145, 403
    digital certificates, 409, 411, 412-413
    Domain Name Serving, 415
    encryption algorithms, 409
    firewalls, 414-417
    Global Server Certificate, 412
    hardware cryptography, 410
    HTTP Server for AS/400, 411
    IBM Payment Server V1.2 for AS/400, 413-414
    Integrated PC Server (IPCS), 415, 416, 417
    Internet Connection Secure Server (ICSS), 405, 409
    Network Address Translation (NAT), 417
    Network Gateway, 415
    Public Key Cryptography Standard (PKCS), 411-412
    SafeMail Mail Relay, 417
    Secure Electronics Transaction (SET), 411-414
    Secure Sockets Layer (SSL), 411, 415-416
    Security Wizard, 414-418, 505-509
    SET Internet Security Manager, 411-414
    sniffing programs, 415
    Socks Client program, 417
    software encryption, 410
    symmetrical encryption, 412
    Traffic Blocking, 415
    user profiles, 411
    validation lists, 411
    virtual private networks, 295
    WebSphere Application Server (5769-AS1), 418
Inventory for Multiple Systems (Management Central), 332
inventory reduction, 461
I/O
    bus, 70-71
    devices, migrating from System 3/X, 478-479
    processors, 68, 70, 73
Iona Orbix, 362
IOPs (Input/Output Processors), 132-136, 143
IPDS (Intelligent Printer Data Stream), 103, 110-112, 266
IPL (Initial Program Load), 53-54, 142, 315
IPX (Internet Packet Exchange, Novell), 7
ISDN Basic Rate Interface Adapter, 164

ISDN Data Link Control (IDLC) protocol, 164
ISDN (Integrated Services Digital Network) protocol, 167-168, 292
ISLD (Interactive Source Level Debugger), 343

J
Java
    application development facilities for, 343, 357, 362-369
    AS/400 Developer Kit for Java, 363-364, 365
    Borland J-Builder, 369
    bytecodes, 362
    Class Libraries, 362
    at the client, 369
    compiler, 362-363
    DB2 for AS/400, 283
    defined, 362
    with Domino, 424, 425
    Enterprise Java Beans (EJB), 369
    Extensible Markup Language (XML), 368
    just-in-time compilers, 363
    Panel Definition Markup Language (PDML), 368
    Program Call Markup Language (PCML), 368
    Secure Sockets Layer (SSL), 364
    Structured Query Language Java (SQLJ), 364-365
    virtual machine, AS/400, 363-364
Java Database Connection (JDBC), 283
Java Developer's Kit (JDK), 362
Java Transformer, 363
Java Virtual Machine (JVM), 362
JBA International-JBA System 21, 41
J-Builder, 369
JBuilder/400 IDE, 343
JDBC (Java Database Connection), 283
JDK (Java Developer's Kit), 362
job scheduling, 227-230
journaling, 316-317
just-in-time compilers, 363
JVM (Java Virtual Machine), 362

K
KB (kilobytes), 14, 15
kernel threads, 345-347, 426
knowledge-based tools, 344
Knowledge Tool/400, 344

L
L2TP (Layer 2 Tunnel Protocol), 295
Lakeview technology, 50
LANs (Local Area Networks), 145-161. *See also* communications
    #6618 Integrated NetFinity Server, 155
    access points, 159
    Asynchronous Transfer Mode (ATM), 157-159
    Carrier Sense Multiple Access/Collision Detect (CSMA/CD), 146-147
    Ethernet, 146-147, 392
    event logs, 151
    Fiber Distributed Data Interface (FDDI), 150
    firewalls, 152
    Integrated PC Server (#6616), 154
    Integrated PC Server (#6617), 154-155
    Integrated PC Server (IPCS), 150-157
    Lotus Notes/Domino, 151
    message frames (packets), 148-149
    message queues, 151
    NetServer, 151-152
    nodes, 148
    Novell NetWare, 151
    On-Line Transaction Processing (OLTP), 158
    PCI 25-Mbps UTP ATM (2811), 158
    PCI 34-Mbps Coax E3 ATM (2819), 158
    PCI 45-Mbps Coax T3DS3 ATM (2812), 158
    PCI 155-Mbps MMF ATM (2816), 159
    PCI 155-Mbps SMF OC3 ATM (2818), 159
    PCI 155-Mbps UTP OC3 ATM (2815), 158
    PCI Integrated PC Servers (#2854, #2851, #2857), 156-157
    PCI Integrated PC Servers (#2865), 155-156
    Shielded Twisted-Pair Distributed Data Interface (SDDI), 150
    terminals, 115-116
    token frames, 148-149
    token passing protocol, 148-149
    token-ring, 148-150, 392
    wireless local area networks, 159-161, 162, 163
large business environment, hardware selection for, 451-454
Large Objects (LOBs), 262
laser printers, 109-112
latency of platters, 82
Layer 2 Tunnel Protocol (L2TP), 295
LCS (Local Controlling System), 94, 95
LDAP (Lightweight Directory Access Protocol), 428-429
LDAs (Local Data Areas), 229
lease or buy decision, 464-465
libraries, 80
Lightweight Directory Access Protocol (LDAP), 428-429
Lilly Software Associates-Visual Manufacturing, 43
line-at-a-time printing, 102
LOBs (Large Objects), 262
Local Area Networks. *See* LANs
Local Controlling System (LCS), 94, 95
Local Data Areas (LDAs), 229
lock management, 264, 279
logical files, 276-277
logical partitioning of Symmetrical Multi-Processors (SMPs), 48-49, 439-440
loosely coupled computing, 66-67
loss prevention, 472-473
Lotus Domino.Doc, 427
Lotus Enterprise Integrator (NotesPump), 239-241
Lotus Learning Space, 427

Lotus Notes 5.0, 151, 236, 237-239, 312-313
Lotus Script, 427
Lotus Simple Mail Transport Protocol/Mail Transfer Agent (SMTP/MTA), 426

M
machine interface, technology-independent, 5, 10
Magstar MP 3575 Tape Library Dataserver, 139
main storage expansion options, 117-121. *See also* memory or main storage
   for AS/400 Advanced Entry Model 150, 117
   for AS/400e server 170, 117-119
   for AS/400e server 720, 119-120
   for AS/400e server 730, 120-121
   for AS/400e server 740, 121, 122
   for migrating from System/3X, 477
maintenance tools for applications, 342-343, 344-345
Managed System Services (MSS), 297, 332-333
Management Central, 329-332
Management Collection objects, 331
Manufacturing Accounting and Production Information Control System/Database (MAPICS/DB), 243
manufacturing environment, hardware selection for, 444-446
MAPICS/DB (Manufacturing Accounting and Production Information Control System/Database), 243
MAPICS-MAPOCS XA, 41
Massachusetts Institute of Technology (MIT), 288
massively parallel database, 284
Maximum Press Web Site, xxiii-xxiv
MB (million bytes), 14, 15
medium business environment, hardware selection for, 446-451, 454-456
memory or main storage. *See also* auxiliary storage; main storage expansion options
   cache memory, 68, 69-70
   capability-based addressing, 80
   check bits, 77
   Compact Disk-Read Only Memory (CD-ROM), 84, 141-142
   disk storage, 78, 477
   libraries, 80
   non-volatile storage, 78
   object-oriented access, 79-80
   overview, 68, 69-70
   packaging for, 86
   Single In-line Memory Module (SIMM), 23
   single-level storage, 79, 80
   storage management, 77-81
   swapping, 79, 80-81
   thrashing, 79
   virtual storage, 79, 80-81
   volatile storage, 78
   as workspace, 76-77
message
   defined, 355
   frames (packets), 148-149
   queues, 151

Messaging and Queuing Interface (MQI), 398-399
metadata, 233
method, 355
MFIOP (Multi-Function I/O Processor)
   auxiliary storage options, 124, 133-134, 143
   custom application servers, 44
   system unit members, 26, 27, 32, 36
   workstations, 94
microprocessors, 11-18
Microsoft's Policies, 308-309
migrating application programs
   to AS/400, 245, 358-371
   from System 3/X, 479-482
migrating from System/3X, 475-488
   0059 Transition Data Link for, 181-182, 478
   9402, 9404, 9406 Models, 482-483
   Advanced Series 20X/30X System Units, 483
   application programs, 479-482
   C, D, E, F 9402, 9404, 9406 Models, 482-483
   CISC to RISC, 483
   data, 479-482
   disk storage needed for, 477
   I/O devices, 478-479
   main storage needed for, 477
   and performance, 477
   sizing a replacement AS/400, 476-478
   from System/34, 482
   from System/36, 479-480
   from System/38, 480-482
   System/38 Performance Measurement Tools for, 477
   System/38 Utilities for, 482
   Systems Management Facility (SMF) tools for, 477
migration paths for AS/400 upgrades, 54-56, 510-522
million bytes (MB), 14, 15
MIME (Multipurpose Internet Mail Extensions), 430
MIPS (Million Instructions Per Second), 14, 15
MIT (Massachusetts Institute of Technology), 288
Mixed Object Document Content Architecture-Presentation (MODCA-P), 265
Mobile Worker, 295
MODCA-P (Mixed Object Document Content Architecture-Presentation), 265
Model 150. *See* AS/400 Advanced Entry Model 150
Model 170 server. *See* AS/400e server 170
Model 720 server. *See* AS/400e server 720
Model 730 server. *See* AS/400e server 730
Model 740-SB1, 44
Model 740 server. *See* AS/400e server 740
Model 2100 Versatile Storage DataServer, 131-132
models, upgrading, 54-56
Model S40-SB1, 44

Model SB1
  disk options, 130-131
  overview, 43-44
modems, 169-171
MODULE (module object), 347-348
module object (MODULE), 347-348
Movex System, 41
MPTN (Multiprotocol Transport Networking), 399-401
MQI (Messaging and Queuing Interface), 398-399
MSS (Managed System Services), 297, 332-333
multi-application computer systems, 250
multiform printers, 105
Multi-Function I/O Processor. *See* MFIOP
Multimedia, 223-227
Multiprotocol Transport Networking (MPTN), 399-401
Multipurpose Internet Mail Extensions (MIME), 430
multi-system coupling, 47, 49
multitasking computer systems, 250
multiuser computer systems, 1, 249-250, 435-436
multivendor application program interfaces, 397-399

N
NAT (Network Address Translation), 292-293, 417
Net.Commerce
  Domino.Merchant versus, 428
  overview, 420, 422-423
Net.Data, 420-421
NetFinity for AS/400, 333-334
net present value, 463
NetQuestion, 421-422
NetServer, 151-152, 310-311
Netsoft Router, 301, 308
NetView/Remote Manager (NV/RM), 297
Network Address Translation (NAT), 292-293, 417
Network File System (NFS), 263-264
Network Gateway, 415
networking blueprint. *See* IBM's networking blueprint
network presentation and printing technology, 101
network printing support, 309
Network Remote Facilities (NRF), 297
Network Station #8361, 97-100
neural networks, 344
New York Committee for Occupational Safety and Health (NYCOSH), 468
NFS (Network File System), 263-264
nodes, 148
noise comfort, 470-471
nonimpact printers, 103, 109-112
Non-Programmable Terminal (NPT), 249
non-volatile storage, 78
Novell Internet Packet Exchange (IPX), 7
Novell NetWare, 7, 151
NPT (Non-Programmable Terminal), 249
NRF (Network Remote Facilities), 297
NV/RM (NetView/Remote Manager), 297
N-way multiprocessor architecture, 71, 72
NYCOSH (New York Committee for Occupational Safety and Health), 468

O
object, 354
Object Archive, 320
object code, 195
ObjectConnect/400, 393
object-oriented
  access, 79-80
  languages, 350, 357-358
  server applications, 5, 9
Object Packaging and Distribution Graphical Interface (Management Central), 331
Object Request Broker (ORB), 355, 362
object technology
  and AS/400, 357-358
  benefits of, 356-357
  C++, 349, 358
  class, defined, 355
  Common Object Request Broker Architecture (CORBA), defined, 355
  defined, 353-354
  dynamic binding, defined, 355
  encapsulation, defined, 355
  frameworks, defined, 355
  inheritance, defined, 355
  instance, defined, 354
  Java, 283, 343, 357, 362-369
  message, defined, 355
  method, defined, 355
  object, defined, 354
  object-oriented languages, 350, 357-358
  Object Request Broker (ORB), defined, 355
  part, defined, 356
  polymorphism, defined, 355
  procedural programming comparison to, 354
  SmallTalk, 357, 358
OCL (Operation Control Language), 252
ODBC (Open DataBase Connection), 267, 281, 282, 309
OfficeVision, 201-209, 426
OfficeVision JustMail (5798-TBT), 209
OLAP (On-Line Analytical Processing), 232-233
OLE DB, AS/400 Software Development Kit for, 343
OLTP (On-Line Transaction Processing), 158, 230
op code, 12
Open DataBase Connection (ODBC), 267, 281, 282, 309
OpenDoc, 361
open interfaces of data mining, 235
Open Standards (UNIX), 369-371
open systems computing, 4, 5-6
operating lease, 464-465
operating systems, 246-254. *See also* OS/400
  Application Program Interfaces (APIs), 247, 252-253
  batch versus interactive processing, 248-249
  Client Access support, 301, 302-307

Index **537**

client/server environment, 250-251
concepts, 247-248
interactive versus batch processing, 248-249
layer of software model, 185, 186, 187
multi-application computer systems, 250
multitasking computer systems, 250
multiuser computer systems, 249-250
Non-Programmable Terminal (NPT), 249
Operation Control Language (OCL), 252
System Support Program (SSP), 247, 252-254
operational data, 230-231
Operation Control Language (OCL), 252
Operations Console, 94-95, 196, 197
Operations Navigator, 269, 311-312, 318-320
Operations Productivity Pak (5716-OPK), 377
optical libraries, 84-85
optical storage, 141-143
OptiConnect/400
    performance, 66-67
    for system availability, 49, 71-76
optimal decoding, 12
Optimizer, 269-270
options and peripherals. *See* adapter (other) options; auxiliary storage options; LANs; main storage expansion options; packaging options; power options; printing technology; WANs; workstations
Orbix product, 362
ORB (Object Request Broker), 355, 362
OS/400, 254-257. *See also* AFP (Advanced Function Presentation); application development facilities; Client Access; communications support; DB2 for AS/400; IFS (Integrated File System); System 3/X; SystemView
OS/400 Directory Services, 428-429
outgoing balancing, 293

P
packaging options, 174-180
    1 1/4-Inch Tape Unit Cage (#7130), 178
    3 1/2-Inch Disk Unit Cage (#7128), 177
    1063 Mbps PCI Expansion Tower #5065, 176, 177
    Advanced Series #2686 Optical Link Processor (266 Mbps), 179-180
    Advanced Series Base Optical Bus Adapter (#2696), 178-179
    Advanced Series Optical Link Processor (#2688), 180
    for memory or main storage, 86
    packaging technology, 3, 85-86
    PCI Card Cage (#9329), 176-177
    SPD Bus Card Cage (#9331), 176
    Storage Expansion Tower (#5083), 178, 179
    Storage Expansion Unit (#5058), 178
    System Expansion Tower (#5073), 178
    System Unit Expansion (5064/9364), 174, 176
page-mode printing, 102
Page Printer Formatting Aid (PPFA), 210
paging support, 229
Panel Definition Markup Language (PDML), 368
parallel access path maintenance, 268

parallel capability, 439
part, 356
partitioned database, 281, 283-284
partner locations, 391
payback period, 463
Payment Server V1.2 for AS/400, 413-414
PCI 25-Mbps UTP ATM (2811), 158
PCI 34-Mbps Coax E3 ATM (2819), 158
PCI 45-Mbps Coax T3DS3 ATM (2812), 158
PCI 155-Mbps MMF ATM (2816), 159
PCI 155-Mbps SMF OC3 ATM (2818), 159
PCI 155-Mbps UTP OC3 ATM (2815), 158
PCI Card Cage (#9329), 176-177
PCI Cryptographic IOA (#4800), 181
PCI Integrated PC Server, 134
PCI Integrated PC Servers (#2854, #2851, #2857), 156-157
PCI Integrated PC Servers (#2865), 155-156
PCI (Portable Computer Interface), 23, 27, 30, 113
PCML (Program Call Markup Language), 368
PCs (personal computers), 95-96, 435-436
PDML (Panel Definition Markup Language), 368
Peer Web Services, 310
performance, 56-67
    benchmark testing, 57-66
    Commercial Processing Workload (CPW) benchmark test results, 61-62, 63
    of data mining, 234-235
    of DB2, 270
    of disk units, 82-83
    of distributed computer communications, 392-393
    interactive jobs, 61
    interactive performance, 66, 67
    loosely coupled computing, 66-67
    and migration from System 3/X, 477
    OptiConnect performance, 66-67
    overview, 56-57
    response time, 57
    RPMark95, 66
    server jobs, 61
    server performance, 62, 64-66
    Symmetrical Multi-Processors (SMPs) for, 62, 64
    system default priorities for, 61
    throughput, 56-57
    of virtual storage, 79, 81
Performance Tools (5716-PT1), 332
personal computers (PCs), 95-96, 435-436
PFS (Physical File System), 263
phosphors, 91-92
physical files, 275-276
Physical File System (PFS), 263
pipelining, 12
PKCS (Public Key Cryptography Standard), 411-412
Point to Point (PPP) communications, 292
polymorphism, 355
POP3 (Post Office Protocol, Version 3), 212, 430
portability
    of AS/400 systems, 5
    of software, 196
    UNIX C, 370-371

Portable Computer Interface (PCI), 23, 27, 30, 113
POSIX Application Program Interfaces, 345
Post Office Protocol, Version 3 (POP3), 212, 430
power options, 174, 175
PPFA (Page Printer Formatting Aid), 210
PPP (Point to Point) communications, 292
prewritten application programs, 199-200, 440, 441
printers, 2, 89, 103-112
printing technology, 100-117
    3270 protocol, 116
    5250 protocol, 116
    Advanced Function Printing, 102-103, 110
    and applications, 100, 102-103, 209-211, 338-340
    ASCII workstation controllers, 114-115
    band printers, 104, 105-107, 108
    cable-thru, 113
    cold fusion printing, 109, 111
    and costs of printing, 101
    and document archival, 101
    and document characteristics, 100, 101-103
    electronic documents, 101-102
    and environmental considerations, 101
    impact printers, 103-108
    inkjet printers, 109, 110
    Intelligent Printer Data Stream (IPDS), 103, 110-112
    LAN-connected terminals, 115-116
    laser printers, 109-112
    line-at-a-time mode, 102
    and location of printers, 100
    multiform printers, 105
    and network presentation, 101
    nonimpact printers, 103, 109-112
    page-mode, 102
    Portable Computer Interface (PCI), 113
    printer pass-thru, 298-299
    printers, 2, 89, 103-112
    and print window, 101
    protocol converters, 116-117
    and relative importance, 100
    shared network printers, 111-112
    shuttle-matrix printers, 106
    and special forms, 101
    twinaxial workstation controllers, 113-114
    and volume, 100-101
    wire-matrix printers, 104, 105, 107, 108
    workstation controllers, 112-116
Print Services Facility/400, 338-339
problem log, 329
procedural programming comparison to object technology, 354
procedures, 195
production forecasting, 229
productivity improvement, 461-462
Program Call Markup Language (PCML), 368
Program Development Manager, 337-338
program interaction, 197-198
programming. *See also* application development facilities; application programs; business and Application Systems; *specific languages*
    application development facilities for, 343

languages, 194, 334-335
Programming Request Per Quote (PRPQ), 76, 393
Program Temporary Fixes (PTFs), 332, 333, 380, 382
protocol converters, 116-117
PRPQ (Programming Request Per Quote), 76, 393
PTF Management Wizards (Management Central), 332
PTFs (Program Temporary Fixes), 332, 333, 380, 382
Public Key Cryptography Standard (PKCS), 411-412

Q
QDLS, 261
QIC tape formats, 138
QLANSrv, 261, 262
QNTC for Windows NT, 259
QOPENSYS, 261
QOPT, 262
QSYS.LIB, 260, 262
quality improvement, 462
Query/400, 212-214, 340-341
question-and-answer database for communications, 383

R
RAD (Rapid Application Development), 238
RAID-5 disk controllers, 327-328
Rapid Application Development (RAD), 238
RCS (Remote Controlling System), 94
R/DARS (Report/Data Archive and Retrieval System). *See* EDMSuite OnDemand for AS/400 (5769-RD1)
Record Archive, 320
record level locking, 286
Reduced Instruction Set Computer (RISC), 11-12
relational database system, 232
relative importance and printing technology, 100
remote
    data model, 352
    journaling, 316-317
    office connections, 295
    presentation model, 352
    workstation controllers and lines, 171-174
    workstations, communications for, 383-385
Remote Controlling System (RCS), 94
Remote File System, 264-265
Remote Procedure Calls (RPCs), 263-264, 286-287, 398
Report/Data Archive and Retrieval System (R/DARS). *See* EDMSuite OnDemand for AS/400 (5769-RD1)
residual value of computer system, 464
response time, 57
retail
    environment, hardware selection for, 442-443
    terminals, 403-404, 405, 406-408
    workstations, 96-97
RETAIN network, 382
RISC PowerPC AS microprocessors, 11-18

Index

RISC (Reduced Instruction Set Computer), 11-12
RISC System/6000 computers and business, 436-438
root file system, 261
RPCs (Remote Procedure Calls), 263-264, 286-287, 398
RPG, 343, 348-349
RPMark95, 66

S

S/390 communications support, 299-300
SafeMail Mail Relay, 417
San Francisco Framework, 360-361
SAP-Base R/3 Package, 43, 46
SAP R/3 AFP Print, 211
SAP-Ready to Run R/3, 43
save while active feature of SystemView, 317
scalability of data mining, 235
SCIL (Serial Control Interface Logic), 16, 18, 35
Screen Design Aid (SDA), 337
SDA (Screen Design Aid), 337
SDDI (Shielded Twisted-Pair Distributed Data Interface), 150
SDK (Software Developer Toolkit), 309
SDLC (Synchronous Data Link Control) protocol, 167
Secure Electronics Transaction (SET), 411-414
Secure Sockets Layer (SSL), 294, 310, 313, 364, 411, 415-416
Secure Web Server, 409
security
  and business, 471-474
  functions of distributed computer communications, 391
Security Wizard, 319, 414-418, 505-509
seek time of disk units, 82
separate storage control chip (STGCTL), 16, 18
Serial Control Interface Logic (SCIL), 16, 18, 35
Serial Line Internet Protocol (SLIP), 430
server. *See also* AS/400e servers; client/server computing
  jobs, 61
  layer of advanced application architecture, 5, 9
  performance, 62, 64-66
  selection, 454-456
  server-based development tool, 343
service, 474-475
session endpoint filter lists, 391
SET (Secure Electronics Transaction), 411-414
SEU (Source Entry Utility), 337
shared network printers, 111-112
Shielded Twisted-Pair Distributed Data Interface (SDDI), 150
shuttle-matrix printers, 106
SIMM (Single In-line Memory Module), 23
Simple Mail Transfer Protocol (SMTP), 294, 430
Simple Network Management Protocol (SNMP), 430
Single In-line Memory Module (SIMM), 23
single-level storage, 79, 80, 334
Six-Line Communications Controller (2629), 164, 165
sizing a replacement AS/400, 476-478

SLIC (System Licensed Internal Code), 5, 10, 70, 185, 187-189, 190
SLIP (Serial Line Internet Protocol), 430
small business environment, 442-443, 444-446
SmallTalk, 357, 358
SMAPP (System Managed Access Path Protection), 325-326, 327
SMF (Systems Management Facility), 477
SMPs (Symmetrical Multi-Processors)
  and DB2 for AS/400, 268
  logical partitioning of, 48-49, 439-440
  overview, 71, 72
  for performance, 62, 64
  in system unit members, 25, 29, 33, 35-36, 44
SMTP (Simple Mail Transfer Protocol), 294, 430
SNADS (System Network Architecture Distribution Services), 74, 391
SNA (Systems Network Architecture)
  communications support, 297, 379-380
  and distributed computing, 391
  IBM's networking blueprint for, 394
  and Wide Area Networks (WANs), 167
sniffing programs, 415
SNMP (Simple Network Management Protocol), 430
Socks Client program, 417
software, 184-198. *See also* application development facilities; application programs; business and Application Systems; *specific programming languages*
  application architecture, 195-198
  application program layer, 185, 186
  of AS/400, comparison to traditional, 189-191
  Common User Access (CUA), 198
  compatibility, 193-198, 371-372
  compiling a program, 195
  encryption, 410
  EZ Setup Wizard, 196-197, 500-504
  layers working together, 191-193
  license agreement, 465
  maintenance costs, 458-459
  for medium business environment, 449-451
  model for, 185-188
  object code, 195
  operating system layer, 185, 186, 187
  Operations Console, 196, 197
  portability, 196
  procedures, 195
  program interaction, 197-198
  programming languages, 194, 334-335
  selection, 440-441, 449-451
  source code, 194
  SSP operating system, 195
  standard user interface, 198
  and System/3X programs, 193-194
  System/38 environment, 195
  for system availability, 47
  System Licensed Internal Code (SLIC), 185, 187-189, 190
  Systems Application Architecture (SSA), 195-196, 198
systems programmers for, 189
Technology Independent Machine Interface

(TIMI), 188
  Welcome Center, 197
Software Developer Toolkit (SDK), 309
source code, 194
Source Entry Utility (SEU), 337
SPCN (System Power Control Network), 46-47
SPD Bus Card Cage (#9331), 176
special forms and printing technology, 101
Spool File Archive, 320, 321
SQL Development Kit, 262-263
SQLJ (Structured Query Language Java), 364-365
SQL (Structured Query Language), 74, 267, 269, 281, 340
SSA-BPCS Client/Server or Mixed Mode, 40
SSA (Systems Application Architecture), 195-196, 198
SSL (Secure Sockets Layer), 294, 310, 313, 364, 411, 415-416
SSP operating system, 195
SSP (System Support Program), 247, 252-254
standard user interface, 198
stateless design, 264
STGCTL (separate storage control chip), 16, 18
Storage Expansion Tower (#5083), 178, 179
Storage Expansion Unit (#5058), 178
storage management, 77-81. *See also* memory or main storage
stream files, 259-260, 261
Structured Query Language Java (SQLJ), 364-365
Structured Query Language (SQL), 74, 267, 269, 281, 340
Subnetworking layer, 401-402
Sun Java Developer's Kit (JDK), 362
superscalar, 12
swapping, 79, 80-81
symmetrical encryption, 412
Symmetrical Multi-Processors. *See* SMPs
synchronization, 277-279
Synchronous Data Link Control (SDLC) protocol, 167
system
  console, 2
  default priorities for performance, 61
  monitor, 264
  performance tables, 483-487
  processor, 68-69
System/3X. *See also* migrating from System/3X
  AS/400 comparison to, xxvii-xxx
  compatibility, 193-198, 371-372
  history, xxv-xxviii
System/34, migrating from, 482
System/36, migrating from, 479-480
System/38, migrating from, 480-482
System/38 Performance Measurement Tools, 477
System/38 Utilities, 482
System/390 computers and business, 438-439
system availability, 46-56
  Byte Stream File (BSF) replication, 52
  cluster nodes, 52
  Cluster Resource Groups/Services for, 50-52
  continuous availability clustering for, 47, 50-52, 71-76, 392-393
  Continuously Powered Main Storage (CPM), 53-54
  data resiliency and application resiliency for, 47, 50
  disaster tolerance for, 47, 52-54
  hardware solutions for, 46-47
  heartbeat monitoring, 52
  horizontal growth, 54
  Initial Program Load (IPL), 53-54
  logical partitioning for, 48-49, 439-440
  models, upgrading between, 55-56
  models, upgrading within, 54
  multi-system coupling for, 47, 49
  OptiConnect for, 49, 71-76
  OS/400 subsystems and logical partitioning for, 48-49, 439-440
  software solutions for, 47
  Symmetrical Multi-Processors (SMPs), 48-49, 439-440
  System Power Control Network (SPCN), 46-47
  system unit swap, upgrading through a, 54
  Uninterruptible Power Supply (UPS), 53
  upgrades for AS/400, 54-56, 510-522
  vertical growth, 54
System Expansion Tower (#5073), 178
System Licensed Internal Code (SLIC), 5, 10, 70, 185, 187-189, 190
System Managed Access Path Protection (SMAPP), 325-326, 327
System Network Architecture Distribution Services (SNADS), 74, 391
System Power Control Network (SPCN), 46-47
Systems Application Architecture (SSA), 195-196, 198
systems management. *See* SystemView
Systems Management Facility (SMF) tools, 477
Systems Manager/400, 328-329, 387, 390
Systems Network Architecture. *See* SNA
Systems Network Management, 295-297
systems programmers, 189
System Support Program (SSP), 247, 252-254
System Unit Expansion (5064/9364), 174, 176
system unit members, 19, 20-40
  AS/400 Advanced Entry Model 150, 19, 20-24
  AS/400e server 170, 3, 19, 25-27, 28
  AS/400e server 720, 19, 27, 29-31
  AS/400e server 730, 19, 31-34, 35, 36, 37
  AS/400e server 740, 19, 34-40
  BasePak for, 24
  constrained performance, 23
  Continuously Powered Main Storage (CPM), 27, 30, 33, 39
  Error Correction Code (ECC), 23
  growth version, 21, 23-24
  Multi-Function I/O Processor (MFIOP), 26, 27, 32, 36
  Portable Computer Interface (PCI), 23, 27, 30
  Serial Control Interface Logic (SCIL), 35
  Single In-line Memory Module (SIMM), 23
  Symmetrical Multi-Processors (SMPs), 25, 29, 33, 35-36
  unconstrained performance, 23

system unit swap, upgrading through a, 54
SystemView, 313-334
   Adstar Distributed Storage Manager (ADSM), 324-325
   Advanced Function Presentation (AFP) index fields, 321
   AnyStore, 320
   application dimension, 313-316
   Application Storage Pools (ASPs), 323, 325, 326
   AS/400 Performance Tools (5716-PT1), 332
   backup/recovery, 317-328
   Backup Recovery and Media Services (BRMS/400), 321-323
   BRMS Advanced Functions Feature, 323
   BRMS Network Feature, 323
   checksum, 327-328
   Collection Services (Management Central), 331
   commitment control, 316
   Common User Access (CUA), 313
   data dimension, 313, 314
   data mirroring, 328
   data protection methods, 328
   disk failure recovery, 327-328
   EDMSuite OnDemand for AS/400 (5769-RD1), 320-321
   end-use dimension, 313, 314
   Hierarchical Storage Management (HSM), 323, 325, 326
   HTTP Server for AS/400, 319
   Initial Program Load (IPL), 315
   Inventory for Multiple Systems (Management Central), 332
   journaling, 316-317
   Managed System Services (MSS), 297, 332-333
   Management Central, 329-332
   Management Collection objects, 331
   NetFinity for AS/400, 333-334
   Object Archive, 320
   Object Packaging and Distribution Graphical Interface (Management Central), 331
   Operations Navigator, 318-320
   problem log, 329
   Program Temporary Fixes (PTFs), 332, 333
   PTF Management Wizards (Management Central), 332
   RAID-5 disk controllers, 327-328
   Record Archive, 320
   remote journaling, 316-317
   save while active feature, 317
   Security Wizard, 319, 505-509
   Spool File Archive, 320, 321
   System Managed Access Path Protection (SMAPP), 325-326, 327
   System Management Utilities, 382-383
   Systems Manager/400, 328-329, 387, 390
   utility failure recovery, 327

T
tape libraries, 139
tape storage, 85, 136-140
TCP/IP Simple Network Management Protocol (SNMP), 430
TCP/IP TELNET, 430
TCP/IP (Transmission Control Protocol/Internet Protocol), 292-295, 496-499
TCSEC (Trusted Computing Systems Evaluation Criteria), 474
technical data, 233
technical support costs, 459
Technology-Independent Machine Interface (TIMI), 188, 457
telephone book, 274-275
telephone system application programs, 222-223
TELNET, 430
Terminal Multiconnector and Telephone Twisted-Pair Adapter, 182-183
terminals, 2, 89
Terminal Server Edition (TSE), 310
testing tools, 344
theft prevention, 473-474
thin client. *See* IBM Network Station
thrashing, 79
threadsafe functions, 345-347
throughput, 56-57
TIMI (Technology-Independent Machine Interface), 188, 457
token frames, 148-149
token passing protocol, 148-149
token-ring networks, 148-150, 392
Traffic Blocking, 415
Transaction Performance Council, 62
Transmission Control Protocol/Internet Protocol (TCP/IP), 292-295, 496-499
Transport Network layer, 399-401
Trusted Computing Systems Evaluation Criteria (TCSEC), 474
TSE (Terminal Server Edition), 310
twinaxial workstation controllers, 113-114

U
Ultimedia Business Conferencing/400, 225-227
unconstrained performance, 23
Uniform Resource Locator (URL), 271, 430-431
Uninterruptible Power Supply (UPS), 53, 174
United States Department of Defense (DoD), 474
UNIX, 369-371
UNIX C portability, 370-371
upgrades for AS/400, 54-56, 510-522
UPS (Uninterruptible Power Supply), 53, 174
URL (Uniform Resource Locator), 271, 430-431
User Defined Functions, 272
User Defined Types, 272
user profiles, 411
utility failure recovery, 327

V
validation lists, 411
ValuePoint/400, 96
ValuNets, 295
vertical growth, 54
vertical market application programs, 441
Very Large Scale Integration (VLSI), 85
VIPA (Virtual IP Addressing), 293
Virtual IP Addressing (VIPA), 293

virtual machine, AS/400, 363-364
Virtual Private Networks (VPN), 294-295
virtual storage, 79, 80-81
VisiBroker, 362
Vision Solutions, 50
VisualAge/SmallTalk, 358
Visual Manufacturing, 43
VLSI (Very Large Scale Integration), 85
volatile storage, 78
volume and printing technology, 100-101
VPN (Virtual Private Networks), 294-295
VRPG Client, 343

W
WANs (Wide Area Networks), 161-174. *See also* communications
    5394 Remote Workstation Controller, 172
    5494 Remote Workstation Controller, 172-174
    analog communications, 167
    Async protocol, 166
    Bisync protocol, 166-167
    communications protocol, 162
    D Channel, 164
    digital communications, 167
    frame relay, 168
    Integrated Analog Modem #2761, 169-170
    Integrated FAX Adapters, 168-169
    Integrated Services Digital Network (ISDN) protocol, 167-168
    interface, 162, 163
    ISDN Basic Rate Interface Adapter, 164
    ISDN Data Link Control (IDLC) protocol, 164
    modems, 169-171
    remote workstation controllers and lines, 171-174
    Six-Line Communications Controller (2629), 164, 165
    Synchronous Data Link Control (SDLC) protocol, 167
    Systems Network Architecture (SNA), 167
    X.25 protocol, 167
Web Publisher, 239
Web Site for Maximum Press, xxiii-xxiv
WebSphere Application Server (5769-AS1), 418
WebSphere Studio, 418
Welcome Center, 197
WGS (Workstation Gateway Server), 431
Wide Area Networks. *See* WANs
Windows NT File System, 259, 265
Window Tool/400, 341-342
wireless local area networks, 159-161, 162, 163, 297-298
wire-matrix printers, 104, 105, 107, 108
WMRM (Write Many, Read Many), 85, 141
word processing, 205-206
Workfolder Application Facility, 219, 220
Workplace Server Benchmark, 66
workspace, memory as, 76-77
Workstation Gateway Server (WGS), 431
workstations, 89-100
    Client Access, 94
    comfort, 469-470
    computer terminals (display station), 89
    controllers, 112-116
    defined, 89
    IBM Network Station #8361, 97-100
    InfoWindowII 3486/3487 Display Stations, 90-92
    InfoWindowII 3488/3489 Modular Display Station, 93-94
    intelligent workstations, 96
    Local Controlling System (LCS), 94, 95
    Multi-Function I/O Processor (MFIOP), 94
    Operations Console, 94-95
    Personal Computer (PC) terminal emulation, 95-96
    phosphors, 91-92
    printers, 89
    Remote Controlling System (RCS), 94
    retail workstations, 96-97
    terminals, 89
    ValuePoint/400, 96
WORM (Write Once, Read Many), 84-85, 141
Write Many, Read Many (WMRM), 85, 141

X
X.25 protocol, 167
XML (Extensible Markup Language), 368

Y
Year 2000 challenge, 459, 475

Reader Feedback Sheet

Your comments and suggestions are very important in shaping future publications. Please email us at *moreinfo@maxpress.com* or photocopy this page, jot down your thoughts, and fax it to (850) 934-9981 or mail it to:

Maximum Press
Attn: Jim Hoskins
605 Silverthorn Road
Gulf Breeze, FL 32561

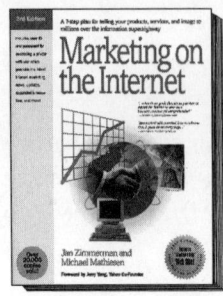

Marketing on the Internet, Third Edition
by Jan Zimmerman and Michael Mathiesen
445 pages, illustrations
$34.95
ISBN: 1-885068-26-3

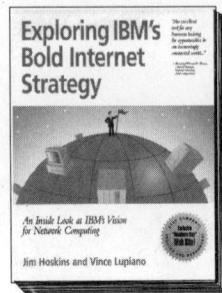

Exploring IBM's Bold Internet Strategy
by Jim Hoskins and Vince Lupiano
184 pages
$34.95
ISBN: 1-885068-23-9

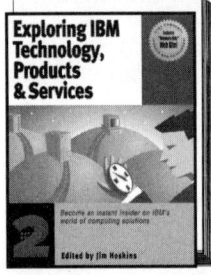

Exploring IBM Technology, Products & Services, Second Edition
edited by Jim Hoskins
240 pages, paper
$54.95
ISBN: 1-885068-31-X

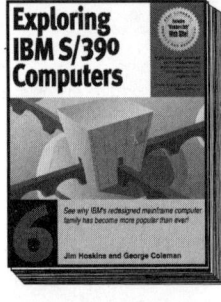

Exploring IBM S/390 Computers, Sixth Edition
by Jim Hoskins and George Coleman
472 pages, illustrations
$39.95
ISBN: 1-885068-30-1

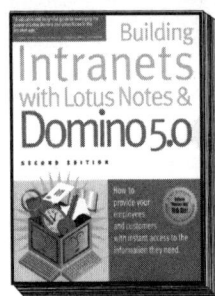

Building Intranets with Lotus Notes & Domino 5.0, Second Edition
by Steve Krantz
$32.95
ISBN: 1-885068-24-7

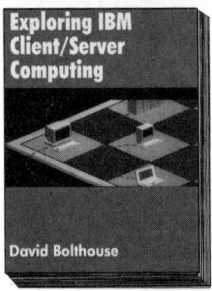

Exploring IBM Client/Server Computing
by David Bolthouse
471 pages, illustrations
$32.95
ISBN: 1-885068-04-2

Exploring IBM RS/6000 Computers, Ninth Edition
by Jim Hoskins and Doug Davies
444 pages, illustrations
$39.95
ISBN: 1-885068-27-1

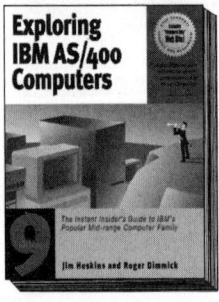

Exploring IBM AS/400 Computers, Ninth Edition
by Jim Hoskins and Roger Dimmick
576 pages, illustrations
$39.95
ISBN: 1-885068-34-4

To purchase a Maximum Press book, visit your local bookstore or call 1-800-989-6733 (US) or 1-850-934-4583 (International) or visit our homepage: *www.maxpress.com*

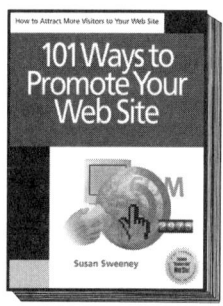

101 Ways to Promote Your Web Site
by Susan Sweeney, C.A.
288 pages, illustrations
$29.95
ISBN: 1-885068-37-9

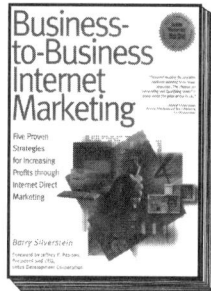

Business-to-Business Internet Marketing
by Barry Silverstein
425 pages, illustrations
$19.95
ISBN: 1-885068-35-2

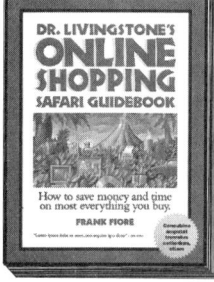

Dr. Livingstone's On-line Shopping Safari Guidebook
by Frank Fiore
501 pages, illustrations
$24.95
ISBN: 1-885068-07-7

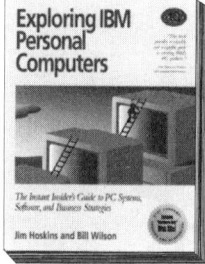

Exploring IBM Personal Computers, Tenth Edition
by Jim Hoskins and Bill Wilson
384 pages, illustrations
$34.95
ISBN: 1-885068-25-5

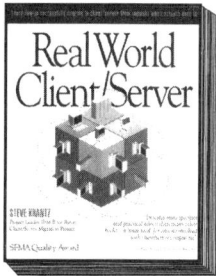

Real World Client/Server
by Steve Krantz
344 pages, illustrations
$29.95
ISBN: 0-9633214-7-1

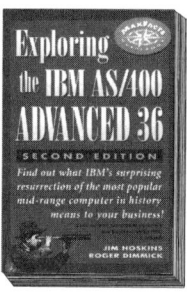

Exploring the IBM AS/400 Advanced 36, Second Edition
by Jim Hoskins and Roger Dimmick
105 pages, illustrations
$26.95
ISBN: 1-885068-11-5

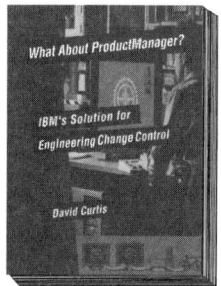

What About ProductManager?
by David Curtis
200 pages, illustrations
$34.95
ISBN: 0-9633214-4-7

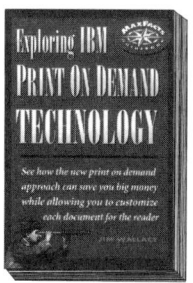

Exploring IBM Print on Demand Technology
by Jim Wallace
122 pages, illustrations
$22.95
ISBN: 1-885068-06-9

To purchase a Maximum Press book, visit your local bookstore or call 1-800-989-6733 (US/Canada) or 1-850-934-4583 (International) or visit our homepage: *www.maxpress.com*